Commercial Agency Agreements:
Law and Practice

Fifth Edition

Dedication

To my daughters – Rachel, senior solicitor at Macfarlanes and Rebecca, solicitor, Head of Legal at M&C Saatchi, London. To my twin sons Joe and Sam who graduate in 2020. To my oldest son Ben, who has escaped the legal net and works for Ocado.

To my grandchildren Rose and Frederick – you have it all before you.

To my late mother Anne Morgan, 1929–2004, teacher, whose early educational efforts with us, her children in the 1960s and 1970s, is one reason that I am a solicitor, publisher and writer.

To my late father, Dr Peter Morgan, 1928–2008 who enjoyed practising psychiatry to the age of 77. Without knowledge of basic psychology, how could many of us handle clients, colleagues and indeed litigation?

To my ex-colleagues at Nabarro Nathanson (now CMS), Slaughter and May and Bristows who taught me so much.

To the team at Bloomsbury, including Andy Hill and Ellie MacKenzie, for all your help. And to my clients at Singletons, Solicitors – agents, principals, trade associations, companies and solicitors, and also past delegates at my commercial agency courses, without all of whom I would have no experience and little knowledge of commercial agency law.

Commercial Agency Agreements: Law and Practice

Fifth Edition

Susan Singleton, LLB,
Solicitor, Singletons
www.singlelaw.com

Bloomsbury Professional

LONDON • DUBLIN • EDINBURGH • NEW YORK • NEW DELHI • SYDNEY

BLOOMSBURY PROFESSIONAL
Bloomsbury Publishing Plc
41–43 Boltro Road, Haywards Heath, RH16 1BJ, UK

BLOOMSBURY and the Diana logo are trademarks of Bloomsbury Publishing Plc

Copyright © Bloomsbury Professional, 2020

British Library Cataloguing-in-Publication Data

A catalogue record for this book is available from the British Library.

ISBN:	PB:	978 1 52651 187 4
	ePDF:	978 1 52651 189 8
	ePub:	978 1 52651 188 1

Typeset by Evolution Design and Digital, Kent, UK
Printed and bound by CPI Group (UK) Ltd, Croydon, CR0 4YY

To find out more about our authors and books visit
www.bloomsburyprofessional.com. Here you will find extracts, author information, details of forthcoming events and the option to sign up for our newsletters

Preface to the fifth edition

When the first edition of this book was published in late 1998 by Butterworths, the Commercial Agents (Council Directive) Regulations 1993 which implemented the EU Agency Directive in the UK had only been in force for a few years. I had only been advising on the Regulations for four years. Now over 25 years since the Regulations have applied, many agents have received compensation and principals have grappled with deserving and undeserving agents' claims. I am delighted to have the opportunity to bring out a fifth edition in 2020 published by Bloomsbury Professional (which also published the third and fourth editions, and second through Tottel Publishing). In my solicitor's practice, Singletons, which I founded in February 1994 just as the Regulations came into force, I have handled hundreds of cases under the Regulations for both agents and principals.

The lack of certainty as to when an agent is entitled to compensation or an indemnity payment continues to be a problem, even after the *Lonsdale* case which is prayed in aid merrily by solicitors on both sides in much litigation, sure that it helps their case. Whilst it is helpful to know there is no set tariff such as the French two years' commission as compensation, the reality is that although valuers are familiar with valuing private companies (and that in itself is a difficult art with valuation fees often £20,000 and higher), there is no market as such for sale of agencies in the UK and thus no real life comparators. Many agents earn too little to justify engaging a valuer unless the matter is going to court, and valuers although now sure they look at what the agency is worth on the date of termination for compensation cases, still do not have particularly helpful guidelines to aid them in their task. Some things are clear – if the agent has taken all the customers or left a legacy of failure and few sales, the agent is not likely to receive much compensation, and for smaller cases it can be worth using as a rule of thumb one year's commission as a reasonable early offer for settlement. However, the heart of the issue is what is the agency worth, ie what would someone pay to buy that revenue stream of commission the agent would have continued to have had had the agreement continued. The absence of many new interesting cases does not make the task any easier. For the fifth edition there are more cases than usual, which is helpful. As the years go by more case law emerges.

For this fifth edition, and indeed the third and fourth editions, I am grateful for the contribution (Chapter 7) written by Charles Lazarevic, chartered accountant,

Managing Director of Vero Consulting Ltd (previously at Moore Stephens LLP) who has acted as valuer/expert witness in agency cases. Given that one of the hardest issues under the Regulations is how much to pay the agent on termination, the more guidance available on this topic, the easier it will be both for principals and agents to know where they stand and what offers to accept.

Some companies have been put off using agents because they are expensive to fire. This can be short sighted. I have had several cases, including one in 2019, where the agent earned more than anyone at the company including the Board of Directors, but that is because they have generated sales. Agency in a sense is capitalism at its best. The agent only eats what they kill, and if the agent does well the company does even better.

The Regulations are arbitrary, unfair and in parts badly drafted. On 25 July 2014, the European Commission began a consultation on the Regulations which closed on 31 October 2014. This concluded in July 2015 that '*the Directive meets its objectives and functions well. The Directive's benefits outweigh its costs, it remains relevant and continues to have EU added value. Based on these findings, it is recommended that the Directive is maintained in its current form*'. In 2016, the UK voted to leave the EU in a referendum, but this is unlikely to affect this area of law and the European Union (Withdrawal) Act 2018 ensures that the Regulations continue after the UK leaves the EU, and given the majority Government after the December 2019 election, a 2020 departure of the UK on or about 31 January 2020 from the EU on the basis of the EU/UK Withdrawal Agreement and passing of the European Union (Withdrawal Agreement) Act 2020. Although some businesses regard the protection for agents as too wide, there appears, at the time of writing, to be no proposal from the Government or business to abolish or amend the Regulations.

Agents who market 'goods' may be paid one to two years' commission on termination of their agreement unless the contract provides for an indemnity payment on termination. Agents handling services in the UK receive nothing. That is just one apparent anomaly. I have acted for companies with millions of pounds worth of turnover who have successfully claimed compensation which were perhaps not the original intended beneficiary of the protection of the EU Agency Directive. I have also acted for agents in their 80s wanting to carry on working and principals with agents who are performing badly, but not badly enough that they can be sacked without payment. As with all litigation, legal costs issues and the size of claims are equally as important as the legal issues and the litigation changes – to the effect that conditional fee uplifts and insurance premia may not be recovered from the defendant if the case is won, as well as the 2015 large increases in court fees. This means it is often better, if both sides agree, to take agency disputes to mediation and can mean principals have more of an upper hand when disputes occur. It remains good advice for principals to include many duties on agents in the contract to ensure that it is easier to argue substantial breach of contract on termination when seeking to terminate the contract of an incompetent agent without payment of compensation.

This book addresses both the drafting of such agreements and termination and compensation. I always tell solicitor clients that they ought to inform clients of the risks of appointing agents. Perhaps a distribution arrangement or use of employed representatives may be less risky/expensive, particularly on termination. On the other hand, an agent has a powerful incentive through commission payments to maximise sales whilst also not being a burden or overhead on the company. Do not dismiss agents out of hand because of the costs and risks of termination of agency agreements, but do be aware of those risks right at the start. I have advised in more agency disputes where the agent has no written contract or simply a two-line letter of appointment than those with contracts. This is not good for either party and, in particular, principals will find their legal rights much stronger if they have written agreements with clear duties on the agent.

Many agency agreements around the world fall outside the scope of the EU Agency Directive and this book does not attempt to provide advice on foreign laws. However, some of the practical issues addressed, such as imposing duties on principal and agent, and commercial issues such as commission and restrictive covenants are relevant wherever an agency agreement will operate.

There are many standard, detailed works on the theory of agency law and this book does not intend to be a substitute for those. Instead this book looks at the standard commercial agency agreement where an agent is self-employed (or a limited company) and paid a commission on sales they generate for the principal. It is those agents who fall within the Regulations and whose position is primarily addressed here.

The book includes some examples of agency contracts, but in practice these are as varied as the types of industry sectors which use agents and every agreement should be assessed from scratch. In addition, the book includes coverage of most of the UK judgments, to date, on commercial agency. There have been more in recent years than for earlier editions of this book. However, many cases likely to reach a trial are settled so it can be difficult to obtain details of the typical settlements which agents and principals negotiate. At the time of writing, only three cases with which I have been involved, where I acted for the principal, came to trial in June and July 2005 and July 2014, but hundreds have settled which I have handled. That is a typical statistic for most lawyers in terms of the proportion that go to trial of those where claims are made. It is hardly surprising that the vast majority of cases have been settled.

The Regulations substantially changed UK agency law. Before they came into effect principals and agents could largely determine the contractual position between themselves. If the contract specified that three months' notice of termination should be given and the principal gave such notice that was the end of the matter. Under the Regulations, even if the principal follows the provisions of a contract to the letter, the law steps in and in many cases the agent is entitled to a large lump sum, except in cases of substantial breach of contract on the part of the agent. How large a payment is the most difficult question of all. I usually tell agents if they receive a year's gross commission early on and without litigating it they should take it. If they go to court they might possibly receive up to two years' commission (unless the contract contains a written indemnity cap), or possibly more, although in some cases they run a risk of receiving nothing. If the agency does not yield much commission income, then its value to a putative buyer may be little or nothing. This means those agents earning large commission sums tend to find it easier to negotiate a payment. Agents earning £20k to £40k a year find it harder as the costs of litigation can make it risky to litigate even if a conditional fee basis for fees were possible. So tread carefully.

Copies of no new court judgments have been added for this fifth edition to Appendix 3 as judgments are now more readily available on the internet than they were in 1998 when the I wrote the first edition of this book, and there are too many judgments to include in the book.

The law is described as at 1 January 2020. No imminent changes in the law in this field are expected. Those agents operating in the EU will need to consider issues of enforcement of judgments between the EU and the UK, in particular the transitional withdrawal agreement extending the Brussels regulation on jurisdiction of disputes, at least to the end of the transition period.

I welcome any comments or suggestions as to how the book might be improved in any subsequent edition, and details of new UK agency cases. Comments may be directed to:

Susan Singleton
Singletons
The Ridge
South View Road
Pinner
Middlesex
HA5 3YD

www.singlelaw.com
Tel: 020 8866 1934
Email: susan@singlelaw.com
twitter @singlelaw

Susan Singleton
January 2020

Chapter 7 – details of the author

Charles Lazarevic, Managing Director of Vero Consulting Ltd

Charles has over 35 years' experience as a chartered accountant with leading firms in central London including Moore Stephens LLP. He has acted as an expert witness in over 350 cases in a wide range of fields covering business valuations, commercial and contractual disputes and forensic investigations, and has given evidence at international arbitrations, tribunals and courts.

In 2016, he founded Vero Consulting to work closely with his clients and their lawyers to present their cases.

https://charleslazarevic.com/

Contents

Table of Cases

Table of Statutes

Table of Statutory Instruments

Chapter 1

Introduction and definitions

'Commercial agents were not a class of agent that had hitherto enjoyed any special protection under English common law. The protection that the Regulations seek to provide originated in the civil law systems of France and Germany where there existed two distinct legal regimes. In Germany, upon termination of a commercial agency, the agent became entitled to an equitable payment, known as an "indemnity". In France, the system involved the award of "compensation." The two regimes operated differently, and could lead in any particular case to different results.'

(Mrs Justice Sharp, *Berry v Laytons* [2009] EWHC 1591 (QB))

1.1   This book examines agency law and, in particular, commercial agency law. It does not examine the many forms of agency at common law but leaves that to the detailed theoretical textbooks. Instead it addresses the law relevant to those who use commercial agents in the course of their business. In particular it concentrates on the commission agent.

1.2   In commercial relationships there are many different types of agency. In one sense anyone acting under the instructions of another is an agent. However, in business a narrow definition is useful.

1.3   In its July 2014 consultation Public consultation on the Evaluation of the Commercial Agents Directive (86/653/EEC), the European Commission described the EU Directive and Commercial Regulations as follows:

'Commercial agents are self-employed intermediaries authorised on a permanent basis to negotiate the sale or purchase of goods in the name and on behalf of another person (the principal). The objective of the Commercial Agents Directive was to move towards a single market for commercial representation and improve the conditions of competition by facilitating the conclusion and operation of commercial representation contracts across borders through harmonised rules.

For this purpose, the Directive defines the commercial agents falling under its scope and harmonises the rights and obligations of commercial agents and

1

their principals, and defines rules for the remuneration of the commercial agent, the conclusion and the termination of the contract and the restraint of trade after the termination of the contract.'

The 2015 report arising from the consultation is reproduced in Appendix 2.4 of this book.

The agent and distributor

1.4 The commercial agent, the subject matter of this book, is not trading on his or her own account. He or she is not a 'distributor'. In practice many businesses call their agents their distributors and vice versa and it is crucial for legal purposes to ascertain the legal status of the individual or company. The most pertinent question to ask is about title to the goods being sold. Does the 'agent' buy the goods and resell them? If so, the agent is a distributor or dealer and not a true agent. If the agent never owns the goods but simply finds customers for the supplier, no matter how extensive the agent's role otherwise is, then the agent will be in all probability a commercial agent of the supplier. The person appointing the agent is known as the 'principal' and this term is used throughout this book. In *AMB Imballagi Plastici Srl v Pacflex Ltd* [1999] 2 All ER (Comm) 249, mentioned below, the judge referred to the one English witness who had called agents 'both middlemen who bought and re-sold and middlemen who acted as agents for a commission'. In that case the court found that all trading was done on a sale and re-sale basis. The term 'intermediary' in the Directive does not include distributors. Pacflex was not therefore an agent for the principal even though the principal would have let it trade on that basis. It decided not to do so.

Who is an agent or distributor

Case example – *Sagal (t/a Bunz UK) v Atelier Bunz Gmbh* [2009] EWCA Civ 700 (CA)

1.5 Mr Sagal was in the jewellery business and had had his own shop. He started to undertake business for Bunz GmbH. The judge found that:

(i) Mr Sagal was to take orders from UK customers and fax them to Bunz;

(ii) Bunz would deliver jewellery pursuant to those orders and invoice Mr Sagal;

(iii) Mr Sagal would invoice the UK jewellery customers;

(iv) Mr Sagal's terms to the UK customers were to be payment within 3 (in fact 30) days of delivery or 3% discount if cash paid on delivery;

(v) Mr Sagal would have 60 days within which to pay Bunz;

(vi) Bunz would provide a sample line to Mr Sagal (known as 'the UK Collection') and would insure that sample line;

(vii) Mr Sagal would receive a 20% discount on Bunz's wholesale prices and would thus pay 80% of that price.

By July 2002 Mr Sagal had launched himself under the trade name 'Bunz UK', procured note paper so headed and began to seek and secure orders. He sent letters to customers informing them of the 'launch of Bunz UK - the UK branch of Bunz' and he also sent them brochures and price lists. The judge found that the price to UK customers was arrived at

> 'by dividing the list price [namely Bunz's wholesale prices] by 2.2, a result which would give Mr Sagal a 25% margin.'

The judge then recorded the method of business that operated between 2002 and September 2005 when relationships deteriorated and grievances began:

(i)   Bunz UK took an order from a customer sending out a confirmation of purchase order in its own name; it then placed a purchase order on Bunz (to whom I shall now refer as 'Bunz GmbH');

(ii)   Bunz GmbH would confirm the order to Bunz UK giving Bunz UK's reference number and showing the appropriate (20%) discount; Bunz GmbH then invoiced Bunz UK;

(iii) Bunz UK sent its own invoice to its UK customers requesting payment to it;

(iv)   Bunz UK's invoice referred to 'Standard Conditions of supply' regulating the contract between the UK customer and 'the company' which the judge, correctly, held was a reference to Bunz UK.

It was on the basis of this documentation, evidencing the contract made between the UK customer and Bunz UK (Mr Sagal) on the one hand and the contract between Mr Sagal and Bunz GmbH on the other hand, that the judge concluded that Mr Sagal had no authority from Bunz GmbH to negotiate or contract on its behalf.

However, Sagal held no stock and Bunz GmbH insured the goods but Sagal charged what he liked when he resold the stock.

In practice commercial lawyers regularly are instructed in situations where it is not clear if an agency or distribution arrangement is envisaged. Some clauses suggest agent and commissions and direct sale from principal to customer and others suggest the 'agent' buys and resells. It is crucial to establish what is meant. There is also a category of agent at common law known as undisclosed agent where the customer does not know they are dealing with an agent's principal where there is no case law as to whether the regulations apply.

In the *Sagal* case the court of appeal decided Sagal was not an agent. The following passage from the Court of Appeal usefully summarises the court's view on several relevant points in this area:

> 'Construction of the Directive
>
> This question is whether the Directive applies only to agents who bring their principals into direct contractual relationship with their customers or whether

it can also apply to agents who make their own contracts with their customers. The defining words of the Directive itself are almost identical to the words in the regulation but it is perhaps important to recite Article 1(2) of the Directive itself:

> "For the purposes of this Directive 'commercial agent' shall mean a self-employed intermediary who has continuing authority to negotiate the sale or the purchase of goods on behalf of another person, hereinafter called the 'principal', or to negotiate and conclude such transactions on behalf of and in the name of the principal."

The difficulty with a construction which includes agents, who make contracts in their own name and on their own behalf is that there would then be no need for the second limb of the definition. If someone is an agent for another he will invariably have authority to negotiate (namely, to find out the terms on which a third party wishes to contract) on behalf of his principal; the question may then arise whether he has authority to contract on behalf of his principal. The first limb of the definition envisages that the agent does not have authority to contract on his principal's behalf but only has authority to negotiate terms on behalf of his principal and then refer back to him to see whether he wants to make a contract on certain terms with a third party customer. To my mind the definition further envisages that, if the principal does want to make a contract with the customer, he will then do so and there will then be a contract made directly between the customer and the principal which will be made in the name of the principal. It does not envisage that, after the agent refers back to the principal and obtains the go-ahead for making a contract, the agent will enter into a contract in his own name with the customer; the reason for that is that, although he will then have authority to conclude a contract which is not in the principal's name, he will not come within the second limb of the definition which is the limb dealing with authority to contract. In other words agents with authority to contract (as opposed to authority to negotiate) are only commercial agents for the purposes of the Directive if they have authority to contract (and do contract) in the name of the principal as well as on his behalf. That is precisely the authority which Mr Sagal did not have since, as the documents show, he never contracted in the name Bunz GmbH but only in the name of Bunz UK which was (as Mr Stuart recognised) a mere trade name for himself.

It is, of course, possible as a matter of English law for a principal to authorise an agent to make a contract on behalf of the principal but in the name of the agent rather than in the name of the principal. To my mind agents who contract in that way do not come within the definition of "commercial agents". It is perhaps not difficult to see why this should be so. If a principal is unidentified or undisclosed on the face of the contract it will often be difficult to ascertain whether a particular contract is, or contracts in general are, made on his behalf or not. It may require oral and undocumented evidence of the parties' intention. I doubt if the framers of the Directive thought that courts should receive detailed oral evidence over many days about the details of the parties' commercial relationships in order to decide whether someone was a "commercial agent". If the Directive only applies where the principal's name appears on the face of the contracts made with the third parties, the inquiry can be a quick and straightforward inquiry, only requiring disclosure of the parties' contractual documentation.'

1.6   While the English authorities have not had to grapple directly with this particular debate about the proper construction of the Directive, they are by no means inconsistent with the above conclusion. In *AMB Imballaggi Plastici SRL v Pacflex Ltd* [1999] 2 All ER (Comm) 249, BAILII: [1999] EWCA Civ 1618 the judge had found that there was no formalised contract between the claimant principal and the defendant agent but that the way the agent had chosen to do his business was on the basis of a sale (by the principal to the agent) and a re-sale (by the agent to the customer or third party); the agent charged a mark-up chosen by it and not dictated by the claimant. This court held that the agent was not a commercial agent within the Regulations because it had throughout acted on its own behalf not on behalf of any principal. The court does not appear to have had any argument addressed to it about the detailed terms of the contractual documentation but held that an arrangement whereby the agent was entitled to choose his own mark-up on resale to the third party was unlikely to constitute a 'commercial agency'. (No doubt this holding accounted for the detailed argument below on the question whether the price to the UK customer was imposed or only advisory.) Waller LJ said (page 252):

> 'If a person buys or sells himself as principal he is outside the ambit of the regulations. That is so because in negotiating that sale or purchase he is acting on his own behalf and not on behalf of another.'

In that case therefore it was clear, as a matter of fact, that the so-called agent was not in fact acting on behalf of the so-called principal. It does not follow that every agent acting on behalf of the principal is necessarily a 'commercial agent' especially if contracts are made in his own name and not in the name of the principal.

> 'Mark-up is not, however, conclusive against commercial agency. In *Mercantile International Group Plc v Chuan Soon Huat Industrial Group Ltd* [2002] 1 All ER (Comm) 788, [2002] EWCA Civ 288 the defendant principal was content for the claimant agent to retain an undisclosed margin on contracts made with third parties in the United Kingdom. But all the contracts made with those third parties stated that the contracts were made with the principal and that the claimant was acting as agent only. This court held that that documentation had to be conclusive unless the documentation could be shown to be a sham, other factors allegedly inconsistent with the claimant being an agent (eg the mark-up) could not be relied on to displace that documentation. Rix LJ cited the *Pacflex* case and the earlier case of *Re Nevill ex p White* (1871) LR6 Ch App 697 in both of which it had been held that the parties were in truth seller and buyer rather than principal and agent but he then said (page 798a) that it was critical in both cases that there had not been contractual documentation stating that the contracts were made between the third party and the principal. So, where there is documentation, that documentation is critical. Here the

documentation is to the opposite effect to that in the *MIG* case and, to my mind, the opposite conclusion must follow namely that there is no commercial agency.

HH Judge Mackie QC said that, in a case where the picture presented by the documents was clear, oral evidence from many witnesses about the details of the parties' relationships

"was not going to change that clear picture."

I agree with that conclusion and would, therefore, conclude that Mr Sagal was not a commercial agent within the meaning of the Directive.'

Case example – *Bailey and D&D Wines International Ltd in liquidation v Angove's Pty Ltd* [2014] EWCA Civ 215

1.7 In the *Bailey's* case D&D International Wines Ltd, the second defendant, was in liquidation so Angove gave notice to D&D to terminate their agreement immediately. Just like many of the muddled client-drafted agreements which come across the writer's desk on a regular basis, the agreement appointed D&D as its sole agent and distributor. Angrove's applied to court for a ruling on whether it was entitled to A$570,843.22 and A$302,773.86 which sums were being held in escrow pending the decision and arose from the sale of wines to third party customers. On appeal the Court of Appeal set aside the judgment below and ordered the sums to be paid to the liquidators representing the agent. The Supreme Court overturned this in 2016.

The sums D&D received were not held on trust for the principal and could be used to pay the creditors for D&D.

The moral is not to let the agent receive and handle money. First, because that can make it hard to prove if an agency relationship arises and second, it runs the risk to the principal that the money is lost. Consider setting up distribution arrangements with the distributor paying in advance for the goods as an alternative rather than having an agent at all if the agent might otherwise have to handle money.

Definitions

1.8 A definition is given of 'commercial agent' in the Commercial Agents (Council Directive) Regulations 1993, SI 1993/3053 (see Appendix 1). These Regulations are known as 'the Regulations' throughout this work and they set out certain important rights and obligations which apply to agents. The Regulations apply in Great Britain. There is a separate set applicable to Northern Ireland (see Appendix 1). There are no material differences between the two.

1.9 Some agents are not within the definition in the Regulations and yet are clearly 'agents' so the term must be used more broadly than this. For example, the Regulations provide protection for agents who market 'goods' but not agents who market services. Those who market services are just as much 'agents' in many legal senses, and are paid commission and do not contract on their own behalf, but they have no protection (in the UK, though they may in other countries like Spain) under the Regulations or indeed the EU Directive on which the Regulations are based. A copy of the Agency Directive appears in Appendix 2. It is called the Directive throughout.

1.10   How an agreement is drafted can provided assistance. The Court of Appeal in a decision *Mercantile* decided in a case where the individual could have been either agent or distributor that reading the contracts and terms in place, the arrangement was intended and was one of agency (see *Mercantile International Group Plc v Chuan Soon Huat Industrial Group Plc* [2002] 1 All ER (Comm) 788, Court of Appeal). In that case the first instance judgment which was confirmed on appeal held that payment by way of 'mark up' not commission was not to be regarded as inconsistent with an agency agreement.

1.11   Regulation 2(1) of the Regulations provides:

> 'In these Regulations – "commercial agent" means a self-employed intermediary who has continuing authority to negotiate the sale or purchase of goods on behalf of another person (the "principal") or to negotiate and conclude the sale or purchase of goods on behalf of and in the name of that principal; but shall be understood as not including in particular:
>
> (i)   a person who, in his capacity as an officer of a company or association, is empowered to enter into commitments binding on that company or association;
>
> (ii)   a partner who is lawfully authorised to enter into commitments binding on his partners;
>
> (iii) a person who acts as an insolvency practitioner (as that expression is defined in s 388 of the Insolvency Act 1986) or the equivalent in any other jurisdiction.'

1.12   The Regulations go on to provide that they do not apply to unpaid agents, agents operating on commodity exchanges or in the commodity market, or the Crown Agents for Overseas Government and Administrations, as set up under the Crown Agents Act 1979 or its subsidiaries.

Relevance of application of the Regulations

1.13   All those involved in drafting and advising on commercial agency agreements should first ask themselves if the Regulations will apply. This is because in general terms, if the Regulations do apply, then certain obligations are implied in the agreement and, in particular, as will be seen in Chapter 6, the agent has the right to claim compensation or an indemnity when the contract is terminated. If the Regulations do not apply, then largely the parties are free to agree whatever they like in their commercial agreement subject to the rules applicable to commercial agreements. The law will rarely interfere and clauses will all be upheld by the courts. Sometimes an agency agreement breaches the competition rules (considered in Chapter 3), in article 101 of TFEU where it affects trade between EU Member States (or the Chapter I prohibition in the Competition Act 1998 which applies in the UK), but this is rare. However, in some countries abroad compensation is paid on termination of contract of agents marketing services as well as good so always take local law advice.

1.14   Compensation for agents just like protection for employees and protection against anti-competitive agreements will be superimposed over choice of law. One cannot avoid English employment law by appointing English staff in the UK under the laws of some foreign state with no such protection. In the same way compensation for agents cannot easily be overridden by choice of law and jurisdiction even though the EU Rome I Regulation (593/2008) (on choice of law in contractual matters) and Brussels Regulation (1215/2012) (which replaced for new agreements the predecessor Brussels Regulation from 10 January 2015 (44/2001) – see further in Chapter 8) on jurisdiction in theory mean that in the EU choice of law and jurisdiction in a contract is largely respected. The position after the UK leaves the EU is likely to remain similar.

1.15   The basic principle is that if the Regulations apply then the law intervenes in the agreement; otherwise the parties have a free rein. This is why this chapter concentrates on who is an 'agent' within the narrow definition of the Regulations. Agents who are at common law agents but not 'agents' as defined by the Regulations will normally in practice have a written commercial agreement which will set out the powers and obligations of the parties. The extent of the agent's powers will normally be set out in such contract. If not, then common law may intervene. For example, an agent who is held out as such will bind his principal. In practice, companies are advised to ensure that there is always a written agency agreement setting out the rights and obligations of the parties.

1.16   Do not use standard agency contracts for agents within the regulations who are outside the regulations as too many rights will be given to the agent when there is no need to do so such as an indemnity payment on termination, post termination commission, longer notice periods and the like.

Self-employed

1.17   The Regulations first require that the agent be a 'self-employed intermediary'. Thus, an agent who is employed cannot be protected by the Regulations. He may be protected by employment law, for example if unfairly dismissed, but the Regulations will not apply. The first question to be asked of an agent is whether he is employed or not. There are many employment law cases in the UK which seek to define 'employment' and set out the relevant test. Control is an important issue. Just because an agent is called an 'employee' or called 'self-employed' does not mean that those terms are strictly accurate. For tax reasons many companies seek to ensure employees are deemed 'self-employed', but in practice they really are employees acting for one employer only. Tax changes placing the burden of proof on employers other than small businesses to establish the tax position of a consultant were (until the December 2019 election) expected to be brought into force by the Finance 2019/20 Bill, but were only to apply to consultants operating through limited companies under rules known as IR35, not sole traders or partnerships. In any event, most commercial agents are unlikely to be employees although some principals even in 2019 keen to be rid of agents without compensation have suggested the agent 'must' become an employee in April 2020. This is usually not the case. The questions to be asked are:

- what is the title given to the person?

- does he hold other non-competing agencies?

- is he allowed to take on other agencies?

- is he paid a fixed sum or just commission? (though some true agents are paid a retainer and commission)

- does the agent bear his own expenses?

- does the agent decide when and where he works?

1.18   Some have sought to avoid the application of the Regulations by paying agents a very low monthly retainer – so low that it is below the tax and national insurance threshold – and then commission in addition, and in some industries this type of payment structure is common. Indeed, some employees (eg telesales operators) are paid entirely on the basis of commission, while some estate agents make the bulk of their income from commission. They may still be employees, as it is not always easy to make the distinction between employees and the self-employed. If there is only one client of a 'self-employed' agent, it is likely that he is an employee rather than self-employed, though this is not invariably the case.

1.19   In *James Craig Donald/Craijan Ltd v Worcester Marine Windows Ltd* Case No: 2WR00372 (January 2013 http://www.bailii.org/cgi-bin/markup. cgi?doc=/ew/cases/Misc/2013/41.html&query=Craijan&method=all)   in which the writer acted for the claimant agent, the agent was being paid initially £7,650 per year by way of retainer. The defendant sought to argue that this precluded the application of the Regulations and the county court held that the agent was still protected and was a self-employed agent. Commission was paid in addition to this agent and the retainer stopped after an initial period in any event.

'The letter of the 13th March 2008 set out that a declining retainer would be paid during the first year and a product commission structure would operate throughout. The purpose of these arrangements was to allow the first Claimant to spend time familiarising himself with the business and researching opportunities for its development. I calculate the retainer to aggregate to £7,650, although the Defendant pleads in the defence "£7,950 (wages)". Nothing turns on arithmetical difference. The payment was not wages and even the Defendant asserts self-employment, not employment.'

1.20　Two cases examined these issues. In one an employee seeking to avoid Child Support Agency income deductions went self-employed and became an agent. The Court of Appeal upheld the relationship as agency because of its form (surprisingly, normally substance counts for more). The case was *(Smith (Julian) v Reliance Water Controls Ltd* (1993). In the second case *(Mercantile International Group Plc v Chuan Soon Huat Industrial Group Plc* [2002] 1 All ER (Comm) 788, Court of Appeal) again form won over substance. Looking at distribution and agency where sometimes it is hard to assess the nature of the relationship, in this decision the Court of Appeal held that the man was an agent despite certain notable features which suggested distributorship. The court thought the fact that the contracts between agent and principal and with customers described the relationship as agency and were not treated as a sham and must be considered.

Agents who are companies

1.21　The use of the word 'self-employed' has caused some to question whether the Regulations apply if the agent is a limited company. The term 'self-employed' is not normally applied to companies and the Regulations also refer to compensation being payable when an agent 'dies', which would appear to rule out companies.

1.22　However, the Government guidance notes on the Directive (which are reproduced in Appendix 1) suggest the Regulations do apply to agents who are companies. Although the guidance is not on the Department for Business website, the law has not changed and the guidance remains of interest. It is also referenced at https://publications.parliament.uk/pa/cm199697/cmselect/cmeuleg/036i/el0119.htm.

The Guidance states:

'The expression "self-employed" is derived from articles 52 and 57 of the Treaty of Rome [as they then were] (which deal with freedom of establishment and freedom to provide services) and is consistent with Community law, to be understood as including, for example, companies as well as self-employed individuals.'

1.23　It was always intended corporate agents would be protected. In F Randolph and J Davey, *Guide to the Commercial Agents Regulations* (2nd edn, 2003), this is examined:

'Indeed the draft Directive which was the subject of the Commission's Explanatory Memorandum of 14 December 1976, appended to the Law Commission Report, expressly allowed the exclusion of certain of the agent's rights where the paid-up share capital of the agent exceeded a given figure clearly indicating that corporate entities will fall within the definition of commercial agent.' (p 40)

1.24   The Regulations expressly do not apply to officers of a company who have authority, such as a director might have, to bind the company to contracts. Of course, Government guidance notes are not a definitive statement of the law. However, in practice many settlements have been achieved where the agent is a limited company and most businesses proceed on the basis that the Regulations apply in such a case. The *AMB Imballagii Pastici Srl v Pacflex Ltd* case concerned an agent, Pacflex Ltd, which was incorporated. The case contains some interesting comments:

'It was submitted by Mr Stood on behalf of AMB that Pacflex was not a commercial agent within the meaning of the Regulations (and the Directive) for three reasons. These are:

(a)   The Regulations and the Directive apply only to individuals and do not apply to companies;

(b)   Pacflex did not negotiate the sale of goods on behalf of AMB or conclude the sale of goods on behalf of AMB; Pacflex purchased goods from AMB and resold them to the end users and so acted as a distributor of goods rather than as an agent;

(c)   Pacflex's activities in connection with goods supplied by AMB were 'secondary' within the meaning of regulation 2(3) and so the Regulations did not apply.'

The court considered first whether the Regulations applied to companies. The judge decided the Regulations did apply to companies 'on the basis of a purposive construction of the Directive, Regulations and of articles 57 and 58 of the Treaty [*as they then were – numbering since changed*] and do so despite references in the Regulations which suggest that the draughtsman had individuals primarily in mind'. The court said that the phrase 'self-employed' did not refer to self-employment in the 'special meaning of English law but as a meaning akin to "independent", perhaps as it is used in the term "independent contractor" in English law'. In *Pacflex* the arrangement was not agency and the agent determined resale prices and this was a distributorship agreement. This decision was reviewed in *Mercantile International Group Plc v Chuan Soon Huat Industrial Group Plc* [2002] 1 All ER (Comm) 788 to which reference should be made.

Partnerships

1.25   Some agencies are run as partnerships and these are also covered by the Regulations. The agency contract needs to address issues relevant to such means of trading. For example, if there are two partners and one dies, would the principal wish to continue the agreement with the remaining partner, particularly if the one who died did all the work and had all the experience? The other complex issue addressed generally (see Chapter 5) is whether the compensation due to an agent on 'death' is payable if only one of two partners dies. Probably it is not, as 'the agent' continues in existence despite the death of one partner.

Continuing authority

1.26 The Regulations only apply where the agent has continuing authority to negotiate the sale or purchase of goods on behalf of another person or to negotiate and conclude the sale or purchase of goods in the name of the principal. If the agent is contracting in his own name, then he will normally be a distributor and not an agent. However, he may be an undisclosed agent. The customers may believe he is the principal in the sales transaction. In the *Pacflex* case mentioned above, the judge thought that the fact that an agreement allowed Pacflex to act as agent whereas Pacflex acted all along as distributor meant there was no 'continuing authority' under the Regulations.

1.27 There are two alternatives in this provision: either the agent just negotiates, or he negotiates and concludes transactions. Probably the vast majority of commercial agents just negotiate but do not have the final say in whether a particular customer will be supplied. Indeed, most agency agreements make it clear that the principal has the right to determine whether to do business with a particular customer. The customer may have a bad reputation in the trade or be a bad payer. Normally the principal retains complete discretion as to whether or not to accept an order.

1.28 In other agencies the agent not only finds the customers but also concludes the transaction. He may even ship the goods to the customer and receive the payment due to the principal from which the agent deducts his commission, forwarding the balance to the principal. This gives the agent considerable control, and some arrangements of this type are hard to distinguish from distribution agreements.

Example

1.29 The JJ Company supplies electrical products. It uses Mr H as a so-called agent. Mr H markets the products at the prices stipulated by JJ Company and receives the proceeds of sale. He then sends the money he has received back to JJ Company, less his agreed 'commission'. However, he invoices the customers in his own name. Is he an agent or distributor?

This type of arrangement is all too common and is a complete muddle from the legal point of view. As far as the customers are concerned Mr H is selling as principal. He is an undisclosed agent, if he is an agent at all. The fact he invoices customers suggests he is in reality a distributor rather than an agent. However, the fact the prices at which he 'sells' are stipulated by the principal, JJ, suggests he is an agent. If Mr H is a distributor then JJ has broken both UK and EU competition law in setting the resale price. Resale price maintenance is prohibited.

What is negotiation?

1.30   For many the term 'negotiation' in the Regulations has appeared as a major loophole as the Regulations only apply where the agent 'negotiates'. It can be argued that most agents cannot negotiate, as they have no freedom to depart from the principal's price list and terms of business. Their contract may state this or may only allow them to vary those items with consent of the principal. Their agency contract, drafted with the Regulations in mind, may also make it clear that they have no continuing authority to negotiate. This point is raised again and again between commercial solicitors litigating commercial agency disputes.

1.31   UK Government guidance notes state:

'Some agents only effect introductions between their principals and third parties. The question arises as to whether such agents are commercial agents for the purposes of the Regulations. Such agents are sometimes known as "canvassing" or "introducing" agents. As such, they generally lack the power to bind their principals and are not really agents in the true sense of the word. However, to the extent that such an agent "has continuing authority to negotiate the sale or purchase of goods" on behalf of his principal, even though, as a matter of fact, he merely effects introductions, it seems that he would fall within the definition of "commercial agent" in regulation 2(1). It is clear that an "introducing" agent who lacks such authority falls outside the scope of the definition of "commercial agent". It may be that the courts would give a wide interpretation to the word "negotiate" and that, as a result, "introducing" agents will, in general, have the benefit of the Regulations.'

It is unlikely that the term 'negotiation' is a major saving grace for principals in avoiding the Regulations. It may be construed by the courts as meaning little more than that the agent is sent out to persuade customers to buy. If persuasion is the same as negotiation, then such agents are covered. However, principals can do themselves no harm by stipulating in agency contracts that the agent has no power to negotiate and then seeking to claim that the Regulations do not apply in due course. This argument may succeed, for taking the ordinary meaning of 'negotiation' such agents genuinely do not negotiate. Chapter 3 looks at when a website might amount to an agency or a distribution arrangement although the CMA 2015 investigation (Skyscanner) considered in Chapter 3 may provide more light on this topic in due course. Websites purely with 'click through' revenue are probably simply introduction agencies (they are certainly not distribution agreements although with some other online selling it is sometimes unclear as to who is an agent and who a distributor.

1.32   Negotiation was looked at in the decision of *Parks v Esso Petroleum Company Ltd* [2000] Eu LR 25. Mr Parks ran a garage for Esso, the oil/petrol company. He was paid a commission on sales but all he did was run the garage and have a discretion which credit cards to accept. The court held he did not have the necessary negotiating power required for the Regulations to apply. Negotiate means more than mere self-service but less than haggling. The court said:

> 'If the word "negotiated" is given its ordinary English meaning, I feel myself quite unable to avoid the conclusion he [Mr Parks] is not a commercial agent. He does not negotiate the sale of motor fuel. The price at which motor fuel is sold is fixed by the principal. He concludes the sale as agent, but does not negotiate in any sense at all.

> Did Mr Parks negotiate and conclude the sale of petrol owned by Esso to those who attended his forecourt? I take the normal meaning of the word from the Oxford English Dictionary definition. . . . This definition does not require a process of bargaining in the sense of . . . haggle. But equally it does require more than the self-service by the customer followed by payment in the shop of the price shown on the pump.'

1.33   In *Accentuate Ltd v Asigra Inc* [2009] EWHC 2655 (QB) (see further below) a case about arbitration clauses and service outside the jurisdiction, the court usefully summarised the law on 'negotiate' as follows:

> 'The Distributor submits that for the purposes of defining a commercial agent pursuant to Reg. 2(1), the term "negotiate" is to be given a very wide definition.'

1.34   For example, in the case of *Nigel Fryer Joinery Services Ltd v Ian Firth Hardware Ltd* [2008] EWHC 767 (Ch); [2008] 2 Lloyd's Rep 108, at paras 17 and 18 Patten J (as he then was) said:

> 'The word "negotiate" is not defined in the Regulations but Bowstead on Agency [18th ed] (at para 11–018) suggests that 'one who canvasses on what one would call a retained basis' could be a commercial agent unless actually forbidden to solicit contractual offers'.

The finding in *Fryer* was informed in part by the earlier decision of Fulford J in *PJ Pipe & Valve Co Ltd v Audco India Ltd* [2005] EWHC 1904. Both those cases in turn are based on the definition of 'negotiate' in commercial agency cases in *Parks v Esso Petroleum Co Ltd* [1999] 18 Tr L Rep 232; [2000] Eu LR 25. In that case there was extensive argument, including reference to the German text of the version of the Directive which was then current. Morritt LJ (as he then was) held that 'negotiate' meant what the Oxford English Dictionary said it meant: 'to deal with, manage or conduct' (see at 32D to 33F).

1.35   The *Pipe & Valve* decision is particularly worth reading in relation to who is an agent. The agent had no authority to negotiate or deviate from terms or prices but was building up significant goodwill and the court held this was sufficient to bring the agent within the Regulations. In that case the judge said:

> 'The purpose of the Directive, in my view, was to provide protection to agents by giving them a stake in the goodwill which they have generated for the principal, and as a result the courts should avoid a limited or restricted interpretation of the word "negotiate" that would exclude agents who have been engaged to develop the principal's business in this way, and who successfully generated goodwill to the manufacturer, to the latter's benefit after the agency terminated.'

1.36   In *Invicta UK v International Brands Ltd* [2013] EWHC 1564 the court said:

> 'I agree that the word "negotiate" (and its equivalents in the other languages of the EU) is to be widely construed. In the case of *Parks v Esso Petroleum Co Ltd* [1999] 18 Tr L Rep [at 33E–34B], a definition along the lines of "deal with, manage or conduct [a sale]" was accepted. There is no need for the agent necessarily to be involved in a process of bargaining over price. In the case of *P J Pipe & Valve Co Ltd v Audco India Ltd* [2005] EWHC 1904 (QB) [154] [at 155] it was held to be no bar to the claimant's reliance on the Regulations that it was found not to have been engaged to solicit orders at all, but rather to promote the principal's capabilities to contractors generally and seek its designation as an transactions are "... concluded as a result of his action" and "... concluded with a third party whom he has previously acquired as a customer for transactions of the same kind".

Thus, the activities of a commercial agent extend to procuring transactions and acquiring customers for repeat orders. Neither of these activities need include negotiating the terms of the transaction, provided that the agent gets business in for the principal.

The Claimant submits that whether an agent has continuing authority to negotiate is to be determined, in the first instance, at the time when the agency agreement was made. This, they say, is consistent with the court's approach to a similar question raised in *Tamarind International v Eastern Natural Gas* (whether one transaction is likely to lead to further transactions with the same customer or to customers in the same geographical area). It follows that whether that authority comes to be exercised less frequently (or even not at all) as the agency continues and customer relationships are established and then cemented, is neither here nor there, unless the continuing authority is withdrawn.

Therefore, one must establish whether Invicta in 2008 (more precisely at about 21st August 2008) was a commercial agent not whether Invicta in 2009 was a commercial agent, as if the relationship at the outset was one of commercial agency, then the transferred agency continues as a commercial agency with the rights and liabilities passed to the transferee. That must be assumed to be so as a purchaser would not purchase the commercial agency if the commercial agency functions were no longer being performed. I agree with the claimant's submissions on this point'.

However, the judge did say what happened later in the agency could be relevant – although in this case the agent did have continuing authority and the agent's activities were not 'secondary' and the Regulations applied. Approximately £124,000 was awarded for compensation. The agent had other agencies and a total turnover (commission income) of £1m of which only £60,000 was generated by the International Brands agency which was the subject matter of this case.

The decision is also worth consideration by readers in relation to the issue of assessment of compensation in agency cases as well as the question above of the construction of 'continuing authority to negotiate'.

1.37   In *Green Deal Marketing Southern Ltd v Economy Energy Trading Ltd* [2019] EWHC 507 (Ch D), £1m compensation was awarded under the Regulations. This is possibly the largest award in a court decision (although the writer has had one of that size where she acted for the agent in a settlement, and there are highly likely to be other settlements exceeding this). In relation to the issue of 'continuing authority to negotiate' the principal argued that the agent did not have authority to negotiate, and did not negotiate, the sale of power to customers; 'its role was limited to soliciting customers to switch their supplier to EE, so that the customers could thereafter buy power from EE, but it had no part in any consequent sale of gas or electricity'.

The court said in *Green Deal*:

'I accept that GDM had authority to, and did, negotiate the sale of goods on behalf of EE. It is correct, as Mr Green points out, that GDM did not directly negotiate sales of energy but rather acted in respect of signing the customers up to a switch of energy providers, who then made the sales themselves. However, the courts have construed the Regulations broadly so as to bring work such as that done by GDM within the scope of the definition. In *PJ Pipe Valve Co Ltd v Audio India Limited* [2005] EWHC 1904 (QB), Fulford J treated "negotiate" as meaning "to deal with, manage or conduct", a construction he derived from the judgment of Morritt LJ in *Parks v Esso Petroleum Company Limited* [2000] E.C.C. 45: see [30]-[32] in Morritt LJ's judgment. In *Nigel Fryer Joinery Services Ltd v Ian Firth Hardware Ltd* [2008] EWHC 767 (Ch), Patten J said the meaning attributed to "negotiate" by Fulford J was "obviously a much wider meaning of the word than to negotiate a sale in the sense of engaging in the bargaining process or haggling over terms or price", and at [20] he approved that construction of the Regulations:

"I prefer the approach of Fulford J. It seems to me that the inclusion in reg. 2(1) of two definitions of commercial agent (negotiate the sale or negotiate and conclude the sale) indicates that the first of these alternatives can include the wider meaning which he gave to the word 'negotiate' in the first of the two definitions. This can, I think, include an agent whose role (like that of Mr Fryer) is to get the client interested in the product; suggest possible prices subject to confirmation by the principal; and to encourage the customer to place an order at those prices. This seems to me to come well within the ordinary meaning of 'negotiate'."

Consistently with this approach, both in *Tamarind International [Tamarind International Ltd v Eastern Natural Gas (Retail) Ltd* [2000] Eur LR 708] and in the *Devers* case [*Devers v Electricity Direct (UK) Ltd* (unreported, 7 November 2008)], where the facts were, in the relevant respect, materially identical to those of the present case, the court accepted that the definition of commercial agent in regulation 2(1) was satisfied, notwithstanding the fact that the agents in those cases had no ability to alter the offered terms and were not involved in the actual sales of energy.'

1.38   In *James Craig Donald/Craijan Ltd v Worcester Marine Windows Ltd* Case No. 2WR00372 (January 2013, County Court), where the writer acted for the successful agent claimant (who won three years' commission as compensation), His Honour Judge Hooper said the activities:

'fell within the proper broad interpretation of the word "negotiate". He [the agent] dealt with the customers, conducted the relationship with them and exercised his skill and experience in doing so. His role was to build up the goodwill of the business. He acquired a large number of new customers and encouraged existing customers to switch from regular windows to the more profitable S-type windows'.

1.39   In practice the writer tells clients that negotiate means little more than persuade to buy otherwise most agents would be outside the regulations as few agents have power to vary prices or terms.

Del credere agents

1.40   It is the view of Government guidance that *del credere* agents do benefit from the Regulations where they exhibit the characteristics of the definition of commercial agent in the Regulations. These are quasi-agents who take the commercial risk on transactions. The guidance states:

'The Department does not consider that the additional features of a *del credere* agency causes the agent to fall outside the definition. Questions can, however, arise as to whether a person is an agent at all who, in consideration of extra remuneration, guarantees to his principal that third parties with whom he enters into contracts on behalf of the principal will duly pay any sums becoming due under those contracts (and thus appears to be a del credere agent) or, whether that person is really acting on his own account.'

This is the difficult test – is the agent acting on his own account? Does he take the commercial risk on the transaction? However, even this test is not definitive in determining whether the Regulations apply, as the Regulations themselves provide that if a customer defaults (eg refuses to pay through shortage of funds) the principal can require the agent to repay commission. Therefore, the Regulations contemplate that agents can take commercial risks in relation to transactions of which they are an agent. The position is therefore unclear.

One-off agents

1.41 Sometimes an agent is appointed for one transaction only. A new power plant may be built and an agent appointed to arrange various purchases or sales. The Regulations only apply where an agent has 'continuing' authority. The DTI say that 'if an agent is appointed for a specified number of transactions, then he could be excluded from the scope of the Regulations, owing to his lack of continuing authority'.

Case example – *Hunter v Zenith Windows* (13 June 1997, Norwich County Court, unreported) (see Financial Times, 7 July 1998)

1.42 In this case the court examined a claim by an agent who was responsible for the activities of a number of double-glazing agents. The agent had principally an administrative role, but the Regulations still would have applied. However, the court found that as one transaction made by the agent (ie double-glazing installation) would not be unlikely to lead to further transactions with the same customer then the agent's activities were 'secondary' and he was excluded from the Regulations. The Regulations include a detailed and rather confusing Schedule on 'secondary activities' described below. Where the activities of an agent are secondary, such as where he is mostly a distributor trading on his own account and only does a small amount of agency work, then the Regulations do not apply at all.

1.43 If an agent is appointed for a series of one-off transactions, perhaps simply to avoid the impact of the Regulations, it is highly likely the court will look to the reality of the situation and determine that there is indeed continuing authority.

1.44 Where the agent is appointed as agent for one customer only the Regulations are likely to apply. Indeed, the compensation provisions, when addressing what benefits an agent has brought to the principal, take into account not only whether the agent has found new customers but also whether he has increased the volume of business with existing customers.

Purchasing agents

1.45 The Regulations apply equally to agents who are procuring purchases. Regulation 2(1), which defines 'commercial agent', includes agents who have authority to negotiate the purchase of goods on behalf of another person. For example, members of a trade association might seek to obtain discounts on bulk orders by clubbing together and using an agent to obtain supplies for them, perhaps one of the purchasing agency companies which exist for this purpose. Those agents will be protected by the Regulations.

Non-commission agents

1.46   Some agents are paid a fixed monthly sum or retainer in addition to commission. This depends on the industry concerned. In some industries, only commission agents are used. In others, where the agent will be involved in a lot of initial expense in fulfilling the agency, a retainer will be paid too. This does not necessarily make the agent an 'employee' and outside the Regulations. Some agents are just paid a retainer and no commission at all, but they can still benefit from the Regulations. This is quite clear, because regulation 6(3) provides that 'Where the commercial agent is not remunerated (in whole or in part) by commission, regulations 7 to 12 below *[which deal with commission]* do not apply'. The rest of the Regulations would apply in those circumstances. Therefore, it is not true to say that just because an agent is paid other than on a commission basis then the Regulations do not apply. However, it may be easier to show an agent is an employee where he is paid a fixed monthly sum. Other factors too would be relevant in any such analysis, and reference should be made to employment law and tax books in relation to any such examination.

1.47   In *Duffen v FRA* (30 April 1998 [2000] Lloyd's Rep 180), the court awarded an indemnity payment on termination of an agency in a case where the agent was paid a £4,000 monthly retainer in addition to commission. There is no doubt that a retainer does not of itself affect the application of the Regulations.

Who is the principal?

1.48   Sometimes a dispute arises as to who is the principal. Many agency arrangements begin with two clearly defined parties and then over the years businesses are sold or divided and the principal ultimately is a different company from that which originally contracted. However, in most cases the new principal has paid commission and taken on the role, albeit not always documented in writing, and thus becomes the 'principal' in law even if no agreements are signed. English contract law does not require a written agreement in any event, simply offer, acceptance, consideration and intention to create legal relations.

Case example – *Light v Ty Europe Ltd* [2003] EWCA Civ 1238

1.49   In *Light v Ty Europe Ltd* [2003] EWCA Civ 1238 the claimants entered into exclusive agreements with a company called SCS – a company with exclusive rights to market the defendant company's goods. SCS had no assets and ceased to trade. The claimants continued to act on behalf of the defendant thinking they were authorised to do so but without written agreement. They rejected contracts of employment offered to them by the defendant. They sued for compensation under the Regulations. The judge said they were commercial agents at first instance. However, the Court of Appeal disagreed.

There was no contract between the agents/claimants and the defendant. So, no compensation was due as the regulations did not apply.

1.50   Agency agreement do not need to be in writing for the Regulations to apply. In *Wells v Devani* [2019] UKSC 1106 the Supreme Court held that an agency agreement arose notwithstanding that there was no written contract. The case concerned estate agency services and was not a case relating to the Regulations, but even so, the principle that no written contract is needed for an agency to arise is generally applicable to situations where agencies within the Regulations arise.

Exclusions

1.51   The following are expressly excluded from regulation 2 and the Regulations do not apply to them:

1   *Officers of a company*

1.52   Directors, company secretaries and other officers of a limited company act on behalf of a company and often directors are not even employees. However, under regulation 2 they are not commercial agents either. This is the case even where they are empowered to bind the company.

2   *Partners*

1.53   Partners who are lawfully authorised to enter into commitments binding on other partners are not commercial agents. This of course is an entirely different question from that of whether the partnership itself is a commercial agent (which indeed it might be and which has been previously considered). Thus, a partner in a law firm who is dismissed cannot claim compensation under the Regulations.

3   *Insolvency practitioner*

1.54   A person who acts as an insolvency practitioner as defined in s 388 of the Insolvency Act 1986 or the equivalent in any other jurisdiction is, by virtue of regulation 2(1)(iii), not a commercial agent. Unfortunately, this does not cover all the different types of insolvency 'agents' which exist, but it is envisaged the courts will construe the provision broadly and exclude other similar persons.

4   *Unpaid agents*

1.55   Regulation 2(2)(a) provides that the Regulations do not apply to agents whose activities are unpaid. It is likely that 'payment' relates both to money and other benefits so that an agent paid in kind in some way may still benefit from the Regulations, whereas an agent truly acting as agent for nothing would not.

5 Commodity exchanges

1.56   Commercial agents when they operate on commodity exchanges or in the commodity market are excluded from the Regulations (regulation 2(2)(b)). There is some elaboration on this exclusion in the Government's guidance notes:

> 'A "commodity" is any tangible good. So called "commodity exchanges" deal in such goods and, to a large extent, in commodity "futures", ie the right to buy or sell a particular commodity at a particular price at a particular time in the figure, hence eg "coffee futures".'

Such people do not benefit from the provisions of the Regulations even though they are buying for clients the right to purchase certain goods in the future.

1.57   In *Pluczenik Diamond Co NV v W Nagel (A Firm)* [2018] EWCA Civ 2640 the court looked at the commodity exchange exclusion in a case involving a diamond broker. The court found that just because the product was traded on a commodity exchange did not mean an agent marketing diamonds was excluded from protection. Overturning the court below, the Court of Appeal held that sale of diamonds at 'sights' did not result in the exclusion applying.

The court looked at the purpose behind the EU Agency Directive and the commodity market exclusion. The Directive aims to reward agents for their efforts and goodwill and to exclude commodity exchanges as they are automatic. Hardwicke Chambers writing in *Corporate Briefing* journal (March 2019) summarised this part of the case as follows saying that the Court of Appeal followed:

> '*Tamarind International Ltd v Eastern Natural Gas (Retail) Ltd* [2000] CLC 1397, where, taking into account the continental jurisprudence, it was held that the purpose of the Regulations was: "*to protect agents by giving them a share of the goodwill which they have generated and from which the principal has benefited after the agency agreement has been terminated.*"

> Leggatt LJ therefore concluded that the rationale for excluding sales on the commodities markets or exchanges from the scope of the Regulations was because: "... *trading which takes place on a commodity exchange is not an activity by which members of the exchange who buy and sell on behalf of clients build up goodwill for their principals with counterparties. It is trading of a nature where the identity of a counterparty is largely irrelevant. Sales are made to whoever is able and willing to pay the agreed price. Considerations of customer or supplier loyalty and goodwill are of little or no significance. Indeed, the rules of an exchange are usually intended to promote this by providing confidence that any contract made between members of the exchange will be honoured. Thus, it would be implausible for a commodity broker to suggest that, because it has executed many trades on behalf of a particular principal over a long*

period, it has thereby helped to develop valuable relationships between the principal and other traders from which the principal will continue to benefit if it decides to use a different broker."

Leggatt LJ found that the relationship between Sightholders and brokers was the antithesis of such impersonal trading; noting that allocations were made on the basis of brokers maintaining goodwill with De Beers and lobbying and promoting their individual Sightholders. He therefore found that the agency relationship between the parties was exactly the kind to which the protections afforded by the Regulations would be most expected to apply. In the absence of any 'clear and countervailing purpose' which would be served by excluding the case from the scope of the Regulations, Leggatt LJ found that adopting the broad definition applied by the court below would frustrate its purpose. This would be contrary to the principle of EU law that exceptions from the general scope of a Directive should be interpreted strictly, although not in such a way as to deprive the exceptions of their intended effect.

Leggatt LJ agreed with the submission that the definitions of 'commercial agent' and 'commodity exchange or market' were two distinct questions which needed to be addressed separately. However, it did not follow that the two concepts did not share a common underlying purpose. Thus, although: *"... the creation of goodwill for the principal is not an element of the definition of a commercial agent: it is a concept which informs its interpretation. It ought likewise to inform the interpretation of the commodity market exception – all the more so in the absence of any other identified purpose for it."* Leggatt LJ concluded therefore that the Regulations applied.'

Hardwicke Chambers continued:

'The decision has clarified several areas of uncertainty regarding the interpretation of "commercial agent" and the scope of the commodities market exception. Key points of general application include:

- the interpretation of "commercial agent" as defined by Regulation 2(1) is flexible; at least where the commodities market exception is raised as an issue. In such cases, the question of whether the agent has generated goodwill for the principal individually will fall to be considered.

- the defining feature of a "commodity exchange" or "commodity market" is free trading between participants whose identities – and with them, concepts of goodwill and loyalty – are largely irrelevant to the negotiation and execution of individual sales.'

6 Crown agents

1.58 The Regulations do not apply to the Crown Agents for Overseas Governments and Administrations, as set up under the Crown Agents Act 1979 or its subsidiaries (regulation 2(2)(c)).

Goods and services

1.59   Perhaps one of the most important factors in relation to the application of the Regulations is their application only to agents who market goods. Obviously, what all agents provide is services (agency services) rather than goods, but the Regulations look at what the agent is marketing for the principal. If it is not goods then the Regulations do not apply at all. The original draft of the EU Agency Directive had referred to services but this was deliberately removed. Therefore, one of the first questions for the lawyer drafting an agency contract is whether the products concerned are goods or not. In many cases there is no doubt – the agent is marketing car spare parts, frozen fish or whatever, products which are clearly goods on any definition. In other cases it is not at all clear. In some cases, it is clearly services, in which case the Regulations will not apply. Examples of services which agents market include:

- car hire or car leasing (though obviously not car sales);

- package holidays;

- rental of houses and flats and leases of leasehold flats;

- subscriptions to satellite television channels;

- insurance and other financial services.

1.60   In their guidance notes on the Regulations the Government says:

> '"Goods" clearly has to be interpreted in accordance with the EC Treaty and, of that reason, the Regulations do not define the word. However, it is considered that the definition of "goods" in s 61(1) of the Sale of Goods Act 1979 as including, inter alia, all personal chattels other than things in action (eg shares) and money, may offer a reasonable guide, without necessarily being absolutely co-extensive with the Directive meaning.'

1.61   The definition in s 61(1) is:

> '"Goods" includes all personal chattels other than things in action and money, and in Scotland all corporeal moveables except money; and in particular "goods" includes emblements, industrial growing crops, and things attached to or forming part of the land which are agreed to be severed before sale or under the contract of sale.'

The Consumer Rights Act 2015 contains implied conditions for digital downloads, thus accepting that many electronic products downloaded online are not traditional 'sale of goods'.

The reference from the Supreme Court in 2019 to the Court of Justice of the EU (CJEU) on the issue of software may well result in some useful further information when a judgment is issued in 2020 or 2021.

1.62   There will be some contracts where the agent is marketing both goods and services, such as double-glazing contracts where both glass and wood and the work involved in hacking out and replacing old windows is involved. It is likely that the court will take a pragmatic approach and look at whether there is a reasonably substantial element of 'goods' in a particular transaction and decide accordingly, or may assess the matter based on whether there are separate contracts for each as in *Crane v Sky* (see para **1.95** below). For example, if the 'goods' element is worth only about 5% of the transaction, either the courts will say the Regulations do not apply at all or that the compensation paid to an agent who is dismissed is based on the proportion of the commission attributable to that 5%. For that reason, in 'mixed' contracts of this kind it can be wise to split the commission between the goods and services elements. Indeed, some companies might choose to have two separate agency contracts for the goods and services elements.

1.63   In some cases, the agent is marketing goods but is also acting as agent for certain after-sales services such as warranty work. If the goods develop faults, the agent attends to them on behalf of the principal and is paid a separate commission for that. That element is services and not covered. In other cases, the agent acts as agent for the sale of the goods but as principal in relation to the provision of spare parts to the customer once the goods are supplied or as principal in relation to an ongoing maintenance contract with the principal once the goods are sold. The relevance of that issue is that it may be sufficient in certain cases to result in the agent's agency activities being 'secondary' (see later in this chapter) if the maintenance contracts or contracts for supply of spare parts are more time-consuming than the agency work. In those cases, the issue is not whether the contract is for goods or services but whether the services element or the direct supply of goods part of the contract has assumed more importance than the original agency, sufficient to result in the Regulations not applying at all. Where the work is separated into goods and services contracts, the Regulations may in some cases be avoided from the services element (see the *Crane v Sky*, at para **1.95** below).

1.64   *Pace Airline Services Ltd v Aerotrans Luftfahrtagentur GmbH* (Case C-64/99) [1999] OJ C121/123 concerned the sale of cargo space. Surprisingly the court indicated this might be 'goods' which seems extremely unlikely. The case was to be referred to the European Court of Justice but was settled before it reached that stage.

1.65   For contracts involving two or more EU jurisdictions reference should be made to the *Unamar* case (Case C-184/12 CJEU) considered in Chapter 8. In that case, even though the parties had chosen in the contract that Bulgarian law should apply (which like English and EU law only provides protection for agents marketing goods, not services), the agent could claim compensation only available to agents operating in Belgium. The court held that it was consistent with the Rome Convention that the Belgian agent could claim Belgian law agency compensation under Belgian law as Belgian law went further than the EU Agency Directive and provided compensation to agents marketing services as well as goods. This was despite the parties' choosing

Bulgarian law which offered no such compensation for agents marketing services.

Financial services

1.66   Frequently financial services agents paid on commission selling insurance policies and the like approach commercial lawyers who advise on the Regulations hoping compensation may be available. In fact, it is clearly not so, however unfair that may seem to those involved who might as easily have been peddling baked beans as life insurance products. In *Abbey Life v Yeap* [2001] EWCA Civ 706, CA the European Court of Justice looked at this when the Court of Appeal in November 2001 referred the issue to them. The court was asked to look at whether policies for life assurance, annuities, health and pension business, unit trusts, offshore funds business, personal equity plans and other contracts offered by Abbey Life were goods for these purposes. The court held that financial services were outside the EU Agency Directive and although good and services had been in early drafts of the Directive, services had been deliberately removed.

Software contracts

1.67   There are some products in relation to which the courts have not yet ruled definitively whether a particular item is goods or services. An example is computer software. In *St Albans v ICL* (1996) 15 Tr LR, CA, the court did not have to rule definitively on the issue, but it was stated, obiter, that the court considered software to be 'goods'. This was a material issue in that case, as if software were 'goods' then the implied terms in the Sale of Goods Act 1979 might have applied – ie that the goods were to be of satisfactory quality and fit for their purpose, but not if services were supplied. From October 2015, the Consumer Rights Act 2015 implies conditions into contracts for digital downloads for the first time as mentioned above. However, this will not resolve the issue of whether sales of software supplied other than on disk are supplies of services, goods or IP. In fact, it could make it harder for software agents to be protected as the Act by implication makes it clear digital downloads are different from sales of goods, although the common law implied conditions which have run along statutory sale of goods terms since the Sale of Goods Act 1894 could still provide protection under common law. In 2020/21, a decision from the CJEU is expected on this issue following a reference there from the Supreme Court in 2019 in the *Software Incubator* case (see para **1.76** below).

1.68   In the USA a better and more detailed principle seems to have emerged – that if software is specially written for a customer then professional services have been supplied, whereas if off-the-shelf software has been 'bought' then that is 'goods'. In *St Albans* a rather artificial distinction was proposed – if the software were supplied on a computer disk, whether the disk was 'sold' or 'leased' to the customer then it was goods. If, instead, the supplier installed the software or a distributor/dealer installed it or it was supplied electronically and not on a disk, such as via e-mail, then it would not be goods. The fact the disk might be worth 50p and the software £250,000 (ie payment for valuable intellectual property, the licence of copyright) was not considered.

1.69 The Court of Appeal in *St Albans* said:

'In both the Sale of Goods Act 1979, s 61 and the Supply of Goods and Services Act 1982, s 18 the definition of "goods" is "includes all personal chattels other than things in action and money". Clearly a disk is within this definition. Equally clearly a program, of itself, is not.'

The judge went on to say:

'Suppose I buy an instruction manual on the maintenance and repair of a particular make of car. The instructions are wrong in an important respect. Anybody who follows them is likely to cause serious damage to the engine of his car. In my view the instructions are an integral part of the manual. The manual including the instructions, whether in a book or a video cassette, would in my opinion be "goods" within the meaning of the Sale of Goods Act and the defective instructions would result in a breach of the implied terms in s 14.

If this is correct, I can see no logical reason why it should not be correct in relation to a computer disk onto which a program designed and intended to instruct or enable a computer to achieve particular functions has been encoded. If the disk is sold or hired by the computer manufacturer, but the program is defective, in my opinion there would prima facie be a breach of the terms as to quality and fitness for purpose implied by the Sale of Goods Act or the Act of 1982.'

1.70 However, in *St Albans* the program was not sold and it was probable it was not hired either and so the implied terms did not apply. It was possible that common law implied terms might apply but that was a separate issue. The court did not have to make a finding on whether software was 'goods' in order to decide the case and it is therefore not a binding legal precedent on the issue.

1.71 In *Green Deal Marketing Ltd v Economy Energy Trading Ltd* [2019] EWHC 507 the court held that both gas and electricity are goods for the purposes of the Regulations.

1.72 Those who market computers, of course, are selling goods even though part of what they are selling is computer software already loaded in such computers.

1.73 There are some EU states, such as Spain, where local regulations implementing the Directive provide for compensation for agents marketing services as well as goods, and therefore the local law position should always be examined (see the *Unamar* case mentioned at para **1.65** above and described in Chapter 8). It is very important to check this point with local lawyers even if English law is specified in the agreement because sometimes local law may prevail and the agent have protection. Ascertaining if this is the case before the agent is appointed is wise.

Case example – *Accentuate Ltd v Asigra Inc* [2009] EWHC 2655 (QB)

1.74   In this case the High Court looked at a Master Reseller Agreement under which Asigra appointed Accentuate as agent to market Asigra's software and hardware. The agreement said it was subject to the law of Ontario and disputes would be settled by arbitration in Toronto. Accentuate did submit to the arbitration but argued its Agency Directive compensation fell outside the arbitration. It began UK proceedings and the principal appealed in the English courts over the issue of whether proceedings could be served on it and in particular whether the Regulations applied at all.

The judge was perhaps a little unclear about the software/ hardware issue. Hardware was only supplied later once a software licence was entered into. Even the judge said that:

'The hardware . . . is to be provided to the end user only after the end user has become a party . . . to the software licence agreement.'

In practice then there was no sale of hardware to the licensee and the supply of hardware was only after the end user signed the licence agreement and the hardware supply was a small matter compared with the software element of the contract.

The judge said:

'It may be that the draughtsman of the MRA envisaged that there would be sales of hardware by the Licensor to the Distributor, and sub-sales by the Distributor to the end user who was to enter into the Software License Agreement. But supply of hardware is so subsidiary a part of the subject matter of the MRA that this interpretation seems very technical, not to say a little unrealistic. Although Schedule A includes the words ". . . the Software [the Distributor] purchases from [the Licensor]" (see para 44 above), I can see no way in which the Distributor could be said to purchase software (whether or not it purchased hardware). Schedule C makes clear that a direct contractual relationship was envisaged between the Licensor and the end user, not a licence to the Distributor followed by a sub-license from the Distributor to the end user.

Although the supply of the hardware is ancillary to the supply of the software, the supply of the hardware is critical to the Distributor's case. The Regulations apply to a person who negotiates the sale or purchase of "goods": see Regulation 2(1) cited in para 26 above. If no hardware was to be supplied under the MRA, then the Regulations would not apply at all.

Software is intellectual property, not a chattel, but hardware is a chattel. In so far as the performance of the MRA leads to the formation of a Software Licence Agreement in the form of Schedule C, then that is an agreement made between the Licensor and the end user.

In so far as the performance of the MRA leads to the supply to the end user of hardware, the legal analysis is not so clear on the evidence before me.

In my judgment there is a real prospect of the Distributor succeeding on its submission that the substantive obligation of the Distributor was to find end users who would enter into Software Licence Agreements with the Licensor. In respect of this aspect of the Distributor's contractual obligations the Distributor can plausibly be seen as acting as an agent.

In the present case, in so far as the Software Licence Agreement is concerned, it is clear that the Distributor did not have authority to contract on the Licensor's behalf. What the Distributor did seems to me likely to be found to come within the definitions of negotiation adopted by Patten J and Morritt LJ in *Fryer* and *Parks*.

Accordingly, I find that the Distributor has satisfied me that it has a real prospect of success on the merits of its claims'.

In other words, as even the smallest part of hardware was sold, there is an arguable case the Regulations could apply. However, this decision was in an initial application regarding services of proceedings. It is possible higher authority might hold if most of the contract relates to supply of services then the regulations do not apply particularly if the software is not even supplied on CD Rom.

Case example – *Fern Computer Consultancy Ltd v Intergraph Cadworx & Analysis Solutions Inc* [2014] EWHC 2908

1.75   In this case, the court decided software on a CD may well be goods as the judge said:

'The effect of all this authority [*St Albans* case above and *London Borough of Southwark v IBM UK Ltd* [2011] EWHC 549 (TCC)], and of the principles underlying the argument in those cases, is that where software is supplied on CDs there is a real prospect of success in arguing that that is the supply of goods. Where that supply is accompanied by a physical dongle and documentation then the argument is even stronger. While there is an argument that what is really being supplied is software, which is not goods, that argument is not so strong as to make the contrary argument unsustainable. Indeed, if I had to decide it I would probably decide that it is wrong, but I do not have to go that far. I bear in mind that the Regulations do not contain a definition of goods corresponding to the Sale of Goods Act, and that the analysis of the expression is not constrained by reference to the word "chattels", so it becomes easier to argue that such a supply is the supply of goods.

I therefore find that the argument that the sale in the present case (if there was a sale) was a sale of goods raises a serious question to be tried and passes the merits test for service out.'

The judgment then looked at the issue concerning the fact that the software was not sold but was licensed – a second hurdle facing those litigating agency agreements for the 'sale' of software. *Usedsoft Gmbh v Oracle International Corp* [2012] 3 CMLR 4, a case concerning whether a fairly standard ban in software licences not to 're-sell' or pass the software on to another user held that such clauses breach article 101 of TFEU and are anti-competitive where the software has been licensed perpetually to a user. In *Fern* the judge said:

> 'It is in my view arguable that "sale" and "purchase" in the Regulations should have an autonomous meaning and should not be confined to the concepts of transfer of property which underpin the Sale of Goods Act and would be capable of applying to a transaction based on a licence. While the concept of licensing might not be widespread in relation to goods other than those associated with computer programs, the observations in paragraph 49 of the *Usedsoft* judgment might apply to the Regulations as well. It may be that that point would have to be the subject of a reference when all the facts are determined, but I do not need to determine that. Nor do I need to determine whether or not the argument is actually correct. It is sufficient if the point is arguable enough to give rise to a serious question to be tried, and I hold that it is.

> … The decision in *Usedsoft* seems to depend on the licence being for "an unlimited period". If the successful argument in that case is to be deployed on the facts of the present case there must be case for saying that the licence or licences in the present case were similarly unlimited in time. I have referred above to the limited nature of the evidence in this case. There are no pre-2009 end user licences. However, the evidence does give rise to a serious question to be tried as to whether the licences were unlimited. The 2009 licence expresses itself as being effective until terminated "in accordance with the terms of this Licence Agreement".

> The circumstances which the licence specifies as giving rise to a termination are the transfer of possession of any copy of the "licensed program(s)" to a third party (without procuring that the third party became subject to the terms of the licence), a voluntary termination by the end user by destroying the material, and an "automatic" termination in the event of a failure to comply with any term or condition of the agreement. It is otherwise perpetual. That would appear to be an "unlimited" licence in accordance with the reasoning in *Usedsoft* . The 2010 licence introduces the concept of time-limited licences because it provides for two types of licence - a perpetual licence and a lease licence (one granted for a specified time duration). However, there is no evidence that these licence terms were ever in operation in relation to Fern's customers before the termination of the agreement, and even less that there was ever a lease licence. There is, in my view, a serious question to be tried (at the very least) as to the perpetual nature of the licences with end users'.

Case example – *Software Incubator v Computer Associates* Case ID: UKSC 2018/0090, on appeal from the Court of Appeal decision of [2018] EWCA Civ 518

1.76   In this case the Supreme Court looked at whether software supplied to customers electronically and not on any tangible medium constitutes 'goods' within the meaning of regulation 2(1) of the Regulations.

The Supreme Court summarised the case in 2019 as follows:

'The Respondent produced software which was supplied electronically as a download. In March 2013, the parties entered into an agency agreement whereby the Appellant agreed to promote the software in the UK and Ireland ("the Agreement"). In September 2013, the Appellant entered into a similar agreement with another company, Intigua, whereby it agreed to promote and market Intigua's software in the UK and Ireland.

In October 2013, the Respondent terminated the Agreement summarily on the basis that the Appellant was in repudiatory breach of its obligations under the Agreement to devote "substantial time and effort" to performing its obligations, and not to engage in any activity competing directly with the Respondent's software. Thereafter, the Appellant commenced High Court proceedings for damages for breach of contract and compensation under the Regulations.

The Respondent argued that the Regulations did not apply because software supplied electronically did not amount to "goods" within the meaning of regulation 2(1). The High Court disagreed and awarded damages to the Appellant under the Regulations, as well as for breach of contract. The judge held that a sale of electronically supplied software was a sale of "goods" within the meaning of regulation 2(1). The Court of Appeal allowed the Respondent's appeal on the meaning of "goods" in regulation 2(1)'.

At a hearing in March 2019, the Supreme Court decided to refer questions to the European Court including concerning the issue of whether software when not delivered in material form at all can be goods. The Court of Appeal in this case held it could not be goods and the agent had no protection and the High Court below had ruled that software was goods in such cases.

The CJEU's decision is likely to be available in 2020 or 2021.

Sub-agents

1.77   Many UK businesses are appointed as UK agent of a foreign supplier and then are entitled to appoint 'sub-agents'. The sub-agents operate under them in particular parts of the UK. The 'agent' is therefore both principal and agent. If the principal were to dismiss the agent, part of the agent's compensation claim might include the compensation the agent itself would have to pay to its own agents. Of course, if the contract precludes the delegation of any of the agency duties or appointment of a sub-agent (as many contracts do) then no such claim could be made.

1.78   In some casesd the agent who appoints sub-agents may in fact place the sub-agents in a direct contractual relationship with its principal. In such cases it might be possible to argue that the agent is not the UK principal at all and instead the sub-agents must look to the foreign supplier as their principal and for compensation. In most cases this will be difficult to establish. In *Stuart Light v Ty Europea Ltd* [2003] EWCA Civ 1238 the court found that as the sub-agents in that case had no contract with the ultimate principal, they had no right to claim compensation against the principal. In this case the judge also considered the agent (SCS) saying:

> 'As its commercial agent I cannot see why SCS did not have a Regulation 17 claim for compensation against the appellant [ultimate principal] based on the claimants' and its success in promoting and selling Ty products, subject to the effluxion of time question. The claimants were probably not SCS's commercial agents because they were not selling on its behalf, but I can see no reason why as SCS's agents they should not have been able to establish a stake in SCS's compensation claim. Whether they could have compelled SCS to make such a claim is more problematical, but a combination of commercial pressure and resourceful lawyers might have done the trick. So I see no need to try and give the Regulations a meaning they will not bear in order to confer a right to compensation on sub-agents such as the claimants.
>
> If in order to avoid liability to its commercial agents under the Regulations a principal sets up a sham structure the courts would be entitled to ignore it, applying well-known general principles, but it is not suggested that this is such a case.'

It seems clear from the *Ty* case that the usual contractual rules apply – sub-sub agent claims against sub-agent, sub-agent against his principal (the agent) and that agent against the ultimate principal.

1.79   The UK agent in the worst position is one appointed under the laws of a country where compensation for agents does not apply (such as the laws of a US state) who is dismissed and has appointed UK sub-agents to whom it has to pay compensation. In theory the UK agent can still claim compensation as English law prevails) but in practice the UK agent may not have the funds to argue an international jurisdictional matter of this sort against its US principal.

1.80   In *Guide to the Commercial Agents Regulations* the authors consider whether a sub-agent might have rights against the ultimate principal as the sub-agent would have continuing authority to negotiate and the Regulations do not specify on whose behalf that authority must be. *Pace Airline Services Ltd v Aerotrans Luftfahrtagentur GmbH* Case C-64/99 [1999] OJ C121/123 looked at this issue, although the case settled before it was referred to the European Court so a final view was not obtained. The Court said it needed guidance on whether the Regulations applied to sub-agencies at all. However, it is more likely that they do and that the sub-agent has a claim against its principal – the agent and part of that agent's claim against its principal would be any compensation it had to pay to the sub-agent. There is a risk a principal might argue as there is judicial doubt on whether sub-agents have compensation rights that an agent pays compensation to its sub-agents at its only risk and expense without any recompense claim to the principal. The *Guide* mentioned above agrees with this point and suggests principals should always ensure they look at the terms of any sub-agency agreement before appointment of the sub-agent and that if the sub-agent is used on the advice of the principal which costs the agent money then this contracted service (and the compensation arising from termination thereof) could be an unamortised cost for which the agent could claim on termination.

1.81   Clearly there are useful points which can be made in litigation about the rights or otherwise of sub-agents. In drafting contracts for principals include a provision that the principal can vet and amend sub-agency agreements (eg to put indemnity caps in them) and perhaps expressly say the agent chooses and appoints its own agents. If the principal is abroad, eg in the US where no compensation is payable but the agent is appointing EU or UK sub-agents then it is crucial the agent takes legal advice as it may be in a situation of having to pay sub-agents compensation (if there is such a right) but be unable to claim from the principal. In such a case a contract clause stating that where there is a legal obligation to pay compensation or an indemnity to a sub-agent arises the principal will fully indemnify the agent on termination may suffice if the principal abroad will accept that provision.

1.82   Always consider the Contracts (Rights of Third Parties) Act 1999. Check first if it is excluded from a particular contract. Assuming it is not, then the contract between principal and agent where the parties contemplate sub-agencies or even name the sub-agents may well be for the benefit of the sub-agent who on termination of that head agency contract may have a claim against the principal arising from the breach of the main agency agreement which has caused the sub-agent loss. However, the sub-agent under that legislation cannot claim if the agent has claimed as there is no double recovery under the legislation. If the agent is in liquidation or bankrupt but had a claim against the principal, the sub-agent (unable therefore to obtain compensation from the impoverished agent) might be able to bring a claim under the agent's contract with its principal under the 1999 Act.

Secondary activities Schedule

1.83   The EU Agency Directive on which the Regulations are based gives Member States the right to decide whether their national law will have provisions relating to secondary activities. The UK has chosen to do so in a somewhat unclear Schedule to the Regulations. In general, if the agent is mostly a dealer or distributor and simply does a small amount of agency work, then the Regulations do not apply because the agency activities are 'secondary'. This means that when an agent is taken on, he must be asked what other activities he undertakes so the principal knows what else he does and whether the Regulations apply. In addition, the principal will want to know of any changes to this over the years of the agency, as an agent who at the beginning was not covered by the Regulations may become so if distribution activities cease. Indeed, the contract might, to protect the principal in such cases, include a clause that the agent must not take on or give up any other activity without the principal's permission or at the least without the principal being notified.

1.84   It should also be considered when the agent might be best advised to operate through a separate limited company for its agency work to ensure that it is all channelled through one entity which benefits from the Regulations and the secondary activities of distribution are dealt with through the agent as a sole trader or a separate limited company. Advice on the tax implications of this should always be sought, particularly if there is any chance the agent may be an employee (full or part time) of the principal in which tax rules only applicable to those running small companies (known as IR35) might apply to the disadvantage of the agent. Most agents, however, whether operating through limited companies, are not usually clearly self employed and are not employees for tax purposes – given the risks they run and expenses they bear and the control they have over their working life and range of principals for whom they act.

1.85   This Schedule has nothing to do with the number of other agencies the agent handles. Many agents run four or five or even more non-conflicting agencies. The principal usually knows about these and even if the agent's activities for the principal comprise only a small proportion of the overall agency activities the Regulations still apply. The secondary activities Schedule is directed at cases where the agent engages in other business activities which are entirely separate from agency.

1.86   Regulation 2(3) provides that the Schedule has effect in determining when the agent's activities are considered secondary. Regulation 2(4) states that the Regulations do not apply to an agent whose activities are secondary. Normally a relationship will be one of agency where paragraph 2 of the Schedule applies. This says:

'An arrangement shall fall within this paragraph if:

(a)   the business of the principal is the sale, or as the case may be purchase, of goods of a particular kind; and

(b)   the goods concerned are such that:

    (i)   transactions are normally individually negotiated and concluded on a commercial basis; and

    (ii)   procuring a transaction on one occasion is likely to lead to further transactions in those goods with that customer on future occasions, or to transactions in those goods with other customers in the same geographical area or among the same group of customers; and

that accordingly it is in the commercial interests of the principal in developing the market in those goods to appoint a representative to such customers with a view to the representative devoting effort, skill and expenditure from his own resources to that end.'

1.87   Notice that the provision makes clear again that the Regulations apply to agents marketing goods, rather than services, and that the principal can be involved either in purchase or sale. The sale of the goods will normally be negotiated on a commercial basis (so no free sales or perhaps no sales between subsidiaries which are not on a commercial basis). There is also the requirement that the agency is more than a 'one-off'. The customer is expected to buy on more than one occasion or may lead to transactions in those goods with other customers. This seems clear. The customer may not be expected to order again (as in the *Hunter v Zenith* example at para **1.42** above). It is sufficient if the agent is finding customers who each may order on a one-off basis.

1.88 It must be intended that the agent will expend effort, skill and expenditure from his own resources. Most agents do pay for their own computers, cars, petrol, stationery and other expenses. Where the principal pays all expenses, that suggests an agent may in fact be an employee, but this will not be the only relevant factor.

1.89 There are unlikely to be many problems in practice with paragraph 2 above. Much more difficult are the lists of indications in paragraphs 3 and 4. Paragraph 3 says:

'The following are indications that an arrangement falls within paragraph 2 above [*ie the Regulations will apply*], and absence of any of them is an indication to the contrary:

(a) the principal is the manufacturer, importer or distributor of the goods;
(b) the goods are specifically identified with the principal in the market in question rather than, or to a greater extent than, with any other person;
(c) the agent devotes substantially the whole of his time to representative activities (whether for one principal or for a number of principals whose interests are not conflicting);
(d) the goods are not normally available in the market in question other than by means of the agent;
(e) the arrangement is described as one of commercial agency.'

Obviously, some of these factors are more important than others. If the parties call a distribution agreement or employment contract a 'commercial agency', then factor (e) above is unlikely to be decisive. The name is simply wrong. If (a) were decisive then some of the agents who have sub-agents appointed under them would not be regarded as principal in relation to their own sub-agents (though many are importers and thus covered by (b)).

Secondary activities in the Tamarind case

1.90 The words in the secondary activities Schedule have been judicially criticised. In *Tamarind International Ltd v Eastern Natural Gas (Retail) Ltd* [2000] Eu LR 708 the court considered some preliminary issues (the case settled subsequently before a full trial). The two issues were whether the Regulations did not apply because the agents' activities were secondary, and secondly would the Regulations apply anyway because of what the agreements said. The court said that the UK's original thoughts on the secondary activities issue was that unless the agent was wholly or mainly engaged in agency activities then he or she was not protected by the Regulations. That is point (c) from paragraph 2 in the Schedule quoted above and appears to be the logical and sensible basis for determining protection or otherwise. Agents who mostly make a living through distribution, employment or whatever would not be protected. Those who were mostly agents, even if that were five different agencies for five different non-conflicting principals (as is the norm for many agents) would be protected. That is not what the Regulations say nor the Schedule as point (c) is but one point of a number of factors to consider.

1.91   On the facts of *Tamarind* 85%–98% of employees' time was devoted to Eastern's business. The defendants estimated the time spent on Tamarind representative activities at 60%. On either basis the judge thought that Tamarind was devoting substantially the whole of its time to representative activities for Eastern 'let alone for any other principal'. Eastern was part of a group with a turnover of about £5 billion. The agents were small businesses in comparison. The court then examined each of the factors in the Schedule and found the Regulations did apply.

Secondary activities and the Gailey case

1.92   In a Scottish case *Gailey v Environmental Waste Controls* [2004] Eu LR 423 the judge examined all the previous relevant case law on this. These provisions were considered, obiter, by the Court of Appeal in *AMB Imballagi Plastici Srl v Pacflex Ltd* [1999] 2 All ER (Comm) 249. In that case, Waller LJ commented as follows (at 254d–g):

1.   Article 2(3) of the Directive seems to allow a Member State to disapply the Directive where the activities of the agent as agent are secondary, as compared with the rest of the agent's business.

2.   The Schedule then seems to contemplate an assessment not of the activities of the agent as 'a commercial agent' as compared with his other business, but an assessment of the agent's arrangement with a principal. That this was probably unintentional is confirmed by the guidance notes issued by the Department of Trade and Industry which include this paragraph in relation to the Schedule: 'The comparison to be made is between the agent's activities as a commercial agent and his other activities and not the relationship with the principal.

3.   Paragraph 1 of the Schedule refers to a primary purpose 'other than as set out in paragraph 2'. But paragraph 2 does not set out a purpose; it describes aspects of the arrangement with a particular principal.

4.   Paragraphs 3 and 4 suggest pointers are being supplied as to whether an arrangement is within paragraph 2, but provide no assistance as to what is being compared with what for the purpose of deciding what might be secondary as compared with what might be primary, nor any assistance as to whether other factors are excluded.

In *Gailey* the Lord Advocate said:

> 'These criticisms of the Regulations appear to be based on the view that article 2.3 of the Directive used the word "secondary" to denote a straightforward numerical comparison of the agent's activities as a commercial agent and his other activities. As I have already sought to explain, however, I do not think that this is the only possible meaning of article 2.3, and in my opinion the 1993 Regulations have chosen to give a different, but permissible, significance to the word "secondary". If that is done, I think that the Schedule becomes reasonably intelligible. In particular, a rational basis is provided for applying the pointers in paragraphs 3 and 4 to the question of whether an arrangement falls within paragraph 2; thus much of the force is taken out of these criticisms. There does appear to be some force in the third criticism, but it can easily be met by reading into paragraph 1, between "is" and "other", the words "to achieve an arrangement".'

1.93   In *AMB Imballagi Plastici Srl v Pacflex Ltd*, Waller LJ stated that there was much force in the argument that, if an agent has an arrangement with a principal that falls within paragraph 2, then it must be taken that the business is not secondary. That view is supported by the opinion of Morison J in *Tamarind International Ltd v Eastern Natural Gas (Retail) Ltd* [2000] Eu LR 708, at paragraph 21; where Morison J states:

> 'Because there is no easily recognisable way of measuring whether or not activities are secondary, it is, I think, unnecessary, and perhaps misleading, to seek to find an antithesis to the word "secondary". All I can say is that the activities of this agent are, for the purposes of the Regulations, to be regarded as secondary, and he is an agent to whom the Regulations do not apply; whereas an agent whose activities are not regarded as secondary is covered by the Regulations. The contrast is simply between the agents who are covered and the agents who are not. It is not necessary to say, for example, that the activities of an agent who is covered by the Regulations are "primary"; they are, simply, not secondary.'

In *Gailey* the judge said:

> 'I agree that it is necessary to examine the provisions of the Schedule in order to determine whether an agent's activities as a commercial agent are to be considered secondary as a matter of Scots or English law. Nevertheless, it seems to me that there is a clear policy underlying the Schedule, and a mischief against which the Regulations are directed; the Schedule should be interpreted in the light of that mischief.'

The *Gailey* opinion is at http://www.scotcourts.gov.uk/opinions/CA41.html and reported at [2004] Eu LR 424.

Secondary activities and the Zako v Sanidel case (CJEU)

1.94   In *Zako SPRL v Sanidel SA* (Case C-452/17) [2019] Bus LR 343, [2019] 1 Lloyds Rep 377, the CJEU held that just because the agent engaged in some activities which were not agency related, this did not preclude the application of the Regulations. Nor did it make any difference that the agent worked from the same premises as those which the principal provided, since the agent's independence was not compromised.

The case was sent to the CJEU for a preliminary ruling from the Belgian courts.

The CJEU said:

> 'The answer to the first question is that Article 1(2) of Directive 86/653 must be interpreted as meaning that the fact that a person who has continuing authority to negotiate the sale or the purchase of goods on behalf of another person, or to negotiate and conclude such transactions on behalf of and in the name of that person, performs his activities from the latter's business premises does not prevent him from being classified as a 'commercial agent' within the meaning of that provision, provided that that fact does not prevent that person from performing his activities in an independent manner, which is for the referring court to ascertain.'

It went on:

> 'Thus, in the present case, the referring court must ascertain whether the fact that the applicant in the main proceedings performs, for the same person, his activities as a commercial agent together with other activities having the same importance has the effect, taking account of all of the circumstances of the case, such as the nature of the tasks performed, the manner in which they are carried out, the proportion those tasks represent with regard to the overall activities of the person concerned, the method of calculating the remuneration, or the reality of the financial risk incurred, of preventing him from performing the first kind of activities in an independent manner.

> In the light of the foregoing, the answer to the second and third questions is that Article 1(2) of Directive 86/653 must be interpreted as meaning that the fact that a person not only performs activities consisting in the negotiation of the sale or purchase of goods for another person, or the negotiation and conclusion of those transactions on behalf of and in the name of that other person, but also performs, for the same person, activities of another kind, without those other activities being subsidiary to the first kind of activities, does not preclude that person from being classified as a 'commercial agent' within the meaning of that provision, provided that that fact does not prevent the former activities from being performed in an independent manner, which it is for the referring court to ascertain.'

Secondary Activities

Case example – *Crane v Sky In-Home Service Ltd* [2007] EWHC 66 (Ch)

1.95   In this case Sky fought off an agency compensation claim. Mr Justice Briggs rejected the claimant's claim that the Schedule to the Commercial Agents Regulations was *ultra vires*. The raising of this point had lead to the intervention of Secretary of State for Trade and Industry. The High Court also provided guidance as to the proper construction of the much maligned schedule and the meaning of a 'secondary' commercial agent. It held it was not ultra vires and commented as follows:

'It was suggested to me that paragraph 2(a) would not be satisfied unless the sale (or purchase) of the relevant goods was the sole or main business of the principal. I disagree. The purpose of the Regulations as a whole is (consistent with the Directive which it implements) the protection of a particular class of self employed intermediaries. The same agent may be appointed for the development of the same market in the same particular goods by, on the one hand, a large unitary corporation with many different businesses, including the sale of those goods, and on the other hand by a group of companies in which each different business is carried on by a different group company. It would be curious if the relevant group company was liable to pay compensation on termination, but the large unitary corporation not liable because the sale of those goods was not its sole or main business. The purpose of paragraph 2(a) is not to make that distinction, but to focus the analysis on the commercial interests served by the development of a market for goods of the relevant kind, rather than, for example, a market for related services.

It was common ground before me that the "indications" for and against a conclusion that an arrangement falls within paragraph 2, in paragraphs 3 and 4 respectively, are not to be used in some slavish numerical way. They are a non-exclusive list of pointers, each of which may be of differing weight in different cases. Viewed in the aggregate they do provide some assistance towards an understanding of the elusive concept of secondary activities which the Schedule seeks to define by its identification of the opposite. Taken as a whole they appear to me to be directed at distinguishing between a relationship where the agent develops goodwill (in relation to the market for the particular goods) which passes to the principal, and one where that does not happen, either because the agent's activities are not typically generative of such goodwill, or because the principal generates goodwill mainly by other means.

I was referred to a number of cases in which the meaning and application of the Schedule has been reviewed, in particular *Tamarind International Ltd v Eastern Energy Ltd* [2000] Eu.L.R. 708; *AMB Imballagi Plastici SRL v Pacflex Ltd* [1999] 2 All ER (Comm) 249; and *Edwards v International Connection (UK) Ltd* [2006] EWCA Civ 662. I believe that the analysis which I have set out above, focused as it is upon the resolution of the issues in this case, is consistent with the reasoning to be derived from those authorities. I remind myself that like any other statutory provision, the Schedule is not to be paraphrased. It means what it says. I therefore turn to the application of the Schedule to the facts, starting with paragraph 1, which calls for an identification both of the relevant arrangement and the principal.'

The judge then goes on to conclude that the agency activities are secondary:

'Mr Dhillon submitted that 'representative activities' in paragraph 3(c) [of the Schedule to the Regulations] must mean activities in relation to goods rather than services, so as to exclude Mr Crane's sale of Sky Digital subscriptions.

I disagree. In my judgment paragraph 3(c) is directed to a focus on the question why (ie for what primary purpose) the agent was appointed. If his agency is ancillary to other non-representative activities, then it is unlikely that he was appointed for the exploitation of his skills as an agent. The question is simply whether the person in question is a full time agent (ie sales or purchase representative). Since the question addresses the purpose of the appointment, it is best answered at the time of the appointment. Otherwise he might drift in and out of qualifying commercial agency during the currency of the arrangement.

Notwithstanding my rejection of Mr Dhillon's submission about the meaning and purpose of paragraph 3(c), the evidence nonetheless fails to persuade me that Mr Crane was, either at the start of, during or at the end of the period of his agency devoting substantially the whole of his time to representative activities. Paragraph 3(c) is not therefore satisfied. In the circumstances it is unnecessary for me to rule on Mr Dhillon' other submission based on the undoubted fact that most of Mr Crane's activity was carried out for the financial benefit of his company Say It Loud Marketing Limited.

Paragraph 3(d) is plainly not satisfied. Box packages were throughout the relevant period available direct from the Sky Group, and the majority were actually sold direct. As for paragraph 3(e), COPA speaks for itself. It is an agency agreement, both by its title and by its terms. Mr Dhillon submitted that the exclusion of compensation on termination in clause 5.5 of COPA means that the arrangement is not described as a commercial agency within the meaning of the Regulations. I disagree. A person may be (and in Mr Crane's case is) disentitled to compensation by reason of the Schedule, even though he is a commercial agent within the meaning of Regulation 2(1), because he fails the secondary activities test.

Paragraph 4 (a) and (b) are clearly satisfied on the evidence; ie those are indications against the arrangement falling within paragraph 2. The evidence did not enable me to reach any clear conclusion in relation to paragraph 4(c).

It will be evident that my conclusion that Mr Crane's activities were secondary within the meaning of the Schedule does not depend upon any fine analysis of the indications in paragraphs 3 or 4. In my view he failed to pass the tests in paragraph 2(b)(ii) and in the last four lines of paragraph 2. If the answer had depended on that fine analysis, then his failure to satisfy paragraph 3(c) and (d) would have told heavily against him, as would the indications in paragraph 4(a) and (b). Whether they would have been fatal if the facts relevant to the paragraph 2 tests which he failed had been different is a hypothetical question which I must leave to others.'

1.96   This case was considered by the judge in *Fern Computer Consultancy Ltd v Intergraph Cadworx & Analysis Solutions Inc* [2014] EWHC 2908 in relation to the issue of whether computer software is 'goods' (see para **1.75** above).

In *Fern* counsel had raised an argument that the principal value of what the agent marketed was the ephemeral software elements, any hardware or software disks being de minimis.

However, the judge said the situation differed from *Crane v Sky* as there had been two separate contracts (for goods and services). That illustrates how sometimes the form of arrangements not just the intent can help principals structure arrangements to minimise the risk the Regulations might apply, although this is never easy given EU law is purposive in its interpretation.

The judge commented:

> 'I do not consider that Mr Dhillon is obviously correct in his arguments. There is no complete parallel with *Sky* because in *Sky* there were two contracts, and two agencies. The primary agency was held to be the subscription-related agency. The agency for sale of goods was secondary to that because it failed to pass the test in the schedule. In the present case there was just one contract and one agency. What was sold was a package. It is arguable that that package was a sale of goods within the Regulations. Those goods were not just a blank, and therefore pointless, CD or a blank, and therefore pointless, ESL. Those items carried the software and unlocking codes respectively. They were the medium via which the software was carried and unlocked. That was part of the agency. They cannot be split out as being separately sold, and then analysed for their primary or secondary qualities. There wasn't an agency for software and an agency for goods. There was an agency for selling a package. There is therefore a serious question to be tried in relation to the question of whether the agency for the sale of goods was primary or secondary. I do not need to develop the point any more than that'.

Case example – *James Craig Donald/Craijan Ltd v Worcester Marine Windows Ltd* Case No: 2WR00372 (January 2013, County Court)

1.97   In the *Donald* case where the writer's firm, Singletons, acted for the agent (see earlier in this chapter and Chapter 6) the judge said:

> 'I am bound to conclude that paragraph (3)(d) [in the Regulations' secondary activities schedule which says the following is indicative the relationship is **not** agent "(d) the goods are not normally available in the market in question other than by means of the agent"] read alone and in the context of the other indicative and non-indicative criteria is overwhelmingly in favour of commercial agency, not contradictory of it, particularly in the overall balance of the factors generally being either indicative or not indicative as the Regulations particularly prescribed and that the importance to be attached to each one should be weighed by the judge. I recognise the significance of brochure and website contact, but in my judgment that does not displace the overall impact of the first Claimant's involvement.'

Pyramid selling

1.98   There are some very complex pyramid selling type schemes which require analysis under the Regulations. If most of the payment is for recruiting others to the network, that is likely to be a payment for services rather than commission. If instead there are genuine sales on commission to sub-agents who market on to sub-agents etc, then the Regulations may apply. If at each stage of the transaction the goods are bought and then resold, the Regulations of course do not apply as that is distribution rather than agency. Reference should be made to the Trading Schemes Act 1996 which has applied from 6 February 1997 and the Consumer Protection from Unfair Trading Regulations 2008 (SI 2008/1277). Schedule 1 to the said 2008 regulations makes it a criminal office to undertake the following:

'14. Establishing, operating or promoting a pyramid promotional scheme where a consumer gives consideration for the opportunity to receive compensation that is derived primarily from the introduction of other consumers into the scheme rather than from the sale or consumption of products.'

1.99   Paragraph 3(c) of the Schedule to the Agency Regulations is arguably the most helpful – the agent devotes substantially the whole of his time to representative activities. Note that it refers to time not profit, so if an agent made 90% of his profits from distribution activities which took up only 10% of his time he would still be protected by the Regulations. It also refers to the agent being allowed also to represent other companies, if these are non-conflicting. In the rare case where an agent carries several competitive lines for different principals it appears that the Regulations will not apply. In *Pacflex*, referred to previously, the judge had already decided that the 'agent' was not in fact an agent but went on to consider whether the agency activities would have been secondary had he been wrong. The agent produced no evidence to show its agency activities outweighed its manufacturing activities, despite stating that this was the case. The judge thought that if this were truly the case the agent should have had no difficulty producing the relevant evidence. The judge answered the questions in paragraphs 2–4 of the Schedule and decided the activities would have been secondary.

1.100   Paragraph 3(d) of the Schedule is more difficult. It suggests that if the goods can be bought from someone other than the agent in the market then the Regulations may not apply. This is extremely important because many agents are not 'exclusive'. Indeed the paragraph must be wrong. The Regulations themselves, as discussed in later chapters, refer to certain rights to commission which depend on whether the agent has an exclusive area or not and therefore clearly contemplate that non-exclusive agents benefit from the Regulations. Paragraph 3(d) suggests the opposite. It is probably therefore better ignored.

1.101   In the *AMB Imballaggi v Pacflex* decision (mentioned above) the court examined the secondary activities provisions and their meaning. However, they were looking there at where the agent's agency activities were not his primary activity. The court said that if the agent's agency work was not his primary function then the Regulations were not needed to protect him. The court appears to have commented that the Schedule is worthless. In practice this is likely to be correct except perhaps in so far as it indicated that if an agent is mostly a distributor the Regulations may not apply.

1.102   Paragraph 4 of the Schedule states that the following factors indicate that the agent is not protected:

(a)   promotional material is supplied direct to potential customers;

(b)   persons are granted agencies without reference to existing agents in a particular area or in relation to a particular group;

(c)   customers normally select the goods for themselves and merely place their orders through the agent.

Most agents are given promotional materials by the principal, sometimes for payment, sometimes supplied free. In some cases, the principal supplies the material direct which is supposed, under the Schedule, to be a contra-indication to the Regulations applying. It is submitted that if that is the only factor then the Regulations are likely to apply. Paragraph 4(b) repeats the point about non-exclusive agencies above and is not regarded as materially significant by the writer. Paragraph 4(c) might cover agencies where an agent simply has a catalogue open in his shop and the customers just place the orders through the agent.

Internet shopping

1.103   It might also mean that where an agent, for example, operates an internet selling page or catalogue for various principals, which is becoming increasingly common and might be called a 'virtual shopping mall', the agent may not be protected. In such cases the contract of sale is normally between the various principals and the consumer, but the 'agent' sets up the websites and may even arrange contracts with banks etc relating to the payment by credit card which customers make. The agent receives the money on behalf of the principals and deducts its commission before sending the money to the principals. In such cases it appears likely that the customer is selecting the goods himself and is just placing orders through the agent. However, the agent may have made substantial efforts to ensure the web page is attractive and has the right links to ensure customers find the page. In those cases the agent's activities are not much different from those of an agent walking from shop to shop with his bag of samples, and the Regulations may provide protection.

Software distribution

1.104   It is common for solicitors to be presented with complex agency/distribution arrangements relating to software distribution where even the client is unsure if the arrangement is agency or distribution. Sometimes the arrangements involve attempts by the copyright owner to impose resale price maintenance on a dealer (which is illegal under EU and UK competition law) whereas if the arrangements were agency and the copyright owner licenses directly to the end user, invoices the end user then the arrangement may well be agency and such price agreement is not illegal. These cases need to be examined on a case by case basis to ascertain who invoices whom and on whose behalf.

Mail order and consumer credit agents

1.105 The final category of agents addressed in the Schedule, and thereby expressly excluded from the Regulations, are mail order catalogue agents of consumer goods and consumer credit agents (paragraph 5). Notice that the mail order exclusion is only for consumer goods. Therefore, a catalogue agent for products for businesses would still be protected provided the other requirements of the Regulations are met. However, a person who is an 'agent' of a clothing catalogue company and obtains orders from friends and neighbours does not have protection.

Jurisdictional issues

1.106 One of the most complex and most interesting areas of the Regulations is their jurisdictional extent. This issue must always be addressed before consideration of whether the Regulations apply. The departure of the UK from membership of the EU should not affect the issues below other than any impact on enforcement of judgments between the UK and EU, although there is a risk that over time UK and EU case law will begin to differ. The situation should be closely watched.

Northern Ireland

1.107 The Regulations do not apply to Northern Ireland (regulation 2(5)). However, there is an equivalent set of Regulations applying to Northern Ireland which is almost identical and which also appears in Appendix 1. These are the Commercial Agents (Council Directive) Regulations (Northern Ireland) 1993, SR 1993/483.

Activities in Great Britain

1.108 Regulation 1(2) provides that the Regulations govern the relations between 'commercial agents and their principals and, subject to paragraph (3), apply in relation to the activities of commercial agents in Great Britain'.

Other EU law applies

1.109 Paragraph (3) states that the Regulations do not apply 'where the parties have agreed that the agency contract is to be governed by the law of another Member State'. The Commercial Agents (Council Directive) (Amendment) Regulations 1998 (SI 1998/2868) amended the Regulations to refer to contracting states of the EEA, not just EU Member States.

Amended regulation 1(3)(a) says that parties to an agency contract can be bound by the laws of another Member State.

UK parties

1.110 In most cases there is no problem. The contract is between a GB principal and agent and is for work to be done in Great Britain. Either the parties have specified that English or Scottish law applies or they have not, in which case it automatically applies because of the Rome Convention (as implemented in the UK by the Contracts (Applicable Law) Act 1990).

Other EU law specified

1.111 In other cases, a GB agent is appointed for part of the UK by an EU principal and the contract specifies French, German, Italian or other EU law. In those cases, sub-paragraph (3) means that that foreign law applies. Therefore, not all agents operating in the UK will be subject to the Regulations. However, in the *Unamar* decision (*United Antwerp Maritime Agencies (Unamar) NV Navigation Maritime Bulgare* (Case C-184/12), see at para **1.65** above and in Chapter 8) the agent was operating in Belgium under a Bulgarian law contract and the CJEU said the agent was entitled to compensation under Belgian law (this being an agent marketing services where under Bulgarian and EU law no compensation is payable, whereas it is in the more generous Belgian law). The court did hold that the case could be heard in Bulgaria because of the exclusive jurisdiction clause in the contract which would also be consistent with the revamped Brussels Regulation 1215/2012 in force 10 January 2015 (see Chapter 8).

No written contract

1.112 In some cases, there is no written contract and there is a foreign but EU principal. In those cases, normally English (or Scottish) law will apply because of the Rome I Regulation 593/2008 and, in particular, the fact that the agency activities are being carried out in the UK. In the absence of a choice of law where the Rome I regulation applies article 4 provides that the choice of law shall be the law of the country where the service provider has his habitual residence (ie where the agent lives). The arrangements negotiated after the UK leaves the EU will need to be considered in this regard once they are available, however, to see how the position changes between UK/EU.

Draft contracts

1.113 In other cases which the writer has found common in practice one party, agent or principal, has in the past sent out a draft contract. This may have specified which country's law applied but one party did not sign it. Then the position becomes more complicated. Under English law if there is no other contract and the other party did not reject the draft contract and the parties proceeded to operate on the basis of the contract then the law specified in the draft contract may apply. In other cases, the draft contract was specifically rejected and is unlikely to apply even if there was no adverse comment on the choice of law provision. Reference should be made to legal textbooks on international law in relation to this issue.

Using GB law in other countries

1.114 The Regulations in regulation 1(3)(b) as amended provide:

'A court . . . shall . . . (whether or not it would otherwise be required to do so) apply these Regulations where the law of another Member State corresponding to these Regulations enables the parties to agree that the agency contract is to be governed by the law of a different Member State and the parties have agreed that it is to be governed by the law of England and Wales or Scotland.'

The effect of this provision is that as long as one of the other EU/EEA states' national laws allow this, the parties can agree English law will apply say to an English company appointing an agent for Spain. It is possible where two Member States' laws conflict on agents' rights the agent may be able to argue for the application of one even if the contract chose another. Further case law on this would be useful. Article 66 of the EU/UK Withdrawal Agreement continues the existing EU/UK rules during the post-Brexit transition period.

1.115 Before the Regulations were amended it was unclear whether an English company appointing a foreign agent could effectively provide an agent with no Agency Directive protection – as English law would apply but without the protection of the Regulations because they did not apply outside the UK.

1.116 This is also an interesting issue as regards the differences in various Member States between agents who sell services being protected and those which do not. The Directive does not require protection for services agents. Thus, an English company with agents for services would usually appoint agents for places such as Spain and Belgium which protect services agents under English law. In theory because of the Rome Convention those countries should respect that choice of law and this was the thinking until the *Unamar* case (Case C184/12, see para **1.65** above) although even before that case the agent probably had a good chance of persuading a local court otherwise on public policy grounds. Since the *Unamar* decision it would be unsafe to assume a services agent could not use local law to override a choice of law clause and it would be wise to seek local legal advice in the jurisdiction where the agent will operate to check in advance if local law protects agents who market services as well as goods.

1.117 There seems no reason why (for non-GB contracts) the parties cannot contract in to the Regulations expressly if they wish. So, a UK company appointing a UK agent who will operate only in Australia (in which case by default no protection under the Regulations would apply) could actively choose to extend protection to the agent by providing that the agent would have the protection as if the Regulations applied, it is more likely an agent rather than the principal would request such a clause.

Government guidance says:

> 'The provisions of the Regulations, where the Agent carries on his activities outside Great Britain, do not, however, prevent the parties from choosing the law of a part of Great Britain (for example the law of England and Wales) and incorporating in the agency agreement some or all of the provisions of the Regulations which the parties might wish to agree should apply as though the agents [sic] activities were, in fact, to be carried on in Great Britain. However, in such a case, if litigation arises, the court hearing the action may or may not: (i) uphold the choice of law, and (ii) accept the validity of such incorporation.'

Case example – *Lawlor v Sandvik Mining and Construction Mobile Crushers and Screens Ltd* [2013] EWCA Civ 365

1.118 In *Lawlor* the Court of Appeal (upholding the decision of the court below) found that Spanish law applied to a commercial agency agreement. The agent would have received more compensation under English than Spanish law hence this issue was litigated first as a preliminary issue. He began as an employee without an employment contract, then became a commercial agent – again without a written agreement. The Court of Appeal said that:

> 'The claimant's strongest point was the judge's finding that his previous contract of employment was probably governed by English law. If there had been an express agreement to that effect, there would have been force in the argument that the same law should be presumed to have been intended to apply to the agency contract in the absence of anything being said to the contrary. However, the judge [at first instance] found it unlikely that the parties had expressly agreed that the employment contract should be governed by English law. The contract of agency created a different legal relationship in different factual circumstances. The judge was in my view correct in regarding the fact that the employment contract had been governed by English law, being the law most closely connected with the contract, as insufficient to establish with reasonable certainty that there was an implied agreement that the same law should apply to a contract of a different nature made in new circumstances.'

Agent appointed under non-EU law

1.119 The agent appointed for the UK under a contract specifying, say, the laws of the State of New York, will still be protected by the Regulations. This is because it is only when another EU state's laws are stated to apply that the GB Regulations are avoided. The Regulations are an example of UK legislative measure where the parties' choice of law is overturned on public policy grounds. UK employers would not get very far before an industrial tribunal in saying they had chosen the laws of an obscure island in the South Pacific to apply to their employment contracts in the UK (to avoid unfair dismissal provisions), and it is the same in the field of agency. This was decided in *Ingmar GB Ltd v Eaton Leonard Technologies Inc* [1999] Eu LR 88 (and ECJ: C-381/98 [2001] 1 CMLR 9) where the contract between the parties specified Californian law for agency duties performed by an English agent in the UK and the European Court of Justice on a reference from the English court held that even so the agent was protected by the EU Directive.

1.120 See also the software arbitration case above *Accentuate Ltd v Asigra Inc* [2009] EWHC 2655 (QB) where the contract specified non-EU laws and arbitration but a commercial agency claim was regarded as outside that or at least arguably so and following Ingmar the case could proceed.

Forum shopping

1.121 Some agents and principals will have a choice as to which EU state's laws to choose. The EU Commission's report into compensation and indemnity through the EU states (see Appendix 2) provides some guidance. For example, an agent may do best with French law because two years' commission is normally paid. He may do worst in Italy where a very low indemnity scale based on a trade union negotiated arrangement applies, which may result in Italy going before the European Court for failure to implement the Directive properly. He may feel comfortable with German law where a maximum of a year's commission as indemnity is payable and the rules are clear, as they have operated for some years.

1.122 UK principals have had a very difficult task in determining these issues because of the lack of precedent even after the *Lonsdale* decision on compensation amounts but this is addressed in Chapters 6 and 7 and there has been more case law of late bringing more clarity.

Agent operating in several states

1.123 The Regulations apply to the activities of the agent in Great Britain. Some agents operate in several states including GB. They would be protected by the Regulations as regards the GB work. If they also, say, operate in

France, then unless the agreement says to the contrary, they would be protected by French agency law for that activity. If they also operate in the US, then for that part of their activities they would have no protection. It is not clear in the absence of case law whether the courts would base any compensation on termination, for example, only on commission earned in relation to GB and exclude, say, the US commission or whether the court would find some part of the activities were carried on in GB and therefore all commission is used in assessing compensation. The answer is probably the former because of the way regulation 23 is worded. Also, this is a judicial nightmare because the agent would have to litigate in several states in some cases.

1.124 In other cases, it is not easy to see where the agent is carrying on his activities. If he is based in the UK but marketing abroad using e-mail and the Internet where are his activities?

1.125 Government guidance notes (see Appendix 1) include an annex at the back to which reference should be made. They give various examples of choice of law and when the Regulations apply and make the point that where an exclusive jurisdiction clause is chosen, rather than simply choice of law, then the courts may respect this and thus the US principal may avoid the application of the GB Regulations to its UK agents. It may be material whether the US principal has any sort of presence of assets in the EU.

Obtain foreign law advice

1.126 In general, in any case where there is a foreign element, it is sensible to obtain advice on foreign agency law before a contract is signed, before notice of termination is given, and when a compensation claim is made or other dispute arises, even if English law and jurisdiction are specified.

Transitional arrangements

1.127 The Regulations are very clear in relation to 'old' agency agreements. Regulation 23 provides:

'Notwithstanding any provision in any agency contract made before 1 January 1994, these Regulations shall apply to that contract after that date and, accordingly, any provision which is inconsistent with these Regulations shall have effect subject to them ... Nothing in these Regulations shall affect the rights and liability of a commercial agent or a principal which have accrued before 1 January 1994.'

1.128 Some principals have sought to argue that commission rates in the UK have traditionally been higher in the UK because agents were not entitled to compensation on termination. There is no evidence to suggest that this is the case. In other cases, principals have argued that only the work done by the agent since 1 January 1994 when the Regulations came into force is counted in ascertaining the level of compensation or indemnity payable to an agent. Again, this is wrong.

1.129   In *Duncan Moore v Piretta Pta Ltd* [1999] 1 All ER 174 the court examined a case where the agent had had a series of agency contracts with the same principal one after the other. The court said they were aggregated and treated as one. 'The agency contract' meant the overall arrangement. The judge said, 'In my judgment the phrase 'the agency contract' means simply 'the agency'. The word 'contract' after 'agency' adds nothing'. In that case counsel for the principal sought to argue that it would be retrospective and unfair if activity of the agent before the 1 January 1994 were taken into account. However, the judge said that legislation often displaces this principle:

> 'Regulation 23(1) applies the Regulations to contracts, whenever made, which are in existence on 1 January 1994. On the face of it the Regulation incorporates regulation 17 [*the compensation provision*] into contracts existing on that date.'

He made an analogy with employment law which applied retrospectively in the same way and also stated that of course where the agency was properly terminated before 1 January 1994 (as many were in anticipation of the then new law) then no compensation was payable nor would the Regulations have applied.

No written contract

1.130   Finally, readers need to be aware that even if an agency is entirely oral, the agent is still protected by the Regulations. Principals often tell agents they have no rights because nothing is in writing. In fact, often the agent is in a stronger position through having no written contract because most written contracts are written by the principal and designed to reduce the agent's rights as far as is legally possible.

Although not a case under the Regulations, the Supreme Court decision in *Wells v Devani* [2019] UKSC 1106 looked at unwritten agency agreements and provides useful guidance. The case concerned a property developer who was introduced to an estate agent as the developer was having trouble selling his block of flat. There was no written contract. The agent was promised a 2% finder's fee for finding a buyer. The parties did not agree when the fee would be due, but even so, the Supreme Court held there was a binding contract. However, s 18 of the Estate Agents Act 1979 requires this kind of contract to be in writing, and if not, it is unenforceable subject to the court's discretion. The court in this case exercised its discretion but decided to reduce the agent's fee by a third.

Checklist

1.131   This chapter is arguably the most important in the book as it seeks to provide guidance on when the Regulations apply. In ascertaining this, the following checklist may assist:

- Is the agent marketing goods or services? If services, the Regulations do not apply (except in some foreign states such as Spain and Belgium).

- Is the agent operating in Great Britain or Northern Ireland? If not, local law may apply depending on what the contract says.

- Even where operating in Great Britain or Northern Ireland, is another Member State's law chosen? If so that other country's laws will apply.

- Are the agent's activities secondary? Ask the agent before he starts what other work he does.

- Check the form in which the agent trades, though the Regulations apply to sole traders, partnerships and companies who are agents and also to agents who appoint sub-agents under them.

- Do any of the exclusions apply, such as for unpaid agents or agents acting as officers of a limited company?

- Is the agent a true self-employed commercial agent or in reality an independent distributor buying and reselling goods on his own account or an employee, in which case the Regulations will not apply.

- Has the agent continuing authority to negotiate?

Further information

1.132   The Regulations are considered on websites such as that of:

Fox Williams – www.agentlaw.co.uk

The Manufacturers' Agents' Association – www.themaa.co.uk

Chapter 2

Duties of the agent and principal – choosing and using an agent

2.1   This chapter looks at some of the most important provisions in a commercial agency agreement – the obligations of the agent and principal respectively. Most of these are left, by the law in the UK, to the parties to the agreement to agree between themselves. The Commercial Agents (Council Directive) Regulations 1993 (or their Northern Irish equivalent) will apply to most UK agency agreements where the agent markets goods rather than services. Whether the Regulations apply should be considered carefully as it has some impact on the duties of the parties. The circumstances in which the Regulations apply were considered in detail in the last chapter. However, even where the Regulations apply, they do not provide much detail on the respective duties of the parties.

Choosing an agent

2.2   Normally lawyers will not be used in the choice of agent. However, businesses will find that many of the legal difficulties addressed in this book will not arise if the right agent is picked in the first place. It is also sensible to take an agent on a trial basis, although be aware that there is no exclusion from the Regulations for short term agencies unless they are one-off for one short project.

2.3   The following issues should be considered before the agent is taken on:

1.   What experience does the agent have?

2.   Take up references.

3.   Do credit and other checks such as, if the agent is a limited liability company, ascertaining what it has filed at the relevant registry in the UK or abroad.

4. What the differences are under any local law? Some countries stipulate the form of agency agreement and require it to be registered in advance.

5. Be cautious of giving a large area exclusively to the agent. To have different agents covering parts of a large country may be a better arrangement.

6. What other agencies does the agent already have with other companies? Some companies restrict the number the agent may take on to four or five to ensure the agent has enough time to handle this agency. Others allow the agent only one agency.

7. Is the agent subject to a restrictive covenant which might prevent his entering into this agreement or obligations of confidentiality which prevent his using business and customer information in his possession?

8. For foreign agents check whether language skills are sufficient.

9. Computer links can be important – ascertain whether the agent has the necessary software and e-mail links and/or is prepared to use any software/apps you require such as 'Salesforce'. If you require the agent to use software which checks or verifies where the agent has attended at customers' premises, check compliance with the Data Protection Act 2018 and the General Data Protection Regulation (GDPR).

10. Make a note of what customer information is handed over to the agent when he starts. If he is taking over from another agent or is handed details of existing accounts, then account can be taken of this if he is paid an indemnity on termination of the agency (see *Moore v Piretta PTA Ltd* [1999] 1 All ER 174).

11. In some jurisdictions a new agent can be persuaded to pay the principal an up-front lump sum which is used to pay off any indemnity claim to the outgoing agent. This is not usual in the UK but common, for example, in Germany and is similar to a franchise fee a franchisee might pay for exclusivity over a particular area.

12. In certain cases, for an interim period the agent can be persuaded to share commission with an outgoing agent and indeed the agency Regulations make provision for this (see Chapter 4). The agent must be told and agree to such matters before the agency begins.

13. Make sure the agent is absolutely clear about whether he will be contracting as agent or principal. It can be helpful to go through the agreement clause by clause with him so every provision is clear, and have a translation arranged if the agent is abroad although in such a case it should be made clear by a clause in the agreement that, in the event of a conflict between the wording in the translation and the original, the original will prevail.

14. Register trade marks abroad in the principal's name before the agent starts to use them otherwise goodwill may accrue in such names abroad in the name of the agent. Ensure that the contract addresses this issue too.

15. Do not allow the agent to start work until an agency agreement is signed.

Agent to act in good faith

2.4   The main duty in the Regulations, which apply to most agents marketing goods in the UK and indeed under the agency directive most agents in the EU, is that the agent must look after the interests of his principal and act dutifully and in good faith (regulation 3(1)). Good faith is a concept not often implied into most commercial relationships but certainly imposes duties on an agent. For example, it may be hard for an agent to argue that he has acted in good faith if he has also in secret handled competing products.

Case examples

2.5   The author has been involved in several cases where the agent has handled a product which the principal says is competing. In some cases, there was a clause restricting the agent acting for competing principals and in others none. Where there was no clause the principal sought to argue that the omission of such a clause was not material because the duty to act in good faith would require that the agent not handle competing products. Whether that is so or not remains to be seen. In cases where there was an express clause the principal is in a stronger position. However, in the cases concerned the dispute was over whether the product concerned did or did not compete and/ or whether the principal knew. Sometimes a principal later adds to its list of products a competing product, having already had full disclosure from the existing agent about other product lines covered, or the principal knew the agent was carrying a competitive line and never objected and therefore later may be estopped from objecting.

Rossetti Marketing Ltd v (1) Diamond Sofa Company, (2) Solutions Marketing Ltd **[2012] EWCA Civ 1021**

2.6   In this case RML, an agent, represented Diamond in marketing its furniture products in the UK. The judge at first instance was asked to look at 35 preliminary issues to save costs (although it seems in the end to have added to costs by having preliminary issues considered separately). The first instance judge made his initial ruling and also ordered substantial payments for interim costs and for interim damages (£300k and £500k respectively, overturned by the Court of Appeal). The agent had claimed under regulations 7, 8, 15, and 17 of the Regulations in the region of £90,000, £600,000, £210,000, and £1.5m.

    There was no written contract. In an email RML's predecessor had told the principal about two other agencies but had not highlighted that they were or could be competing agencies. The Court of Appeal said:

> 'In an email sent to Mr Charoenyos on 30 January 2004, shortly before the agency agreement was concluded, Mr Willan said that Diamond's "product range does not clash with either of our upholstery companies Linkwise and

ArtPeak who are both based in China", and then went on to suggest that Diamond appoint SML as its agent for a trial period of a year.'

The Court of Appeal went on:

'As a general proposition, an agent occupies a fiduciary position vis-à-vis his principal. He owes what Millett LJ called "the single-minded duty of loyalty" to his principal, so that he "must not place himself in a position where his duty and his interest conflict", and he "may not act for ... the benefit of a third party without the informed consent of his principal" – *Bristol and West Building Society v Mothew* [1998] Ch 1, 18A–B. To the same effect, and more specifically to the present case, Lord Browne-Wilkinson, giving the judgment of the Privy Council in *Kelly v Cooper* [1993] AC 205, 214D, said that "it is normally said that it is a breach of an agent's duty to act for competing principals".'

...

An agent can act for two principals with conflicting interests in two types of case. The first is, as already indicated, where both principals agree. In such a case, it is for the agent to show that the principal not merely consented, but that the consent was given on a fully informed basis – ie that the agent had made full disclosure to the principal – see per Tuckey LJ in *Hurstanger Ltd v Wilson* [2007] EWCA Civ 299, [2007] 1 WLR 2351, para 35 (approving a passage in the then-current edition of *Bowstead & Reynolds on Agency*, now in para 6-039 of the 19th edition).

The second type of case where an agent can act for competing principals is where, as in *Kelly* [1993] AC 205, the principal must have appreciated that the nature of the agent's business (in that case a residential estate agent) is "to act for numerous principals". As Lord Browne-Wilkinson explained, "despite the conflict of interest", residential estate agents "must be free to act for several competing principals; otherwise they will be unable to perform their function" – [1993] AC 205, 214C.

In this case, it seems to me that there was no reason for concluding that the normal non-compete principle should not apply, when the agency agreement was made. Accordingly, it follows that SML could not act as agents for competitors of Diamond. It was certainly not agreed that SML could act for competitors of Diamond: as the Judge found, nothing was said about it. The email sent by Mr Willan to Mr Charoenyos on 30 January 2004, and quoted in para 19 above, supports this conclusion: Diamond was being told that the two named furniture manufacturers for whom SML acted had ranges which would not clash, or compete, with those of Diamond. That plainly supports, rather than undermines, the argument that Diamond would have expected SML not to act for any of Diamond's competitors.'

2.7   Interestingly the Court of Appeal has simply referred to the common law of agency, rather than the implied duty of good faith under the regulations.

The Court of Appeal set aside the interim payment order as at full trial the principal might be able to argue a right of set off arising from breach of contract by the agent even though the issue of breach arising from the 'competing agencies' was only raised after termination.

2.8   The moral of the case is ensure there are written agency contracts and that litigation can go either way in these cases and should be avoided where possible. Also, it should not be assumed that dealing with certain preliminary issues first in litigation always saves costs.

Computer Associates Ltd v Software Incubator Ltd [2018] EWCA Civ 518

2.9   This case arose when the principal, Computer Associates, terminated Software Incubator's agency agreement because Software Incubator had signed an agreement with another software firm, Intigua.

The Court of Appeal held that holding additional agencies did not render the agent in breach of contract. However, this case has gone to the Supreme Court on appeal, from which questions about 'software as goods' have been referred to the CJEU. A decision is expected in 2020 or 2021.

2.10   The Court of Appeal looked at the alleged breach of the agency agreement and breach of agency duties. On the agreement and whether it had been breached by taking on the new agency, the court said:

'The relevant clauses in the Agreement show that this is clearly a non-exclusive agency. TSI [the agent] agreed to devote a "substantial amount of time and effort" to its principal. It was possible for it to do this and to work for more than one principal. CA's argument to the contrary only succeeds if "substantial amount of time" means the "majority of time;" a conclusion which I am not persuaded the Agreement supports. Further, it is telling that the two commercial parties did not choose to expressly restrict TSI's ability to act for another principal. I agree with the judge at [76] that, provided there was no conflict under Clause 3.6, the Agreement allowed for TSI to take on another principal.

In addition, I conclude that the judge was perfectly entitled to find on the facts that there was no breach of the Agreement because TSI was not in fact prevented from carrying out, and/or did not fail to carry out, its duty to devote a substantial amount of time to its work for CA.'

2.11   The Court of Appeal did not then examine breach of the Regulations as it had held that the Regulations did not apply as software was being sold, not goods (although, as stated above, this has been appealed so may become relevant once the Supreme Court hears from the CJEU).

2.12   Finally, the Court of Appeal looked at whether there had been a breach of the common law duties of agents (which apply whether or not the agent is protected by the Regulations) and agreed with the High Court that there had not been such a breach saying:

'In relation to the common law position, I accept Mr Dhillon's submission that TSI was bound by the common law proposition of law that an agent may not put himself in a position or enter into a transaction by which his personal interest or duty to another principal may conflict with his duty to his principal, unless his principal with full knowledge consents. The judge accepted that TSI owed a duty to CA to avoid any conflict of interest, but he distinguished the authorities relied upon by CA on their facts. He concluded there had been no breaches of the conflict of interest rule, or, if there had been breaches of that principle, they were minor breaches, which were not repudiatory at [91]–[125] and [129]–[131] of the judgment.

For the purpose of determining this issue, it is necessary to consider the Agreement. Clause 12.1 prevented TSI from being engaged "in any activity competing directly with the actual and/or planned activities and/or [Product] of [CA]."

There are two sub-issues of fact here: first, whether the respective natures of CA's product and of the Intigua product were such that TSI acted in actual/potential conflict of interest in promoting both products in the relevant period; second, whether TSI devoted a substantial amount of time to Intigua during the relevant period which put it in conflict with its duty to devote the same time to CA.

As to the first sub-issue, the judge [in the high Court] heard considerable evidence on this point. He dealt accurately and thoroughly with that evidence at [81]–[89] of the judgment. In my view, he was entitled to accept TSI's case that the two products did not realistically compete at all; and that the two products could not become competitive by combining Intigua's product with a free third-party product.

As to the second sub-issue, I agree with the judge's finding at [113] that, if one takes the terms of the Intigua Agreement at face value, so that TSI was obliged to and did spend a substantial amount of time on Intigua, it was unlikely that it could do the same for CA. However, in the judge's view, this did not happen. I do not think that there is a sufficiently strong evidential basis for this court to depart from that finding'.

2.13   This is a useful case in practice as frequently companies do wish to terminate the agency agreement when an agent takes on a competing product or one which the principal believes to be so. The case illustrates the importance of being very sure that the product does in fact compete with the principal's products. Most agencies are non-exclusive and most agents carry a range of products, rather than acting only for one principal.

One Money Mail case – restrictive covenants and enticement

2.14   In *One Money Mail Ltd v (1) Ria Financial Services (2) Sebastian Wasilewski* [2015] EWCA Civ 1084 the Court of Appeal held that non-competition clauses in an agreement where an agent was marketing payment services were valid and reasonable both during the agency contract and after it ended. This was not a case under the Regulations, but is still useful with regards to restraint of trade law. The competing agency did raise with the agent whether the agent was allowed to take the new agency on as it expected there to be a restrictive covenant in place and the Court of Appeal did not award damages against that competitor principal although found it had procured a breach of contract by the agent.

2.15   In practice sometimes a new proposed principal does become embroiled in a dispute between an agent and the principal. The passage below from the *One Money Mail* case provides some guidance and suggests principals should not rely on an agent assuming there is no restriction. The new principal should take no active steps and certainly should not sign a contract with the agent until the new principal is certain there are no such restrictions.

> 'As to the first of these submissions, I would not interfere with the judge's finding that Ria [the competitor proposed principal] "knew of the exclusivity provision" in Mr Wasilewski's [the agent] contract. It was amply justified on the evidence and even if true "knowledge" could only be obtained by reading the contract itself, there was sufficient Nelsonian blindness to justify an alternative finding that Ria were reckless as to the existence of the exclusivity provision. Miss Smith submitted that Mr Wasilewski had given Ria an assurance that there was no exclusivity provision but the evidence was only that he said "he did not think" so (para 42) which hardly amounts to an assurance. Even if it could be described as an assurance, it was not worth the paper it was not written on coming from someone whose first language was not English and who could not be relied on to have read, understood and remembered all the provisions contained in a closely printed 10 page contract. There was in my judgment every intention to sign Mr Wasilewski up as an agent in circumstances in which Ria knew of (or were reckless as to) the existence of an exclusivity clause.
>
> As to the second submission, Miss Smith said that cases in which an "active step" was held to be a sufficient procurement or inducement for the purpose of the tort, such as *BMTA v Salvadori* [1949] Ch. 556 and *Rickless v United Artists Corporation* [1988] QB 40 had been impliedly overruled by *OBG v Allen* [2008] 1 AC 1. This argument depended on the disapproval by the House of Lords of the theory that the tort of inducing a breach of contract was part of a more general tort of causing loss by unlawful means and their criticism in that respect of *D C Thomson v Deakin* [1952] Ch 646. Miss Smith took us through the authorities at a speed consonant with the 1½ day estimate for the hearing and it was (at any rate to me) a fascinating exercise of an advocate's skill. But as Mr Davies pointed out, the exercise was unnecessary because, on any view, Ria's acts were more than merely an "active step" enabling Ria to compete with OMM since Ria had signed a contract with Mr Wasilewski which meant that the procurement of the breach by Mr Wasilewski of his contract with OMM actually occurred and continued to occur for a period of 3 years until it was terminated.
>
> *OBG v Allen* certainly decided that inducing breach of contract was a tort of accessory liability. As Lord Toulson JSC pointed out in *Fish & Fish Ltd v Sea Shepard UK* [2015] AC 1229, 1239 para 21:
>
>> "To establish accessory liability in tort it is not enough to show that D did acts which facilitated P's commission of the tort. D will be jointly liable with P if they combined to do or secure the doing of acts which constituted a tort."

In the present case Ria and Mr Wasilewski combined to the extent of making a contract which was or made provision for the very act which was a breach of Mr Wasilewski's contract with OMM.

I would uphold the judge's finding that Ria unlawfully procured a breach of Mr Wasilewski's contract with OMM, and enter judgment for OMM on that basis; but since OMM cannot quantify their loss I would do no more.'

2.16   Agents should be very careful about competing agencies and not just declare them to the principal but obtain clear informed consent from the principal that they may operate the other agencies. Indeed, in the *Rosetti* decision (para **2.6** above) the Court of Appeal said it had not yet been established that the other agencies were necessarily competing although both parties seemed to be assuming that they might be.

2.17   Clearly the duty of good faith implies important obligations into the relationship between the parties. The agent must not make a secret profit from his relationship. He should not take bribes. He should not act as agent for the buyer as well as for the seller and take commission from both. For certain types of agencies these activities are proscribed by statute. For example, since 1 June 2019, letting agents are not allowed to charge flat hunters a fee where they are also paid a commission by those seeking to let out their properties (and many years before used also to be banned).

2.18   Reference should be made to the standard works on agency law for further information in relation to the fiduciary duties of agents at common law. The *Crocs Europe BV v Craig Lee Anderson* [2012] EWCA Civ 1400 case did hold that not every breach of fiduciary duties and of regulation 3 of the Regulations is serious enough to justify immediate termination without payment of compensation to the agent.

2.19   Although regulation 3 is helpful it is much better to set out in detail in the agency agreement what duties the agent has. He may be obliged to look after the interests of his principal, but does this mean visiting customers every six weeks or once a year, for example? The contract can make this clear.

2.20   Regulation 3(2) goes on to provide that the commercial agent must:

(a)   make proper efforts to negotiate and, where appropriate, conclude the transactions he is instructed to take care of;

(b)   communicate to his principal all the necessary information available to him;

(c)   comply with reasonable instructions given by his principal.

These provisions elaborate on the agent's duties.

Negotiation by agent – prices and terms

2.21   Paragraph (a) of regulation 3(2) makes it clear that in some cases the agent has authority to conclude a deal. However, in practice it is normally better that the principal decides whether a particular account will be opened or customer taken on. In most cases the agent simply negotiates. There was discussion in Chapter 1 about 'negotiation' because the Regulations only apply where the agent has authority to negotiate and many agents may not do what to most people amounts to negotiation. Indeed, some agency contracts, in order to seek to avoid the application of the Regulations, specifically provide that the agent has no authority to negotiate.

2.22   The following checklist may assist:

- Is the agent allowed to vary the standard price list of the principal?

- Does the agent have power within a fixed band to vary prices?

- What impact does a reduced price have on commission levels? (Normally it results in a reduction under the commission provision of the contract.)

- Does the agent set the prices on his own?

2.23   Agency is used in many industries and it is impossible to say what arrangement is correct for all industries. However, in practice one of the main advantages of using an agent over a distributor who buys and sells on his own account is that the agent can be controlled. He can be told the price at which he must market the goods. If the supplier wants to stipulate prices to a distributor, on the other hand, he can be fined up to 10% of turnover for breach of article 101 of TFEU (where EU competition law applies) or the Chapter I prohibition in the Competition Act 1998 in the UK. In most contracts it is provided that the agent can only vary prices with the prior consent of the principal.

2.24   Normally the agent is obliged by a contract term to market the goods on the standard terms and conditions of sale of the principal. Rarely is an agent entitled to use his own terms of business. If he is, there is a danger that the arrangement becomes one of distribution rather than agency, or the agent becomes an undisclosed agent because the customer believes it is dealing only with the agent and the terms and conditions may have the agent's name upon them rather than that of the supplier (see the *Sagal v Bunz* decision considered in Chapter 1).

2.25   Note that paragraph (a) of regulation 3(2) refers to transactions of which the agent is instructed to take care. It is clear that the principal decides which customers are taken on. Many agency contracts include a mechanism whereby the principal is given details on a regular basis of customers who want supplies and the principal then decides whether to supply them. The principal may find after a credit check that a particular customer is a bad credit risk and may decide not to supply. There are obligations on the principal, where the Regulations apply, for the principal to keep the agent informed about this, as otherwise the agent may think he will be due a large commission when, in fact, the request for supplies has been turned down by the principal.

Communication of information

2.26   Paragraph (b) of regulation 3(2) requires the agent to communicate all necessary information to the principal. There is no legal requirement that such a term be set down in the agency contract, when the Regulations apply but it will be implied anyway. Regulation 5 states that no provision of regulations 3 or 4 can be derogated from. Therefore, any term in the contract which allows the agent to act in bad faith or not to keep the principal informed is void. No principal would draft such a contract in any event.

2.27   However, in practice it would foolish simply to rely on paragraph (c) of regulation 3(2) because there are many duties the principal may want to impose on the agent relating to information. What they are depends on the industry concerned. Those advising companies should ask what the agent is expected to do in practice and then write those obligations into the contract. Some companies will have an Agents' Manual or other detailed document setting out how the agent operates, how orders are accepted etc, and where this is the case then the contract should make provision for such document being part of the contract, subject to a right of the principal from time to time to make reasonable changes.

2.28   In most other cases where the detail is not set out in some other document, then at least some of the practical aspects of the agency should be set out in the agreement.

2.29   Those are the only duties of the agent set out in the Regulations. The rest of this chapter looks at other clauses which might be included in an agency agreement, but in relation to which there is no legal obligation. Much of what follows is common sense rather than law, but seeks to provide an overview of commercial issues relevant to the drafting of an agency agreement.

Written or oral?

2.30   Where the Regulations apply there is only an obligation for the terms to be reduced to writing where one party requests it. The protection given by the Regulations applies whether or not the agreement is in writing. The agreement can be in the form of a letter or signed agreement. It is generally best for principals to ensure that full duties of an agent are set out in a written contract signed by both parties so there can be no dispute later about what was agreed.

Variation of agreements

2.31   One issue which arises frequently in practice is the variation of agency agreements. Under English law an agreement can only be varied with the consent of both parties *unless* the contract says otherwise. Some agency agreements include, perfectly lawfully, for example a clause which entitles the principal to:

- vary the product range at its discretion from time to time;

- change the agent's territory;

- change the agent's commission rate;

- alter the commercial terms.

2.32   No agent should willingly cede such power to the principal. There is nothing in the Regulations which prohibits a principal acting in such a manner where a contract term provides it, although sometimes it is argued by solicitors in correspondence that such a clause could be void as contrary to the principal's obligation to act in good faith.

2.33   Those last words are important. If there is no contract term allowing a change then the agreement can only be altered by agreement. Frequently agents have foisted on them a reduction in commission levels, sometimes to such a level as the agency becomes uneconomic to operate. In such cases the agent may have a right to resign and claim compensation or an indemnity under the Regulations' equivalent provision to 'constructive dismissal'. However, if a change is minor to the agency terms then that right is unlikely to apply. If the contract allows the principal to vary the terms, then normally the English courts would stand by such a provision. It is important, therefore, for an agent not to sign an agency agreement with such substantial rights of variation given to the principal.

2.34   In practice many principals unilaterally even without a contractual right to do so alter agents' product ranges and territories and take back bigger accounts ('house accounts'). Frequently the agent simply has to accept this in practice as the alternative with which they are presented is termination of their agency. Some the writer has advised have at termination sought to recover the lost commission from those earlier changes although their 'acceptance' however reluctant of those changes might amount to acceptance of the change. The legal position is not clear. The agent has little power and forced changes may be unenforceable. However, by analogy with employment law, in recessions employees are often offered a four-day week or redundancy and thousands have accepted a four-day week. Those are usually lawfully agreed changes to a contract accepted in writing by both sides and enforceable despite the imbalance of power.

Case example – changing the contract: *Vick v Vogle-Gapes Ltd* [2006] EWHC 1665 (QB)

2.35   Mr Vick was taken on as an employee for Vogle-Gapes trading as Town and Country in 1996 and changed his status to that of a commercial agent for the company three years later. The contract ended in 2004. The principal was unhappy about his performance, but he ignored them. In 2004 the company said they would reduce his territory and his market which was permitted under the agency agreement's terms.

2.36   Both parties said the other had breached the contract. The court said as the contract provided for it then the company could change the territory and the market. The agent argued this breached the duty of good faith and the only change should have been a reasonable and proportionate one. Indeed, the writer has argued before now that reducing a territory from say 100 to 0.01 in an effort to avoid compensation and say the agreement was still continuing would be seen as an artificial device to avoid the Regulations and be contrary to good faith and void.

2.37   The court did not disagree totally with that stance but said here as the agent was doing badly the action was proportionate and reasonable.
  The agreement said:

'7.1 If in the reasonable discretion of the Principal, the Agent is failing to maximise sales opportunities within the Territory, the Principal may by one month's written notice to the Agent amend the Territory.

7.2 The Principal may by one month's written notice to the Agent amend the Market by adding or deleting specific customers or categories of customers.'

In the *Vick* case the court said:

'Mr Segal [counsel for the agent] submitted that the obligation to act towards Mr Vick dutifully and in good faith was at least as wide as the obligation implied on the part of both an employer and an employee in a contract of employment to act towards the other with mutual trust and confidence. The content of that obligation was considered by the House of Lords in *Malik v Bank of Credit and Commerce International SA* [1997] ICR 606 [an employment law case]. The formulation approved by the House of Lords was that the relevant party (in that case the employer):

"shall not, without reasonable and proper cause, conduct itself in a manner calculated and likely to destroy or seriously damage the relationship of confidence and trust between employer and employee."

'I accept those submissions of Mr. Segal. However, it is material to notice that, in the formulation approved by the House of Lords, a number of elements fall to be considered on the way to reaching a conclusion as to whether the obligation has, on particular facts, been breached. The first is that whatever has been done which is said to have amounted to a breach of the obligation must have been done without reasonable and proper cause. If what was done was done reasonably and for good cause, it is not a breach. Second, what was done which was said to have been a breach must have been calculated and likely either to destroy or to seriously damage the relationship of trust and confidence. It appears that what is required is deliberate, rather than inadvertent conduct, but that the conduct in question need not be targeted at the other party to the contract, as opposed to someone else. As Lord Steyn said in *Malik v Bank of Credit and Commerce International SA* at paragraph 60:

> "The motives of the employer cannot be determinative, or even relevant, in judging the employees' claims for damages for breach of the implied obligation. If conduct objectively considered is likely to cause serious damage to the relationship between the employer and the employee a breach of the implied obligation may arise." '

2.38   If the agreement is unsigned and there is no other agreement and the agency has proceeded, then it may be deemed accepted. The agent therefore must expressly reject any such draft terms. As will be mentioned later in this chapter many agency agreements now include target figures or minimum sales requirements which the agent must meet. This is normally designed to ensure that the principal can more easily be rid of an underperforming agent.

2.39   In practice it is important to establish whether the agent has accepted the target figure or not. Agents who have been sent a target for the first time and do not agree with it must expressly reject it, otherwise it may become part of their agreement by default. Variations to an agreement must normally be supported by 'consideration' – normally money or money's worth, but this may constitute as little as the principal agreeing to extend the agency agreement by a further year (where it is for a fixed term).

2.40   Principals, on the other hand, may find rights to vary factors such as territories and commission levels very helpful indeed, and in most cases agents simply sign the standard terms of the principal which are put to them; such clauses are accepted on a regular basis by agents and are legally binding.

2.41   In *Page v Combined Shipping and Trading Co Ltd* [1997] 3 All ER 656 the written agreement between principal and agent could have allowed the principal to reduce the volume of business with the agent and reduce commission to very little had the principal decided to operate the provisions of that agreement in that way. However, the court said that should not be looked at in assessing the agent's loss on termination because part of the principal's duty is to act in good faith.

Parties

2.42   The agreement should begin by setting out the names of the parties and their addresses. It may seem facile even to mention this point, but many agreements upon which advice is sought are unclear, particularly where foreign entities are concerned. In the event of legal proceedings being brought later, it is essential to know who the defendant should be. Ensuring that the name is correctly spelt and the right group company is chosen, where the company is part of a group, is important, particularly with foreign organisations which may be difficult to trace subsequently. It is good practice to give the registered number of companies, and asking the client for sight of the agent's notepaper is one basic way in which some of this information can be gleaned. Company or business registry searches should also be undertaken to verify the information given.

2.43   Many agents trade as individuals and in the contract their proper full name should be given as well as their trading name. The phrase *trading as* will be familiar to most people. If in future there is a reconstruction or reorganisation or a change of name within the company or in relation to the agent, then a letter noting that fact should pass between the parties and the agreement varied accordingly. Frequently when an agency dispute arises there has been a complex series of past transfers. Including a clause in the contract which requires the agent to notify the principal when it changes its name or mergers with another entity should assist, and details of the variation should be noted between the parties. It should also be made clear in the contract whether the principal and the agent are entitled to assign their rights under the agreement. An agreement under English law which contains no restriction on assignment can be assigned by both parties. Normally, the principal is free to assign the agreement and the agent is not – which illustrates how one sided most agency agreements are, but also shows how important it is for the principal to know that the agency will be performed personally by an individual chosen for their particular skills. It is very common in practice to find that the agency agreement is with one entity – e.g. a sole trader agent but the commission has been paid at a later stage to a limited company the agent has set up or vice versa. It can be difficult to ascertain which legal entity is the 'agent'. Usually looking at who has been paid the commission helps decide the issue and shows an implied assignment accepted by both parties even if undocumented by a written contract change. It is obviously much better if the parties agree written variations at the time of changes. It becomes very material if the agent dies or becomes too old or ill to carry on, which of course cannot be the case with an agent which is a limited company. Some agents for limited companies split income by way of dividends with a non-working spouse to use both annual tax allowances and tax bands, and indeed often simply to limit their liability. However, the downside is that they will have no compensation claim during old age or on death or illness.

Appointment clause

Exclusivity

2.44   The agency agreement or letter should appoint the agent either as exclusive or non-exclusive sales agent for the products in the territory. The next chapter on competition law looks at exclusivity in detail. The parties should make it clear what they mean by the terms used. For example, the agreement might provide that the principal shall not appoint other agents in the agent's territory nor itself market the products there (this would be normal for an exclusive agreement). Sometimes the agreement becomes non-exclusive if the agent does not meet the sale targets.

2.45 A 'sole' agreement conversely means that the principal itself can compete. However, such clauses should always be read in conjunction with the commission clause (commission is addressed in a later chapter). This is because the commission clause often provides that the agent is entitled to all commission on orders arising from his territory whether generated by him or not. This is normally what an exclusive agent expects. Therefore, even if the principal is allowed to compete, it is not true competition because the agent is paid commission in any event.

2.46 In practice in termination or dispute situations the parties often argue over whether an agreement which simply appoints an agent for a named geographical territory without saying if the territory is exclusive or nonexclusive, have by implication or case law appointed the agent exclusively. In *Georgios Kontogeorgas v Kartonpak AE* (Case C-104/95, [1996] ECR I-6643) the then European Court of Justice held that the agent was exclusive even though the contract did not say so. It is best if the word non-exclusive is used if the parties do not intend exclusivity to be given.

2.47 The Regulations provide that exclusive agents are entitled to commission on all orders from their territory. In *Heirs of Paul Chevassus-Marche v Group Danone (Case C-19/07)* (see also [2008] 2 All ER (Comm) 1093) the court held that where a customer bought via a central buying office even if they were situated in the exclusive agent's territory in terms of where goods were delivered, no commission entitlement arose.

2.48 This is an important practical issue. Very often big groups of companies operating internationally choose to move to centralised buying and wise principals include clauses in the contract allowing them subsequently to nominate those accounts to be house accounts on which no commission or lower commission is payable.

Products

2.49 What is meant by *the products* should be defined, especially if exclusive rights are being given. The principal may branch out into other product areas later and may not want to be bound to offer those additional products to the agent. The agent, on the other hand, may want the rights to market all the products of the principal from time to time.

2.50 Some principals seek to avoid the application of the agency Regulations by providing that they have a right to change the 'products' definition from time to time. An agent handling twenty products could have this reduced, lawfully, to one but not have his contract terminated, so would have no right to claim compensation. However, there remains a risk that an agent in such circumstances could argue this was tantamount to a termination and seek to claim compensation.

Territory

2.51   Similarly, the area of the territory should be defined. This does not have to be an entire state, but could be a region, but this should be clear from the agreement. Often a map is included.

Commencement date

2.52   The date from which the agreement commences should be clearly stated. Particularly where the agent is given exclusive rights, an appointment for a short, limited term may be desirable. A period of a year gives a supplier the opportunity to see whether the agent is, in fact, doing his job properly and would also give the agent a sufficient period in which to prove himself. Trial periods are common. However, compensation may well be payable when a trial period ends although the agent probably will not by then have built up much goodwill or value and thus compensation may be low or non existent on termination.

2.53   There is no reason why the agreement cannot be expressed to be for a year and then to continue automatically unless terminated under the termination clause or on notice. This is then an indefinite contract. Regulation 14 provides:

> 'An agency contract for a fixed period which continues to be performed by both parties after that period has expired shall be deemed to be converted into an agency contract for an indefinite period.'

The risk with a one-year term, for example, is that if it overruns by even one day it becomes, where the Regulations apply, an indefinite contract. In practice, however, many companies do not find it practicable to renew agency agreements each year and prefer an indefinite contract in any event, with, of course, rights to terminate on notice. Termination is dealt with in a later chapter and the rights to compensation on such termination.

Obligations of the agent

2.54   The following are examples of obligations which might be imposed on an agent:

(a)   to use best endeavours to promote and sell the products in the territory by procuring orders for them and to achieve minimum sales levels;

('best endeavours' represents a fairly strong obligation in law although not as strong as originally thought so principals are better off having binding sales requirements; agents will want to alter this to 'reasonable endeavours');

(b) supplying reports or returns or other information in relation to sales of the products (it is best to have a detailed provision in relation to this – many agents hate paperwork and are bad at it, but love selling, yet the principal needs the information and often the contract will specify the form in which the information must be supplied);

(c) informing the principal of all information which would be of benefit in relation to marketing the product and making proper enquiries about the financial stability of customers who place orders through the agent;

(d) not to be involved in selling similar or competing goods (this provision might make it clear that the agent should not be so involved whether on his own or directly or indirectly, and whether by way of importation, manufacture or sale or supply of such competing goods; where there is any doubt about what is a competing product then this should be fully defined);

(e) not to make any promises or warranties or representations about the products or give any guarantees in connection with them unless the supplier consents;

(f) not to sell the goods except at the price which has been notified to the agent and on the terms and conditions of sale which the supplier provides;

(g) not to incur any liabilities nor pledge credit for the supplier without obtaining his consent;

(h) not to undertake any advertising or promotion without consent. In some cases, there may be provisions dealing with joint advertising campaigns or agreements by the principal that he will spend a certain sum on advertising the products in the territory. Both parties should be clear about their obligations in this area;

(i) to keep books of account up to date with records showing all enquiries and transactions handled by the agent. A principal should have the right to visit, or send his authorised representatives to, the premises of the agent to examine the books and records;

(j) pass on complaints made by customers to the supplier and not settle or compromise or prejudice any claims in relation to the goods without obtaining the prior written consent of the supplier;

(k) notify the supplier of any actual or threatened infringement of its rights such as patents, trade marks and copyright and assist the supplier in bringing and running legal proceedings (at the supplier's expense); and

(1)   not to use or register any name used by the supplier without express authorisation. Some agents have registered the principal's names as trade marks in their own territory and the principal has found itself unable to get back its own marks. The provision can be extended to Internet domain names too.

Sales targets

2.55   Some agency agreements are almost too vague to enforce. It is not clear what is expected of the agent and therefore hard to ascertain whether the agent is in breach of contract or not in any particular instance. It is much easier to claim – 'you have failed to visit each customer twice in each selling season as specified in clause 6 of our agreement' than 'you have failed to make proper efforts under the agreement'.

2.56   Therefore, principals are advised to set out the agent's duties in detail even if these will change over time. Change control provisions can be added to make it clear how the duties may be varied in due course. In particular, it is wise for principals to impose minimum sales figures on any agent given an exclusive area otherwise the principal has locked itself out of that area and the agent could sit back and do nothing and the principal would have no legal recourse.

2.57   Some companies have two target figures – one a figure for which to aim and another a base line figure which if the agent does not exceed can result in his dismissal. Whether there is one figure or there are two, it should be made absolutely clear what the consequence of failure to meet the figure is. As will be seen in the chapter dealing with termination and compensation, if an agent under the Regulations is in substantial breach of contract which justifies immediate termination then no compensation is payable. It can be very hard to prove this in practice. Agents often say they did not meet a target because the principal did not supply the goods to customers or only very late or to a low standard or sales were down because of a recession or other reasons than the agent's fault. The aim for principals will be to put a target figure into that category of a breach of contract by careful drafting. Some principals require the agent to use mobile phone applications such as www.salesforce.com's products which will track agents and their visits to customers.

2.58   There are other commercial aspects beyond the scope of this book which are also relevant in relation to target figures. The agent needs an incentive to do well and many companies will have 'salesman of the year awards' for those who succeed particularly well. There may be special bonuses when particular rates are achieved. The target should ideally be arranged in consultation with the agent. Some companies set unrealistically high targets which the agent could never meet.

2.59   Some agents are sacked for failing to reach their target when it has been poor quality products and bad after-sales service which has led to the target not being reached. Agents are therefore advised to ensure that any target is: (i) not legally binding; and (ii) even if it is, they are not held in breach of it through circumstances which are outside their control. This would include not just failures by the principal but also a fall in business generally, such as a recession or collapse of a particular market, e.g. following a food health scare.

2.60   The specimen agency contract in the Schedule includes some additional obligations too. Some agents will have to visit customers a particular number of times each year. Others will have certain exhibitions they must attend. The agreement should make it clear who pays expenses – agent or principal – for attending events such as trade shows and generally in relation to the agency.

2.61   There may well be other obligations which the principal would want to impose on the agent and those should be set out clearly in the agreement.

Principal's obligations

2.62   The Regulations, when they apply, impose in regulation 4 certain duties on the principal. These include:

'**4.**—(1) In his relations with his commercial agent a principal must act dutifully and in good faith.'

In *Cooper v Pure Fishing (UK) Ltd* [2004] EWCA Civ 375 the agent refused to take on new products which Pure Fishing (the principal) wanted the agent to sell. The agent's refusal was due to the fact the agent was already selling products which competed with the new products for another principal. At paragraph 9 of the Court of Appeal's judgment, the court refers to the fact that the High Court had found that the principal had only asked the agent to take on the new products to engineer a termination of the agency as the principal knew the agent would not be prepared to take on the new products. This was a breach of the duty of good faith the principal owes the agent under regulation 4. Although the case was about termination and expiry of agency agreements and found the principal did not terminate the agreement for breach so could not thus avoid its obligation to pay compensation, the case does touch on the duty to act in good faith.

Regulation 4 goes on to provide:

'(2)   In particular, a principal must:
   (a)   provide his commercial agent with the necessary documentation relating to the goods concerned;
   (b)   obtain for his commercial agent the information necessary for the performance of the agency contract, and in particular notify his commercial agent within a reasonable period once he anticipates that the volume of commercial transactions will be significantly lower than that which the commercial agent could normally have expected.

(3)   The principal shall, in addition, inform his commercial agent within a reasonable period of his acceptance or refusal of, and of any non-execution by him of, a commercial transaction which the commercial agent has procured for him.'

2.63   Regulation 4(2)(a) is largely self explanatory. Most principals supply documents such as price lists and glossy booklets. Many provide samples of the relevant products for which the agent pays. The agreement then needs to include clauses dealing with the payment for such samples and what happens to them on termination. In a number of agency disputes on termination the agent has withheld payment for samples to set against compensation allegedly due. This can be anticipated and addressed in the agency contract.

2.64   Derogation is not permitted from the obligations in regulation 4 (regulation 5 provides this), although they do not have to be expressly stated in the agency agreement. They will apply whether or not the agency agreement says so. Some agents abroad have a better knowledge than the principal of matters such as volume of likely transactions; however, where the principal determines which orders are accepted (which is normally the case), the principal must ensure it puts in place mechanisms to enable it to keep the agent informed of orders accepted and orders cancelled.

2.65   The obligations to be imposed on the supplier or principal will depend on what the parties have negotiated. A typical provision is that the supplier will send samples of advertising and promotional material to the agent for him to use in the territory. Also, the principal may send representatives to the territory to promote the products and may, as mentioned above, run an advertising campaign himself in that country.
   The principal should include an express right to decline, for any reason, any order.

Confidentiality

2.66   If the agent will have access to confidential information, whether it is a customer list or business information or secret technical details concerning the manufacture of the products, then an obligation on the agent not to divulge the confidential information nor use it otherwise than in the course of carrying out his normal duties may be imposed. The agent can under the Regulations be restricted from competing for up to two years after the agency is over if there is a clause to this effect (regulation 20(2) of the Regulations).

Personal performance

2.67   As the principal has carefully chosen the agent, he does not want the agent to farm out his duties to sub-agents nor assign the agreement, so restrictions on those events should be imposed. Of course, this depends on the particular circumstances and in some cases the agent is given a right to appoint sub-agents. Where the agent is a limited company it is clearly envisaged that employees of the company will carry out the duties concerned. However, a common issue arises where the agent, whether incorporated or not, wants to involve their son or daughter or a spouse in the selling activities and the principal does not agree. It is best to clarify these matters before the agency agreement is signed by clear provisions to the effect that, e.g., Ms Jones shall perform the [limited company] agent's duties only and no other director, shareholder or employee may be used in the performance of the agency duties without the principal's prior written consent. Where there is a change of control of the limited company then the principal may reserve a right to terminate the agreement. Similar issues arise with partnerships where one is the expert selling partner and the other does the book keeping and the revenue is shared – usually in a family situation. In such cases the principal will want to ensure the contract prevents the non-expert administrative partner taking over the selling activities for which they may not have the necessary experience.

2.68   Conversely, agents wanting to involve family members such as their adult children may specifically want this stated in the contract or at the least to ensure the limited company which is the agent is not limited as to which directors or employees it uses in performance of the agency services.

Exclusion of liability

2.69   Many contracts exclude all liability of the principal for consequential, indirect and financial loss including loss of profit, revenue and goodwill which an agent might incur in performing its duties under the agreement. In any event both parties should ensure that they have adequate insurance cover against the products causing damage. The principal may wish to accept some liability for direct loss caused to the agent, perhaps up to a fixed financial limit. In relation to exclusion clauses, note that the Unfair Contract Terms Act 1977 may have an impact, but not the unfair terms provisions of the Consumer Rights Act 2015 which only apply to consumer transactions (agents are in business). However, the agent is not contracting with customers so it is unlikely that any liability will attach to the agent in the course of the performance of his duties.

2.70   The writer has had one case advising on such liability but the potential litigation against the agent client was misconceived and the matter resolved. Many agency contracts require the agent to help with difficult customers and issues over returned products and defects. Agents need to be careful to ensure they act only as agent of the principal rather than providing stand alone or even paid for assistance directly to the customer as that might lead to liability.

2.71 The agent may, whether in breach of a contractual term or not, make a misrepresentation about the products which induces the customer to purchase the products. In such cases the principal may be bound by a misrepresentation made by the agent, depending on the circumstances and on whether exclusions for such matters are included in the standard terms of business between the principal and the customer.

2.72 A principal in a strong negotiating position might also like to obtain from the agent an indemnity providing that the principal will be fully compensated for all costs, losses and expenses arising from the activities of the agent in undertaking his duties under the contract.

2.73 The matters which could cause liability arising from the agent's activities include the agent in breach of the agreement making untrue representations about what the product can and cannot do and customers purchasing the product from the principal on that basis. The agent should be responsible for such statements made in breach of the agreement. Also, the agent might tamper with the products and they could cause damage to a purchaser. Indemnities are only as valuable as the financial worth of the agent and will not provide a 'cast iron' guarantee of recompense in the event of such a dispute. Certain liability cannot be excluded or limited by law, such as liability for death or personal injury including liability under the Consumer Protection Act 1987 (which implemented the EU product liability directive in the UK). The Unfair Contract Terms Act 1977 provides that any contract term purporting to exclude liability for death or personal injury caused by negligence is void. Liability for fraud also cannot as a matter of law be excluded by a contract term.

Insurance and agents

2.74 Despite these risks, most agents do not need, nor do they take out, insurance. However, if the agent is an employer, the agent will need employers' liability insurance as that is required by law. Some distribution and consultancy agreements include clauses that the distributor/consultant must have in place at all times a particular insurance policy including, for example, professional liability cover or (for distributors) product liability coverage. There is nothing in law to prevent a principal also requiring agents to have some kind of insurance cover.

General points – boilerplate

2.75 Other general clauses, often known as *boilerplate*, include a provision stating how formal notices should be given under the agreement. For further information on boilerplate clauses see Anderson *A-Z Guide to Boilerplate and Commercial Clauses* (4th edn, 2017, Bloomsbury Professional). In the case of foreign agents, it is sometimes useful, if it is possible, to require that they specify in the agreement a UK person or company which will be its representative in the UK and accept service of legal proceedings on its behalf.

2.76   General clauses excluding rights to compensation of an agent are unenforceable where the Regulations apply. Clauses relating to commission and termination are addressed in later chapters of this book.

2.77   A clause stating that previous agreements between the parties are terminated and a clause that the agreement is the entire agreement between the parties and that there are no other oral or written agreement or arrangements which are part of the agreement, are helpful provisions to include.

2.78   Finally, the choice of English law and the parties' submission to the jurisdiction of the English courts should be added. Chapter 1 considered the impact of the Regulations and certain jurisdictional issues. As stated in that chapter even if English law and jurisdiction are chosen and even if the Rome I and Brussels regulations apply in the EU it is possible on public policy grounds the choice of law may be set aside to enable an agent to claim compensation, although the latest Brussels regulation 1215/2012 which applies to proceedings commenced from 10 January 2015 can make this harder – see Chapter 8 for further details. The situation after UK departure from the EU should always also be considered including article 66 of the EU/UK Withdrawal Agreement.

2.79   It is useful to have a statement that the headings of the agreement are simply for convenience and do not affect its interpretation and that where one party needs time to enforce its rights, failure to do so will not result in a waiver of such rights.

Signature

2.80   Both parties should sign the agreement. If an agreement is sent to an agent for signature and it is not returned no goods should be shipped until the agent has returned it.

Checklist of clauses

2.81

1.   Parties, addresses and date of agreement

2.   Appointment of agent – exclusivity, the products, the territory, the term

3.   Obligations of the agent

4.   Obligations of the principal

5.   Commission

6.   Confidentiality

7.   Termination

8.   Consequence of termination and non competition after termination

9.   Personal performance

10. Exclusion and limitation of liability of the principal and indemnity from the agent

11. Clauses as discussed earlier required by the 1993 Regulations such as duty to act in good faith

12. Boilerplate clauses

Foreign agents – special points

2.82   In some countries a standard form of agency agreement must be used and choice of English law is invalid, even if specified in the agreement. The UK Government has some guidance for those considering exporting their goods or services – see https://www.great.gov.uk/. For further information on this topic see Chapter 8.

2.83   See also rules on export control – information at https://www.gov.uk/government/organisations/export-control-organisation.

Further information

2.84   A large amount of dealing with agents in practice is nothing to do with the legal issues, which are the subject matter of this book, but more with commercial management and indeed psychology and the ability to manage and motivate people well. Information on those topics is beyond the scope of this book but websites, such as Agent Base (British Agents Register) and Professional Sales Agents Association, may provide assistance.

Agent Base (The British Agents Register) offers guidance on operating an agency sales force – see 'Planning your Agent Strategy' at https://www.agentbase.co.uk/principal-companies-area/planning/. They also sell a model agreement and guidance package for £495 (2020 prices) at https://www.agentbase.co.uk/principal-companies-area/contracting/.

Agent Base
Talisman House
11 Talisman Square
Kenilworth
Warwickshire
CV8 1JB, UK
Tel: +44 (0) 1926 864 200
Email: enquiries@agentbase.co.uk

www.salesforce.com offers products which enable principals to track and monitor agents sometimes through 'phone apps.

Some agents are represented by The Manufacturers' Agents' Association (MAA), http://www.themaa.co.uk/, which has represented agents in the UK and Ireland since 1909.

Trade unions also provide support to agent members. Unite has a new sector, 'Service Industries', which covers workers in the UK and Ireland. It consists of CMA which covers Royal Mail, Post Office and Parcelforce managers along with professional sales agents, hotel, hospitality, casino, security, cleaners, maintenance, non-food retail and care home workers. See www.unitetheunion.org.

Further details from Rhys McCarthy, Service Industries sector national officer, email rhys.mccarthy@unitetheunion.org.

There are also sectoral specific bodies such as that for sports – the Association of Professional Sales Agents. This is a specialist trade association representing sales agents operating in the sports sector operating under the umbrella of the Federation of Sports and Play Associations. They represent commercial agents selling sporting goods. See https://www.apsa.org.uk/home.

Chapter 3

Competition law and agency agreements

3.1   UK and EU competition law rarely cause problems in relation to agency agreements. The agent is not entering into contracts separately in the marketplace, and so any restrictions in the contract between the agent and his principal are not generally regarded as anti-competitive. However, this is not invariably the case which makes it particularly regrettable that competition law is so unclear in this field. The EU competition law is set out in part of the European Commission's Vertical Agreements Guidelines (2010 version – a new version should be out during 2020). These are likely to remain relevant after Brexit as UK and EU competition law are similar. Previously there was a specific agency notice on competition law issued in 1962. The relevant extract – paragraphs 12–21 from the guidelines is reproduced in Appendix 2.

EU competition law and agency

3.2   EU competition law relevant to agreements is contained in article 101 of TFEU (renumbered in December 2009 – previously article 81 and before that article 85). It prohibits anti-competitive agreements where they have an effect on trade between Member States. It is therefore relevant to the EU/EEA states if an agency agreement relates to a territory outside these states then it is unlikely to be subject to EU competition law unless it has effects in the EU.

3.3   For distribution agreements the law is clear. The Commission has a detailed block exemption Regulation which applies to vertical agreements including distribution (which will also apply to agency agreements where they do not meet the test of true agency). This is helpful because it means they can be block exempted from the EU competition rules in any event.

3.4   Fines for vertical price fixing (fixing a price between supplier and distributor i.e. those acting in a 'vertical relationship' to each other down the distribution chain) are common under UK and EU competition law. The European Commission, for example, fined four companies for RPM (resale price maintenance) in July 2018: Philips, Pioneer, Asus, Denon.

3.5 In the UK, the Competition and Marketing Authority (CMA) has fined companies for online RPM in several cases, including: one in August 2019 in the digital pianos and digital keyboards sector; one in August 2016 in the light fittings sector and two in May 2016; one in the bathroom fittings sector; and one in the commercial refrigeration sector.

In October 2019, the CMA said it was starting a case (not yet proven) against a guitar supplier. The CMA issued a Statement of Objections to Fender Musical Instruments Europe Ltd, which supplies guitars to UK retailers. The CMA provisionally decided that between 2013 and 2018 Fender Europe operated a policy designed to restrict competitive online pricing, requiring guitars to be sold at or above a minimum figure.

3.6 The cases above relate to distributors who buy goods and resell them on their own account. However, where instead an agency agreement exists and the agent does not sell to the customer, but the contract of sale instead is between the principal/manufacturer/supplier and customer with the agent simply paid a commission – then it is not illegal for the principal to determine the price paid by its own customer. Indeed it would be usual to give the agent no or little latitude in negotiating the price between principal and customer.

Article 101(3) – Beneficial restrictive agreement

3.7 In addition, for all agreements even if they are restrictive if they meet the requirements under article 101(3) of helping consumers and providing technological advances they will be automatically exempt. Until May 2004, such exemption was by way of notification to the European Commission but since that date it has been automatic.

3.8 Article 101(3) sets out four conditions which must all be met. It provides that the prohibition in article 101(1) is inapplicable in respect of any agreement:

'which contributes to improving the production or distribution of goods or to promoting technical or economic progress, while allowing consumers a fair share of the resulting benefit, and which does not:

(a)   impose on the undertakings concerned restrictions which are not indispensable to the attainment of these objectives
(b)   afford such undertakings the possibility of eliminating competition in respect of a substantial part of the products in question.'

3.9 The equivalent wording of s 9(1) of the UK Competition Act 1998 is similar to that of article 101(3) except that in the first condition in s 9(1) the phrase 'of goods' is not included. The UK Office of Fair Trading (now the Competition and Markets Authority) in their Guidance Notes on Vertical Agreements (December 2004 edition) says 'The omission of these words is intended to make clear (consistent with the practice of the European Commission in relation to article 101 (3)) that improvements in production or distribution in relation to services may also satisfy the first condition in section 9(1).'

Block exemptions

3.10   There is a separate block exemption regulation for ordinary vertical agreements (including franchising agreements) – 330/2010 (which expires on 31 May 2022 but is likely to be replaced with a similar such regulation) and another for motor vehicle distribution agreements relating to repairs and spare parts – 461/2010. The Technology Transfer Regulation 316/2014 block exempts many patent, knowhow and software licence agreements. However, as was seen in Chapter 1, agency agreements are very different in law from distribution agreements. The block exemption Regulations are very helpful indeed because if an agreement is drafted to fall within their detailed provisions then it is exempt from EU competition law and automatically the UK Competition Act 1998. Therefore, many distribution agreements around the EU take their wording in part directly from the block exemption. For example, it permits the appointment of an exclusive distributor but prohibits any absolute ban on the distributor exporting from his territory. It allows restrictions on the distributor competing with the supplier but prohibits any restriction on the price at which the distributor will resell the goods.

3.11   In some cases, an agency agreement does not affect trade between EU Member States. The European Commission issued a notice on agreements of minor importance (2014 version) which provides that in most cases of 'vertical' agreements (between parties at different levels of supply such as agent and principal or distribution and supplier) where the parties have a market share of less than 15% then the EU competition rules will not apply where they are non-competitors and 10% where they are competitors. There is no de minimis where hard core restrictions are present such as to resale price of goods or absolute export bans or 'restrictions by object'. However, because it is very hard to define the relevant market many do not like to rely on this notice and it is not legally binding on the Commission in any event.

Brexit

3.12   The UK's departure from the EU will not immediately make any material change to the law described in this chapter. The UK Competition Act 1998 is almost identical to EU competition law. It is possible that over time UK and EU case law will diverge. The UK may even revert to a UK vertical block exemption regulation as it first had when the Competition Act 1998 came out, and UK-specific provisions (such as the specific UK provisions in the Resale Prices Act 1976 relating to 'loss leaders' on resale of products) or other UK exemptions may be introduced. Any change though is likely to be gradual in relation to agency agreements. Those buying and selling goods for their own account as distributors by contrast who may be wanting to take advantage of the EU single market are more likely to be materially affected. Article 95 of the EU/UK Withdrawal Agreement contains provisions relating, inter alia, to article 101 after Brexit and continuing cases.

Consequences of infringing EU and UK competition law

3.13   Where an agency agreement infringes EU or UK competition law:

- the restrictions in the agreement will be void and therefore unenforceable. It is not the whole agreement which is void in the UK and most agreements contain a severance clause;

- the parties are at risk of a Commission (or UK Competition and Markets Authority (CMA) (previously the Office of Fair Trading (OFT))) investigation and ultimately European Commission or CMA fines of up to 10% of worldwide turnover. Both principal and agent can be fined (after Brexit if the arrangement only affects the UK and the parties are in the UK, the position should be carefully considered having regard to the EU/UK Withdrawal Agreement);

- third parties have a right to bring claims for damages when they have suffered losses through the operation of an anti-competitive agreement of this sort, though such claims are rarely brought. The author acted for the claimant in the first in the UK *Arkin v Borchard Lines* (2002) where £150m damages for breach of articles 101 and 102 were claimed in the English court ([2003] EWHC 687 (Comm) – (judgment at http://www.bailii. org/ew/cases/EWHC/Comm/2003/687.html). In *2 Travel Group plc (in Liquidation) v Cardiff City Transport Services Ltd* [2012] CAT 19 exemplary damages were awarded to the claimant (judgment at [2012] CAT 19) http://www.bailii.org/uk/cases/CAT/2012/19.html. There have been some confidential settlements, but damages claims are rare. The Consumer Rights Act 2015, Sch 8 makes provision for collective opt-in competition damages actions which may lead to more competition damages claims, such as the collective action on behalf of consumers claiming £14bn for breach of competition law brought by solicitor Walter Merricks against Mastercard – an initial Supreme Court decision being expected in 2020 and a case summary of which is at http://bit.ly/35Ygdgg).

Only if the agreement contains restrictions is there going to be a problem with article 101 or indeed any other competition law.

Guidelines on Vertical Restraints

3.14   Paragraphs 12–21 of the Commission's Guidelines on Vertical Agreements set out the Commission's current views in this area and expressly state they are also to be read in conjunction with the Agency Directive 86/653.

3.15   Paragraph 14 of the Guidelines states:

'There are three types of financial or commercial risk that are material to the definition of an agency agreement for the application of Article 101(1). First, there are the contract-specific risks which are directly related to the contracts concluded and/or negotiated by the agent on behalf of the principal, such as financing of stocks. Secondly, there are the risks related to market-specific investments. These are investments specifically required for the type of activity for which the agent has been appointed by the principal, that is, which are required to enable the agent to conclude and/or negotiate this type of contract. Such investments are usually sunk, which means that upon leaving that particular field of activity the investment cannot be used for other activities or sold other than at a significant loss. Thirdly, there are the risks related to other activities undertaken on the same product market, to the extent that the principal requires the agent to undertake such activities, but not as an agent on behalf of the principal but for its own risk.'

3.16   The notice says that the agency agreement will fall outside the provisions of article 101(1) where the agent does not bear any significant risks in relation to the contracts concluded. It goes on to say that where the property in the contract goods does not vest in the agent or for services arrangements where the agent does not perform the services then the arrangement will not fall within article 101(1) where a list of seven factors is satisfied. The seven factors are as follows (from the 2010 version of the guidelines):

'(a)   does not contribute to the costs relating to the supply/purchase of the contract goods or services, including the costs of transporting the goods. This does not preclude the agent from carrying out the transport service, provided that the costs are covered by the principal;

(b)   does not maintain at its own cost or risk stocks of the contract goods, including the costs of financing the stocks and the costs of loss of stocks and can return unsold goods to the principal without charge, unless the agent is liable for fault (for example, by failing to comply with reasonable security measures to avoid loss of stocks);

(c)   does not undertake responsibility towards third parties for damage caused by the product sold (product liability), unless, as agent, it is liable for fault in this respect;

(d)   does not take responsibility for customers' non-performance of the contract, with the exception of the loss of the agent's commission, unless the agent is liable for fault (for example, by failing to comply with reasonable security or anti-theft measures or failing to comply with reasonable measures to report theft to the principal or police or to communicate to the principal all necessary information available to him on the customer's financial reliability);

(e)   is not, directly or indirectly, obliged to invest in sales promotion, such as contributions to the advertising budgets of the principal;

(f)   does not make market-specific investments in equipment, premises or training of personnel, such as for example the petrol storage tank in the case of petrol retailing or specific software to sell insurance policies in case of insurance agents, unless these costs are fully reimbursed by the principal;

    (g)   does not undertake other activities within the same product market required by the principal, unless these activities are fully reimbursed by the principal.'

This is a non-exhaustive list. Restrictions on the customers the agent may serve, the territory in which he may sell and the prices at which he will sell or purchase the goods are thus taken outside of article 101.

3.17   The Commission says:

'Exclusive agency provisions will in general not lead to anti-competitive effects. However, single branding provisions and post-term non-compete provisions, which concern inter-brand competition, may infringe Article 101(1) if they lead to or contribute to a (cumulative) foreclosure effect on the relevant market where the contract goods or services are sold or purchased (see in particular Section VI.2.1). Such provisions may benefit from the Block Exemption Regulation, in particular when the conditions provided in Article 5 of that Regulation are fulfilled. They can also be individually justified by efficiencies under Article 101(3) as for instance described in paragraphs (144) to (148).'

(paragraph 19 Guidelines on Vertical Restraints).

3.18   If the agreement facilitates collusion, then even if the principal bears all risks the agreement could breach article 101 such as when a number of principals use the same agents while collectively excluding others from using those agents or where agents collude on marketing strategy or exchange sensitive information between principals.

3.19   For the purposes of applying article 101(1), the agreement will be qualified as an agency agreement (see para 15 of the Guidelines) if the agent does not bear any, or bears only insignificant, risks in relation to the contracts concluded and/or negotiated on behalf of the principal, in relation to market-specific investments for that field of activity, and in relation to other activities required by the principal to be undertaken on the same product market. However, risks that are related to the activity of providing agency services in general, such as the risk of the agent's income being dependent upon its success as an agent or general investments in for instance premises or personnel, are not material to this assessment.

3.20   By paragraph 13 if the agency could fall within article 101 then the guidelines and the exemption regulation for vertical agreements can be applied to exempt the agency agreement where applicable.

Case example – *Re European Sugar Cartel (Suiker Unie)* (Case C-40–48, 50, 54–56, 111, 113 & 114/75, December 1975, [1975] ECR 1663, [1976] 1 CMLR 295)

3.21   In *Re European Sugar Cartel (Suiker Unie)* (Case C-40–48, 50, 54–56, 111, 113 & 114/75, December 1975, [1975] ECR 1663, [1976] 1 CMLR 295) the

Court of Justice had to consider whether restrictions on 'agents' handling the contract goods on their own account or on behalf of third parties amounted to an anti-competitive agreement. It was held necessary to ascertain whether the agents were 'agents' in the legal sense and the court stated:

> 'The position is different if the agreements entered into between the principal and his agents, whom the trading parties call "trade representatives", confer upon those agents or allow them to perform duties which from an economic point of view are approximately the same as those carried out by an independent dealer, because they provide for the said agents accepting the financial risks of the sale or of the performance of contracts entered into with third parties.'

Case example – *CEPSA Estaciones de Servicio SA v LV Tobar e Hijos SL* (Case C-279/06)

3.22   In this case the agent had no authority to market goods which were the product of the principal. Instead, the agent was obliged to pass on orders to the principal. The contract related to supply of vehicle fuels at a petrol service station. The Court of Justice of the EU (CJEU) held that the 'agent' was indeed a genuine agent. This case is also footnoted in the European Commission's 2010 Guidelines on Vertical Restraints (which is reproduced in Appendix 2.3 of this book).

3.23   Referring to an almost identical earlier case, *Española de Empresarios de Estaciones de Servicio* [2006] ECR I-11987 ('CEEES'), the CJEU held that the test was the same – whether the agent had sufficient independence. Here, the agent was trying to avoid the contract and its exclusive supply obligations on the grounds they breached EU competition law. If instead the agent were a true agent not a distributor, then the competition rules would not apply.

3.24   As there are so few competition law cases on agency agreements, it is worth quoting below from the CJEU's judgment on this issue in full:

> '38 As regards, first, the risks linked to the sale of the goods, the service-station operator is presumed to bear them when he takes possession of the goods, at the time he receives them from the supplier, when he assumes directly or indirectly the costs linked to the distribution of the goods, particularly the transport costs, when he maintains stocks at his own expense, when he assumes responsibility for any damage caused to the goods, such as loss or deterioration, and for damage caused by the goods sold to third parties, or when he bears the financial risk linked to the goods in the event that he is required to pay the supplier the amount corresponding to the quantity of fuel delivered instead of that actually sold (see *CEEES*, paragraphs 51 to 58).
>
> 39 Second, as regards the risks linked to investments specific to the market, namely those required to enable the service-station operator to negotiate or conclude contracts with third parties, it is necessary to establish whether that operator makes investments in premises or equipment, such as a fuel tank, or in

advertising campaigns. If so, such risks are transferred to the operator (*CEEES*, paragraphs 51 and 59).

40   It must, however, be pointed out that the fact that the operator bears only a negligible share of the risks does not render Article 81 EC [now Article 101] applicable (see, to that effect, *CEEES*, paragraph 61), since such an operator does not become an independent economic operator when selling fuel to third parties. In that case, the relationship between the operator and the supplier is identical to that between an agent and his principal.

41   It also follows from paragraphs 62 and 63 of *CEEES* that, even in the case of an agency contract, only the obligations imposed on the intermediary concerning the sale of the goods to third parties on behalf of the principal, including the fixing of the retail price, fall outside the scope of Article 81 EC [now/article 101]. By contrast, exclusivity and non-competition clauses which concern the relationship between the agent and the principal as independent economic operators are capable of infringing the competition rules in so far as they entail locking up the market concerned. The prohibition laid down in Article 81(1) EC [now Article 101] is therefore applicable to those clauses.

42   If an examination of the risks leads to the conclusion that there is an agreement between undertakings within the meaning of Article 81 EC [no Article 101] , as regards the sale of goods to third parties, the fixing of the retail price of those goods constitutes a restriction of competition expressly provided for in Article 81(1)(a) EC [now Article 101(1)(a)] which brings that agreement within the scope of the prohibition laid down in that provision to the extent to which all the other conditions for the application of that provision are satisfied, namely that that agreement has as its object or effect to restrict appreciably competition within the common market and is capable of affecting trade between Member States (see, to that effect, Case C-230/96 *Cabour* [1998] ECR I-2055, paragraph 48).

43   Moreover, as regards in particular exclusive purchasing agreements, the case-law of the Court of Justice should be recalled, according to which, even if those agreements do not have as their object the restriction of competition within the meaning of Article 81 EC [now Article 101] , it is nevertheless necessary to ascertain whether they have the effect of preventing, restricting or distorting competition. The effects of an exclusive purchasing agreement have to be assessed in the economic and legal context in which the agreement occurs and where it may combine with other agreements to have a cumulative effect on competition. It is therefore necessary to analyse the effects of such an agreement, taken together with other agreements of the same type, on the opportunities of national competitors or those from other Member States to gain access to the relevant market or to increase their market share (see Case C-234/89 *Delimitis* [1991] ECR I-935, paragraphs 13 to 15, and Case C-214/99 *Neste* [2000] ECR I-11121, paragraph 25).

44   In the light of the foregoing considerations, the answer to Question 1(a) and 2(a) [questions referred by the Spanish court to the CJEU] must be that an exclusive supply contract for petroleum products is capable of falling within the scope of Article 81(1) EC [now Article 101(1)] where the service-station operator assumes, in a non-negligible proportion, one or more financial and

commercial risks linked to the sale of those products to third parties and where that contract contains clauses capable of infringing competition, such as that relating to the fixing of the retail price. If the service-station operator does not assume such risks or assumes only a negligible share of them, only the obligations imposed on the operator in the context of services as an intermediary offered by the operator to the principal, such as the exclusivity and non-competition clauses, are capable of falling within the scope of that provision. It is for the referring court to ascertain, moreover, whether the contract at issue in the main proceedings has the effect of preventing, restricting or distorting competition within the meaning of Article 81 EC [now Article 101].'

3.25   As can be seen above, exclusivity and non-competition clauses can be anti-competitive in agency agreements. However, the Agency Directive and UK Regulations permit non-competition clauses, indeed lasting up to two years after the agency agreement ends, so rarely is there a problem in that respect.

Book Publishers and Apple – Ebooks Agreements 2012

3.26   Another example was where a number of publishers chose to move from a distribution model to an agency model because they wanted to be able to stipulate the resale price for ebooks online. The competition authorities held that when several publishers took that decision to move from a distribution to an agency model collectively, that breached competition law. Had one publisher simply decided it preferred distribution to agency that would not have been a breach of article 101 TFEU (or the Chapter I prohibition in the Competition Act 1998).

The case brought by the European Commission was settled in December 2012 without a formal decision. The publishers were Hachette Livre, HarperCollins, Simon & Schuster and Macmillan. The European Commission found that Amazon and other sellers had to contend with 'what we suspect was a concerted and coordinated demand' by the publishers to agree to the agency model. This, it said, would have allowed the publishers, rather than retailers such as Amazon, to set the prices of ebooks and that 'the coordination of commercial behaviour between competitors – here, with the help of Apple – is forbidden by our competition rules'. The Commission also sought undertakings from Pearson which owned Penguin books and indeed the US justice department also reached agreement with Pearson over the same issues in the USA. Pearson in an agreement with the European Commission later (in 2013) also agreed to abandon the agency agreements and to make other commitments (see http://bit.ly/32BKMX2).

Online hotel bookings

3.27   Often websites market goods or services and it is not made clear who is the seller – the website or the supplier. Some sites make this very clear eg Amazon is either selling direct or a third party seller is selling to the customer, and the site and the order process makes this clear. However, frequently the writer is asked to draft terms for websites when even the intermediate supplier is unsure whether they are setting up some form of agency agreement (in which case it is usually lawful to set the resale price to the consumer) or a distribution arrangement (where it would be unlawful for the supplier/manufacturer to stipulate the price sold by the website).

The websites were Expedia, Booking.com and InterContinental Hotels Group.

3.28   The Competition Appeals Tribunal in 2014 required that undertakings agreed between various parties with the then Office of Fair Trading (OFT) had to be abandoned. The OFT had looked at two issues – one was most favoured customer clauses (not relevant here), and the second was whether an online platform could allow suppliers to set the prices of products sold through the platform – was that resale price maintenance? The OFT is now the Competition and Markets Authority (CMA).

3.29   The then OFT's view was that usually suppliers' restrictions on resale price could breach competition law. For hotels and online travel agents the OFT believed that there could be efficiencies if some price control were exercised so they accepted undertakings in relation to that part of the case as long as websites could discount the room charges up to the level of the commission they were paid in closed user groups. The OFT did not believe that these websites were genuine agents.

See summary of the initial part of the case at http://bit.ly/1CPnzBS.

3.30   The issue then went before the Competition Appeals Tribunal which reached its decision on 26 September 2014 [2014] CAT 16 in *Skyscanner Ltd (supported by Skoosh International Ltd – Intervener) v Competition and Markets Authority (supported by Booking.com BV, Expedia Inc and Intercontinental Hotels Group plc)*. The appeal was brought by Skyscanner which operates a price comparison website allowing consumers to search for and compare flight, hotel and car hire deals globally.

3.31   The CAT held that the undertakings could not stand

3.32   The CAT ordered the CMA to pay Skyscanner £186,096.81 in respect of its costs.

3.33   The CMA says:

'As a result of the CAT's judgment, the investigation has been re-opened. The CMA is considering next steps in the investigation in light of the CAT judgment and market developments, including developments in the investigations of other European competition authorities.

The European Commission has announced the launch of market tests in anti-trust investigations by the French, Swedish and Italian competition authorities in the online hotel booking sector. Comments on the proposed commitments in those investigations can be submitted to the relevant national competition authorities by 31 January 2015. More information can be found on the European Commission's website.'

The European Commission's web page on its launch of market tests in December 2014 is at http://europa.eu/rapid/press-release_IP-14-2661_en.htm.

3.34   However, the EU case just relates to the issue of most favoured nation (MFN) clauses rather than the price fixing issue which is more relevant to the agency issue.

3.35   The EU stated:

'The European Commission announces the launch of market tests in antitrust investigations by the French, Swedish and Italian competition authorities in the online hotel booking sector. The three national competition authorities have concerns that so-called "parity clauses" in contracts between online travel agent Booking.com and hotels may have anti-competitive effects, in breach of EU and national antitrust rules. Booking.com has proposed commitments to remedy these concerns, which – if the market tests confirm their adequacy – the national competition authorities can make legally binding on Booking. com. The Commission is coordinating the national investigations but has not opened its own investigation.

The parity clauses in the contracts between Booking.com and hotels oblige the hotel to offer Booking.com the same or better room prices as the hotel makes available on all other online and offline distribution channels. The French, Swedish and Italian competition authorities consider that these clauses may harm competition, in breach of their respective national competition laws as well as Article 101 and/or Article 102 of the Treaty on the Functioning of the European Union (TFEU). In particular, they have concerns that they may restrict competition between Booking.com and other online travel agents ("OTAs") and hinder new booking platforms from entering the market.

To alleviate these concerns, Booking.com has proposed to abandon the parity requirement in respect of prices which the hotel makes available to other OTAs. This would enable hotels to offer different room prices to different OTAs. However, the hotel would still have to offer the same or better room prices to Booking.com as are offered on the hotel's own online and offline booking channels. The commitments are intended to apply EEA-wide.

The French, Swedish and Italian competition authorities are continuing their investigations into the parity clauses of other OTAs.'

3.36   In April 2015, Booking.com settled a dispute with French, Italian and Swedish competition authorities who with the EU had accused the company of fixing prices over hotels on its website to make sure it always had the cheapest rate. The case was settled (with no formal decision). Since then Booking.com has allowed the hotels on its site to offer cheaper rates through other online travel agents and on the telephone, although not on those other companies' websites so the settlement is clearly a compromise. Early in 2015 the German competition authorities held Booking.com had been non-compliant with competition law in this field. The company has more than 41 per cent of Europe's €43.9bn market for air travel and hotel bookings, according to one source. 'Hotels would have to undercut their own websites and also pay commission to offer a better rate to a smaller online travel agent,' said the general counsel of Skyscanner which has challenged Booking.com and Expedia in the UK. 'It doesn't help competition and it's terrible for the consumer – hotels can't offer them anything but the same price they offer Booking.com. And there are very few rival travel agents in the market,' said Dorian Harris, the chief executive of Skoosh, an online travel agent which brought the first competition complaint in the UK in 2010.

3.37 On 25 June 2015 Booking.com BV announced that from 1 July 2015 it would abandon its price, availability and booking conditions parity provisions with respect to other online travel agencies in its terms with all accommodation partners across Europe, including in the UK.

3.38 In April 2019, the Japanese competition authorities began an investigation into alleged hotel room price fixing of Rakuten Travel, operated by Rakuten Inc., Booking.com and Expedia.

Online hotel bookings and price fixing

3.39 On 6 April 2017, the European Competition Network (ECN) published its report on the results of a monitoring exercise in the hotel online booking sector. The CMA took part in the monitoring work, along with nine other national competition agencies and the European Commission.

It concluded that many hotels were not aware that since summer 2015, Booking.com and Expedia no longer enforce 'wide' parity clauses – whereby a hotel agrees not to undercut the room prices that the online travel agent (OTA) charges for their hotel. Nor were they aware of what this means for hotels' ability to differentiate their prices across OTAs.

3.40 The CMA therefore announced it was 'taking steps to raise awareness among UK hotels of the changes'.

As part of this work, the CMA has sent a '60 Second Summary' to UK hotels highlighting that Expedia and Booking.com used to require hotels to guarantee that they would not offer their rooms more cheaply on other OTAs.

3.41 As a result:

- hotels can choose to offer a lower price on other OTAs than they offer on Expedia and/or Booking.com;

- hotels can also decide to offer other OTAs better availability or conditions (such as room extras or 'breakfast included') than on Expedia and/or Booking.com.

3.42 In light of the findings in ECN report, the CMA decided not to prioritise further investigation on the application of competition law to pricing practices in this sector at this stage.

2019 undertakings – hotel booking companies and advertising law

3.43 In February 2019, the CMA secured undertakings from Expedia, Booking.com, Agoda, Hotels.com, ebookers and trivago about unfair practices as regards online hotel bookings potentially in breach of the Consumer Protection from Unfair Trading Regulations 2008, SI 2008/1277 (consumer law protecting consumers against unfair advertising). However, no finding of infringement of the law was found by the CMA as the cases were settled. The companies were given until September 2019 to improve their advertising practices. See https://www.gov.uk/government/news/hotel-booking-sites-to-make-major-changes-after-cma-probe.

EU Online Intermediation Services Regulations 2019

3.44 The European Commission adopted EU Regulation 2019/1150 on 'promoting fairness and transparency for business users of online intermediation services'. This sets out principles of fairness in contracts between online platforms and business customers who use them, such as rights to terminate if contract terms change. It does not deal with issues of who is an agent. The Regulation applies in the EU from 1 July 2020 and will therefore apply in the UK after Brexit during the transition period and potentially thereafter, as this date falls within the transition period in the Withdrawal Agreement. Those advising on online agency/intermediation services, online platforms and the like in the EU will need to ensure they accommodate the provisions of this Regulation along with the wide raft of other legislation applicable to selling, including the EU Services Directive 2006/123 (and the UK Provision of Services Regulations 2009, SI 2009/2999).

A good summary of the various cases and the latest regulations can be found at http://bit.ly/31DS8YW.

Advice to ascertain if a website is an agent or not

3.45 In general, the writer's advice is that when advising on the issue of whether a website is acting as an agent or not, information should be sought in order to ascertain if the model is similar either: (1) to an Amazon direct sell; or (2) an Amazon Marketplace sale. The following questions should be asked:

1. Who sells to whom?

2. Does the website ever own the goods (where the sale is goods)? When does title pass and to whom and who insures the goods?

3.   Whose books does the revenue pass through for accounting purposes? For example, a real commercial agent has a turnover which is its commission, not the turnover of the gross sale of products from the principal to the ultimate customer.

4.   Can the client show some other websites which are similar to their proposal, as the lawyers for those websites may have already decided which is the better legal model (agency with the risks of compensation on termination, or distribution where there are no such risks, but price fixing is not allowed)?

3.46   It should not be assumed that what the parties call the arrangement is correct, nor even that the client knows if what they propose is agency or distribution. The agreements for agency and distribution are very different so modifications should never be sought to a precedent to change from one to the other. The process should be started from scratch if the client wants to change from agency to distribution.

3.47   Finally, if a website simply makes click-through revenue, where users are directed from that first website to another, in the writer's view that is not commercial agency but little more than an introduction agent (although each case should be analysed on its facts). There is no continuing authority to negotiate – see Chapter 1 of this work for the tests to be satisfied before the Commercial Agents (Council Directive) Regulations 1993 apply.

Other cases

3.48   In *Pittsburgh Corning Europe* (OJ 1972 L272/35) the Commission held that the 1962 Notice did not apply in the absence of economic dependence between the agent and the principal. In *Aluminium Imports from Eastern Europe* (OJ 1985 L92/1) the Commission said that even if a company were to be considered to be an agent it could still be subject to article 85 (now 101) where the decision to enter into or remain within the agency agreement placed restrictions upon competition in the market for the provision of an agent's services.

3.49   Other cases which have attempted to interpret the Notice are the *IMI Rules* (paragraph 62) OJ 1980 L318/1, [1981] 2 CMLR 498, *Fisher Price* (paragraph 18) OJ 1987 L49/19, [1989] 4 CMLR 553 and *ARG/Unipart* (paragraph 26) OJ 1987 L45/34, [1988] 4 CMLR 513. For discussion of the Commission's previous Notice see Swanson & Brown 'Agency Agreements: the Commission's new Draft Notice' [1991] 2 ECLR 82.

3.50   In the *Flemish Travel Agents* (Case C-ll/85 [1987] ECR 3801, [1989] 4 CMLR 213), a reference was made to the European Court of Justice under then article 177 of the EEC Treaty concerning questions arising from the interpretation of the Treaty which had arisen in proceedings in Belgium. In Belgium a licence was required to carry on a travel business. A system of agreements was in place between travel agents and tour operators and between travel agents themselves which was intended to oblige agents to observe the prices set by tour operators and this was held to infringe article 85 (now 101) (not surprisingly). The court also held that there is a duty on an EU Member State not to adopt or maintain in force measures which would deprive articles 101 and 102 of their effectiveness.

3.51   However, the nub of the decision is the way it treated agents under the competition rules. The Belgian government had denied that article 101(1) could apply to a relationship between a tour operator and a travel agent. They said the relationship was one of principal and agent and the agent must therefore be regarded as an auxiliary organ of the tour operator. To support this argument the Belgium government emphasised that a travel agent does not enter into contracts with clients in his own name, but in the name and on behalf of the tour operator organising the travel in question.

3.52   The court stated:

> 'However, a travel agent of the kind referred to by the National Court must be regarded as an independent agent who provides services on an entirely independent basis. He sells travel organised by a large number of different tour operators and a tour operator sells travel through a very large number of agents. . . . a travel agent cannot be regarded as an auxiliary organ forming an integral part of a tour operator's undertaking.'

In this case the court was already beginning to think along the lines of the vertical agreements notice. The restrictions in relation to the prices which the agents could charge were therefore unenforceable under article 101.

3.53   In *Daimler Chrysler AG* (2001), one of the rare cases there have been at EU competition level on commercial agency agreements and the competition rules, the EU imposed a fine for export bans in agency agreements.

3.54   The Commission in *Daimler Chrysler AG* imposed a fine of EUR 71.825 million on Daimler Chrysler AG for three types of infringements of article 101 of the EC Treaty in the area of car distribution. The decision concerns measures adopted by Daimler Chrysler in order to impede parallel trade in cars and limit competition in the leasing and sale of motor vehicles. This was the fourth Commission decision imposing a fine against a car manufacturer that does not respect EU competition rules.

3.55   The Commission started the investigation concerning the distribution of motor vehicles of the Mercedes-Benz make after receiving complaints from consumers about restrictions on the export of new cars in various Member States. In principle, article 101 is not applicable to restrictions agreed between an undertaking and its commercial agents as has been seen above. As commercial agents exercise an economic activity, they have to be considered as undertakings within the meaning of the EU competition rules. The Commission said 'But due to the fact that they act on behalf of another undertaking, they operate as auxiliary organs forming an integral part of the principal's undertaking. The restrictions contained in agreements between the principal and its commercial agents are, therefore, in general not considered as restrictions of competition within the meaning of article 101. But in the present case, the application of article 101 to the restrictions agreed between Daimler Chrysler and its German agents results from the fact that these agents have to bear considerable financial and commercial risks linked to their activity'. From the point of view of EU competition law, they had, therefore, to be treated not as commercial agents but as dealers.

3.56 The case was Daimler Chrysler AG decided on 10 October 2001 – see Commission Press Release IP/01/1394 of 10.10.2001 (*Daimler Chrysler AG*) http://europa.eu./rapid/press-release_IP-01-1394_en.htm?locale=en. It was examined in the February 2002 Antitrust newsletter of the Commission (pp 56-57) http://ec.europa.eu/competition/publications/cpn/cpn2002_1.pdf.

What to do in practice

3.57 Those advising in relation to competition law of the EU (and the EEA) as it affects agency agreements cannot do so in isolation without asking questions. The degree of risk taken by the agent and the other relevant factors set out in the Vertical Guidelines should be examined. It is rarely the case that a standard commercial agency agreement causes any problems whatsoever under competition law. Indeed sometimes where a supplier wants to control the price to customers it is better to make a distribution arrangement an agency agreement where such a practice is lawful.

Further information

3.58 The European Commission's Vertical Guidelines are in Appendix 2.3 of this book in relation to the section on agency agreements.

The EU block exemption for vertical agreements no 330/2010 (other than motor vehicle parts and repairs covered by regulation 461/2010) is on the EU's website with other EU anti-trust legislation at http://ec.europa.eu/competition/antitrust/legislation/vertical.html. The regulation is due to be updated by 2022 along with its accompanying Vertical Guidelines, and in 2019 a consultation on this was issued – see https://ec.europa.eu/competition/consultations/2018_vber/index_en.html.

Information on UK competition law is at https://www.gov.uk/government/organisations/competition-and-markets-authority.

The CMA Guidelines on Vertical Agreements are at https://www.gov.uk/government/publications/vertical-agreements (although have not been updated to reflect the fact that land agreements are now fully caught by UK competition law).

Chapter 4

Commission and other payments

4.1 Most commercial agents are usually paid a percentage of the net sales value of the goods which they market for their principal. In many cases, where the agent has an exclusive territory, he is entitled to commission on all sales in his territory whether generated by him or not. This chapter looks at commission and other means of payment for agents. Agents and their principals often fall out over commission issues. Ensuring the contract clauses are very clear as to what is due and when can avoid some of the most common disputes. It can be particularly difficult to draft commission clauses for non exclusive agents and particular care should be given to such arrangements. Where an agent is outside the Regulations then under English common law the parties are free to agree whatever they choose as regards commission and should not automatically use a precedent based on the regulations as this may give the agent more commission entitlement than is legally necessary.

The Regulations

4.2 The Commercial Agents (Council Directive) Regulations 1993 apply to many agency agreements in the UK. Chapter 1 examined the circumstances in which the Regulations apply. Part III of the Regulations deals with remuneration of the agent.

Form and amount of remuneration under the Regulations

4.3 The Regulations provide that in the absence of any agreement as to remuneration between the parties:

'A commercial agent shall be entitled to the remuneration that commercial agents appointed for the goods forming the subject of his agency contract are customarily allowed in the place where he carries on his activities and, if there is no such customary practice, a commercial agent shall be entitled to reasonable remuneration taking into account all aspects of the transaction.' (Regulation 6(1).)

Although many agents operate without any written contract at all, the one matter which is usually agreed, whether verbally or in writing, is their commission rate. However, even here cases are known where the precise rate had not been specified but the parties appeared to have agreed that commission would be paid, for example at a rate of between 3% to 8%. However, such cases are rare. There is normally no doubt about the commission rate agreed. Often it varies depending on turnover or even type of customer.

What rates are customary?

4.4   The question frequently arises as to what is a normal commission rate, to which there is no answer. Agents can ask what others in their industry are paid or ask their trade association if they are a member of one. They can look at advertisements for agents, where there are any. In the majority of the agency cases in which the author has been involved rates of about 5% to 6% have been common. However, in certain industries, such as computer software or marketing or high value journals or educational products, books etc, rates of 20% to 30% are not unknown. Often a higher rate reflects additional duties of an agent, such as collection of money or processing of invoices.

4.5   Some agents separately offer their principal a 'distribution' type service. This normally means that the agent is still a true agent and the goods are sold by the supplier to the customer in the supplier's name and on his invoice, but the agent takes over the sending out of such invoices and also arranges transport and deliveries, often billing the supplier separately for those services. The supplier is there contracting out to the agent what is normally a duty of the supplier.

Changing commission rates

4.6   Many an agency dispute has come about because the principal has unilaterally altered commission rates. A reduction from 5% to 3% may make it uneconomic for the agent to continue with the agency. The legal principles are clear. No commercial agreement can be varied without agreement of the parties, unless the contract says so. The legal issues arising from contract clauses which allow a principal to change contract terms after the agreement was entered into were examined in Chapter 2 such as *Vick v Vogle-Gapes Ltd* [2006] EWHC 1665 (QB) (but this was alteration of territory and market not commission rates). As long as this is proportionate the courts regard it as acceptable and not contrary to the requirement of 'good faith' implied into agency agreements. Some commercial agency agreements provide that the principal reserves the right to alter commission rates. Agents may find it hard to accept that such a right can be valid in law, but it usually is in English law. This may not be the case in civil code jurisdictions abroad. The English courts do not look to whether parties to contracts have made a bad bargain or not.

The agent did not, in legal theory at least, have to accept such an onerous term and if he did, then he must live with the consequences. However, it is possible that even in the UK very onerous terms may be breach of the duties 'good faith' agent and principal owe each other under the Regulations so only impose very one sided contract terms with caution when drafting agreements.

4.7   Even if the agent did not return the contract duly signed, then provided there was no earlier written contract which continued, the fact the agent has not rejected the written contract may be sufficient under English law for it to apply as the terms between the parties. There are no other terms and the agent has not rejected it.

4.8   Therefore, agents should always either reject or accept written contract terms or put forward their own set. Doing nothing is risky and likely to amount to agreement to the principal's terms.

4.9   There may be cases where the reduction in commission is tantamount to termination in all but name and bad faith can be found, but agents should take legal advice before assuming all onerous clauses in contracts will be void. In many civil code countries, however, there is a much stronger requirement to ensure contracts are balanced and fair between both parties. This is a very alien concept to the 'buyer beware' common law system which tends only to protect consumers. Some agreements do not give the principal the right to vary commission rates – probably the majority. In those cases, the agent may refuse to accept the reduction.

4.10   In *Scottish Power Energy Recall Ltd v Task Force Contracts Ltd* ([2008] CSOH 110) the agreement gave the principal the right to terminate the agreement if one major client terminated (Sainsbury's) which at the start and throughout was 92% of the business. The Agent stopped working as agent when the customer, Sainsbury's, ceased to purchase from that source. The principal wrote to the agent requiring him to start work. He refused and when the matter came to court the court said that the agreement itself was not terminated as the parties had allowed for the possibility in its terms that this 92% customer might cease its business with the principal and the 8% left could continue and thus there was no compensation.

Case example

4.11   In the *Skingsley v K J C Carpets Ltd* case (Bristol County Court Case BS517069, 4 June 1996) the court had an example of an agent whose commission rate had been altered. It is a badly argued judgment which misrepresents German law. The agent was aged 61 when his contract was terminated in 1994 and was a sales agent in the carpet industry. He was entitled to 4% commission on all sales in his area and he had previously been an employee of the company. He worked as an agent for seven years for the principal. During this time when the company was taken over in 1993 his commission rate 'was unilaterally reduced to 3.5% and he felt that he had no way of objecting to this. Clearly this was in breach of the terms of the agreement', the judge said.

4.12 The first part of his claim was the difference between 3.5% and 4% on sales he achieved between 1 January 1994 (when the new commission rate came in) and 26 September 1994 when he was sacked. This sum was about £2,000 and VAT was chargeable on it. The first part of the damages he was awarded was for this amount. The judge does not say if the agent objected to the reduction in his commission at the time and assumes as he was not in a position to object then his rights were somehow preserved. It is correct that agents are in a very weak position to argue over such reductions.

4.13 In some cases, the agent has been dismissed for objecting. The agent objects to the reduction. The principal says take it or leave it. The agent insists he does not accept the unilateral alteration to his contract and he loses the agency. He may well have a right to claim damages under the Regulations as discussed in a later chapter, because this right exists where the principal is at fault under a kind of constructive dismissal provision, but that is a right which it can be time consuming and expensive to enforce. If the agent has been given other benefits to compensate for the reduction in commission, such as a wider area, the court might think the change is reasonable. There is an analogy here with employment cases where the courts will accept small changes to an employee's terms, such as coming to work 15 minutes earlier, or small alterations to job descriptions, but not major changes unless they are agreed. The *Skingsley* case is not a precedent, as it is simply a local county court decision. However, solicitors advising agents who have been sacked may like to use it in including in their claims compensation for reductions of commission where rates have been varied.

On what is commission paid?

4.14 Commission is normally paid on the sales generated either by the agent in his territory (and possibly though not usually outside his territory) or on all orders received from the agent's territory (where he has an exclusive territory). This then includes orders received direct by the principal and those where another agent has generated the order. This issue is really the guarantee of an agent's exclusivity. If he has a so-called exclusive territory but is only paid commission on the orders he generates, then that exclusivity can quickly become undermined in practice.

4.15 In practice most exclusive agents receive commission on every order in their territory. However, principals should consider the following issues:

1. Should a clause be included stating that where a customer objects to dealing with the agent (as they sometimes do on personality or other

grounds or because they think they can obtain better prices if they cut out the agent) the account does not then generate commission for the agent or only commission at a lower rate? Such accounts are sometimes called 'house accounts'. It may be justifiable that the agent receives less or no commission if he is doing no work on the account. On the other hand, with some agencies agents have few continuing duties with a particular existing customer anyway and yet receive commission. Agents, of course, should object to such a provision as it gives the principal an arbitrary method of ensuring it can take any profitable account it likes away from the agent.

2. Should a clause be included that certain large accounts such as nationwide chains be excluded or a lower level of commission paid? These are true 'house accounts' and get around the problem of which agent to pay when a nationwide chain places an order from its head office which may by chance be in one agent's territory. If the agent will still be visiting stores in his area, keeping display stands fresh, soliciting local orders from the local branch, then commission may justifiably be paid to him though possibly at a lower rate. The contract should also cover the position where a small local branch is taken over by a 'house account' or large chain, when perhaps later it can become a house account after the takeover.

3. Should there be provisions for commission to be split with another agent where both he and the first agent were responsible for generating the order? It is best to anticipate this by a clause in the contract which allows such a split than trying to negotiate with the agent over it later. It depends on the industry whether such joint work is likely to occur. Agencies differ tremendously from the sole trading man who markets, say, car parts of fairly low value to the agent marketing machines costing £100,000 a time, and therefore the nature of the work the agent does to procure one order varies and no fixed formulae on commission can be set out as always applicable. The important point for the lawyer is to ask the right questions and make sure that commission provisions are included which cover the issues likely to arise in the relevant field.

4. On what is the commission paid? Often the contract includes a definition of 'net sales value'. Frequently this would be the price at which the goods are sold with deductions for items such as carriage and insurance and any sales tax (VAT) or import or other duties. The lawyer should ask what elements there are in pricing to a customer and work from that. Deductions can make a substantial difference to the commission received.

5. For foreign agents it is important that the currency in which the commission is paid is clear.

6. Often a big customer will negotiate a much lower price than that on the standard price list. Many agency agreements therefore include a clause

stating that in such cases the agent will be paid a lower commission. Most agents are not allowed themselves to negotiate prices lower than those on the principal's standard price list, but whether the principal has agreed a lower price it is common for the agent to be paid less commission under a formula laid down in the contract.

Commission on orders during the agency agreement

4.16   Where the Regulations apply, they provide in regulation 7(1)(a):

'A commercial agent shall be entitled to commission on commercial transactions concluded during the period covered by the agency contract:

(a)   where the transaction is concluded as a result of his action; or

(b)   where the transaction is concluded with a third party whom he has previously acquired as a customer for transaction of the same kind.'

There is no provision, however, saying that the parties cannot change regulation 7(1)(a) in their agreement, although other provisions in the Regulations clearly state that those other provisions cannot be altered to the detriment of the agent. The fact there is no such statement here means, in the author's opinion, that parties to agency agreements can alter these provisions. However, others have argued that as the words are so forceful – the verb 'shall' is used – one cannot depart from the legislation. In practice most agents are paid on the basis set out above in any event. It is the later provisions of regulation 7 which cause more problems in practice.

4.17   Regulation 7(2) provides:

'A commercial agent shall also be entitled to commission on transactions concluded during the period covered by the agency contract where he has an exclusive right to a specific geographical area or to a specific group of customers and where the transaction has been entered into with a customer belonging to that area of group.'

The Agency Directive (see Appendix 2) provides that Member States can choose whether agents are entitled to commission on all orders from their area where they have non-exclusive rights as well. This does not make much sense because if a principal has six agents in the same area, he cannot give them all full commission on every order in the territory or he is paying six times over. Not surprisingly, the UK government used the alternative provision in its implementation of the Directive as set out in regulation 7(2) above.

EU case

4.18   In *Georgios Kontogeorgas v Kartonpak AE* (Case C-104/95) [1997] 1 CMLR 1093, the European Court of Justice held that a commercial agent appointed under the Agency Directive 96/653 who is in charge of a particular geographic sector has a right to a fee even to contracts concluded without his intervention.

4.19   Notice that even regulation 7(1) entitles the agent not only to commission on orders he generates but also 'repeat orders' from customers he has found in the past. If principals wish to vary this then they need a commercial term to that effect (and note the comments above about the lack of a non-derogation provision). It is not every old customer whose new order results in payment of commission. It must be a customer whom the agent has found for transactions of the same kind. Thus, an agent who has found a customer for the company's range of curtains is not entitled to commission when that customer orders the latest range of production line equipment for the factory floor (unless the agency contract so provides). Some agency contracts are so sloppily drafted that the agent may in some cases have a commission entitlement in such cases and indeed sometimes this is intended in any event. The agent may have been appointed for the full range of the principal's products from time to time.

4.20   So, under regulation 7(2), most agents who are given an exclusive territory or group of customers are entitled to all commission from that territory or that group of customers, but the contract may provide otherwise. The then DTI in their guidance notes say that regulation 7(2) includes 'house accounts held by the principal, ie where the principal deals directly with the third party although the agent has the rights to that area'. Therefore, companies wanting to pay less commission on such accounts or no commission must say so, otherwise the agent is entitled to full commission.

4.21   In the *Duncan Moore v Piretta PTA Ltd* [1999] 1 All ER 174 the judge commented that 'Thus the first sub-regulation requires some action on the part of the agent to earn the commission, the second does not'. This neatly sums up regulations 7(1) and (2).

4.22   In *Heirs of Paul Chevassus-Marche v Group Danone* (Case C-19/07) the Court of Justice of the EU (CJEU) held that where a customer bought via a central buying office even if the customer was situated in the exclusive agent's territory in terms of where goods were delivered, no commission entitlement arose. The Commission summarised the case as follows:

'The first indent of Article 7(2) of Directive 86/653 on the coordination of the laws of the Member States relating to self-employed commercial agents must be interpreted as meaning that a commercial agent entrusted with a specific geographical area does not have the right to a commission for transactions concluded by customers belonging to that area with a third party without any action, direct or indirect, on the part of the principal.

Although that provision merely refers to any 'transactions concluded during the period covered by the agency contract', without any other requirement than that those transactions have been entered into with a customer belonging to a geographical area or a group of customers for whom the commercial agent is responsible, it nevertheless follows from the combination of Article 10(1) and Article 10(2) of Directive 86/653 that the commercial agent's right to commission arises either when the principal has or should have carried out his obligation, or when the third party to the agency contract, that is the customer, has or should have carried out his obligation. In each instance, the presence of the principal in the transactions for which the commercial agent can claim commission is indispensable. That is supported by the wording of Article 11(1) of that directive, according to which the commercial agent's right to commission can be extinguished only if and to the extent that it is established that the contract between the third party and the principal will not be executed, and that fact is due to a reason for which the principal is not to blame.

It is for the national court to establish whether or not the evidence before it, assessed in the light of the aim of protecting the commercial agent which is one of the objectives of that directive and of the obligation on the principal to act dutifully and in good faith under Article 4 of that directive, allows it to establish the existence of such action, be that action of a legal nature, for example through the intermediary of a representative, or of a factual nature.'

See:

(a)   http://curia.europa.eu/jcms/jcms/j_6/.

(b)   (2008) Sol Jo 5 August.

Commission after the contract is over

4.23   Regulation 8 provides:

'Subject to regulation 9 below [*apportionment of commission between new and previous agent*], a commercial agent shall be entitled to commission on commercial transactions concluded after the agency contract has terminated if:

(a)   the transaction is mainly attributable to his efforts during the period covered by the agency contract and if the transaction was entered into within a reasonable period after that contract terminated; or

(b)   in accordance with the conditions mentioned in regulation 7 above, the order of the third party reached the principal or the commercial agent before the agency contract terminated.'

4.24   The then DTI in their guidance notes suggest that the 'principal and agent may attempt to define 'reasonable period' in their agreement. However, in the event of a dispute, despite any such definition, the matter would be ultimately for the decision of the court'. Some agency contracts have provided that a period of one month or three months is regarded by the parties as reasonable. There may be difference between an agent selling small value goods after a visit to a customer's shop and an agent selling expensive industrial equipment in relation to which he may have been working on securing an order from a customer for a period of six months with many visits to that potential customer. In the latter case a reasonable period might be a much longer period of time.

4.25   The 'conclusion' of the contract is taken by the Government to mean when the customer and principal enter into a contract. The words 'the transaction' was mainly 'attributable' to the agent's efforts' bear consideration. Thus regulation 8 is one of those which is relevant when an agency is terminated and part of most agents' claims is to claim commission under regulation 8 (in addition to compensation/indemnity as discussed in a later chapter). The debate in practice is often over whether the agent must have been responsible for that particular order or whether it is enough that the agent had introduced that customer (ie it is a repeat order from an existing customer introduced originally by the agent). The wording of the regulation is clear. It refers to the efforts of the agent during the period of the agency contract. That clearly might be an effort made 15 years before to introduce a customer to the principal.

4.26   Is there a set off between compensation and regulation 8(a)? If an agent is entitled, say, to one year's commission as an indemnity on termination of the agency agreement, can he also claim commission on orders for a reasonable period after termination? Does this not mean he is claiming twice or should the indemnity payment be reduced by the sums paid in this 'reasonable period'? It is submitted that the indemnity is separate and there should be no set off or reduction. However, the provisions do not sit easily with a compensation payment which looks at what the agent would have earned had the contract carried on. The court examined this in *Tigana v Decoro* [2003] EWHC 23 (QB) 3 February 2003 which is looked at in more detail in Chapter 6 and one fact in setting the level of regulation 17 compensation on termination was the fact the agent was awarded US$606,836 under regulation 8. The judgment is in Appendix 3.

4.27   In this case the principal unilaterally stopped the agent towards the end of the agency contract contacting customers. However, orders received were still held to be through the agent's earlier efforts.

4.28   At paragraphs 64 onwards of the judgment the judge held:

'64.   It is to be noted, however, that the provisions of Regulation 8(a) are conjunctive and cumulative: the transaction concluded is to be mainly attributable to the agent's efforts during the period of the agency contract and if the transaction is entered into within a reasonable period after the agency contract terminated. Thus the second part of Regulation 8(a) delimits the first part.

65.   What is a reasonable period in this case? I have come to the conclusion it is nine months. I so conclude for essentially the following reasons:

65.1   By October 2000 Mr Feltham-White had become established as Decoro's agent in place of Mr Coleman.

65.2 Up to October 2000, Mr Feltham-White's activities had been confined to consolidating and administrating the customers introduced by Mr Coleman: by then, he had become familiar with existing customers and thereafter he also started to introduce some new custom himself.

65.3 By October 2000, there had been (or were about to be) High Point, and other trade fairs, where new Decoro models were displayed. Repeat orders for 1999 models were thus tending to disappear.

65.4 The significance of Mr Coleman's erstwhile involvement with Decoro would by October 2000 be likely substantially to have diminished in the eyes of even his most loyal supporters.

65.5 For the purposes of Regulation 8(a), nine months seems to me to be a fair reflection, in the circumstances, both of the nature of Tigana's agency and of the actual period of such agency.

66.   Accordingly, while I think that a proportion of the orders placed up to the end of 2000 (and, perhaps, even in the First part of 2001) could be said still to be mainly attributable to Mr Coleman's efforts, in my judgment nine months is to be determined as the reasonable period for the purposes of Regulation 8(a).'

Obviously, a lot of that turns on its facts – in that case agents did much work for big orders which came in some time after their efforts were put in. Nine months is probably a longer 'reasonable period' than would be found in most cases.

4.29   In *Monk v Largo Foods Ltd* [2016] EWHC 1837 the court decided that a regulation 8 payment would only affect regulation 17 compensation if a notional buyer of the business would pay less because regulation 8 commission was due.

4.30   Regulation 8(b) is more straightforward and simply entitles the agent to commission on orders received before the contract was terminated. Often the termination date is not clear. Sometimes a principal gives an indication of termination verbally and the agent asks for it in writing later or the precise date of termination is argued over. However apart from those difficulties normally regulation 8(b) is easy to interpret.

4.31   There is nothing in regulation 8 to state that the parties cannot vary it. Unlike regulation 10(2) and (3) discussed below where it is provided that nothing in the section can be derogated from, regulation 8 is silent. As mentioned above in relation to regulation 7, the inference must therefore be that the parties can alter this if they wish to. There is some doubt about this because the wording uses 'shall'. Principals therefore may like to provide that the agent is only entitled to commission on orders received by the principal before the date of termination or even only on orders where the goods are shipped to the customer before the date of termination. The principal could even provide that where the agent is in substantial breach of contract which has resulted in the agreement being terminated, the agent will not be given any commission 'due' at all. English freedom of contract rules should entitle such a position to prevail if the parties do agree though in practice many agency agreements have followed the wording in regulation 8 to be on the safe side.

4.32   There has not been much judicial consideration of regulation 8 and yet in practice in termination cases it is a major issue. In *Berry v Laytons* [2009] EWHC 1591 the judge did not agree to consider the interaction between regulations 8 and 17. The valuer for the defendant had suggested that were an award made under regulation 8 then the compensation should be adjusted to ensure there was not double recovery.

4.33   One issue raised in practice is whether an order from a longstanding customer the agent had found which is placed after termination but on which the agent had done no recent work resulted from the agent's efforts. The regulations do not say recent efforts but it is probably implied that this refers to recent 'pipeline' orders. *Monk v Largo Foods Ltd* [2016] EWHC 1837 looked at what the 'agent's efforts' were, in paragraph 113 et seq of the judgment, but only in the context of the facts of that case.

When the Regulations do not apply

4.34   If the Regulations do not apply to an agency agreement, then it is up to the parties to agree when commission may be payable on contracts made before the agency agreement is terminated. This should be set out in the agreement and if it is not there may be some guidance in the general commission clause. If there is nothing, then there is no reason why an agent should be entitled to any commission on orders received after termination. It is much better, though, if the issue can be addressed in the contract in any event.

Apportionment of commission with previous agent

4.35   The agency agreement should state when the agent's commission may be shared with a previous agent which the new agent replaces. This will only be relevant in cases where a new agent is taking over. Regulation 9 provides:

> 'A commercial agent shall not be entitled to the commission referred to in regulation 7 [*general commission entitlement during the agency agreement*] above if that commission is payable, by virtue of Regulation 8 above, to the previous commercial agent, unless it is equitable because of the circumstances for the commission to be shared between the commercial agents.'

This is a vague provision which may provide a recipe for disaster. It would be wise to incorporate such a provision into a contract in clearer terms.

Company A may sack agent B. A appoints agent C in his place. C is entitled to commission on all orders from his territory under regulation 7. However, Company A still has to pay, for a reasonable period, agent B for orders received after termination. If Company A is not careful it will end up paying two lots of commission. The new agent must be told there may be commission sharing. Sometimes the new agent is paid a lower rate of commission at the start or no commission on the old agent's customers for whatever the 'reasonable' period may be.

4.36 Even when the Regulations or the Directive on which they are based do not apply, ie outside the EU, it is best to address this issue in a contract where a new agent replaces an old one. Note that the Regulation provides that it is the new agent who does not receive the commission *unless* it is equitable that the commission be shared. A contract could set out the circumstances in which an equitable sharing should take place, such as where the new agent will be doing a lot of work with customers in obtaining the relevant orders. The then DTI say in their guidance notes:

> 'It is the principal's duty to pay commission owing to agents and where commission is paid inadvertently to one agent which was in fact owed to the other, the agent must repay it or the principal reclaim it. In either circumstance the agent entitled to the commission should receive it.'

When should commission be paid to the agent?

4.37 The section above has examined what the commission is assessed upon. However, the time at which the money should be handed over to the agent is equally important. Regulation 10(1), in cases when the Regulations apply, provides that commission becomes due as soon as and to the extent that one of the following occurs:

(a) the principal has executed the transaction; or

(b) the principal should, according to his agreement with the third party, have executed the transaction; or

(c) the third party has executed the transaction.

4.38 There are further details on commission later in regulation 10 from which derogation is not permitted, but it is clearly the case that regulation 10(1) may be altered by contract. It will therefore only apply where the parties have no other agreement (or indeed no other practice for verbal agency agreements) dealing with the issue or where they agree the provisions of regulation 10(1).

4.39 What is not clear is what 'execution' of the transaction means. The then DTI in their guidance notes say that a transaction should be considered to be executed where:

(i)   when the principal has accepted or delivered the goods;

(ii) when the principal should have accepted or delivered the goods;

(iii) when the third party accepts or delivers the goods; or

(iv) when the third party pays for the goods.

4.40   The then DTI say it is for the two parties to the transaction to decide when payment is made. In many cases agents are paid commission in the month following the goods being shipped to the customer. If the customer subsequently defaults in payment, then the commission is repaid or deducted from later commission payments – see below. In other cases, the agent is paid only when the customer is paid. This is lawful too, subject to regulation 10(2).

4.41   Regulation 10(2) *cannot* be changed. It is one of the provisions of the Regulations which by regulation 10(4) cannot be derogated from to the detriment of the agent. It says commission is due at the latest when the third party has executed his part of the transaction or should have done so if the principal had executed his part of the transaction as he should have. Executing the transaction presumably means when the customer pays. However, it may mean when the customer accepts the goods – in other words the commission must be paid on shipment. The author does not agree with that interpretation and believes principals are free to provide that the agent is only paid commission when the customer pays. However, none of the agency cases in the UK have raised this topic and there are no precedents.

4.42   Note the words 'or should have done'. If the customer has not paid because the principal has not fulfilled his side of the bargain, then the agent is still entitled to commission. In many agency disputes there are arguments over whether the principal has performed its side of the bargain. There may have been delays with deliveries, defective goods, orders not satisfied etc.

4.43   Regulation 10(3) is also relevant, and again, derogation from it is not permitted. It says:

> 'The commission shall be paid not later than on the last day of the month following the quarter in which it became due, and, for the purposes of these Regulations, unless otherwise agreed between the parties, the first quarter period shall run from the date the agency contract takes effect, and subsequent periods shall run from that date in the third month thereafter or the beginning of the fourth month, whichever is the sooner.'

In cases where the Regulations apply this provision may not be altered. However, provisions which favour the agent may be included so that for example if commission is paid monthly, as is often the case, rather than quarterly then the payment on a monthly basis is of course allowed. Normally 'quarters' would be defined by the parties in their agreement rather than relying on the provisions concerning quarters in this regulation. Most agency agreements contain details of when commission shall be paid and due.

Instalments

4.44 The then DTI in their guidance notes on the Regulations refer to instalment contracts and say:

'It is not unusual for goods to be delivered by instalments. If the agency contract does not make specific provision for the matter, the question as to when commission is due would seem to depend upon the precise nature of the sale or purchase transaction. Where each instalment delivery is the subject of a separate contract, it seems likely that a separate commission payment will be due as each separate delivery is made, or should have been made. Where a single contract applies to a number of instalment deliveries, the position is somewhat less clear. However, in view of the words 'to the extent that' in regulation 10(1) the agent may be entitled to the commission which is attributable to each particular instalment delivery.'

Extinction of the right to commission

4.45 Regulation 11 describes when the right to commission shall be extinguished. It may not be derogated from to the detriment of the agent. The agent loses the right to commission only if it is established that the contract between the third party and the principal will not be executed. Again, the word 'executed' is used, which is normally used by lawyers to mean that a document is signed. Yet for most purchases by customers there is no signed contract. Instead the customer purchases on the written terms and conditions of the business of the principal. Execution will mean the customer pays and the transaction proceeds.

4.46 The practical effect of regulation 11(1) is that the agent has no entitlement to commission if the customer does not pay, ie the agent can be made to bear the bad debt risk. However, if the parties wish then for the benefit of the agent this can be altered so that the principal bears the bad debt risk. Whether the agency bears the bad debt risk or not varies widely from industry to industry.

4.47 However, the agent must be paid commission where the principal 'is to blame' for the fact that the contract does not proceed or the customer does not pay. This does not mean that the agent is entitled to commission on every order even if rejected by the principal. It is only where the parties reach the stage that there is in law a contract between the principal and the customer for the supply or purchase of the goods and then the transaction does not proceed. This would include:

1. The principal supplies defective goods. There in most cases the principal is to blame and the agent is still entitled to commission.

2. The principal decides not to charge the customer for the goods – this might include where there is nothing wrong with the goods at all but the principal offers some form of 'no quibble' guarantee and in the interests of customer relations even where the principal is not at fault customers are

refunded their money or are not charged if a dispute arises about quality or delay in a delivery. Here the position is far from clear. The principal is taking a good business decision which should ensure there are future orders and yet in law the principal could have 'stuck to his guns' and made the customer pay. He chooses not to. Should commission be payable?

3.   The customer goes out of business – here the principal is not to blame, unless the agent could argue that by failing to carry out normal credit checks before shipment then the principal is at fault and the agent is still entitled to commission.

4.48   In practice regulation 11(1) is one of the provisions in the Regulations which is often breached in agency agreements. The principal often wants a right to hold back commission even in cases where the principal is 'to blame'. Thus, void provisions may be included in an agreement. This is not advisable. Instead the parties should set out a list of what is a 'to blame' circumstance and what is not. This could be quite narrow when drafted from the principal's point of view. It might simply be that the principal is in breach of contract and this has been established by a court and therefore the customer is not paying.

4.49   Regulation 11(2) provides that any commission which the agent has already received, in cases where the right is extinguished, must be refunded. It does not say when this will be the case however, so it could be, for example, at the end of a particular year or selling season.

Example

4.50   Mr Bloggs is agent for Smith and Jones. He is paid 5% commission. This is paid monthly whether the customer has paid or not provided the goods have been sent. In one month Customer X refuses to pay because it is in financial difficulties. However, it pretends the goods are defective at first. The next month it says the cheque is in the post and the next month it is in liquidation. Must the agent refund the commission? Yes, provided the principal is not to blame for the financial difficulties – which it is not. It is not likely that the delay on the part of Smith and Jones in enforcing the debt would be the reason for the failure to pay in law, though the agent might like to argue that had Smith and Jones been more aggressive in its debt collection the money might have been recovered before the company went out of business.

Smith and Jones is entitled to require Mr Bloggs to return the commission he has had or could set it off against other commission due to him.

Other commission issues

4.51   It is dangerous just to concentrate on the Regulations. They do not apply to all agency agreements and there may be other issues relevant to commission which need to be incorporated into the agreements. These are more a matter of commercial than legal issues. They might include:

1. The currency in which the commission is payable (some businesses may want a right to pay in euros).

2. What variations in commission rates there are perhaps dependent on the customer, whether special deals have been offered, if the customer is a house account (as discussed earlier in this chapter).

3. Exactly to what sum the percentage commission is applied and what is deducted first.

4. Whether the agent is also (or alternatively) paid a monthly retainer. In the *Pacflex* case [1999] 2 All ER (Comm) 249 the agent was paid £4000 per month as well as commission. It should be clear if a retainer is paid whether commission due must exceed a certain amount before any additional commission is paid or whether the retainer is paid in addition to the commission. In *Mercantile International Group Plc v Chuan Soon Huat Industrial Group Plc* [2002] 1 All ER (Comm) 788, the Court of Appeal in the first instance judgment (which was confirmed on appeal) held that payment by way of 'mark up' not commission was not to be regarded as inconsistent with an agency agreement, see http://www.agentlaw.co.uk/site/case_summaries/mercantile_v_chuan. html. In *Invicta Uk v International Brands Ltd* [2013] EWHC 1564 the fact the agent was paid a fixed retainer not commission did not prevent the Regulations applying (although obviously then regulations 7 and 8 commission payments did not arise). The way the agent is paid does not decide the issue of whether the Regulations apply but can be relevant (e.g. an employee paid under PAYE is going to find it hard to establish they are a self-employed agent).

5. The contract should deal with payment of expenses as seen in Chapter 2.

6. Some agents pay for samples of products and booklets. All these types of payment issues should be addressed.

7. Some agents have to pay a lump sum to take over an existing agency along the lines of a franchise fee. This is lawful though cannot always be commercially negotiated. This may be used to pay off the earlier agent's compensation or indemnity payment.

8. The most important issue is to make it clear whether the agent is entitled to commission on all orders from his territory or only those which he has generated. If the latter then the contract must state how it is ascertained whether the agent has generated an order or not and what happens if the principal, another agent and the relevant agent have worked to achieve the sale concerned.

Rights to information and inspection of books

4.52   Agents are entitled to a statement of commission due under regulation 12(1) and in most agency contracts, whether the Regulations apply or not, such a right would normally be included. The statement is usually sent with the commission payment. The Regulations provide that the statement should be sent not later than the last day of the month following the quarter in which the commission has become due, and that the statement must set out the main components used in calculating the amount of the commission.

4.53   Principals will normally want the agent to supply information to the principal about potential orders and, which customers they have visited etc often on a regular basis, so contracts need to address the flow of information from agent to principal as well as vice versa, notwithstanding that the Regulations do not deal with that issue.

4.54   The Regulations provide that there can be no derogation from regulation 12(1).
Regulation 12(2) provides that the agent:

> 'shall be entitled to demand that he be provided with all the information (and in particular an extract from the books) which is available to his principal and which he needs in order to check the amount of the commission due to him.'

Nothing in any enactment or rule of law which recognises the right of an agent to inspect the books of his principal is restricted or removed by this provision (regulation 12(4)). There would be rights on disclosure for example in litigation which may be broader than this provision in regulation 12(2). As the then DTI point out in their guidance notes on the Regulations, the principal is only obliged to provide 'necessary' information and only extracts from his books not the full books. Nor does the provision give the agent any right of entry for himself or his accountant to check the books, though some agency contracts may provide for this and go further than the provisions of the Regulations (which is allowed).

4.55   Some agents ask for this information when their contract has been terminated, particularly when exercising the right described above to commission on orders received after termination. The agent has no way of knowing, other than as he can ascertain through contacts he has with customers, whether particular leads he has generated have led to orders, and some unscrupulous principals will pretend an order did not proceed when in fact it did. This provision in the Regulations protects the agent against such fraud.

What happens if the agent takes a secret bribe?

4.56   In *FHR European Ventures LLP v Cedar Capital Partners LLC* [2014] UKSC 45 the Supreme Court looked at the issue of whether a bribe or secret commission received by an agent is held on trust for the principal or if the principal just has a claim for equitable compensation of an amount to the value of the bribe or commission. If it is held on trust, then the principal has a proprietary claim to it (ie the principal can have the money back). The case was about who owns the bribe, in effect. The court said that the principal was entitled to the sum.

FHR European Ventures LLP v Cedar Capital Partners LLC

4.57   The Supreme Court summary of the decision is reproduced below and provides some useful guidance in this area:

16 July 2014 PRESS SUMMARY *FHR European Ventures LLP and others (Respondents) v Cedar Capital Partners LLC (Appellant) [2014] UKSC 45*

On appeal from [2013] EWCA Civ 17 JUSTICES: Lord Neuberger (President), Lord Mance, Lord Sumption, Lord Carnwath, Lord Toulson, Lord Hodge, Lord Collins.

Background to the appeals

This appeal concerns the issue of whether a bribe or secret commission received by an agent is held by that agent on trust for his principal, or whether the principal merely has a claim for equitable compensation in a sum equal to the value of the bribe or commission. If the bribe or commission is held on trust, the principal has a proprietary claim to it, whereas if the principal merely has a claim for equitable compensation, the claim is not proprietary.

The distinction is important for two main reasons. First, if the agent becomes insolvent, a proprietary claim would give the principal priority over the agent's unsecured creditors. Secondly, if the principal has a proprietary claim to a bribe or commission, he can trace and follow it in equity.

On 22 December 2004, FHR European Ventures LLP purchased the issued share capital of Monte Carlo Grand Hotel SAM from Monte Carlo Grand Hotel Ltd ('the Seller') for €211.5m. The purchase was a joint venture between the claimants in these proceedings, for whom FHR was the vehicle. Cedar Capital Partners LLC provided consultancy services to the hotel industry, and it had acted as the claimants' agent in negotiating the purchase.

Cedar accordingly owed fiduciary duties to the claimants. Cedar had also entered into an 'Exclusive Brokerage Agreement' with the Seller, which provided for the payment to Cedar of a €10m fee following a successful conclusion of the sale and purchase of the issued shared capital of Monte Carlo Grand Hotel SAM. The Seller paid Cedar €10m on or about 7 January 2005.

On 23 November 2009 the claimants began these proceedings for recovery of the sum of €10m from Cedar. The main issue at trial was whether Cedar had made proper disclosure to the claimants of the Exclusive Brokerage Agreement. Simon J found against Cedar on that issue, and made a declaration of liability for breach of fiduciary duty on the part of Cedar for having failed to obtain the claimants' fully informed consent in respect of the €10m, and ordered Cedar to pay that sum to the claimants. However, he refused to grant the claimants a proprietary remedy in respect of the monies.

The claimants successfully appealed to the Court of Appeal, who made a declaration that Cedar received the €10m fee on constructive trust for the claimants absolutely. Cedar now appeals to the Supreme Court on this issue.

Judgment

The Supreme Court unanimously dismisses the appeal. Lord Neuberger gives the judgment of the court. Where an agent acquires a benefit which came to his notice as a result of his fiduciary position, or pursuant to an opportunity which results from his fiduciary position, the general equitable rule ('the Rule') is that he is to be treated as having acquired the benefit on behalf of his principal, so it is beneficially owned by the principal. The dispute in this case is the extent to which the Rule applies where the benefit is a bribe or secret commission obtained by an agent in breach of his fiduciary duty to his principal. While it is not possible, as a matter of pure legal authority, to identify any plainly right or plainly wrong answer to the issue of the extent of the Rule, considerations of practicality and principle support the case that a bribe or secret commission accepted by an agent is held on trust for his principal.

Reasons for the Judgment

The only point on this appeal is whether the claimants are entitled to the proprietary remedy in respect of the €10m received by Cedar from the Seller [4]. The following principles are not in doubt:

1) An agent owes a fiduciary duty to his principal because he is someone who has undertaken to act for or on behalf of his principal in a particular matter in circumstances which give rise to a relationship of trust and confidence;

2) As a result, an agent must not make a profit out of his trust, and must not place himself in a position in which his duty and his interest may conflict; and

3) A fiduciary who acts for two principals with potentially conflicting interests without the informed consent of both is in breach of the obligation of undivided loyalty, by putting himself in a position where his duty to one principal may conflict with his duty to the other [5].

Another well-established principle, which applies where an agent receives a benefit in breach of his fiduciary duty, is that the agent is obliged to account to the principal for such a benefit, and to pay, in effect, a sum equal to profit by way of equitable compensation [6]. The principal's right to seek an account undoubtedly gives him a right in equitable compensation in respect of the bribe or secret commission, which equals the quantum of that bribe or commission. In cases to which the Rule applies, the principal has a proprietary remedy in addition to his personal remedy against the agent, and the principal can elect between the two remedies [7].

What is in dispute is the extent to which the Rule applies where the benefit is a bribe or secret commission obtained by an agent in breach of his fiduciary duty to his principal [9].

The appellant contends that the Rule should not apply to a bribe or secret commission paid to an agent, because it is not a benefit which can properly be said to be the property of the principal [10]. The respondents argue that the Rule does apply to bribes or secret commissions received by an agent, because, in any case where an agent receives a benefit, which is, or results from, a breach the fiduciary duty owed to his principal, the agent holds the benefit on trust for the principal [11].

It is not possible to identify any plainly right or plainly wrong answer to the issue of the extent of the Rule, as a matter of pure legal authority [32]. The respondents' formulation of the Rule has the merit of simplicity: any benefit acquired by an agent as a result of his agency and in breach of his fiduciary duty is held on trust for the principal. In contrast, the appellant's position is more likely to result in uncertainty [35]. Wider policy considerations also support the respondents' case that bribes and secret commissions received by an agent should be treated as the property of his principal, rather than merely giving rise to a claim for equitable compensation.

Bribes and secret commissions undermine trust in the commercial world, and one would expect the law to be particularly stringent in relation to a claim against an agent who has received a bribe or secret commission [42].

The argument that the respondents' version of the Rule will tend to prejudice the agent's unsecured creditors has limited force in the context of a bribe or secret commission. In the first place, the proceeds of a bribe or secret commission consists of property which should not be in the agent's estate at all. Secondly, the bribe or commission will very often have reduced the benefit from the relevant transaction which the principal will have obtained, and therefore can fairly be said to be his property. Finally, it is just that a principal whose agent has obtained a bribe or secret commission should be able to trace the proceeds of the bribe or commission into other assets and to follow them into the hands of knowing recipients [43-44].

Considerations of practicality and principle support the case that a bribe or secret commission accepted by an agent is held on trust for his principal. While the position is less clear when one examines the decided cases, taken as a whole the authorities support the respondents' case [46]. The cases, with the exception of *Tyrrell v Bank of London* (1862) 10 HL Cas 26, are consistently in favour of bribes or secret commissions being held on trust for the principal or other beneficiary until the decision in *Metropolitan Bank v Heiron* (1880) 5 Ex D 319, which was then followed in *Lister & Co v Stubbs* (1890) 45 Ch D 1. The domestic cases subsequent to *Lister* are explicable on the basis that the issue was either conceded, or decided on the basis that Lister was binding. The decision in *Tyrrell* should not stand in the way of the conclusion that the law took a wrong turn in *Heiron* and *Lister*, and that those decisions, and any subsequent decisions in so far as they relied on or followed *Heiron* and *Lister*, should be treated as overruled [47-50].

(The paragraph numbers above refer to those in the full Supreme Court judgment.)

4.58   In *Medsted Associates Ltd v Canaccord Genuity Wealth (International) Ltd* (2019 EWCA Civ 83) the Court of Appeal looked at a case where an agent had made a 'secret' commission and held that, with a sophisticated principal (investors) and where such payments were expected, there would be no breach of the law if the agent failed to disclose the precise details to the investors. The agent in this case was a broker who introduced investors to financial institutions. The court also found that the broker owed a fiduciary duty to the investors. The Regulations were not relevant in the *Medsted* case.

Further information

4.59   The archived but still useful Government guidance notes on the Regulations, the Regulations and the Directive itself provide the best guidance, all of which appear in Appendix 1 to this book.

Commission issues are addressed in Chapter 8 of F Randolph and J Davey's book - *The European Law of Commercial Agency* (3rd edn, Hart Publishing/ Bloomsbury Professional, 2010).

Chapter 5

Monitoring and terminating an agency agreement

5.1   This chapter examines practical issues relating to the monitoring of commercial agency agreements and termination of the agency agreement. Many problems arise because the principal neglects to manage the agent properly so that small problems become larger problems. The next chapter looks at compensation and indemnity payments on termination of the agency.

Monitoring

5.2   The commercial agency agreement should include provisions for a flow of information between the agent and the principal and vice versa. The agent should be regularly informed of matters such as:

1.   product changes and their specifications;

2.   new products;

3.   products withdrawn from sale;

4.   new advice on how to operate products, where relevant;

5.   likely warranty claims;

6.   promotions to be undertaken by the principal;

7.   trade fairs to be attended by both parties;

8.   advertising to be undertaken by the principal;

9.   price changes and changes to terms and conditions of sale;

10.   orders which the agent has put forward which the principal has rejected;

11.   how the agent's sales correspond to his target.

5.3   It is good communication between agent and principal which ensures that an agency agreement operates without difficulties and to the mutual advantage of both parties. Many legal agency disputes arise because of lack of communication – either the agent not voicing concerns or the principal failing to respond to queries from the agent. In some cases, agents do not visit customers as often as they should nor complete necessary paperwork or find it hard to tackle new electronic methods of reporting. The typical agent is good at talking and good at selling and sometimes not so good at paperwork. That may not matter but the principal clearly has to assess each agent on an individual basis in order to obtain the best performance they can from the agent.

5.4   The writer has acted for many agents and many principals. Frequent agent complaints include:

- products not available;
- products supplied so slowly after orders submitted that the customer goes elsewhere;
- defective products;
- commission rates altered without the agent's approval;
- accounts removed from the agent without the agent's approval;
- territories altered without agent's approval;
- products altered without agent approval.

Some of these matters may be lawful under the agency agreement but they are rarely sensible in ensuring a harmonious relationship with the agent. It is often the psychology as much as the law which matters in how the agency and principal relationship is managed.

5.5   The agent should notify the principal of matters such as:

1. complaints from customers;
2. which lines are selling well;
3. proposed advertising or marketing campaigns by the agent (mostly these will require the principal's approval before they proceed, because they may intrude into the territory of another agent or even breach a third party company's trade mark rights);
4. whether national rules concerning the sale of the products (for foreign agencies) have altered. This might include registration for sale of products, packaging requirements, product approval and proposed legislation;
5. any potential breaches of the principal's intellectual property rights which have come to the agent's attention;
6. likely volumes of orders throughout the relevant period;
7. pricing of other competitive products or other terms and conditions relevant to them such as whether other companies are offering discounts;

8.   when the agent proposes to start acting for another principal in non-competing products – sometimes this needs the approval of the principal under the contract terms.

5.6   The principal will need to monitor the performance of the agent. This became a much more important issue when the Commercial Agents (Council Directive) Regulations 1993 came into force because where the agent is in substantial breach of contract which justifies immediate termination then no compensation is payable on termination. In many other cases it is. This is the same in the rest of the EU.

5.7   It is very helpful to the principal if there are a series of letters sent to an agent who has not been performing well. As under employment law the courts are more likely to regard a 'dismissal' of the agent as fair in all the circumstances if he has been given due warning that he is falling behind in his performance. The agent may not be making high enough sales, which is the usual problem. However, this may not strictly be a breach of contract. Even more importantly it may not be the special form of breach of contract which entitles the principal to terminate the agency without compensation – this is in cases where there is a substantial breach which justifies immediate termination. The agency agreement without legally binding written sales requirements breach of which leads to immediate termination is a rarity. Mostly principals have no clear wording stating the agent has to meet a certain standard of performance.

5.8   In some cases, he may breach other clauses, such as handling competing agencies or disclosing confidential information or libelling the principal or failing to visit customer outlets frequently enough or forgetting to pass orders on to the principal or being very slow about doing so. Other potential failures include not filling in the paperwork required by the principal (this is very common). Many agents are good at selling but bad at paperwork.

5.9   Of course, many principals want to dismiss agents when they think the agent is 'earning too much money'. This should be regarded as a sign of success for both principal and agent as the more commission the agent earns the more profits the principal is earning through increased sales and it is in just such cases that the Regulations are there to protect the agent. The principal may feel the agent is just making commission from repeat business and doing no work. However, the Regulations make it clear that in the EU, at least, the agent is entitled to the continuing benefit for such repeat orders.

Meetings

5.10   It is sensible for agent and principal to meet on a regular basis and for each to put any complaints in writing to the other beforehand so that they can be discussed. A meeting on an annual basis is often arranged. Sometimes there is an annual meeting of all the company's agents and targets for the next year are set. The agent can also put any complaints he has to the principal. These might include:

1.   failure to process orders at all or in time;

2.   poor quality products;

3.   insufficient support through national advertising;

4.   poor warranty repair work;

5.   products not available which are listed on the principal's price list or in his catalogue;

6.   unrealistic sales targets;

7.   unilateral changes to commission rates;

8.   too many house accounts with reduced levels of commission for the agent;

9.   unilateral alterations to the agent's exclusive territory – some principals take parts of an agent's territory away and give it to other agents;

10.   lack of communication, failure to reply to telephone calls, failure to visit important customers with the agent when the agent requests it.

5.11   Termination of an agency is not the easy answer. As will be seen in the next chapter for the principal sums of at least a year's commission may need to be paid to the departing agent in compensation. For the agent he may be out of a job and having to fund expensive and time-consuming litigation. It may be better to have an agency which is not as lucrative as before than no agency at all. Neither principal nor agent should rush into termination. Many an agent has been sacked to find that the principal has appointed someone else who was worse and left shortly afterwards, or that an experienced agent was replaced by an employed young representative whom the customers do not like and orders are reduced.

5.12   If an agent is to leave, then the parties should try to negotiate an amicable departure. Even where the agent has to leave involuntarily often the handling can make a great difference to whether the parting is acrimonious or not. Making a reasonable ex gratia offer of a pay out with an expression of thanks for the agent's efforts over the years can result in unpleasant litigation being avoided. However, principals need to ensure any sum offered is offered 'without prejudice' and accepted in full and final settlement.

Notice of termination of the agency

5.13   Many agency agreements are for an indefinite period. The agent is appointed and there is no provision that it is for one year, two or five years etc. In such cases either party may terminate the agency by notice under regulation 15 of the Regulations, where they apply. Under English law even if the Regulations do not apply (eg because the agency is for services not goods) then any commercial agreement can be terminated on 'reasonable' notice where no period is specified.

5.14   Where the contract is for an indefinite period then the minimum period of notice specified under the Regulations is:

(a)   one month for the first year of the contract;

(b)   two months for the second year which has commenced;

(c)   three months for the third year which has commenced and for subsequent years.

5.15   It is a pity that the Regulations state 'and the parties may not agree on any shorter periods of notice' rather than 'this clause may not be derogated from to the detriment of the agent', which the rest of certain clauses in the Regulations provide. However, the wording is so clear that shorter periods are not allowed that no clause in the agreement providing for a shorter period is valid. The Regulations do not say that derogation is void, as other clauses do. This brings into question the effect if the parties do provide for a shorter period in an indefinite term contract (this section is only relevant to indefinite term agencies). Presumably the clause is not void, but instead the agent (or principal) can claim damages for the period of notice which was not given in the normal way. This is how it has been operated in practice.

5.16   In *Alan Ramsay Sales & Marketing Ltd v Typhoo Tea Ltd* [2016] EWHC 486 the claim included damages based on the lack of a proper notice period having been given. In that case the contract provided for 12 months' written notice but only three months' notice had been given. A figure of £45,459 was awarded for the additional nine months of which notice should have been served (in addition to about £130,000 compensation and about £7,500 owed for loss of retainer). The case is also interesting in its examination of when correspondence, whether marked without prejudice or not, is indeed without prejudice, and secondly, as to which party was in repudiatory breach. The agent had continued to work the agency after the parties' negotiations had begun and said he would attend a trade show. He was not told to refrain from attending it, so the court decided earlier discussions did not amount to acceptance of repudiatory breach and termination at that point.

5.17   Notice that the minimum notice of termination period under the Regulations is one month in the first year (not after the first year) etc. So an agent who has served one year and one month, for example, is entitled to two months' notice of termination. Once the agency is over the parties could agree a shorter period as part of a settlement agreement. Often once it is known that an agent is leaving, it is better he goes quickly before damage is done to customer relationships so a shorter period could be agreed by consent.

5.18   Longer periods may be agreed, but for indefinite agency agreements the principal must not agree a shorter period than that which the agent must observe (regulation 15(3)).

5.19   Unless the parties agree otherwise the end of the period of notice (again for indefinite contracts only) must coincide with the end of a calendar month.

Example

5.20   Mr X was appointed agent five years' ago. His principal gives him a month's notice by telephone on 15 January 2005. His contract is indefinite and simply provides that a month's notice must be given of termination (it had not been drafted to take account of the Regulations). As Mr X has been an agent for five years, he is entitled to three months' notice. It does not have to be written notice. Some agents claim that no written notice was given before a dispute arose and therefore the principal has to begin again several months later with notice in writing. The Regulations do not require that notice be in writing, but in practice it is much better if it is. Conversations are sometimes not clear as to whether notice is given – 'I never want to see you again', 'That's it, we're finished' – statements such as these are not always clearly understood.

In this example the principal thinks the agency will end on 15 February – ie one month after the notice was given. In fact, it should expire on 30 April – three months plus the time which takes it up to the end of a calendar month.

Working a notice period

5.21   Some agents assume that at the very least, leaving aside any question of compensation, the agent is entitled to commission in a lump sum for such a period. This is not the case. The agent can be obliged to work his notice. Notice means exactly that – the agent is given warning that the agency will end on a particular date. Sometimes the principal offers money in lieu of notice, as often happens in employment disputes. However, there is no obligation for the principal to offer this and the agent can be obliged to work his notice period and must comply with the contract in that period.

5.22   These provisions of the Regulations apply equally to the agent as to the principal. If the agent wants to resign, he may need to give at least three months' notice and work that period. In practice it may be hard to force an employee or agent to stick to a notice period, but in law this is the right of the employer/principal and many agents are very happy to negotiate for their full notice period as it gives them commission income for a longer period than an immediate termination would give them. The contract may provide that in the notice period the agent shall assist any new agent visiting customers, being introduced to them and learning about the products and the area from the old agent. If the relationship between agent and principal has broken down this will be hard to achieve.

Fixed period agencies

5.23   Agency agreements which are for a fixed period may be converted into an agreement for an indefinite period under regulation 14 if the period expires and the contract continues to be performed 'by both parties'. Some principals appoint agents for a period such as one year only. This can act as a form of trial – though there remains a risk that the agent may be entitled to compensation when the fixed period is over.

5.24   Under the Regulations there is no minimum period of service for compensation claims. Indeed, in one case known to the author the agent worked only six weeks and still made a claim. He had not even signed or negotiated a written contract but he was still an 'agent' under the law. Of course, an agent only acting for a short time may not have given 'substantial benefits' to the principal as required before compensation is payable (see the next chapter) so may not be entitled to much in the way of compensation. However, he may have been very successful in such a short period and have a compensation claim. Trial periods, therefore, although commercially a good idea, do not remove the application of the Regulations.

5.25   In *Conseils et mise en relations (CMR) SARL v Demeures terre et tradition SARL* (Case C-645/16) EU:C: 2018:262 (2018) the court held that compensation/ indemnity is payable even if a contract is not renewed after a trial period. The Court of Justice of the EU (CJEU) said:

> 'The interpretation that no indemnity is payable in the event of termination of the commercial agency contract during the trial period is incompatible with the mandatory nature of the regime established by Article 17 of Directive 86/653. Such an interpretation, which effectively makes the award of redress conditional on whether or not a trial period is provided for in the commercial agency contract, without regard for the performance of the commercial agent or the costs and expenses that he has incurred, contrary to the requirements of that article, constitutes, for the same reasons as those set out in paragraph 32 above, an interpretation detrimental to the commercial agent, who is denied any redress on the sole ground that the contract he has with the principal includes a trial period.

> Consequently, an interpretation of Article 17 of Directive 86/653 that no indemnity or compensation is payable where the termination of the commercial agency contract occurs during the trial period is contrary to the objective of that directive.

> In the light of the foregoing considerations, the answer to the question referred is that Article 17 of Directive 86/653 must be interpreted as meaning that the indemnity and compensation regimes laid down by that article, in paragraphs

2 and 3 respectively, in the event of termination of the commercial agency contract are applicable where termination occurs during the trial period provided for by the contract.'

5.26 It is helpful that this point is now clear although it should never have been in doubt given the express words of the Directive and Regulations. It seems a little unfortunate for the principal here as the agent had made only one sale during the trial period and yet had a target of 25 sales for the first year. However, if few sales had been made, then presumably compensation would therefore be a low amount in any event. The case was referred from the French courts to the CJEU and France has compensation and not indemnity provisions – although the CJEU ruling applies to both compensation and indemnity cases.

5.27 Many companies with fixed term contracts forget to renew them in the following year and therefore the contract rolls over and becomes indefinite. If the renewal is as little as a day late this can be the case. Therefore, companies must make a diary entry and ensure renewal takes place well in advance of the expiry date. Solicitors should tell their clients that this is the responsibility of the client and that the solicitor will not be notifying the principal of the need for a renewal.

5.28 It is likely that an agent under a one-year fixed term contract is entitled to less compensation than an agent under an indefinite contract. In *Tigana v Decoro* (see Appendix 3) the court thought that one factor in assessing compensation was length of the contract. A one-year contract also 'keeps the agent on his toes' in that he does not know if he will have the security of a contract for a further year. Conversely if a one-year contract is repeatedly renewed it is highly likely the courts will see this as in reality an indefinite contract, the principal has to remember to renew and has the hassle of annual renewal, and the agent may not be as loyal if he does not have the certainty of greater security.

5.29 It is also likely that the notice periods for indefinite contracts *may* apply for fixed term contracts. If an agent is appointed under a one-year contract and then that is renewed for a second year is his notice period one month in each year or one month in the first year and two in the second? It is probably the latter.

5.30 In *Duncan Moore v Piretta* [1999] 1 All ER 174 the agent argued that the term 'agency contract' as used in regulation 17(1) meant the contractual agreement between the parties. The principal argued that each newly renewed contract was a separate agency agreement. The court agreed that the entire period of the various agency agreements replacing older ones between the same parties were the overall agreement and there was only an entitlement to compensation or an indemnity when the overall agreement was terminated, not when each renewal took place and that periods of service under the old agreement were examined even if they took place before the Regulations came into effect (on 1 January 1994).

Causes of termination

5.31   The reason why an agency agreement is terminated is crucial when the question of compensation is assessed. Levels of compensation are examined in the next chapter, but the rest of this chapter examines the various circumstances in which an agency is terminated and when compensation may be payable.

Agencies outside the Regulations

5.32   Where the agency is outside the Regulations, eg where the agent markets services or is an employed representative or a distributor (see Chapter 1), then his legal entitlement is simply to whatever the contract specifies. For example, the contract may state he is entitled to a lump sum payment. If that is not then paid, then damages for breach of contract can be sought. This is one of the risks of companies giving agents express rights on termination to compensation or an indemnity, because if they do by a contract term it may transpire that in fact the agent was not a true 'commercial agent' under the narrow definition in the Regulations and they have given more than they needed to give.

5.33   The *W Nagel v Pluczenik Diamond Company NV* [2018] EWCA Civ 2640 case, citing *Volvo Car Germany GmbH v Autohof Weidensdorf GmbH* (Case C-203/09) [2012] Bus LR D13 and *Belgium v Temco Europe SA* (Case C-284/03 [2004] ECR I-11237, held that exclusions and exceptions from the Regulations should be construed narrowly.

5.34   The purpose of the legislation should be used in deciding the construction of both the legislation and contracts (*Green Deal Marketing Ltd v Economy Energy Trading Ltd* [2019] EWHC 507).

5.35   Whether the Regulations apply or not, an agent is entitled to be given the notice required by the contract, as is the principal. If this is not given, then either can sue the other for damages. Thus an agent outside the Regulations, for example, given a day's notice of termination when the contract provides for six months' notice, is entitled to the money he would have earned during the notice period – less his expenses, subject to his duty to mitigate (ie try to reduce) his loss and with some deduction for the fact he has had all the money at once (accelerated receipt). Of course, if he is in breach of contract himself there may be a counterclaim to set off against the agent's damages claim. If the contract does not specify the notice period then at English common law the agent is entitled to a reasonable period of notice, as is the principal. This might be as much as a year for a 20 years of service agent or only a week for an agent who has just started and will be a matter of degree and consideration of all the circumstances. Of course, if the Regulations apply then minimum notice periods of indefinite period agencies are implied as seen above. For fixed term contracts either the contract has to run to the end of the fixed term or there will be a clause, whether the Regulations apply or not, stating that the contract can be terminated in the middle of the term either for breach or simply on notice, though the latter would be unusual for a fixed term and result, in practice, in the fixed term being effectively shortened to the notice period specified.

Breach of contract

5.36   Regulation 16 provides that the Regulations do not affect the application of any enactment or rules of law which provides for the immediate termination of the agency contract because of the failure of one party to carry out all or part of his obligations or where 'exceptional circumstances apply'. The only English law to which this could be referring is the laws on fundamental breach of contract which entitle the other party to terminate the contract forthwith and sue for damages. This is not enacted in any statute but is set out in case law and therefore is a rule of law. However, note the Regulations do not say compensation is payable in such cases – though this will often be the case (see regulation 18(a) below).

5.37   Nor, it is submitted, do the Regulations preclude parties to an agency contract providing rights to terminate in other cases, where the breach is not fundamental. Many commercial agreements provide for rights to terminate for breach which at common law would not be available. The breach is not fundamental. It does not go to the root of the contract, but the parties are still allowed to terminate by virtue of a contract term to that effect. Such rights to terminate are unaffected by the Regulations, though the agent may still be able to claim compensation if the contract is terminated because of a minor breach by the agent.

5.38   For details on when an agent can claim compensation after a termination for breach, see below. Regulation 17, which deals with payment of indemnity and compensation, is considered in Chapter 6. The reference in regulation 16 to 'exceptional circumstances', the Government says in its guidance notes, is thought to include matters falling within the doctrine of frustration. In a sense it does not matter much when regulation 16 applies or not. A contract may be frustrated. The agent may be in breach. However, regulation 16 does not state whether or not compensation is still payable.

When no indemnity or compensation is payable

5.39   Regulation 18 as amended provides that:

'The indemnity or compensation referred to in regulation 17 above shall not be payable to the commercial agent where:

(a)   the principal has terminated the agency contract because of default attributable to the commercial agent which would justify immediate termination of the agency contract pursuant to Regulation 16 above; or

(b)   the commercial agent has himself terminated the agency contract, unless such termination is justified:

(i)   by circumstances attributable to the principal, or

(ii)   on grounds of the age, infirmity or illness of the commercial agent in consequence of which he cannot reasonably be required to continue his activities; or

(c)   the commercial agent, with the agreement of his principal, assigns his rights and duties under the agency contract to another person.'

Each of these provisions is examined in turn below.

Breach by the agent

5.40   This is the most difficult and most important ground for the exclusion of a compensation payment. The agent's right to compensation is excluded where the principal terminates because the agent is in breach to such an extent that this would justify immediate termination pursuant to regulation 16 above. In the earlier draft of this regulation there was a reference to 'fundamental breach' which was removed. However, the breach must still be major. It must be enough to justify immediate termination. Does this have to be under common law or under the contract? There is no rule of law that a minor breach of contract entitles the principal to terminate. The point could be argued either way, as has been the practice.

5.41   It is advantageous for principals to specify in the agreement that a breach such as failure to meet minimum sales targets, or an agent taking on a competing line etc, is a breach which justifies immediate termination. Indeed, it would be better if those drafting such contracts did not give the agent the usual right to remedy a breach within 30 days as it is then not a breach which justifies immediate termination if it can be remedied. The law is unclear on what types of breaches exclude the regulations. The writer's example is agent stealing from the principal rather than slightly under performing. A failure to meet a target whilst expressed as material breach in an agreement may however be found by the court later to have been caused by a recession or other external factor or failure by the principal and does not therefore necessarily mean no compensation will be payable.

5.42   If an agent takes on a competing line, for example, that is likely to be a breach both of his obligation to act in good faith and also a breach of an express clause to that effect in the agreement. If he fails to meet a target by a minimal amount, such as £1, then it is likely compensation is still payable even if the contract says termination can then follow. If he failed to meet the target even by a large margin because of circumstances beyond his control, such as a market downturn or poor performance by the principal, then a compensation claim may still be entertained, it is submitted.

5.43   Most agency contracts do not specify well the duties of the agent. His sales levels may be falling off, but he is not in breach of any specific provision. In such cases he normally has a right to claim compensation. Most principals cannot believe this is correct. The entire concept of having to pay compensation when a freely entered-into contract comes to an end in accordance with its contractual provisions is an alien one under English law though many companies now appreciate that this is the law.

Case examples

Breach of contract

Spectrum Agencies v Crocs Europe BV **[2012] EWCA Civ 1400 (Court of Appeal)**

5.44   In this case the agent selling Crocs (shoes) was unhappy with its principal so published online the following:

'That's a Croc!! Of Shite!!

SPECTRUMS WAR OF LIGHT VS DARK

SOS to the stoned nether regions of the Netherlands, evil dark lord create partys to numb the brains of the workers but couldn't do the galactic job of putting shoes in boxes. Leaving the UK to fend off retailers fighting like storm troopers with phone & email abuse, they fought for a year with a promise of reinforcements. This was an evil plan to draw the UK into the dark abyss filled with Croshite ... in the intense battle that followed, we had offered the crown jewels of UK retail to the dark Lords who then shat all over the retail landscape, leaving behind the strewn waste of the spectrum crew. WE WILL SURVIVE battered, bruised but laughing.'

The principal sought to terminate the agency for breach. The court held that this was not bad enough to justify termination, although it was a breach of regulation 3 (to act in good faith) to criticise a principal.

At first instance the judge held that the claimant's breach was not sufficiently serious to be repudiatory and he found for the agent (damages to be assessed later). The first instance judge said:

'My conclusion here is that it was a breach of Spectrum's duty to BV to put the crawl [the statement above] onto the website, but that the seriousness of that breach fell a long way short of the seriousness required to entitle BV to terminate the agency. A reasonable person would not conclude that it showed an intention on the part of Spectrum not to fulfil the contract. The main factors in my reaching that conclusion are that the crawl was obviously intended to be humorous (and its scatology sounds worse in a court than in the world of the web); that its circulation was very limited, and to persons who would see the joke; that it was very unlikely that a retailer (or any other person seriously interested in Crocs) would see it unless they had the link; and that the situation at BV which was the subject of the crawl's Star Wars humour was well known to Crocs retailers.'

The appeal was dismissed. The Court of Appeal said:

'•   The Crawl did not in terms disparage the goods to any one. It referred to the inability of the defendant to meet delivery obligations, a state of affairs that was well known. The style of the Crawl was obviously jokey, though not everyone might see the joke and though the defendant was not amused. The circulation of the Crawl was limited and temporary. The website was soon shut down for other reasons and the Crawl was removed. The failure to give the requested assurance was not serious, if what the claimant had done was not in fact a serious breach. There was no evidence of harm suffered by the defendant.

•   In my judgment, the disparagement of the defendant in the Crawl was, as the judge held, a breach of contract, but it was not a breach (whether of regulation 3 or of the fiduciary duty under the general law) that went to the root of the agency relationship arising from the contract. It was more in the nature of a one-off incident that did not involve bad faith on the part of the claimant, was not shown to involve a real risk of harm to the defendant by dissemination to the world at large and did not, when viewed objectively, evince an intention to abandon or to refuse to perform the commercial agency contract.'

Gledhill v Bentley Designs (UK) Ltd [2010] EWHC 1965 (QB)

5.45   Here the agent in the furniture field did not want to start using email rather than fax. The principal said it would charge him £100 a month for the inconvenience. The agent emailed the principal:

'I just can't believe you. You are at your happiest when you are always causing grief for people and just try to sort of upset people, people would not support you, and I just think you are a horrible, despicable little man. I really do. I just think you are absolutely gutless. You have just taken £195 from me which covers the hotel, fair enough, and £100 twice plus the VAT. You just seem more intent on sort of ... as opposed to getting the business, the nitty gritty part, you seem more intent on causing trouble to people. I think you are an absolutely shit, I really do. You are a despicable, horrible little excuse for a human being.'

Here the court in a decision earlier than and a little at odds with the *Crocs* case above, held that the principal was entitled to terminate the agency and drew employment law analogies. Indeed, the second CA judgment in *Crocs* refers to employment case law and said the *Crocs* first instance decision might have gone either way and the Court of Appeal would not however interfere with the lower court's finding.

In the *Crocs* case the court does mention *Geldhill* in passing, summarising it as 'contents and tone of personally abusive comments by agent in voicemail and on mobile phone to managing director of principal a repudiatory breach damaging relationship of trust and confidence, which entitled the principal to terminate with immediate effect'.

5.46 In both *Crane v Sky In-Home Service Ltd* [2007] EWHC 66 (Ch) and *Green Deal Marketing Ltd v Economy Energy Trading Ltd* [2019] EWHC 507 the court looked at issues arising from termination for alleged breach of contract. The following passage from the *Green Deal* case below is useful:

'Regulation 16 provides in part:

"These Regulations shall not affect the application of any enactment or rule of law which provides for the immediate termination of the agency contract—

(a) because of the failure of one party to carry out all or part of his obligations under that contract; or ..."

On the facts as I have found them to be, GDM is entitled to compensation pursuant to regulation 17(6). The right to compensation is not excluded by regulation 18, because the termination of the contract by GDM was justified by circumstances attributable to EE, namely EE's renunciation of its obligations under the contract.

If I had reached a different conclusion as to EE's entitlement to terminate the contract by acceptance of a repudiatory breach by GDM, the question would have arisen whether the combined effect of regulation 18(a) and regulation 16(a) excluded the right to compensation. As to this, I comment as follows.

1) In *Rossetti Marketing Ltd v Diamond Sofa Company Ltd* [2012] EWCA Civ 1021, [2013] Bus LR 543, the Court of Appeal left open the question whether the right to compensation was excluded when the ground on which the principal could lawfully have terminated the contract was not known to it at the time of termination: see [58]–[60]. [Reference to paragraphs of the judgment in *Green Deal*]

2) As the Court of Appeal has recently reminded us in *W Nagel (a firm) v Pluczenik Diamond Company NV* [2018] EWCA Civ 2640, a case concerning the Regulations: "It is a principle of EU law that exceptions from the general scope of a Directive should be interpreted strictly, although not in such a way as to deprive the exceptions of their intended effect: see *Belgium v Temco Europe SA* (Case C-284/03) [2004] ECR I-11237, para 17; and (with specific reference to this Directive) *Volvo Car Germany GmbH v Autohof Weidensdorf GmbH* (Case C-203/09) [2012] Bus LR D13, para 42."

3) In *Volvo Car Germany GmbH v Autohof Weidensdorf GmbH* itself, the ECJ decided that an agent was not deprived of the right to an indemnity under the Directive "where the principal establishes a default by that agent which occurred after notice of termination of the contract was given but before the contract period expired and which was such as to justify immediate termination of the contract in question": see [45]. That point does not arise in the present

case. The Court was asked to answer the question whether Article 18(a) of the Directive, the source of regulation 18(a) of the Regulations, ought to be interpreted "as precluding national legislation under which a commercial agent is not entitled to an indemnity in the event of contractual termination of the contract by the principal if a serious ground for immediate termination of the contract because of the agent's default existed at the date of contractual termination but was not the cause of the termination?" However, it declined to answer that question on the ground that it was hypothetical on the facts of the case.

4)   However, the Court's reasoning in the *Volvo* case does have a bearing on the present case. First, the Court relied on the principle, mentioned above, that the exception was to be interpreted strictly. Second, it relied on the words "because of" in Article 18(a) of the Directive, which are repeated in regulation 18(a) of the Regulations, as an indication that "the legislature intended to require that there be a direct causal link between the default attributable to the commercial agent and the principal's decision to terminate the contract in order to deprive the commercial agent of the indemnity provided for in article 17 of the Directive": see [38]–[39].

5)   That reasoning is consistent with the reasoning of Briggs J in *Crane v Sky In-Home Service Ltd* [2007] EWHC 66 (Ch). In his discussion of regulation 18(a) at [82]–[92] he accepted the need for a causal link; see in particular [89]–[91]. For that reason, he did not consider that the right to compensation would be excluded where the principal did not know of the breach at the time of termination: see [90]. However, he did not consider that, for the right to be excluded, it was necessary that the principal should have purported to terminate on account of breach of contract or should even have terminated the contract summarily: see [85].

6)   I respectfully agree with the reasoning of Briggs J in *Crane*. The entitlement to compensation will be excluded only if (a) the principal terminates "because of" default attributable to the agent and (b) that default would justify immediate termination of the agency. A default of which the principal is unaware is unlikely to satisfy the causal requirement of the words "because of". Thus, for example, if the reappointment of Johnny Powell were a repudiatory breach of contract, EE could not be said to have terminated the contract "because of" that default, of which it knew nothing. It may perhaps be that circumstances could exist in which, even if a principal did not know of the breach of contract by the agent, its reasons for terminating the agency contract were such that the termination could nevertheless be said to be "because of" the default for the purposes of regulation 18. It is unnecessary for the purposes of this judgment to decide whether such circumstances could exist.

7)   The argument for EE is that it terminated the contract because of GDM's mis-selling and that the mis-selling justified immediate termination of the contract. As I have said, I accept that the mis-selling was a breach of contract but not that it justified immediate termination of the contract. If I considered that the mis-selling was repudiatory, I would have concluded that EE terminated the contract "because of" that default by GDM and that compensation was excluded by regulation 18(a). That is because the termination was a direct response to

Ofgem's attentions, which were themselves the consequence of GDM's mis-selling. In other words, EE terminated the contract because of mis-selling'. (His Honour Judge Keyser QC in *Green Deal*)

The issue of how bad a breach must be to preclude the application of the compensation provisions of the Regulations arises all the time in practice.

Where the agent terminates the agreement

5.47   Compensation is not usually payable where the agent terminates the contract. Agents are advised not to resign but to wait to be sacked, much as under employment law. Principals are advised to seek to persuade an agent to leave rather than have to sack him. Sometimes it is not clear the contract has been terminated and by whom. The parties have a row. One says 'I never want to see you again' or another says 'That's it, I'm finished'. Is the contract terminated? Regulation 15 does not require that notice of termination be in writing though it is always advisable, except where one party wants to retract a verbal notice, to follow up a verbal notice immediately by one in writing with the precise termination date given in the written notice.

Constructive termination

5.48   Compensation is still payable, even where the agent resigns, where under regulation 18(b)(i) the contract was terminated because of circumstances attributable to the principal. An agent may, for example, not have been paid commission for 12 months. The principal is in breach of contract. The agent terminates and still can claim compensation under the Regulations. The words 'circumstances attributable to the principal' are not very clear but they are intended to cover the position where the principal is at fault and that fault justifies the termination.

5.49   If the principal has reduced commission substantially, or removed an important and lucrative customer from the agent's list, or changed the agent's area so that he will earn less money, then the agent may be justified in terminating and claiming compensation. However, agents should consider this very carefully indeed. A reduced commission for the next 20 years may be better than two years of litigation to obtain compensation which the agent may not win and may not be able to fund the legal costs. If the principal makes a minor change to the contract, such as taking out part of a region but giving the agent a comparable additional area in exchange, then it may not be 'justified' for the agent to terminate and he may have no right to compensation.

5.50   In *Page v Combined Shipping and Trading Co Ltd* [1997] 3 All ER 656 the court had an example, examined later in this chapter, of an agent terminating in circumstances attributable to the principal (the principal was in repudiatory breach of contract in saying its operations would be closed down, so the agent accepted the breach and sued for damages.) The Court of Appeal did not disagree and held there would be an entitlement under the Regulations.

5.51   In *Vick v Vogle-Gapes Ltd* [2006] EWHC 1665 (QB) the judge quoted from an earlier decision in this area and supported the previous judge's findings:

> 'It was common ground that, if I found that Mr. Vick repudiated the Agency Agreement and thereby brought the agreement to an end, he was entitled neither to damages at common law nor to compensation under the Commercial Agents Regulations. So far as the latter was concerned, in *Bell Electric Ltd v Aweco Appliance Systems GmbH & Co KG* [2002] EWHC 872 (QB) Mr. Justice Elias had to consider the effect of Regulation 18 of the Commercial Agents Regulations in a situation in which a commercial agent terminated his agreement with his principal in circumstances in which he was not entitled to treat the principal as having repudiated the agreement at common law. That, of course, is this case, on my findings. The learned Judge's consideration of the issue was:

>> "52.   Mr Coppel submits that in this case the agency contract was terminated by his client, the commercial agent, who was justified in so doing by circumstances attributable to the principal, within the meaning of reg 18(b)(i). He submits that even if the claimant had acted precipitately so as to preclude himself from being able to recover damages at common law, nonetheless, looking at the matter as one of substance, the claimant had been justified in bringing the contract to an end because of the failure by the defendant to pay commission over such a lengthy period of time. Whatever technical rules might exclude his entitlement to recover under English law, they should not affect his rights under the regulations.

>> 53.   Mr Tolley, for the defendant, submitted that the dual effect of regulation 16 and 18, when read together, is that when determining whether a termination is justified under 18(b)(i), it is necessary to apply precisely the same principles as operate at common law. In other words, if the agent is not justified in terminating the contract at common law, because he has affirmed the contract and made an election which leaves him only with his right to damages, then he cannot be any more justified within the meaning of reg 18(b)(i) to terminate the contract pursuant to the regulations.

>> 54.   The drafting of the regulations gives no clear answer as to which construction is correct. Reg 18(a) in terms refers to the case where the principal is entitled to terminate the contract and says that such termination is justified if it would be permitted pursuant to regulation 16. In fact, it seems to me that an agency contract would never be terminated pursuant to regulation 16, since that does not provide any right to terminate which did not otherwise exist. On the contrary, all that provision is doing is preserving such existing common law rules as permit the contract immediately to be terminated because of the failure of the defaulting party to carry out his obligation under the contract. I take it that regulation 18 (a)(i) is intending simply to indicate that there will be no right to compensation where the principal has terminated the

agency contract in circumstances where at common law he would have been entitled to do so because of the agent's failure to carry out his side of the bargain. One might have thought that 18(b) would be intended to preserve the right to compensation in precisely the same circumstances. Surprisingly, however, it does not in terms make reference to regulation 16 in the way in which reg 18(a) does. The reason for this may be that regulation 18(b)(ii) provides for justified termination for reasons which do not involve breaches by the principal at all. That would not have prevented some reference to regulation 16 in 18(b)(i), however, and in the circumstances that would have clarified the position. Nevertheless, in my judgment the better view is that regulations 18(a) and 18(b)(i) ought to be seen as the reverse sides of the same coin. In other words, the compensation is not payable if the principal terminates in circumstances which would be justifiable at common law because of the agent's conduct; but on the other hand it is payable if the commercial agent terminates in circumstances which are justifiable at common law because of the conduct of the principal. ..."

I respectfully agree with the analysis of Mr Justice Elias and consider that the agreement of the parties on the point as to no compensation being payable in the situation with which I am concerned is sound.'

5.52   In *Scottish Power Energy Recall Ltd v Task Force Contracts Ltd* [2008] ScotCS CSOH 110 the agreement gave the principal the right to terminate the agreement if one major client terminated (Sainsbury's) which at the start and throughout was 92% of the business. The agent stopped work when Sainsbury's work gone. Principal wrote to the agent requiring him to start work. He refused and when the matter came to court the court said that the agreement itself was not terminated as the parties had allowed for the possibility in its terms that this 92% customer might cease its business with the principal and the 8% left could continue and thus there was no compensation. The drop-in business to such a low level was not tantamount to termination.

Case example – *Turner v Steinhoff UK Furniture Ltd* [2006] Eu LR 50

5.53   In a case in which Singletons, the author's firm, represented the defendant, *Turner v Steinhoff UK Furniture Ltd*, the court held that lack of supplies did amount to termination. The agent was awarded two months' commission for lack of notice and 15 months' gross commission for compensation and examined the list of then relevant factors for compensation in *Tigana* (this was before the *Lonsdale* (HL) decision).

5.54   The agent was held to have a right to terminate and claim compensation when deprived of product to sell for a relatively short period. The agents knew stocks of products would be exhausted by July 2003. In July 2003 the principal wrote saying new product would be available from September 2003. The judge accepted there was old product to sell to end of August and new product from

September. However, it was held to be an implied term of the agency contract (on the basis of business necessity) that the agent will have goods to sell or offer for sale. The principal's case was that 'there was a mere hiatus of a few months of product shortage' and this was not accepted.

Case example – *Simpson v Grant & Bowman Ltd* [2006] Eu LR 933

5.55   In this case in which Singletons, the author's firm, represented the defendant, the agent wanted changes to his contract which were refused, and he therefore terminated his contract and claimed compensation. It was held that there had been no entitlement for the agent to terminate so no compensation was due.

Case example – *Mann v Flair* (unreported, 15 December 2005)

5.56   In this case the court held that having no products to sell was termination but as the agent rejected a without prejudice offer which was more than she was ultimately awarded she paid costs and ended up with a net loss. *Michael Devane of Martin Shepherd & Co solicitors acted for the Principal with Oliver Segal as counsel.*

Case example – *Claramoda Ltd v Zoomphase Ltd (t/a Jenny Packham)* [2009] EWHC 2857 (Comm)

5.57   In this claim for compensation following the termination of an agency contract, the Court held that the contract between a clothing manufacturer and its agent was not terminated when the agent ceased to negotiate sales.

Age

5.58   If the agent terminates because of age 'in consequence of which he cannot reasonably be required to continue his activities', then he has a right to compensation. Agents sometimes ask if that means they can decide when they would like to retire and claim a lump sum accordingly. A decision in November 2004 appears to suggest they can – see below. If the principal sacks the agent because he has reached a certain age the agent *can* claim compensation. If the agent decides to go when he reaches, say 60 or 65, then it had been thought he would receive nothing unless he is so old he cannot reasonably be required to continue. The court have now decided that merely being 65 is sufficient to enable the agent effectively to cash in his or her asset of the goodwill of the agency.

5.59   *Abbott v Condici Ltd* [2005] 2 Lloyds Rep 450 held that an agent was entitled to compensation in such a case. In that case the agent retired from both his agencies on reaching age 65 years. The court said that age 65 years is 'embedded as a retirement milestone' and it was reasonable he should pick that age even though he was fit enough to carry on.

5.60   In the *Skingsley* case mention was made of the fact the agent was 61 and would have been likely to work until he was 65 and this was relevant in assessing the compensation to which he might be entitled, but that is not the same issue. Although in theory the agent would have to be too old to continue before a right to compensation arises in practice, the case law suggests any reasonable retirement age is acceptable. At 65 he may have years of service left for him. Indeed, the author has known several cases which have settled where the agent was well over 60 and indeed in his 80s in one case, and compensation was obtained by the agent who had been told to go against his will, which is the converse situation. The agent over 80 had a doctor prepared to certify he was fit and well and able to carry on. Where the agent wants to retire at around 65 years, compensation appears to be available; whereas where he chooses to retire early, at say 55 years (assuming he is not also ill), then he may not be able to claim compensation.

5.61   The more frequent case is that where the principal wants to be rid of the older agent. The agent may not be pulling his weight any more, and may be relying on repeat orders and have been with the company for 30 years. He may be earning a lot of commission and it would be expensive to get rid of him. Whether the contract specifies a retirement age or not the agent can claim compensation when he is dismissed because of age. Even employment law has now been changed, such that fixed retirement ages are unlawful in employment contracts and employees can carry on as long as they are able and willing. However, age discrimination legislation in the Equality Act 2010 is complex and legal advice should always be sought as it is not the same as other equality legislation.

5.62   State retirement age for men and women is harmonised and age discrimination is unlawful. Some people live into their 80s and it is in the interests of the hugely increasing retired population that those paying tax and national insurance contributions do so for as long as possible.

5.63   The agency contract should normally, however, include a retirement age. If it specifies, say, 65 years and the agent is told to leave on that date, in many cases he will go without objection so it might work in practice. However, if the agent wants to carry on and he capable of so doing then despite the contractual retirement age he can make a compensation claim. This is similar to the position under fixed term contracts when if the fixed term expires it appears the agent can still claim compensation thereafter (other than where the principal offers another fixed term to run on the same basis immediately thereafter), or where the principal has given the notice period required under the Regulations and the agent still can claim compensation. It may, though, be easier to convince a judge that nothing is payable if there is a specified retirement age than if there is no upper limit at all.

5.64   Where there are partners who are together the 'agent' then the contract should specify what happens when one reaches retirement age and the other does not. In those cases, one of the agents could continue alone so no compensation should be payable.

5.65   Agents contemplating retirement may prefer to appoint sub-agents to act under them, where the agreement allows this or indeed does not restrict it, so that they continue to earn from the agency after they cease doing most of the work. They may also like to consider assigning their agency for a lump sum to someone else. Many bring their children into the business and let them take over. If the agent is a limited company, then the age provisions do not apply and termination by the agent (save where the principal is in breach) means the agent cannot make a compensation claim. The writer has had several agent clients pulled in one direction by the legal advantages of having limited liability (the tax advantages of having a company have now largely gone due to recent changes in dividend tax law, except where the company is used to spread income around a family where some people are not tax payers or lower rate tax payers) – and in the other by wanting the rights to compensation on death, old age and illness to apply only to individuals not companies. Agents cannot have it both ways and need to pick one or other legal status. Some do tactically plan to their best advantage by disincorporating as they become old or incorporating if they wish to bring their son or daughter into the business ready for when they are too old to continue. Where there is no written contract it can be difficult to ascertain who is the agent. Asking where the commission revenue is paid and for the exact name of the entity on the bank statement is usually helpful.

5.66   Government guidance notes on the Regulations ask 'Can an age limit be fixed for a commercial agent?' and state that 'it is thought that it can. Fixed term contracts are permitted and if, for example, a 40-year old agent is appointed 'until he is 60' this is equivalent to a fixed contract for 20 years or until death'. It now appears, however, that compensation or an indemnity would have to be paid. Bear in mind that the guidance has not been updated for years.

5.67   The *Abbott v Condici Ltd* [2005] 2 Lloyds Rep 450 retirement case, mentioned above at para **5.59**, is summarised at http://www.agentlaw.co.uk/site/case_summaries/abbott_v_condici.html.

5.68   This case, like very many others, was brought by the Professional Sales Agents Association (now part of Unite – the trade union) for their members. The court decided that 'if the agent was over 65, they were of such an age where they could be entitled to compensation or indemnity for the agency's loss'. As the PSA said there had been a great deal of debate over what exactly would be an age:

'where you could not reasonably be expected to continue. It needs to be remembered that there is no legislation that applies to the self-employed which determines this issue and hence you would have to prove purely on grounds of the number of candles on your birthday cake that you could not continue. Therefore, the fit and healthy 80 year old would, until this decision, have had difficulty in proving that his age stopped him doing his job. Critics of the legislation argue why an agent should receive anything when he/she decides to leave. The simple answer is to stop thinking of an agent as the equivalent of an employee and consider them more along the lines of them being a small company with just one employee. When that employee retires, becomes too ill or dies, obviously that company has to close and liquidate its assets. The legislation therefore simply states that the organisations this agent works for have the obligation to buy this company's assets as it relates to them in the form of the goodwill.'

5.69 Another case which reached trial on retirement age issues was *Frape v Emreco International Ltd* [2002] Eu LR 10. In that case the agency contract provided the agreement would terminate when the agent reached 65 years of age, as many such contracts do. As Fox Williams solicitors say on their note on the case:

'Unfortunately and as a result of the way in which the judge treated the termination of the relationship, Frape provides no guidance as to an appropriate retirement age or what is meant by the phrase 'cannot reasonably be required to continue' in the Regulations.

If a principal wishes to provide for an agent's retirement at a certain age, as Emreco did, the principal should bear in mind that the UK is obliged to implement European legislation against age discrimination by 2006. Accordingly, from 2006 the agent may have a claim against the principal for age discrimination as well as a claim under the Regulations.'

See also http://www.agentlaw.co.uk/site/briefing_notes/sickness_wealth.html.

5.70 It appears from the *Abbott* (2005) and *Frape* (2002) cases that the courts are amenable to awarding compensation to an agent where he is told to cease work at 65 because the contract provides for retirement at that age. It also appears after *Abbott* (para **5.59** above) that an agent choosing to cease work at 65, even if he has no written contract or even if his contract provided a retirement age of 70 (or even 50 but he had continued working after that with consent), can effectively cash in his chips. It is almost a case that the principal effectively has to buy out the agent's business/goodwill at a date of the agent's choosing once the agent has reached statement retirement age (currently 65 but in due course rising to 67 and beyond) but that the agent may continue to 85 plus if he is performing his duties well enough.

5.71 Agents and principals should think ahead and plan carefully how they will handle retirement voluntarily or otherwise of individual commercial agents.

Illness and infirmity

5.72   The rules are the same for infirmity and illness. If the agent resigns because he is too ill or infirm reasonably to be able to carry on, he can claim compensation. This seems very unfair to principals as it is not their fault the agent is ill. The agent could be obliged by a contract term to insure his own health with the proceeds of the policy written in trust for the principal and the agent obliged to pay the premiums. Alternatively, some principals could tack agents on to their in-company health insurance benefits scheme. This can reduce the risk of a principal having to pay a large sum in compensation when an agent falls ill. In some cases, the agent can arrange a sub-agent to carry on the activities where the contract does not restrict this. In other cases that is forbidden.

5.73   If the agent is likely to be ill for only a short time, then temporary cover could be arranged. If the agent's activities do not require him to do much more than make telephone calls, he may be able to do this from home despite particular illnesses. Principals may like to require agents to submit to health checks before taking them on because of these provisions in the same way that many companies require employees to be examined by a company doctor before they are hired. Agents whose health is failing because, for example, they are very over-weight may be given the benefit of company fitness programmes and health advice.

5.74   The contract may also specify that the agent must notify the principal if he is going to be off sick for an extended period. Often principals will not see their agents for long periods, unlike their employees, so monitoring their health becomes difficult. In cases of doubt doctors' advice will need to be obtained. As with age, if the agent is a partnership and one partner is ill and the other is not, then this provision would not apply as the other part of the partnership could continue the relevant duties.

5.75   If the agent is not fulfilling the contract terms, eg not meeting targets, and the principal sacks him before he can declare he is too ill to carry on, then the principal may succeed in avoiding a compensation claim because the termination is for breach. On the other hand, if the principal sympathetically waits as the agent's health declines until the agent resigns on ill health grounds, then the agent is entitled to compensation. The Regulations do not reward beneficence on the part of paternalistic principals. It is possible that in the former case where the termination is for breach, but the breach is caused by the agent's illness, the agent may still succeed in a claim, though this has not been tested in the courts.

Assignment

5.76   If the agent, with the principal's agreement, assigns his agency to someone else then there is no right to compensation under regulation 18(c) of the Regulations. The principle behind this is that the agent will receive a lump sum and therefore is not entitled to be paid twice for the agency termination. However, the regulation makes no reference to payment so if the agent has assigned the agreement for no payment, he is still not entitled to claim compensation. This is supported in the Scottish case of *King v Tunnock* [1999] 1 All ER 1946 where the court said 'Thus if son succeeds father as agent carrying on as before with the principal's blessing then no compensation will be due to the father'.

5.77   *Rossetti Marketing Ltd v Diamond Sofa Company Ltd* [2002] EWCA Civ 1021 also looked at whether an agreement had been assigned but found it had been novated instead with a new agreement set up. However, despite that, as the old agent had transferred the agency to the new agent, it was still treated as falling under regulation 18(c) due to the words in that regulation.

5.78   If a typical straight construction under the English law rules were taken to regulation 18(c), then where a contract term stated that on expiry of a fixed term agency agreement the agent must assign to the principal's nominee for no money, no compensation is payable. This is an artificial device relying on the clear wording of regulation 18 but completely undermines the purpose of the Regulations. Given that the implementing EU law takes a different, more purposive approach than English law, it is unlikely that such a clause would work in avoiding compensation being payable.

5.79   Similarly, the clause appears only to apply where the agent assigns with consent. If he assigns without consent and receives a massive lump sum either in a case where consent is not needed (English law contracts can be assigned as to their benefits, but not the burden of the contract, without consent unless the contract says otherwise), or where consent should have been obtained but was not, then he is still entitled to claim compensation under regulation 18(c) because of the way it is worded. Again, it is likely a court would look beyond the strict wording, either saying that the absence of a requirement in the contract for obtaining of consent amounts to the 'agreement of the principal', or on the basis that the intention is that if the agent has benefited from the assignment then he cannot claim again by way of compensation.

5.80   In some countries such as Germany a new agent may be required to pay a sum up front as an assignment fee to take on an old agent's contract and to pay the indemnity of the old agent. This practice could also occur in the UK if agents can be persuaded of its merits. It is not standard practice here now.

Death

5.81   The agent's estate is entitled to claim compensation on his death. Regulation 17(8) provides that entitlement to an indemnity or compensation exists 'where the agency contract is terminated as a result of the death of the commercial agent'. It is hard to assess the value of compensation payable on death, which is examined in the next chapter. Principals can protect themselves by insuring the life of the agent or requiring the agent to do so and having the proceeds of the policy written in trust for the principal with premiums paid by the agent. Agents could be included in schemes covering employees for death in service, where the scheme rules allow. The amount for which to insure is hard to calculate – perhaps up to one or two year's commission is all that would be required and this may depend on whether the agent's contract specifies an indemnity, in which case there is a maximum of a year's commission as a ceiling.

5.82   Solicitors in probate departments of law firms need to ensure they remember an agent's rights on his death, as otherwise the firm may be negligent in not recommending that the estate makes a claim. The Manufacturers' Agents' Association (MAA) issues cards which agent members can keep with their will to notify heirs of the rights to claim agency compensation or indemnity payments on death.

5.83   If one of two or more partners dies there will be no right to compensation, unless perhaps there is a contractual term that the entire contract would then terminate. In their guidance notes on the Regulations the Government looks at whether a company going into liquidation would be treated in the same way as an agent who dies, where the agent is incorporated. They say:

> 'Where the principal or agent is a company, at common law the actual authority of the principal or agent will be determined by its winding up or dissolution. It should be noted that where the authority is irrevocable it will not be determined by such events.'

5.84   This is not very helpful. As a company cannot die, the express right to compensation in such cases would not apply. However, if the agreement does terminate on liquidation, as most contracts provide, then the liquidator may be able to make a claim, if the principal exercises its right to terminate. Instead the principal may be advised to wait and see if the liquidator can assign the agency to another company or keep the company going through an injection of new money and thus the principal could avoid the payment of compensation.

5.85   There have been no reported cases on death. In one unreported case concerning an agent in Ireland 'M', the agent only left his family enough money to pay the costs of his burial on death. One of his principals pestered the family for repayment regarding some bad debts of the agency and the Professional Sales Agents Association (now part of Unite, the trade union) advised the compensation on death sum was well in excess of that figure. They obtained payment of a year's commission for the family.

Expiry of a fixed term

5.86   There is nothing in the Regulations to suggest that no compensation is payable where a fixed term contract expires. Regulation 17(7) provides that when assessing compensation, one looks at the commission of which the agent had been deprived which 'proper performance' of the agency contract would have procured for him. If a contract expires then has it not been properly performed, as indeed one could say if proper notice were given? The case law does not suggest this is correct (see *Page v Combined Shipping and Trading Co Ltd*, [1997] 3 All ER 656). In English law 'expiry' occurs naturally when a contract comes to its fixed period's end. Termination requires an active step. Regulation 17(1) says the agent is entitled to compensation on 'termination'. Expiry may be something different. The author's view is that such a pedantic English construction point is not going to succeed with legislation which is based on EU law and the intention that agents be compensated when a contract ends, though the fact the contract is for a fixed term may reduce, or in some cases extend, the compensation paid.

5.87   In *Duncan Moore v Piretta* [1999] 1 All ER 174 the judge stated that 'It is to be noted that the grounds upon which the right to indemnity or compensation can be excluded do not include the expiry of the term of the agency contract or the expiry and renewal or agency contracts'.

5.88   *Duffen v FRA* [2000] Lloyd's Rep 180 concerned an agent appointed under a contract which was for a minimum period of four years. The agreement was dated 1 August 1994 and was terminated by letter dated 11 December 1996 – about half way into the four-year term. The agent was paid a £4000 per month retainer and commission. The case was mostly about a penalty clause which was held invalid under common law. However, the court agreed the agent was entitled to rely on the Regulations to top up his common law entitlement to damages.

5.89   In *Page v Combined Shipping and Trading Co Ltd* [1997] 3 All ER 656, the agent was appointed under a fixed five-year contract and contract was terminated before that period was up and a claim made.

5.90   *Tigana Ltd v Decoro Ltd* [2003] is examined in Chapter 6 as regards what it says concerning assessment of compensation payable on termination of an agency agreement. However, it is also relevant to this section as it resulted in a court award of compensation in a situation where the agency agreement was a fixed term contract which had merely expired, not terminated. It laid rest to any argument that under English law a principal could argue on a literal reading of the words of the Regulations no claim to compensation would then lie. The judge very helpfully quoted from two other earlier cases too and declined to raise the matter with the European court:

'In *Whitehead v Jenks & Cattell Engineering Ltd* [1999] Eu LR 827 Judge Alton (sitting as a Judge of the High Court) in a carefully reasoned decision held that Regulation 17 of the Agency Regulations was apposite to include agency contracts which expired by effluxion of time. She placed – as would I – considerable emphasis on the fact that "termination", depending on the context, variously may be focusing on the time of cessation of the contract or may be focusing on the mechanism by which the contract is brought to an end; and on the use of that word in the former sense in Regulations 8 and 20. Likewise, in the Scottish case of *Frape v Emreco International Ltd* [2002] Eu LR 10, Lord McEwan (sitting in the Court of Session, Outer House), who placed particular emphasis on the policy behind the Directive and on the requirement to seek to construe the Agency Regulations purposively so as to fulfil the policy behind the Directive, reached a similar conclusion. As he put it, the word "termination" was, in this context, 'habile' to cover agency contracts which expire through effluxion of time. He expressly agreed with the decision of Judge Alton. I agree with the conclusion of each of Judge Alton and Lord McEwan.

I would only add (although it is not strictly, I think, relevant) that in this case, in practical terms, as a matter of mechanism the Sales Agreement was brought to an end by the decision of Decoro. True it is that in law the contract expired by effluxion of time, no agreement for renewal having been reached as provided by Clause 1. But the mutual hope and expectation at the outset of the agency was, I am satisfied, that the agency would last for considerably more than a year (that indeed in part explains the existence of Clause 6): and Mr Coleman wished it to continue. In the circumstances, it did not: Decoro unilaterally communicating its intention not to renew the contract by its letters of December 1999. I find it wholly unsurprising that Regulation 17 (and Article 17) should provide for compensation on effluxion of the Sales Agreement in such circumstances.

In my judgment, as a matter of interpretation of the Agency Regulations by reference to their intrinsic terms; as a matter of interpretation of the Agency Regulations by reference to their (and the Directive's) perceived purpose and policy; and on consideration of the authorities to which my attention is drawn, the answer to the question raised is clear. Since all the arrows point in the same direction, that is the direction I propose to follow. Accordingly, I decline to direct a reference to the European Court of Justice for a preliminary ruling; and I hold that Regulation 17 is capable of applying, and does apply, on the expiry of the Sales Agreement by effluxion of time on 31 December 1999 (at paras 81–83).'

5.91   In *Cooper, Watkins, Bartle v Pure Fishing (UK) Ltd* (2004) LTL, 18 March 2004, CA the courts looked at termination and expiry. The principal said it was not renewing the agency agreements concerned because of breach of contract on the part of the agent. Had the principal merely terminated for breach there would have been no compensation. Instead the court said that regulation 18 did not apply and the agents could claim compensation. It was not termination because of default. Had they terminated earlier they would have avoided any compensation. The case seems to have been based on the principal that failure to renew an expired fixed term agency agreement does result in compensation being payable but an earlier termination for breach would have removed the entitlement to compensation.

5.92   The practical advice following this case is to terminate as soon as there is a breach and do not wait for an annual review of performance linked to renewal of a fixed term contract. This is a rather harsh and artificial decision.

A summary of the case is online at http://business.highbeam.com/437582/ article-1G1-201710628/cooper-watkins-and-bartle-v-pure-fishing-limited.

5.93   *Stuart Light v Ty Europe Ltd* [2003] EWCA Civ 1238 also looked at this issue and the Court of Appeal stated:

> 'Since the judge's decision in this case [in the court below] and the two cases on which he relied there is now a fourth case in which courts in the UK have decided that Regulation 17 applies to agreements which come to an end by effluxion of time. The fourth case is *Tigana Ltd v Decoro* [2003] EWHC 23 (QB), [2003] EuLR 189, a decision of Davis J. He dealt with this point between paragraphs 71 and 83 of his judgment. He said that all the intrinsic indications were that "termination" in Regulation 17 meant no more than "come to an end". A purposive construction reinforced this view since there could be no policy or purpose for excluding contracts which expire by effluxion of time in Regulations designed to protect commercial agents.
>
> > "I find Davis J's reasons compelling. I think the word 'termination' is used in an intransitive sense meaning no more than 'comes to an end'. If it had been intended to exclude agency contract which comes to an end by effluxion of time, Regulation 18 could have said so. The inclusion of termination on the grounds of age, infirmity etc makes clear the sense in which the word is used. There is no reason why agents whose contracts which come to an end by effluxion of time should not be afforded the protection of the Regulations."'

5.94   The second judge in the decision also considered this decision and said:

> 'Turning to the second issue, in my judgment the answer given by Davis J in *Tigana Ltd v Decoro* [2003] EuLR 189 is compelling. In my judgment Article 17 and Regulation 17 are apt to provide for payment of compensation where the agency agreement between the principal and the commercial agent expired automatically at the end of a fixed period because: (1) the characteristic of a commercial agent entitled to the protection of the Directive is (as reflected in the schedule to the Regulations) that his services rendered during the period of his agency agreement will continue to produce profits for his principal after his agency agreement has terminated; and (2) it is the purpose of the Directive (and in particular Article 17) to secure that, unless (as provided in Article 18) the principal has terminated the agency agreement because of default by the commercial agent or the agent has himself terminated the agency agreement without justification, the commercial agent shall have a share of these post-termination profits.
>
> The word "terminate" in the context of the Directive is apt to include the situation where an agency contract expires by effluxion of time. It is sufficient for this purpose to refer to Article 20.2 which provides that a restraint of trade clause shall be valid for not more than two years after termination of the agency contract. The term "termination" in this Article must plainly include expiration by effluxion of time. This conclusion may place a premium on a principal, when sufficient grounds exist, terminating an agency contract on grounds of default as provided for in Article 18 prior to expiration of the agreement by effluxion of time rather than allowing the agency contract to run its full course.'

Case example – *McQuillan v McCormick* [2010] EWHC 1112, QB

5.95   Here the agreement could be terminated within two years and that was held by the court to mean the agency was worth less than otherwise might be the case in terms of assessment of compensation – see Chapter 6. There has been criticism of this case, however.

Termination on notice

5.96   The Regulations entitle the agent to compensation or an indemnity even where the full period of notice has been given of termination as required under the contract. This is a substantial departure from English freedom of contract law and one with which companies have found it difficult to come to terms. They follow the contract to the letter as agreed and signed by the agent and still have to hand over a large lump sum on compensation. They argue the agent has already been paid for his efforts during the term by his commission. Why should they pay again? Agents argue conversely that they have built up a business for the principal from which the principal will benefit from years to come and they are therefore entitled to their share on termination. The Directive and Regulations support the agent's position on these matters.

Termination on sale of a business or sale of shares

5.97   Some terminations occur where a principal sells his business to another principal. The author has advised in several cases of this type. The solicitors acting for the principal and the buyer of the business need to consider the Regulations just as much as (for employees only) the Transfer of Undertakings (Protection of Employment) Regulations 2006 (TUPE) which apply to employees perhaps laid off as part of such a deal. Sometimes business purchase agreements need to be examined.

1.   If shares are sold then the agency agreement continues and no termination occurs.

2.   If part of a business is sold off the benefit of the agent's customer list is being transferred.

3.   If the principal sacks the agent before the sell-off, the principal must pay the compensation not the new owner of the business.

4.   If the new owner takes the agent on then the agent may suffer no loss, indeed the agency contract may be assigned. There is no compensation.

5.   If the new owner offers the agent a new contract which he turns down, his compensation from the old principal may be less because he has not properly mitigated his loss.

6. The business transfer agreement may require disclosure of commercial agreements such as agency contracts, and existing legal disputes such as agency disputes. When the agent makes a claim the warranties may need to be examined to see what transfer, if any, of the agency agreement took place.

7. The agency agreement will be freely assignable by the principal unless there is a restriction to this effect, so that the agent may find himself obliged to work for a new principal.

5.98 Often there is simply a transfer of ownership of shares in which case the agency continues but the new owner wants to be rid of the agents. When he dismisses them they make compensation claims against the new principal to whom the contracts have been assigned. The old contracts continue.

5.99 If instead a business has been transferred and the agents offered new contracts with the new principal, there is then a debate about whether an earlier period of service with the old principal is counted. It is possible that the courts would count such service, but not clear as there is no equivalent of the EU Acquired Rights Directive in relation to such matters. However, some employment cases have held agency workers employees for certain purposes of the ultimate client. This is a current trend which has emerged from EU law. Some individuals are 'workers' under EU law with some workers' rights but are self employed for tax purposes. Other workers are employees paid under PAYE. A third category (like this book's author) are sole traders who are purely self employed and are neither employees nor workers for tax or employment purposes. It can be seen in the protection given to 'workers' not just employees in the Public Interest Disclosure Act 1998 and the Working Time Regulations 1998, SI 1998/1833. In certain cases, agents may benefit more under employment law than under the Regulations. These developments should be watched with interest. Chapter 1 looked at the distinction between true agents and agents who are employees.

5.100 In theory if an agent is taken on by the company acquiring a business, rather than someone buying shares in an existing company, there will be a new contract and perhaps time starts to run again. It is the next chapter where length of service and compensation are examined, and it is not always the case that length of service makes a difference to the amount of compensation.

5.101 Frequently there are changes of name of a principal which of course do not affect any claim. Sometimes employees with twenty years' service or more become agents after a while. It is only their period as agent which will count under the Regulations. Sometimes they are designated agents at a later stage but in law are in fact still employees. In any termination situation the first stage is to assess the legal status of the person – employee, agent or distributor – so that the correct legislation can be examined.

5.102 If a business is transferred and the agents laid off by the old principal, the old principal will seek to argue that the agent's entitlement to compensation is reduced or removed because the principal would not have carried on benefiting from the agent's customers as he has sold them off to the new buyer. This is unfair to the agent who is not responsible for that sale. The principal has deliberately reduced his future income from the 'agent's' customers but may well have been paid a very large lump sum by the buyer of the business. The agent is entitled to ask what proportion of the sum paid represents the business he has built up and may see the business transfer agreement on disclosure stage in the litigation. If the principal failed to take account of any agency payoffs in his negotiations with the buyer, that is his fault and the agent should not suffer for it. If his solicitor forgot to mention that type of liability the solicitor may have been negligent. Solicitors should ensure that checklists for business and share sales make mention of the Regulations.

5.103 Sometimes the sellers of a business are taken on as agents/consultants for a year after they were paid for the business and then the agency agreement terminated and then they claim compensate. There may be an argument they have already been paid for the goodwill unless they have built up more in their subsequent year of service.

5.104 Sometimes the agent will take on employees in order to perform the agency agreement. When the agency is terminated and a new agent taken on, or the old one taken on as employee of the principal, the employees of the agent may be able to argue this is a 'service provision change' under TUPE and the employment contracts automatically move over to the new agent or the principal/company. Indeed, there may need to be compulsory consultation in advance of the change under employment law in such cases. The principal may have sacked an agent with useless employees to take on a better agent only to find itself saddled with the previous employees. One suggestion by solicitors at Wedlake Bell is:

> 'In order to avoid such a disruptive and potentially expensive situation, the terms of the contract with the commercial agent should ensure that the agent (if an individual) does not have the authority to appoint employees to work on the services provided to the principal. Alternatively, that any employees employed by the agent are "rotated" so that, on any termination of the agency agreement, the agent's employees cannot claim that they are "assigned" (under TUPE) to work on the contract that the agent has with the principal ("rotation" may also be appropriate if the agent is a corporate entity with existing employees); or, if such employees are to be "assigned", that the agent gives appropriate indemnities in respect of any liability the principal or new agent may incur if it decides to dismiss the inherited employees.'
> (see http://bit.ly/1Enheg1).

Another article on TUPE and commercial agency is at http://www.agentlaw.co.uk/site/briefing_notes/tupe_commercial_agents.html.

Business closed

5.105 In *King v Tunnock* [2000] IRLR 569, the principal 'for sound financial reasons, decided to close their bakery'. The pursuer (Scottish claimant – the agent) suffered financially and the principal 'did not continue to benefit from [his] past activities'. There may be a distinction in law between those who close a loss-making business of which the agent is a part, in which case the agent's compensation may be very little if anything and those who sell off a profitable business for a lump sum and sack the agent in the process, in which case the agent may be able to claim compensation.

5.106 In *Page v Combined Shipping and Trading Co Ltd* [1997] 3 All ER 656 the agent had a complex agreement relating to the sale of commodities. The principal informed the agent that its parent company, Tiger Oats Ltd, had decided to disinvest in the operations of the principal. This meant that the principal's activities had to end. Employees were offered redundancy payments, as they were in *King v Tunnock* [2000] IRLR 569, but not agents. Mr Page took this as repudiation of the agreement by the principal. The agreement should have lasted for four years and had only been signed five months before he received this news. He wrote accepting the conduct as repudiation of the agreement. He began a claim for damages for repudiation. He hung on to goods worth £300,000 to set against his claim. He was allowed to do this on appeal to the Court of Appeal. His compensation claim under the Regulations was recognised.

5.107 One issue in the case was in relation to common law damages. The principal could have operated the agreement so that no commission was payable. Of course, they would have been silly to do so and it would have been very unlikely they would have done so. At first instance the judge thought this was enough to disentitle the agent from holding back the £300,000 of stock. The court said that one normally looks, where the defendant has a choice, at how he would have been assumed to have exercised his choice in the way which 'most reduces the sum which he will have to pay as damages'. However, here the intent of the EU Agency Directive should be examined. Mr Page had a good arguable case for recovering a substantial sum – to be assessed when the case proceeded.

5.108 One judge said that one looks at 'the commission which the plaintiff would have earned if the contract had continued to be performed throughout its further life in a normal manner in which the parties intended [it] to be performed, and not by reference to the amount of the commission which the plaintiff could have earned if the defendant had continued to carry out his obligations under the contract with the view to minimising his liability to the plaintiff and in a manner which lawful, if abnormal, would have been least onerous to him'.

5.109 This is a very important principle because most agency contracts give the principal the right to reject any order put forward by the agent, so that at one extreme the principal could argue 'the agent has lost nothing because, had I chose, I could have accepted none of his orders and his commission would have been zero'. This is clearly not what the Directive intends and *Page* makes this clear.

5.110   There remains doubt though, where a loss-making business is closed down, as to the impact that would have on an agent's compensation. It could be that the business has failed because the principal has handled its business badly or because other agents, but not the agent in question, have done a poor job. There is no reason why the agent should suffer through reduced compensation because of such factors.

5.111   If the principal goes into liquidation, the agent may have a compensation claim to be brought against the company and submitted to the liquidator, but unlike employees whose wages have an element of priority on a liquidation the agent has no such priority, so for commission owed would rank as an unsecured creditor and would only find it worthwhile litigating for compensation if the principal is rescued or there is surplus cash. It is also likely that the agency would have a zero value if the company had gone out of business following the principles in the *Lonsdale* case.

Resignations

5.112   As mentioned above if the agent simply resigns, and this is not because the principal is at fault, then there is no entitlement to compensation. The agent should give the notice period required under the contract otherwise he can be sued for damages.

Sub-agencies

5.113   As mentioned in Chapter 1 to which reference should be made for the detailed discussion of this issue, it is believed that the Regulations apply to sub-agencies. Government guidance notes say that the 'position is not clear', but in principle the Regulations can apply to sub-agencies. In some cases, the ultimate principal requires that a sub-agent of the agent be sacked. However, the agent in the middle of such a transaction is the one who must pay compensation so must make his own decision about termination. He may, for example, only agree if his own principal pays any compensation for him. In other cases, the principal terminates his agent's contract and part of the agent's claim for compensation is the compensation he in turn has had to pay sub-agents.

5.114   *Stuart Light v Ty Europe Ltd* [2003] EWCA Civ 1238 mentioned in Chapter 1, a Court of Appeal decision, held that the sub-agent could not claim against the ultimate principal. That certainly makes sense to most people familiar with the regulations and English contract law and is consistent with how the regulations are drafted. The agent in the middle between ultimate principal and sub-agent might well be subject to a claim if he terminates his sub agents' agreements even if that results from his own principal's termination of his agreement, but it seems clear the sub-agent may not claim directly against a principal with whom he has no contract. The position may be different if the top agency agreement specifically named sub-agents as third parties and perhaps even specifically could state the sub-agents had rights to claim against the ultimate principal if the agent did not do so, under the Contracts (Rights of Third Parties) Act 1999, although no principal is likely to want to accept such a clause. Also note the impact where the sub-agent is in a jurisdiction with stronger or weaker rights to claim and the head agency and sub-agency agreements are subject to different choice of law clauses. With sub-sub-agents the position can be even more complex, but the bottom line is that in most cases each agent and sub-agent should claim up the chain in the usual way.

Other cases

5.115   The next chapter looks at the circumstances in which an agent will obtain compensation or an indemnity when the Regulations apply. Regulation 19 provides that nothing in regulation 18 (or 17) can be derogated from to the detriment of the agent. Thus, a clause which provides for no compensation on death, or no compensation on termination or where the agent is too ill to carry on, will be void. It is not an offence to include such a clause and it may impress ignorant agents into not making claims, but apart from such deterrent effect there is little advantage in the inclusion of such a provision. The author has seen agency agreements containing a statement such as 'The Commercial Agents (Council Directive) Regulations 1993 shall not apply to this agreement'. Such provision is wholly void.

5.116   Where this chapter indicates the agent may have an entitlement to compensation, the next chapter should be also examined because it is not in all cases of termination, death etc that there is an entitlement. The agent must have brought substantial benefits to the principal. The agent in compensation cases must have suffered loss. Those issues are examined in the next chapter. The table below attempts to summarise the various types of termination and their effect under the Regulations, but it is subject to the comments made above in this chapter. Readers should remember there is no requirement to pay any compensation or indemnity payment unless the agent (or if he or she is deceased, his or her estate) makes a claim.

Event	Impact of Regulations
Expiry of fixed term contract	Compensation claim
Termination on notice by principal	Compensation claim

Event	Impact of Regulations
Agent resigns	No compensation unless due to principal's fault
Agent reaches retirement age in contract and principal sacks him	Compensation claim
Agent decides to retire voluntarily	No compensation claim unless he or she has reached 65 or other reasonable retirement age.
Agent dies	Compensation claim for estate
Limited company agent in liquidation	No compensation claim
Agent too ill or old to carry on and resigns	Compensation claim where unreasonable to expect agent to carry on
Agent assigns contract	No compensation claim
Principal sells his business and sacks agent	Compensation claim against principal (not buyer)
Principal terminates agency contract and sub-agents are therefore laid off	Sub-agents can claim against their own principal who in turn claims against his principal
Principal ceases to carry on business	Agent in theory has a claim but if the principal has no money he will not get very far with it.

Chapter 6

Compensation, indemnities and litigation

'The question in this appeal is how the compensation should be determined. But for this purpose it is necessary first to decide exactly what the agent should be compensated for. Only then can one proceed to consider how the compensation should be calculated. On this first question the directive is explicit. The agent is entitled to be compensated for "the damage he suffers as a result of the termination of his relations with the principal." In other words, the agent is treated as having lost something of value as a result of the termination and is entitled to compensation for this loss.'

(Lord Hoffmann *in Lonsdale (t/a Lonsdale Agencies) v Howard & Hallam Ltd* [2007] UKHL 32)

6.1 An agency relationship can work well and to the benefit of principal and agent. Chapter 5 examined the circumstances, however, in which it may break down. One party may simply give notice of termination. The agent may die or fall ill, resign or assign his agency. It was seen in that chapter that in any of the following circumstances the agent may claim compensation (or an indemnity if the agreement provides for an indemnity) from the principal where the Regulations apply:

1. the agent dies;

2. the agent has his fixed or indefinite contract terminated by notice (other than for substantial breach which justifies immediate termination – see *Spectrum Agencies v Crocs Europe BV* [2012] EWCA Civ 1400 (CA) described in Chapter 5) or his fixed-term contract expires;

3. the agent resigns because of circumstances attributable to the principal; or

4. the agent is too ill or old reasonably to be required to continue.

Reference should also be made to Chapter 7 in which Charles Lazarevic looks at compensation value issues.

6.2 The first question therefore is whether the Regulations apply to that particular agency and this topic was addressed in Chapter 1. As to the circumstances of termination of an agency and in which compensation is payable on termination, reference should be made to Chapter 5 where these matters are examined in detail.

6.3 This chapter seeks to explain the compensation or indemnity payment which may be payable under the Regulations. One of the most helpful cases on this is *Lonsdale* (a copy of which is in Appendix 3). It is unfortunate in terms of lack of precedent that there have been so few cases on compensation. The vast majority of the writer's cases settle and usually after a confidential mediation which from the clients' point of view, however, is very sensible. This chapter does not provide guidance on all the different compensation schemes for agents throughout the world. Local law advice should be taken before notice of termination is given in such cases.

Post-termination commission and notice period damages

6.4 It is extremely important also to note that in most agency cases the agent claims regulation 17 compensation (or an indemnity payment) in addition to commission under regulation 8 for orders received after termination for a reasonable period. This is discussed in Chapter 4 which deals with commission. In the *Tigana v Decoro* case (a copy of which is in Appendix 3) considered there and below, the agent received commission, unusually for a nine-month period after termination for such regulation 8 orders in addition to the lump sum under regulation 17.

6.5 In *Monk v Largo Foods Ltd* [2016] EWHC 1837 whether payment of regulation 8 commission would affect the amount of regulation 17 compensation was held to depend on if that affected the sum a notional buyer would pay for the agency when assessing regulation 17 compensation.

6.6 Finally, many agents are not given a proper notice of termination – as seen in Chapter 5 this is often a three-month period so their third head of claim is for what they would have earned in the notice period. Some are also owed commission from before the agency ended which is again a separate claim. Most will claim costs and interest when they litigate as well.

Money claims on termination

6.7

1. The agent is entitled to commission due up to the date of termination and for a reasonable period thereafter on orders generated through his efforts. This was examined in Chapter 4. This is separate from compensation/indemnity.

2.   The agent is entitled to damages along the lines of a wrongful dismissal claim in employment law if proper notice was not given under his contract. Again, this is separate from a compensation/indemnity claim. For example, an agent marketing services is not within the Regulations but if he is not given his contractual notice period he is entitled to claim for common law damages for breach of contract for the profit he would have earned in that notice period, subject to the normal deductions such as for expenses, accelerated receipt and subject to his obligation to mitigate his loss. Indeed regulation 17(5) provides that:

6.8   The grant of an indemnity as mentioned above shall not prevent the commercial agent from seeking damages.

This sentence from the Regulations does not mean the agent can claim both the indemnity and compensation alternatives under the Regulations. It means the agent can claim the indemnity plus common law damages for breach of contract if there is a breach of contract. In many cases there is an obligation to make a payment to the agent where the principal is not in breach of contract. This is what companies find so hard to accept, as it was not previously the position under English law. The principal has followed the contract to the letter, paid all commission due and given the notice period required but still has to pay a large lump sum.

6.9   The rest of this chapter looks at the compensation and indemnity provisions. Regulation 17(1) provides that commercial agents shall, after termination of the agency contract, be indemnified in accordance with regulations 17(3)–(5) or compensated for damages in accordance with regulations 17(6) and (7) below. There are therefore two different bases for payment to an agent which might apply. All other EU states have chosen one or the other – in fact all except France have payments of an indemnity. In France compensation is payable.

Case example – *Charles Shearman v Hunter Boot Ltd* [2014] EWHC 47 (QB)

6.10   This decision held that a clause providing that, whichever of indemnity or compensation resulted in the lower payment, was unenforceable. It went against the purpose of the Directive.

In this case the indemnity yielded £204k whereas the compensation figure on a valuation report was estimated at £1,454,400. However, all the judge was deciding was the preliminary issue on the clause concerned and the parties thereafter settled on confidential terms, so it is not known how much the agent obtained.

The judge stated:

'The structure of Clause 14 is not consistent with the Regulations and, following what appears to be a concession by Hunter, the entire clause falls away so that, if the Claimant is entitled to anything, it is to compensation not indemnity.'

It would be wise to avoid such clauses following this decision.

Case example – *Brand Studio Ltd v St John Knits, Inc* [2015] EWHC 3143

6.11   In *Brand Studio Ltd. v St John Knits, Inc* the parties agreed the agency agreement contained a clause similar to that in the *Hunter Boot* case above, but one party argued part of the clause could be severed and the rest stand. The principal was a Californian fashion company designing women's clothing and the agent operated in the EU.

The material parts of the agency agreement said:

'6.3(a) Upon expiry or termination of this Agreement for any reason:

(a)   If and to the extent that the ... Regulations apply, [the claimant] shall (if and to the extent so entitled in accordance with the provisions of the Regulations) have the right to be indemnified as provided for in regulation 17 of those Regulations. For the avoidance of doubt, [the claimant] shall have no right to any compensation under those Regulations upon termination or expiry of this Agreement *provided that* if the amount payable by way of indemnity under this Clause would be greater than the amount payable by way of compensation, [the claimant] shall ... have the right to receive compensation instead of an indemnity under the regulations ...

7.5 In the event that any provision of this Agreement is held to be invalid or unenforceable, such provision will be deemed to have been severed from the Agreement, while the remained of the Agreement will remain in full force and effect.'

6.12   The court heard a preliminary issue only:

'Whether the Claimant is entitled to compensation (as opposed to an indemnity) pursuant to clause 6.3(a) of the EU Agency Agreement executed by the Claimant and the Defendant on or about 9-14 December 2009, referred to in the statement of case as the "EU Agreement", (as defined in the Amended Particulars of Claim dated 6 March 2015) and pursuant to Regulation 17 of the Commercial Agents (Council Directive) Regulations 1993 (as amended).'

The court answered no to that question. The judge said:

'Once the proviso is severed from clause 6.3(a), as I consider it should be, the clause contains only the valid concession by the agent that in the event of termination of the agency agreement the agent will be entitled to an indemnity rather than compensation. For the purposes Regulation 17 the agency contract therefore "otherwise provides."'

That conclusion is sensible. If the proviso 'provided that and words that follow it' are removed from the clause, the indemnity should stand rather that the entire clause including the option of an indemnity. Notwithstanding the decision that the indemnity choice still stood, in practice it remains wise to put separate provisions in different clauses and not to try complex clauses opting for the lower of indemnity or compensation as this case and *Hunter Boot* show they often do not work given the purposive nature of EU law.

Statistics and settlements

6.13   Since 1994 when the Regulations came into force, there have been many settlements but not a vast number of court judgments on the Regulation, although the number of judgments is increasing as the years go by. So, some issues under the Regulations such as how to assess compensation payments currently remain unclear even after the *Lonsdale* case and other subsequent relevant cases. Generally, where the Regulations appear if there is no indemnity 'cap' then agents will often claim two to three years' commission and many will settle for one to eighteen months. Some agents use their trade union, e.g. Unite (previously the Professional Sales Agents Association (PSA) which is now part of Unite). In 2007 the PSA obtained settlements totalling about £4m without solicitors and £1.5m after solicitor intervention.

Also, the Manufacturers' Agents' Association represents many agents – http://www.themaa.co.uk/.

6.14   PSA 2004 settlements included:

- £193,978 for six ex-Morris furniture agents;

- £52,351 for two more agents in the furniture industry, both of whom had the agency for just over two years each. In this case the principal tried to argue that he was dissatisfied with the performance of the agents despite an increase in the sales volume;

- £40,000 for two members who traded as a limited company for 21 years, and started working for a chemical company. Again, the principal attempted to avoid payment by arguing poor performance, which was apparently unsubstantiated;

- £35,000 for Mr E who introduced well over 100 new customers and became his publishing house principal's top-performing agent during his contract of only two years and two months. Several unfounded and unsubstantiated allegations were made toward the latter part of 2002 and as a result his agency was terminated;

- £52,000 for Mr G who during his ten-year textile agency was responsible for opening over 75% of all the customers in the area;

- £50,000 for a different Mr G who works in the food industry and who was paid partly by retainer during his brief two-year seven-month agency, which was lost due to the principal reorganising.

Compensation or indemnity – which applies?

6.15   In the UK, companies have a choice at the contract drafting stage but not later. Regulation 17(2) sets out that choice in saying that 'except where the agency contract otherwise provides, the commercial agent shall be entitled to be compensated rather than indemnified'.

6.16   Therefore, if the parties have not addressed the issue, compensation will be payable but not an indemnity. If a written contract is silent on the point, then compensation is payable. In the early days of the Regulations most contracts did not include an indemnity provision but now it is very common as most contracts are drafted by the principal and they know it limited the payment to at the most a year's commission.

6.17   The Government say in their guidance notes on the Regulations that 'there is nothing to stop the parties from agreeing to use the compensation provisions in some cases and indemnity ones in others when terminating a particular contract'. They also point out that the giving of proper notice or the expiration of a fixed-term contract does not remove the right to claim compensation or indemnity. They say it might 'potentially reduce the level of the indemnity/compensation', and is a matter for the courts to decide. The *Green Deal Marketing Ltd v Economy Energy Trading Ltd* [2019] EWHC 507 case made it clear that compensation is assessed on the assumption the agency contract would have otherwise continued.

6.18   The section below on the indemnity is only relevant where in the UK the contract provides for an indemnity.

6.19   No other country in the EU implemented the Directive with both the indemnity and compensation option. Does that render the UK Regulations void? That has sometimes been argued. In *Hicks v Morris* (2005, unreported) the court looked at this point. The principal attempted to argue this issue. The judge in the Mercantile Court in Leeds did not agree, stating that if this were the case all proceedings that have gone as far as the Court of Appeal in England and to the Inner House, Court of Session in Scotland would be wrong. Clearly, the Law Lords hearing these matters would have indicated this error had it existed and could not have passed judgment in the way in which they did. Of course, those courts might have been wrong or the point perhaps was simply not put to them, however it was given short shrift in this decision.

The indemnity

6.20   The Regulations first provide for the indemnity. It will not be payable where it is excluded by regulation 18, as seen in Chapter 5 – eg where the agent is in default which justifies immediate termination or the agent has resigned or assigned the agency.

Claims within one year

6.21   The indemnity (and compensation) is payable provided the agent makes a claim within one year following termination of his agency contract (regulation 17(9)). Litigation does not need to be started in that period, but the agent must notify his principal that he is pursuing a claim within that period. The period runs from termination of the agency contract, which is presumably later than the date of notice of termination unless the notice is for immediate termination. Subsequently, the normal UK limitation periods for bringing claims would apply under the Limitation Act 1980.

Substantial benefits and equity

6.22   Under regulation 17(3) an agent is only entitled to an indemnity where:

(a)   he has brought the principal new customers or has significantly increased the volume of business with existing customers and the principal continues to derive substantial benefits from the business with such customers; and

(b)   the payment of this indemnity is equitable having regard to all the circumstances and, in particular, the commission lost by the commercial agent on the business transacted with such customers.

6.23   Thus, even if the contract provides that an indemnity is to be payable on termination the agent may not receive anything. This would be the case, for example, where he has not significantly increased business. An agent might have been given a ready-made customer base when he started, and when he finished the job there may be fewer customers or fewer orders, in which case his indemnity entitlement would be zero. There are no subjective factors in regulation 17(3). It does not matter if the business has failed to grow because of a recession or because of incompetence on the part of the principal. If the simple fact is that the agent has not made the significant increase, then he gets nothing. Notice also that the principal must continue to benefit from this increase. If the agent is responsible for an increase, as most are over time, but the agent takes the customers with him when he leaves, then again, no indemnity is payable.

6.24   In *Duncan Moore v Piretta* [1999] 1 All ER 174 the judge examined what is meant by the agent bringing new customers to the principal. The defendants submitted that if, for example, a customer's name appears on a list or if a customer attends a trade fair in response to a circular or advertisement issued by the principal, that customer is not brought to the principal by the agent. The judge did not agree. He said:

> 'A new customer may in practice be induced to place business with a principal by a variety of means – for example, the quality and price of the goods offered for sale by the principal, the reputation of the principal, the general marketing efforts of the principal, the salesmanship of the individual agent, or the introduction, by an agent on whom the customer is accustomed to rely, of the principal to that customer.'

Business may result from a combination of these factors. The judge thought the phrase 'means simply that he [the agent] was instrumental in obtaining the business of new customers for the principal'. The defendants in the case sold fashion clothing to independent retail outlets in the UK. The agent started work in 1988 for them and they already had a customer base. He was given a customer list. Customers also came through contact with the principal at exhibitions and in other ways. However, the agent did most of the work once he had the customer list, and drove 20,000 miles a year in his territory drumming up business. There were 40 customers when the agency ended and all but six or seven were brought in (on the definition used by the judge) by the agent.

6.25   This decision also examined the phrase 'or has significantly increased the volume of business with existing customers'. The judge said this just required that the agent should be instrumental in so doing.

6.26   The judge quoted from the European Commission report on compensation/indemnity of July 1996 (reproduced in Appendix 2) where the Commission refers to German law and says:

> 'The agent must have acquired the new client and in this respect the instrumentality of the agent is crucial. A small level of involvement is sufficient and it is enough that the agent has merely contributed to bringing the new customer. However, the agent must have played an active role and therefore the existence of a new customer who falls within the territorial scope of an exclusive agency agreement will not automatically suffice.' (pages 181–199.)

Even where these factors are satisfied regulation 17(3)(b) requires that the indemnity must be equitable in all the circumstances.

The one-year indemnity cap

6.27   Regulation 17(4) provides that:

> 'The amount of the indemnity shall not exceed the figure equivalent to an indemnity for one year calculated from the commercial agent's average annual remuneration over the preceding five years and if the contract goes back less than five years the indemnity shall be calculated on the average for the period in question.'

6.28   Some agents believe that under the Regulations when an agent is sacked, he is entitled to a year's commission. They get this from a misconstruction of regulation 17(4). In fact, in most cases the agent's contract does not provide for an indemnity and regulation 17(4) is therefore irrelevant. Even where it is relevant, the sum is a maximum of a year's commission averaged over the last five years or a shorter period where the agency has operated over a shorter period.

6.29   There have been few court decisions relating to the indemnity provisions. One was the *Duncan Moore v Piretta* case. The relevant agency contract was made on 18 February 1994 (just after the Regulations came into force) and the clause provided:

'The agent shall be entitled to indemnity on the termination of this agreement for reasons other than a breach of the terms of this agreement by the agent or termination of this agreement by the agent. The parties agree that the indemnity payable to the agent, if any, shall be assessed equitably by applying regulations 17 and 18 of the Regulations to allow the agent the minimum indemnity as permitted by the Regulations.'

The judge looked at the preamble to the Agency Directive and its stated purpose of harmonising EU law on agency. This must be the correct approach. The judge said he therefore was entitled to look to the law of Germany on which the indemnity is based. He also examined the cap of a year's commission and indeed applied it to his calculations.

6.30   In this case the judge said there were three stages in assessing the amount of the indemnity.

1.   Ask what is the value of the business to the principal of new customers brought in by the agent and increases in sales from other customers. Relevant factors are loss of the business of those customers after the agency is over, whether or not due to the agent's or principal's fault, eg the insolvency of a customer or a decision of a customer to buy goods elsewhere or the agent taking the customer with him. If the benefits to the principal may last more than a year after termination, then those benefits can be taken into account.

2.   The payment must be equitable. In particular, the commission the agent would have earned had the contract continued is examined. Also relevant the court said, were the expenses the agent would have had to pay in earning the commission in future and an allowance should be made for accelerated payment. 'The indemnity is accrued as at the date of termination in respect of commission which would have occurred after it,' the judge said. In the DTI guidance notes on the Regulations they say that 'equitable . . . probably means "just" or "fair" rather than necessarily based on the doctrines or principles of equity – the latter, if they exist at all in the law of every Member State, being bound to vary from State to State'.

In *Duncan Moore v Piretta* [1999] 1 All ER 174 the defendants claimed that account should be taken of other earnings the agent may have made in a new job or agency – in other words a kind of mitigation of loss. The court did not agree. The judge said:

The purpose of the indemnity seems to me to be to award a share in the goodwill built up by the efforts of the agent to him on the termination of his agency. Otherwise the whole benefit of that goodwill will remain with his former principal. A concept of mitigation of loss or of anything akin to it seems to me to play no part in this exercise.

In *Tigana v Decoro* both parties' counsel agreed that 'common law principles of mitigation and avoidable loss have no part to play in the assessment'. The judge thought the defendant's counsel's concession in this respect was 'obviously right: having regard, for example, to the availability of compensation on the death or retirement of the agent (regulations 17(8); 18(b)).... As Mr Hollander put it, the focus is on the position at the time of termination: one looks back, not forward'.

In *Duncan Moore v Piretta PTA Ltd*, the judge pointed out that an agent who immediately replaced the lost money should not be in a different position from one who decided to go on holiday for a substantial period. The task is to assess the indemnity, not assess the loss to the agent.

The judge also commented that one does not look into the respective contributions of agent and principal in achieving business because the agent is compensated by the percentage commission they have agreed between themselves for this. If the percentage was grossly disproportionate, he thought that this issue might then be examinable.

3.   The third step is to apply the cap in regulation 17(4). The judge said the 'contract' included earlier contracts, in addition to the current one which the agent in this case had signed in place of the earlier ones, but with the same principal.

6.31   The *Duncan Moore v Piretta PTA Ltd* decision has been described as a 'step back'. Stephen Sidkin in the *Financial Times* (7 July 1998) pointed out that the court considered German law relevant but 'then calculated the indemnity in a way that bore no relation to the approach under German law. Nor was the calculation consistent with English law'.

6.32   The Government Guidance notes on the Regulations say:

'The term "indemnity" has a rather more limited meaning than that which it normally bears in English law in that it:

(i)   appears to fall short of a complete making good of the loss suffered by the principal; and
(ii)   does not necessarily arise in relation to loss caused by the principal.'

The Guidance goes on to say it cannot provide any guidance on the amounts of the indemnity.

Lonsdale *and Indemnity*

6.33   The *Lonsdale* decision (2007) briefly looked at the indemnity provisions although they were not applicable in that case and said:

'It is a condition of the indemnity that the agent should have "brought the principal new customers or . . . significantly increased the volume of business with existing customers" and that the principal "continues to derive substantial benefits from the business with such customers": article 17(2)(a). It follows that in a case such as the present, in which the principal went out of business and therefore derived no benefit from the customers introduced by the agent, no indemnity will be payable: see *Saintier and Scholes*, op.cit, at p. 204 [a book on commercial agency]. In addition, article 17(2)(b) limits the indemnity to one year's commission. In the face of these provisions which will satisfy the policy of the directive, it is impossible to argue that it requires a payment of twice gross commission whether the principal has derived any benefit from the termination or not.'

The indemnity and the Commission's 1996 Report

6.34   The European Commission issued a report in 1996 on indemnity and compensation under the EU Agency Directive: *Report on the Application of article 17 of Council Directive on the Co-ordination of the Laws of the Member States relating to Self-employed Commercial Agents* (see Appendix 2). The report will not be repeated in detail here, but it does provide some useful guidance on the indemnity (and compensation which is dealt with later in this chapter). It seems that the indemnity was modelled on article 89b of the German Commercial Code which has operated since 1953.

6.35   The Commission say that clearly the indemnity is payable at the end of a fixed-term contract and on the bankruptcy of the principal. It is presumed that the principal is deriving substantial benefits from the agency 'even if the principal sells his business or client list if it can be shown that the purchaser will use the client base. If the agent takes the customers with him, he will not get an indemnity'.

The calculation

6.36   The Commission describe various stages under German law in relation to calculation of the indemnity.

Stage 1

6.37

1.   First the number of new customers is ascertained and increases in volume of business from existing customers. Then the commission on those customers is calculated 'for the last 12 months of the agency contract'.

2.   An estimate is made of the likely future duration of these benefits to the principal. The aim is 'to predict the likely length of time the business with the new and intensified customers will last'. If sales have dropped

because of competition or quality of the goods, then the indemnity is *not* reduced. Usually a period of two to three years is examined but sometimes a period of up to five years.

3. Next the rate of migration of customers who move away is examined. This varies. In one case it was 38% per year.

4. The figure is then reduced to take account of accelerated receipt.

Stage 2

6.38 Then equity is considered. Factors examined are whether the agent works for other principals; whether the agent was at fault; rate of remuneration; decrease in principal's turnover; advantage to principal; payment of pension contributions by principal (almost unheard of in the UK); existence of restraint of trade clause (because if the agent cannot work he will earn less – this has led some UK principals to remove restraint of trade clauses as they are hard to enforce anyway).

Stage 3

6.39 The sum calculated under stages 1 and 2 is then compared with the cap under regulation 17(4).

Commission's example – indemnity

6.40

Commission on new customers and/or over last 12 months of agency	50,000 ECUs (euros from intensified customers 1 January 1999)
Anticipated duration of benefits is three years with 20% migration rate	
Year 1 50,000 – 10,000 =	40,000 ECUs
Year 2 40,000 – 8,000 =	32,000 ECUs
Year 3 32,000 – 6,400 =	25,600 ECUs
Total lost commission	97,600 ECUs
Correction to present value say 10% This figure being equal to the equal indemnity.	87,840 ECUs
This figure might be adjusted for reasons of equity (stage 2 above)	

6.41 The Commission says that the method of predicting the indemnity is extremely precise and leads to a predictable outcome and principals can ascertain their risks in advance. It is also better for the agent, as he knows what he can expect.

6.42   The Commission state that in some states the maximum figure of a year's commission is taken rather than lesser awards. The cap is just that – a cap or ceiling. It does not mean that the indemnity will always be that sum; in many cases it may be less. Where the agent has not increased business it could be zero. Indeed, if the agent has breached his contract, he may owe the principal damages at common law for the loss the principal has suffered through the breach.

6.43   Some of those responding to the 2014 consultation by the European Commission on the Agency Directive commented on the compensation regime – the responses are online at https://ec.europa.eu/growth/content/public-consultation-evaluation-commercial-agents-directive-86653eec_en.

6.44   The 2014 consultation led to a decision not to change the Agency Directive. In 2015 the European Commission stated after the results were analysed that:

> 'The conclusion of the evaluation is that the Directive meets its objectives and functions well. The Directive's benefits outweigh its costs, it remains relevant and continues to have EU added value. Based on these findings, it is recommended that the Directive is maintained in its current form'.

The above conclusion is found in the summary on the link above.

6.45   The 36-page EU report on the consultation issued in 2015 (reproduced in Appendix 2.4 of this book) included the following on the indemnity provisions:

> 'Under the indemnity system [Article 17(2)], the commercial agent is entitled to an indemnity if and to the extent to which s/he brought new customers to the principal or had significantly increased the volume of business with existing customers after termination of the contract. The German *Bundesgerichtshof* submitted a preliminary question to the Court of Justice of the EU relating to the definition of "new customers" (Case C-315/14).

> The indemnity represents the continuing benefits (goodwill) to the principal after termination of the contract as a result of the agent's work. The agent receives a commission while the contract is valid, but this does not reflect the value of the goodwill generated for the principal; this is why payment of the goodwill indemnity is commercially justified.

> If no goodwill has been generated, the principal should not pay an indemnity. The Directive sets an indemnity level ceiling equal to one year of the agent's average annual remuneration over the preceding five years (or the average for the period in question if the contract lasted less than five years).

> Under Article 17(2) (c), receiving an indemnity does not prevent the commercial agent from seeking damages. This provision governs situations

where, in addition to the indemnity under Article 17(2) of the Directive, under national law the agent is entitled to seek damages, e.g. for the principal breaching the contract or failing to respect the notice period provided for in the Directive (See the Commission's report on the implementation of Article 17 of the Directive, COM(96)364 final, p. 5.).'

6.46 The 2015 report refers to a case relating to the indemnity in relation to where there may be collective agreements in place such as those which trade unions negotiate, saying:

'Case C-465/04, *Honyvem*

1. Article 19 of Council Directive 86/653/EEC of 18 December 1986 on the coordination of the laws of the Member States relating to self-employed commercial agents must be interpreted as meaning that the indemnity for termination of contract which results from the application of Article 17(2) of the Directive cannot be replaced, pursuant to a collective agreement, by an indemnity determined in accordance with criteria other than those prescribed by Article 17, unless it is established that the application of such an agreement guarantees the commercial agent, in every case, an indemnity equal to or greater than that which results from the application of Article 17.

2. Within the framework prescribed by Article 17(2) of Directive 86/653, the Member States enjoy a margin of discretion which they may exercise, in particular, in relation to the criterion of equity.'

Compensation

6.47 As seen above, unless otherwise agreed, an agent is entitled under the Regulations to compensation rather than an indemnity and this is described below. Where the contract provides for an indemnity the section above on indemnity is relevant instead. The circumstances under which the Regulations apply were addressed in Chapter 1 and those in which an indemnity or compensation is payable were discussed in Chapter 5.

6.48 Regulation 17(6) says that an agent shall be 'entitled to compensation for the damage he suffers as a result of the termination of his relations with his principal'. Regulation 17(7) tries to provide further assistance on this. It says:

'For the purposes of these Regulations such damage shall be deemed to occur particularly when the termination takes place in either or both of the following circumstances, namely circumstances which:

(a) deprive the commercial agent of the commission which proper performance of the agency contract would have procured for him whilst providing his principal with substantial benefits linked to the activities of the commercial agent; or

(b) have not enabled the commercial agent to amortise the costs and expenses that he had incurred in the performance of the agency contract on the advice of his principal.'

The *Lonsdale* case and compensation – Compensation for what?

6.49   In this judgment the House of Lords (now the Supreme Court) provided useful guidance on assessing compensation. The first issue was: what is the compensation for? The court said (Hoffmann J):

'This elegant theory explains why the French courts regard the agent as, in principle, entitled to compensation. It does not, however, identify exactly what he is entitled to compensation for. One possibility might have been to value the total goodwill of the principal's business and then to try to attribute some share to the agent. But this would in practice be a hopeless endeavour and the French courts have never tried to do it. Instead, they have settled upon compensating him for what he has lost by being deprived of his business. That is the "*préjudice subi*". The French case law makes it clear that this ordinarily involves placing a value upon the right to be an agent. That means, primarily, the right to future commissions "which proper performance of the agency contract would have procured him": see *Saintier and Scholes*, op cit, pp 187–188. In my opinion this is the right for which the directive requires the agent to be compensated.'

So, there is no valuation done of the overall business of the principal but instead of the right to be the agent.

Lonsdale case: Future revenue stream

6.50   In *Lonsdale* the court went on to say:

'Having thus determined that the agent is entitled to be compensated for being deprived of the benefit of the agency relationship, the next question is how that loss should be calculated. The value of the agency relationship lies in the prospect of earning commission, the agent's expectation that "proper performance of the agency contract" will provide him with a future income stream. It is this which must be valued.'

So, if there is no future revenue stream because the agent did so badly even if he earned a fortune two years before he would receive nothing on this analysis. It may be argued that if the principal undertook steps which rendered the agency worthless to avoid the regulations or perhaps even without that aim this could be contrary to the duty of good faith and damages for breach of the good faith obligation might instead be payable but that has yet to be proved.

6.51   If the principal through judicious drafting of the agency contract made the value going forwards of the agency worth very little with rights allowing accounts to be removed and territories reduced perhaps again this would breach the good faith obligation and the agent would still be able to claim some form of compensation.

6.52   Valuations on this basis for private companies are done every day in practice. *Daltons Weekly* and other publications are full of companies for sale with their price based on turnover or profits and although it can be difficult and often very expensive (£20k plus in fees is not unusual) to value a private company, there is no market in the UK for resale of agency agreements whether they have a high on- going revenue stream or not. The valuation is therefore a fiction to an extent. However, in some countries like Germany agencies are bought and sold and in the UK franchisees will often pay a fee to become a franchisee and sell their right when they leave to another for a lump sum so the concepts are not totally alien.

6.53   The court in *Lonsdale* says the agency is valued even if the terms provide it is not assignable (as many of them are not) and that the lack of assignability does not affect the valuation.

Lonsdale – no other assumptions

6.54   The issue of lack of assignability can be ignored (if it were not no one would buy the agency and the value would always be zero simply by virtue of the usual no assignment clause). No other assumptions are made however:

'13   On the other hand, as at present advised, I see no reason to make any other assumptions contrary to what was the position in the real world at the date of termination. As one is placing a present value upon future income, one must discount future earnings by an appropriate rate of interest. If the agency was by its terms or in fact unassignable, it must be assumed, as I have said, that the hypothetical purchaser would have been entitled to take it over. But there is no basis for assuming that he would then have obtained an assignable asset: compare the *Crossman* case. Likewise, if the market for the products in which the agent dealt was rising or declining, this would have affected what a hypothetical purchaser would have been willing to give. He would have paid fewer years' purchase for a declining agency than for one in an expanding market. If the agent would have had to incur expense or do work in earning his commission, it cannot be assumed that the hypothetical purchaser would have earned it gross or without having to do anything.'

The court then rejected the French approach of two years' commission on termination on various grounds including that in France agencies are often sold and often for two years' gross commission. That is not the case in the UK.

6.55   The *King v Tunnock* case was not followed and the court said:

'27   *King v Tunnock Ltd* was considered by Judge Bowers (sitting as a High Court judge) in *Barrett McKenzie v Escada (UK) Ltd* [2001] Eu LR 567. The judge was not attracted by the formulaic approach of the Court of Session but said (at p. 575) that the point on which he agreed with Lord Caplan was that –

"one is valuing the agency and its connections that have been established by the agent at the time at or immediately before termination, and it is really a question of compensating for the notional value of that agency in the open market. . . .

I agree that this is what compensation in article 17(3) means. My only caution is that one must be careful about the word "notional". All that is notional is the assumption that the agency was available to be bought and sold at the relevant date. What it would fetch depends upon circumstances as they existed in the real world at the time: what the earnings prospects of the agency were and what people would have been willing to pay for similar businesses at the time.'

6.56   In *James Craig Donald/Craijan Ltd v Worcester Marine Windows Ltd* Case No: 2WR00372 (January 2013 – online at http://www.bailii.org/ew/cases/Misc/2013/41.html) a case in which the writer acted for the agent claimant, the agent won three years' commission. The judge said:

'In particular, but without in this extempore judgment going into any more detail than is necessary to reason my decision, the Defendant's statement in the defence to the effect of the continuing turnover, which on the November to November accounting year basis is to November 2011, some 20 months after the termination of the agency, suggests that snapshotting value at March 2010 there was no reason to predict the adverse financial circumstances which the Defendant now asserts, albeit without any evidence, so that the first Claimant's submission as to **a multiplier of 3** is perfectly reasonable in my judgment. The multiplicand is also in my judgment unarguably correct.'

That was a fairly large multiplier. Most agents feel lucky to win a year's commission.

6.57   The judge went on:

'The first Claimant has properly deducted the level of net income less VAT, together with some 25% for the risk of termination in any event, and lawful termination at that, and has made proper concessions as to attributability of some of his expenses to other uses, including his work for someone called Keith Hunt, albeit that that does not appear to have been any more than a minimal commitment of his time and for social use. In any event, as the Claimant's counsel [Tim Johnston of Brick Court Chambers] properly pointed out in his closing speech, the deductions issue works in the Defendant's favour in reducing the claim and the first Claimant has in my judgment properly and rationally accounted throughout in each relevant way as to this credit. It is neither too much nor too little. I should add that against the claim as a whole the first Claimant has properly given credit for what was paid on termination.'

'As to interest, I prefer the Claimant's counsel's alternative lesser calculation based on 3% over base rate, ie 3.5% total, as being the rate at which a small business might borrow capital during the relevant period. I would apply such an approach in any quasi-commercial case of this kind, and the alternative higher claim based on statutory interest is in my judgment inappropriate. Therefore interest in my judgment totals £5,838.49. I therefore give judgment for the first Claimant against the Defendant in the sum of £59,576.47, together with interest which I assess at £5,838.49.'

There have been very few cases where the courts have assessed compensation and the *Lonsdale* case remains one of the few cases which attempted a full analysis of the exercise of calculation of compensation. Reference should be made to Chapter 7 on valuation by Charles Lazarevic of Vero Consulting Ltd on these issues.

Valuation and expenses

6.58   Many agents have several agencies and because one agency ends does not mean their costs go down although the court did not seem to agree with this point in *Lonsdale* when it said:

'29.   In *Tigana Ltd v Decoro* [2003] EuLR 189 [discussed elsewhere in this chapter] the judge awarded the agent a sum equal to his commission less expenses over the 14 to 15 months during which the agency had subsisted. I would agree that prima facie the value of the agency should be fixed by reference to its net earnings because, as a matter of common sense, that is what will matter to the hypothetical purchaser. Furthermore, in the case of an agent who has more than one agency, the costs must be fairly attributed to each. He cannot simply say, as Mr Lonsdale did in this case, that the marginal cost of the Elmdale agency was little or nothing because he had to see the same customers and go to the same exhibitions for Wendel.

30.   It may well be that 14 months commission adopted by the judge was a fair valuation. But he seems to have had no evidence that anyone would have paid this figure for a comparable business. Instead, he gave (at p. 221) a non-exhaustive list of 14 factors ((a) to (n)), some of them very wide ranging indeed, which he said would require consideration. The list gives no indication of the weight to be attributed to each factor.

31.   More recently, in *Smith, Bailey Palmer v Howard & Hallam Ltd* [2006] Eu LR 578 Judge Overend (sitting as a High Court judge) dealt with claims by other agents who had worked for the respondent in this case. He noted that the Elmdale brand had been sold to a competitor for £550,000 and that, over the three years before the sale, 42% of the sales and distribution expenses had consisted of agent's commission. On these figures, he considered that it would be right to attribute 42% of the value of the brand to the agents. This seems to me a flawed method of calculation. First, it treats the entire value of the brand, i.e. the goodwill of the Elmdale name, as attributable to sales and marketing. No allowance is made for the possibility that some of the goodwill may have been attributable to the fact that the company made good shoes. Secondly, no allowance is made for the fact that the commission, which is treated as the measure of the proprietary interest of the agents in the assets of the company, is what the agents were actually paid for their services. On this theory, the advertising agents should have acquired an interest proportionate to what they were paid. Thirdly, the valuation is based entirely on cost rather than what anyone would actually have paid for the agency.'

Lonsdale – Amount awarded

6.59   Applying the principles described above the court awarded very little to the agent.

> '32.   That brings me to the judgments in the present case. The claim was heard by Judge Harris QC in the Oxford County Court and his judgment was, if I may respectfully say so, a model of clarity and common sense. I shall extract one or two of the most important passages:
>
>> "18.   If it is kept in mind that the damage for which the agent is to be compensated consists in the loss of the value or goodwill he can be said to have possessed in the agency, then it can be seen that valuation ought to be reasonably straightforward. Small businesses of all kinds are daily being bought and sold, and a major element in the composition of their price will be a valuation of goodwill.
>>
>> 19.   But neither side put evidence before the court about how commercial goodwill is conventionally valued. Nor was I told upon what basis claims of this type are conventionally settled. There was no evidence at all about how commercially to value such assets. It is of course for the claimant, as a seeker of compensation, to prove the value of what he has lost."'

6.60   The judge then found that net commission was running at about £8,000 a year and said:

> '33   . . . The value of that agency, the commercial value is what someone would pay for it; to acquire by assignment a business vehicle with a likely net annual income of £8,000 . . .
>
> Commonsense would indicate that few people wanting the opportunity to earn what the claimant was earning would be prepared to pay well over £20,000 for the privilege of doing so, still less would they do so in an industry in remorseless decline, and in which the likely buyers would be men of modest means. . .
>
> Given the absence of evidence about how commercially to value goodwill, or evidence about what price in practice might have been available, the court might be thought to be justified in simply finding that the claimant has failed to prove his case . . .
>
> This was an agency producing a modest and falling income in a steadily deteriorating environment. There is no evidence that anyone would have paid anything to buy it . . . I am strongly tempted to find that no damage has been established . . . But perhaps that conclusion, though I regard it as logical, is a little over rigorous given that the defendant has already made a payment. Doing the best I can, I find that the appropriate figure for compensation is one of £5,000.'
>
> The Court of Appeal approved of this approach. After a thorough review of the authorities, Moore-Bick LJ quoted paragraph 18 of the judgment (see above) and said that the judge was right in his approach. I agree. Furthermore, I do not think that the judge could have been faulted if he had simply dismissed the claim.'

Finding and paying valuers

6.61 The court did comment on the issue of introducing the new requirement for valuations. Although the writers' cases have ranged from an agent paid £1m in compensation to £6,000, many claims are at the lower end and indeed in one case it was cheaper for the principal to pay a nominal lump sum which would have been less than the amount of irrecoverable costs when 'winning' litigation. The winner never recovers all their costs. Recovering two-thirds of legal fees is more likely.

6.62 The court said:

'35. That is sufficient to dispose of the appeal, but there are three additional comments to be made. First, Mr Moser urged your Lordships not to adopt a principle which required valuation evidence. Valuations, he said, were expensive and most claims were too small to justify the cost. Moore-Bick LJ said (at paragraph 57) that "in most cases" the court would be likely to benefit from the assistance of an expert witness but that in some cases it might be sufficient to place all the material before the court and invite the judge to act as valuer. It seems to me that once it is firmly understood that the compensation is for the loss of the value of the agency, relatively few cases will go to court. As Judge Harris said, small comparable businesses are bought and sold every day and it should not be difficult for the parties, with the benefit of advice about the going rate for such businesses, to agree on an appropriate valuation. It should not always be necessary for them to obtain a full scale valuation, involving the checking of income and expenditure figures and the application of the going rate to those figures. But I do not see how, if the matter does go to court, the judge can decide the case without some information about the standard methodology for the valuation of such businesses. In this case, the judge was simply invited to pluck a figure out of the air from across the Channel and rightly refused to do so. Nothing is more likely to cause uncertainty and promote litigation than a lottery system under which judges are invited to choose figures at random.

It may also be possible, after a period of experience in such valuations, for the court to take judicial notice of what would be the going rate in what I might call the standard case, namely an agency which has continued for some time and in which the net commission figures are fairly stable. It should not be necessary to repeat boilerplate evidence in every case. But the judge must be reasonably confident that he is dealing with the standard case. Adjustments would be needed if, as in this case, the market was in decline or had disappeared altogether.'

The valuation issue is difficult and expensive in practice. A straight two years' commission was simpler but clearly the *Lonsdale* basis reflects current law.

The *Tigana v Decoro* case

6.63 *Tigana v Decoro* [2003] EWHC 23 (QB) (a copy of which is in Appendix 3) was a decision prior to *Lonsdale* but still provides interesting reading. In

Lonsdale the court said of *Tigana* 'Instead, he gave (at p. 221) a non-exhaustive list of 14 factors ((a) to (n)), some of them very wide ranging indeed, which he said would require consideration. The list gives no indication of the weight to be attributed to each factor.' This is not exactly judicial endorsement for the factors in *Tigana* listed below.

6.64   The court in a then well argued judgment examined how compensation under regulation 17 was assessed, in a case where commission on orders received after termination under regulation 8(a) had led to a large award (US\$606,836). That was relevant in assessing the regulation 17 compensation. This is an issue in practice which arises all the time – is there any set off between post-termination commission and compensation. Here it was a factor in assessing that compensation but did not by any means distinguish it. That was similar to the view of the court in *Green Deal Marketing Ltd v Economy Energy Trading Ltd* [2019] EWHC 507 and in *Monk v Largo Foods Ltd* [2016] EWHC 1837 (the latter being a case where the parties' experts used 2.5–3 and 7 as their respective valuation multipliers and the court decided on 4x as the multiplier for compensation).

6.65   Here the court thought that the following matters were relevant to assessing regulation 17 compensation (see para 89 of the judgment):

89.1   The period of the agency, as provided for in the contract.

89.2   The period for which the agency in fact lasted up to termination.

89.3   The terms and conditions attaching to the agency as provided in the agency contract.

89.4   The nature and history of the agency and of the particular market involved.

89.5   The matters specifically mentioned in Regulation 17(7) (a) and (b).

89.6   The nature of the client base and of the kind of contracts anticipated to be placed (for example, 'one-off' or repeat).

89.7   Whether the principal has appointed the agent as its exclusive or non-exclusive agent.

89.8   The extent to which the agent has bound himself during the agency to act exclusively for the principal and the extent to which the agent is free to act for others (and whether in the same field of goods or services or not).

89.9   The extent to which the principal retains after termination of the agency benefit (for example, by way of enhanced trade connection or goodwill) from the activities of the agent during the agency.

89.10   The extent to which an agent is free, after termination, to have dealings with customers with whom he dealt during the agency (A restraint of trade clause will be a relevant consideration in this context).

89.11   Whether there are any payments under Regulation 8 (or other Regulations) which ought to be taken into account.

89.12   The manner in which the agency contract is ended: for example by notice given by the principal; or by notice given by the agent; or by effluxion of time; or as the case may be.

89.13   The extent to which the principal and agent respectively have financially contributed to the goodwill accruing during the period of agency.

89.14   The extent to which there may have been loss caused by any relevant breach of contract or duty.

90.   It is clear that the 'damage' suffered by a commercial agent as a result of the termination of the agency (Regulation 17(6)) is – generally speaking (and breach of contract cases aside) – to be regarded as a putative loss and not simply (by common law standards) actual loss. This is shown by the exclusion of principles of mitigation and applicability of the compensation provisions to termination on death or retirement. Clearly one important element, as the recitals to the Directive show, is to avoid a principal being unjustly enriched by retaining for itself without payment the entirety of the benefit of goodwill to which the activities of the agent during the agency have contributed. But another element (which finds both reflection and emphasis in Regulation 17(7) (a)) is to compensate the agent for the loss of a beneficial agency contract. One can perhaps there see some analogy with redundancy payments in an employment context: although the analogy cannot be pushed too far, since the policy considerations behind redundancy payments for employees are rather different.

6.66   This is the nub of the judgment. The agent was awarded the sum of the commission earned over the period of the agency – effectively 15 months less 20% expenses – $452,346. The agent also received regulation 8 commission of US$606,836 and commission which was owed of US$350,000, a total sum of about £1m.

Case example – *Turner v Steinhoff Furniture Ltd* [2006] Eu LR 50

6.67   In this case of the writer, the judge assessed compensation relying on the *Tigana* judgment referred to in this chapter. The following extract from the judgment may provide some guidance for those seeking to advise on compensation and its assessment. The judge said:

'It seems to me that, whilst taking into account the list of suggested factors listed by Davis J, [in *Tigana*] one must not lose sight of the importance of the value which would have been attached to the agency at the date of its termination. Thus one needs to examine what a purchaser would have been prepared to pay for an assignment of the agency (assuming it was not one of those 'personal' contracts which are not capable of assignment). Having regard to the short duration of the agency and its lack of exclusivity, and even taking account of its indefinite duration and protection under the Regulations, it seems to me unlikely that a purchaser would be prepared to offer to pay a price based on two years' earnings – either gross or net.'

Future profitability of the agency was held not to be relevant. The assessment was at termination. The fact the new range of goods being introduced could have led the agent to earning higher commission had the constructive termination not occurred was irrelevant. The agency ran for 20 months only and was non exclusive. Those factors reduced the compensation sum awarded. The court ordered payment of a sum equivalent to the claimant's average gross commission over a period of 15 months ie £14,055.

Case example – *Alan Ramsay Sales & Marketing Ltd v Typhoo Tea* [2016] EWHC 486

6.68   In this case (also considered in Chapter 5), once the court concluded its decisions concerning complex issues over 'without prejudic' correspondence and the parties' conduct which may or may not have amounted to repudiatory breach, it then turned to what compensation to award.

The court quoted at length from *Lonsdale v Howard & Hallam Ltd* and referred to the expert evidence which both principal and agent had obtained in the present case. On the issues of expenses the court examined the evidence of each valuer and said for 'Motor, travel and accommodation - The experts agree that the figure for the cost of motor, travel and accommodation should be about 32% of the total wages bill so that the correct figure, based on Mr MacLaverty's figures, is £47,352'. The court allows in the calculations a deduction of about £25k for employment of a notional employee to provide the agency services (on the basis £50k would be a full time wage, and the agent here paid himself more by way of dividends but that was regarded as irrelevant – he took about £70k a year).

The agent was being paid a retainer of about £260,000 in 2012 and spent three days a week at the principal's office where he engaged in the agency work and work for other principals too.

6.69   In addition to damages for failure to pay retainer and for insufficient notice on compensation, the court said:

'*Conclusion on compensation under Regulation 17*

For all the reasons set out above, I accept Mr MacLaverty's [one expert] figures for the wage costs including for a sales manager equivalent of Mr Ramsay [the agent]. I allow £10,000 for fixed costs and for other variable costs take Mr MacLaverty's figures rather than Mr Hall's [the other expert witness]. On that basis the total costs are £217,375 which means that the pre-tax multiplicand is £42,625. The parties will be able to calculate the post-tax figure. To that must be applied a multiplier of 4. The resultant figure, which will be in the region of £130,000, seems to me a fair reflection of the value of the agency and what a notional purchaser would have been prepared to pay for it.'

6.70   In *Invicta UK v International Brands Ltd* [2013] EWHC 1564, the parties' experts agreed the price for assessing regulation 17 compensation should be based on the price a notional purchaser would pay for the income stream which the agency would have generated to which a multiple of net price should be applied less the direct costs of the agency. The parties' experts' main dispute was over net costs

Mr MacLaverty (one expert – who was also instructed in the *Typhoo Tea* case) suggested a multiplier of 7. Ms Nelder, the expert for the other party suggested 2. The court chose 4.5 thus awarding compensation of £124,213.50 (and £10,000 separately owed in the case).

The court also decided at common law a reasonable notice period would have been six months although they did not need to decide so for the purposes of the case and the court had also decided the Regulations did indeed apply.

Breaches of contract reduce compensation

6.71   In *Green Deal Marketing Ltd v Economy Energy Trading Ltd* [2019] EWHC 507 the court held that even though earlier repeated breaches of contract did not remove entitlement to compensation as they were not substantial and did not justify immediate termination), could result in the agency being valued at a lower level for the purposes of compensation under regulation 17. In that case the court did also consider relevant the fact the agency agreement might not have carried on, in discounting what was payable, but that did not remove the entitlement to compensation entirely.

Net or gross?

6.72   The cases had been contradictory on whether the agent's compensation under regulation 17 should be based on net or gross commission. In the *Tigana* case the court based it on net earnings and took off 20% for expenses (rather high but the sum on the facts of this case). The court specifically did not set a rule that compensation would always be based on net commission. In Lonsdale it was based on net income because in assessing what someone would pay to buy a business or the value of the goodwill of the agency what matters to the buyer is what profit would be made from taking the agency over. Since then, most compensation cases which have reached a court judgment usually involve deduction of expenses and removal of the annual cost of hiring a manager to undertake the agent's work which could, for example, be £40,000 and apply a multiplier such as 4x the resulting sum to work out the overall compensation.

Time limit

6.73   As with the indemnity, a claim must be made within a year of the termination of the contract by the agent notifying the principal he intends to make a claim. It is not provided that such notification should be in writing nor that legal proceedings actually have to be initiated in that time (regulation 17(9)).

The Limitation Act 1980 requires the claim (ie litigation started) to be brought within six years.

Substantial benefits

6.74   Regulation 17(7) is a deeming provision. It describes when the damage for which the agency can claim compensation is deemed to occur. It refers to the agent being deprived of commission. Therefore, the first issue to consider is what is the agent's lost commission – how much was he earning before, and how much would he have been likely to have earned had the contract carried on. In the *Skingsley* case, an agent was awarded four years' commission on the basis he was aged 61 and would have worked until he was 65. It is not a very well argued judgment and it misrepresents German law, but one can see how the judge reached his conclusion given the wording of regulation 17. However. since *Lonsdale* a valuation report should ideally be obtained.

6.75   The agent must have brought substantial benefits to the principal. Where the sum total of the agent's efforts over the period of the agency is to reduce the number of customers in his area, even if the drop in sales is due to the principal's poor products or a recession, it is unlikely the agent can make a claim, but the German and other provisions examined above in relation to a similar substantial benefits provision in relation to the indemnity are relevant (see the indemnity section above in this respect).

6.76   In *Graham Page v Combined Shipping and Trading Co Ltd* [1997] 3 All ER 656 the court looked at what 'proper performance' of the agency contract means. One argument is that if proper notice is given of termination then the principal has properly performed the contract. The agent could not therefore have expected to earn any more than he would have earned in his notice period, and therefore the Regulations do not in that respect alter English law – a principal could still avoid paying anything if he gave the notice stated. This was clearly not the intention of the Regulations or the Directive on which they were based. The Court of Appeal decided the agent had a good arguable case for compensation even though the principal could under the contract have ensured that over the rest of the course of the agency term no commission was earned. The court said it should look at what would have happened had the contract been performed throughout its future life 'in the normal manner in which the parties intended [it] to be performed'.

6.77   In *Green Deal Marketing Ltd v Economy Energy Trading Ltd* [2019] EWHC 507 the High Court looked at whether the *Page* case would be decided the other way these days but did not quite go so far:
   The judge said:

'Mr Dhillon QC [one of the counsel in the case] submitted that the reasoning in *Page* would now be regarded as wrong anyway because, as Lord Hoffmann made clear in *Lonsdale* at paragraph 17, it is for Member States in their discretion to decide what method to use when assuming the value of the indemnity (and by inference also the compensatory award) in relation to which they enjoy a wide margin of appreciation. On that footing, he says that today, *Page* would be decided the other way because the Court should make the common law assumption (as per a damages claim) that the party in breach must be assumed now to have exercised his contractual rights to the greatest advantage to him.

I do not go so far, not because I do not follow paragraph 17 of Lord Hoffmann's judgment but rather because it is plain that a valuation exercise is not the same as a pure damages claim at common law anyway and that difference has to be respected. The better way, therefore, to consider rights of termination is, in my view, to say that they can be factored into account in a valuation which has to be conducted on a 'real-world' basis.

Judge Waksman's decision [High Court in *Software Incubator Ltd v Computer Associates UK Ltd*] was overturned on a different ground in the Court of Appeal [now going from Supreme Court to CJEU in 2020]. However, Mr Green relies on these passages as showing that the court assessing compensation is not required to make a counter-factual assumption that the agency would have endured forever'.

6.78   The judge in *Green Deal* held that the fact that an agency agreement might be terminable at some stage later, was at least to some extent relevant to the valuation of the agency for the purposes of compensation. However, this case and the other case law make clear that a pure common law approach of arguing that if an agency agreement can be terminated on eg three months' notice and therefore has no value, is wrong in relation to the Regulations.

6.79   In *King v Tunnock* [1999] 1 All ER 1946 the court in Scotland on appeal looked at the compensation provisions in detail. The court said that the indemnity and compensation provisions must not be confused and:

'The whole purpose of the 'termination' provisions is to reimburse the agent with the value of the goodwill of the business he has built up, which may be lost to him on termination but retained by the principal. The provisions are not intended to be punitive. They give the agent some security in the form of recompense. He receives no compensation if he assigns to another agency, because he is entitled to payment from the assignee whether he exacts it or not.'

6.80   This was also followed in *Lonsdale*, despite general criticism of that decision. The court said that the indemnity and compensation provisions should be interpreted so that they do not produce significantly different results, because the overall aim was harmonisation of the law: 'although this case is a "compensation" case it is I think both legitimate and indeed necessary to look at the "indemnity" provisions'. The court did not think regulation 17(6) should stand alone. If it did, then if the 'principal retired while the agent was still a young man the principal could find himself liable for a very large sum if all the court was required to consider was the effect on the agent's financial position as a result of termination'. In this case this is what the agent had done – he had estimated the number of working years left to him and estimated his annual earnings and multiplied one by the other and claimed £143,000, even though in this case the principal had decided to close down a loss-making business. It is not the basis now undertaken in assessing compensation after *Lonsdale*.

6.81   In the *King* case there was no finding as to whether substantial benefits accrued to the principal after termination, an important prerequisite before any compensation is payable (or indemnity for that matter). The agent's appeal was not allowed. The court noted that in *Page* supra the sum allowed (at the interlocutory stage) was 75% of a year's commission – ie the agent was allowed to retain goods worth that sum of the principal to set off against his entitlement which would be settled at a later court hearing.

6.82   In *King v Tunnock* the court said 'If the agent has negotiated a five year contract with the principal, and his agency is terminated after one, then the court should try to calculate the benefit that the principal will, in the normal course of business, receive in the following four years and made an award to the agent on that basis – see *Page*. If the agent and the principal have an open-ended contract, then presumably the court must, in its discretion, fix a reasonable period (as the Germans did and as the Regulations do in the indemnity model by providing for a period of one year)'.

6.83   On the issue of whether regulation 17(6) can stand alone, it was pointed out that 17(6) makes no reference to the agent having to show that substantial benefits accrue to the principal. Regulation 17(7), it was argued, was just further explanation – examples of when damage might occur but it did not set out the preconditions. They were in 17(6) and therefore there was no requirement to show the substantial benefits. Regulation 17(7) states that damage is deemed to occur 'particularly' in the circumstances outlined. It does not say 'exclusively'. The Scottish court on appeal in *King* appears to have agreed that there was no need to show substantial benefits even though it is a requirement of French law (which has similar compensation provisions where agents normally receive two years' commission without deductions). The court concluded that the agent had not produced enough figures on items such as his expenses. The court said:

> 'Since the pursuer paid his own petrol and since the payment is a lump sum payment and applying the broadest brush to hand a deduction of 10% in my opinion ought to be made so that the Sheriff's two year gross figure of £27,144 should be reduced to £24,429.60. From that Figure I would have deducted (1) the award already made for severance without notice that is to say £4,762. (2) the benefits which the pursuer received during the two years in question [invalidity and sickness benefit he claimed after termination] and (3) his earnings of £50 per week from the date he commenced part-time employment.

I cannot therefore precisely quantify the award which would have been made if regulation 17(6) stood alone, but no doubt if the matter were to go further the pursuer could produce the figure which would enable a precise figure to be struck if this approach commends itself. On the whole matter the appeal will be refused . . .'

It is a difficult judgment to follow and it is not always clear what the court is saying. It did in its day lend credence to the theory that French law is the most relevant when the compensation provisions are examined but since Lonsdale that is discredited. This was also mentioned in the indemnity case *Duncan Moore v Piretta* discussed previously where the court said the compensation provisions were derived from the law of France. The Commission make the same point in their 1996 Report referred to above.

The Commission's 1996 Report and compensation

6.84   The European Commission in their 1996 Report say that the compensation system was based on French law which dated from 1958. They say French law was based on what a successor to the agent would pay to buy the agency or the time it takes an agent to re-constitute the client base of which he has been deprived. The latter is a better indicator in practice in countries such as the UK where there is no tradition in most industries of new agents 'buying' an area, except perhaps in relation to franchising contracts which are not normally agencies in any event.

6.85   The Commission say:

'By judicial custom the level of compensation is fixed as the global sum of the last two years' commission or the sum of two years' commission calculated over the average of the last three years of the agency contract which conforms with commercial practice. However, the courts retain a discretion to award a different level of compensation where the principal brings evidence that the agent's loss was in fact less, for example, because of the short duration of the contract or where, for example, the agent's loss is greater because of the agent's age or his length of service.'

6.86   The Commission mention the following points:

1.   The sum in France is calculated on all remuneration and not just commission.
2.   It is also based on the gross sum and with no deduction for expenses/costs.
3.   Outstanding commission is included in the calculation.
4.   The sum represents the part of the market lost to the agent and future occurrences are not taken into account such as if the principal ceases to trade, whether the agent continues to work for the same clients or changes in the market place.
5.   There is no duty on the agent to mitigate his loss.

6.87   The Commission also say 'Under French law and practice, compensation awarded in the vast majority of cases amounts to two years' commission which is twice the legal maximum provided for under the indemnity option. This clearly makes the appointment of an agent in France under French law a much more costly enterprise'. This had also led to some principals using other EU law, such as German law for their French agents. The Commission also point out that in the UK some have sought to apply common law principles which are very different from French law. In France the courts do not order two years' commission as compensation where the agent's loss is likely to be less, such as where there had been a short duration of the contract. The sum may exceed two years' commission where the agent's loss is greater because of his age or length of the agency contract.

6.88   Further examples of differences are in the taking account of future developments after termination and the obligation to mitigate a loss. The Commission say they think it unlikely the English courts will reach the two-year sum payable in France:

> 'This no doubt derives from the previous legal position in the UK, that agency contracts could be terminated on notice without any payment being due. This naturally has had consequences for business practices. There was no real concept of goodwill attaching to an agency to which the agent had a right to share in.'

That was written a long while ago and since then the *Lonsdale* case has intervened. It is clear now that there is no two-year rule and what matters is what lasting legacy the principal has after termination.

6.89   The EU's 2014 review of the Agency Directive concluded that no changes were needed – see https://ec.europa.eu/growth/content/evaluation-commercial-agents-directive-86653eec-report-0_en and the resulting report which is reproduced in Appendix 2.4.

Estimating the loss for compensation

6.90   The Government in its guidance notes on the Regulations, questions and answers section, ask if it is possible to include a liquidated damages provision in a contract. This would be where the parties estimate the loss likely to be suffered by an agent on termination. The guidance says this is possible where the sum represents a genuine pre-estimate of damage. However, such clauses risk being rendered void by regulation 19. The parties may however want to set out a valuation basis in their clause in the agreement just as in joint venture/shareholder agreements the parties often agree a valuation basis in advance.

No contracting out

6.91   Regulation 19 provides that the parties may not derogate from regulations 17 or 18 to the detriment of the commercial agent before the agency contract expires. This means that once the contract is over the agent and principal can agree a binding of settlement of any dispute on whatever terms they wish. Therefore, principals may be able to offer the agent a fairly derisory sum which he accepts in writing as a full and final settlement in which case the matter is over. However, when the contract is in operation this cannot be done.

- One point to watch in settlement negotiations before the notice of termination period is over – in theory there the contract is still in operation and therefore a full and final settlement could be avoided later. Therefore, it should be ensured either that the parties document that the agreement is ending early and they accept that, or that the settlement is signed after the period of notice is over and is the correct period of notice.

- Some contracts provide 'three months' commission shall be paid on termination'. This is hardly worth including. It can be overturned because of regulation 19 (unless the Regulations do not apply to the contract). In some cases, it may result in an agent simply accepting the sum proffered but he is under no obligation to do so.

- Other contracts provide 'The Commercial Agents (Council Directive) Regulations 1993 do not apply to this agreement'. Again, this is a completely worthless statement.

- A genuine liquidated damages provision might be included, although it does rather draw the agent's attention to his rights and may be offered in a case where the principal thinks the Regulations apply but they do not. It may even be a case where when the contract begins the Regulations do apply but by the time of termination the agent has taken on other activities which make the agency secondary (see Chapter 1) and thus there is no need to pay compensation at all. However, if the contract says compensation must be paid it must be paid. In *Shearman v Hunter Boot Ltd* [2014] EWHC 47 (QB) the court did say that the Regulations should be interpreted in a purposive EU law manner so in the light of that it is fairly unlikely liquidated damages clauses will work.

The *Duffen* case and penalty clauses

6.92   The decision in *Duffen v FRA* [2000] Lloyd's Rep 180 centred on a clause in an agency contract which provided for a £100,000 payment if the contract were terminated early. It was an unusual contract, as it favoured the agent (most do not). The court found that the sum was unenforceable because it was a penalty clause and not a genuine pre-estimate of losses which would be enforceable by way of a liquidated damages clause. The court therefore found that the agent would be entitled to compensation under the Regulations in the normal way though this was not assessed in this judgment.

The facts

6.93   The agent was appointed exclusive UK and Irish agent of FRA on 1 August 1994 for a minimum four-year period. He was owed £27,000 plus in commission and sued for that as well as £100,000 under the penalty clause or an interim payment pending the full trial. The dispute, not relevant to this chapter, also centred on whether the agent had made a misrepresentation to the principal in a fraudulent way understating an English FRA company's debts in which the principal and agent both had a 50% stake and that he had misrepresented English law in statements he made about rights he had to retain stock. The court found the allegation of fraud incredible and said that it was not surprising that a bad debt was left out as there was no hope of recovering it.

6.94   The clause in question said:

'Upon the termination of this Agreement by the Agent pursuant to clause 6.3 the Principal shall immediately become liable to the Agent for and shall pay to the Agent forthwith the sum of £100,000 by way of liquidated damages which sum is hereby agreed by the parties to be a reasonable pre-estimate of the loss and damage which the Agent will suffer on termination of this Agreement by failure of the Principal to pay the sums which but for the Principal's breach hereof would have been payable to the Agent under the terms hereof.'

The court relied on *Dunlop Pneumatic Tyre Co Ltd v New Garage and Motor Co Ltd* [1915] AC 79, HL, in holding the clause void. The agent was entitled to a £4,000 per month retainer and his commission, and if this were not paid he could terminate the agreement for breach. The court said:

'The sum payable is not graduated. £100,000 is payable irrespective of the unexpired duration of the term. It would still be payable if termination occurred in the last month of the contract's life. The plaintiff could thus recover a substantial windfall. This, to my mind, would be both extravagant and unconscionable.'

The case is a useful warning to those who seek to include clauses providing for the sum paid on termination. They must be carefully considered.

Other contract clauses

6.95   Some contracts provide for the following:

1.   Retirement of the agent at, say, 65 (see Chapter 5). The agent may still claim compensation on termination, although there is little case law on this – see *Abbott v Condici Ltd* [2005] 2 Lloyds Rep 450 and Chapter 5 (para **5.59**).

2.   The consequences of one partner in an agency partnership dying, leaving etc – perhaps the contract continues (no compensation payable).

3.   Payment of an indemnity – the biggest issue of all: at least the indemnity is capped at a year's commission. Perhaps the contract could provide:

> Where the Commercial Agents (Council Directive) Regulations 1993 apply to this Agreement and are so held by a court, the agent shall be entitled to be indemnified where this agreement is terminated under clauses [xxx] where he meets the conditions for an indemnity in the Regulations provided he claims within the statutory period.

(Providing for the lower of compensation or indemnity would not appear to work following the *Shearman v Hunter Boot Ltd* [2014] EWHC 47 (QB) and *Brand Studio Ltd v St John Knits, Inc* [2015] EWHC 3143 (above at para **6.11**).)

4.   Liquidated damages provisions such as:

> Where the Commercial Agents (Council Directive) Regulations 1993 apply to this Agreement and are so held by a court, the agent may be entitled on termination under clauses [xxx] to payment of a sum representing three months' commission for each year in which he has worked for the principal as agent or an indemnity if lower. The parties agree that such sum is a genuine pre-estimate of the agent's losses where he meets the conditions of the Regulations.

It is very doubtful whether a liquidated damages provision would work as it would be so hard in advance to calculate a genuine estimate of the sum concerned, given that compensation is not really damages for breach of contract.

6.96   It is important to ensure that it is only where the Regulations apply that there is an entitlement otherwise the agent may receive more than he is due. The same issues arise if using a precedent designed for agencies within the Regulations when the Regulations do not apply (eg to an agent marketing services not goods) – too much is given to the agent than would need to be under the law in the absence of the application of the Regulations. From the agent's perspective he may be better without a written contract at all, as many of its provisions will be designed to impose onerous duties on the agent with the aim of minimising compensation on termination. Some agents have their own short agreement they have principals sign. There is no need for this to refer to compensation.

6.97   In *McQuillan v McCormick* [2010] EWHC 1112 (QB) the court looked at valuation issues. It said:

> 'Under clause 9.3 [of the Agreement] the License Owner had the right to terminate on one year's notice if the orders did not amount to €300,000 in a calendar year. Under clause 9.4 there was a right to renegotiate every year. If no agreement could be reached the Agreement continued for a further 12 months and then terminates. It is thus realistically arguable that the agreement is in fact

terminable on a year's notice. It will be seen from the second table in the appendix that the revised annualised income (with a multiplier of 1.5 incorporated to allow for the rising market) is £207,928.96 as at April 2008. It was agreed by the experts that the relevant reduction for the costs was £59,000. It follows that the income stream to be valued is approximately £149,000 per annum.

If the contract between Mr McCormick and Pandora A/S comes to an end then there will be no income stream. In that event it is clear from Lord Hoffmann's speech that it is of no value. Thus the question to be asked is what is the value of an income stream of £149,000 which is increasing but which could be terminated within 2 years. When the question is asked in that way it becomes plain to my mind that the discount applied by the expert of 25% is far too small. For my part I doubt if anyone would pay more than 1 years purchase and I propose to value the compensation at £150,000. It is to be remembered that this sum already includes a multiplier of 1.5 over the actual income.'

There has been some criticism of this case. In *Lonsdale* of relevance was the fact that the principal's business was closing down, whereas in *McQuillan* the risk of Pandora business no longer being available perhaps should only have been considered were Pandora to have given notice to terminate its distribution agreement with Mr McCormick, which it had not done.

In practice, the *McQuillan* case is typical – although *Lonsdale* requires a valuation approach, in practice agents often receive one to two years' gross commission as compensation.

Claiming damages for breach of contract in addition

6.98   However, if the agent has a fixed-term contract it may be that he will receive more in relation to common law damages for breach of contract. If the contract, for example, is supposed to run for four years and notice is given at the end of one year, then the agent under English common law may be entitled to three years' commission less any obligation to mitigate his loss etc. Can he also claim compensation too? That is not clear, but he probably can. As has been seen above in some of the decisions to date, the agent has been able to claim damages and compensation and indeed the Regulations (17(5)) expressly state that this is permissible. The fact that it is suggests compensation is for something other than the agent's losses for breach of contract, ie that compensation in some way is looking at the goodwill the agent has built up from which the principal shall continue to derive substantial benefits after termination. The court does examine what the agent has received under other heads such as regulation 8 post-termination commission but does not undertake a 'set off' in assessing the compensation.

Legal costs and agents

6.99   Agents should ensure that they have full details available of expenses, future loss of earnings etc to provide where required when principals successfully bring in other issues, as described below. Some are represented free by their trade association or union.

6.100 Agents may have legal expenses cover through their trade association. This has enabled many agents to make a legal claim who would otherwise not be in a position to do so. Agents may be able to obtain assistance from their local citizen's advice bureau. Where the claim is under £10,000, they may be able to bring a claim in their local county court under the small claims procedure. Agents who are individuals are entitled to bring legal proceedings themselves if they choose not to use lawyers.

Conditional fee agreements

6.101 Some lawyers may be prepared to bring a claim for an agent on a conditional fee agreement basis (no win, no fee) – however the agent would still need to pay disbursements such as court fees and insure against having to pay the other side's costs if they lose and has to bear the conditional fee uplift (normally 100% of the base costs) and insurance out of the agent's damages since the Legal Aid, Sentencing and Punishment of Offenders Act 2012 came into force. This has had a major impact in reducing access to justice for agents. Many agents earn £10k to £20k a year. If they claim compensation through court proceedings inevitably the portion of their base costs they cannot recover from the other party (perhaps a third) plus the 100% uplift and insurance premium may well exceed the sum they will recover. It is vital to calculate this early in any potential litigation as well as assessing whether the principal is likely to survive or go into liquidation.

6.102 The Legal Aid, Sentencing and Punishment of Offenders Act 2012 provided for the first time for 'damages based agreements' all VAT and both solicitor and barrister fees. However, for commercial agency claims this is not likely to be useful in a case where the agent seeks to recover, say £10k damages as 50% (the £5k less VAT) for the lawyers is not going to be sufficient to cover the likely cost and time involved in taking a case to a full trial at the county court.

Also, the small claims limit is now £10k so any agent claiming less will not recover legal costs.

6.103 Finally, court fees are high. Below are 2020 fees for claims of £3,000 and above.

Claim amount	Paper form fee	Online claim fee
£3,000.01 to £5,000	£205	£185
£5,000.01 to £10,000	£455	£410
£10,000.01 to £100,000	5% of the claim	4.5% of the claim
£100,000.01 to £200,000	5% of the claim	No online claims
More than £200,000	£10,000	No online claims

(Online simply means the case is started online. It does not mean hearings are avoided.)

So, a claim for £40k compensation where litigation is used comes with a court fee of £1,800 (£2k if not issued online). This is similar to the fees charged for formal arbitration under the Arbitration Act 1996 which some contracts specify. Many litigation cases end up in mediation anyway so it may be more sensible for the parties to pay for mediation before they incur court fees.

6.104 It is not surprising that agents try to negotiate compromises of their agency claims under the Regulations and that principals have become increasingly bullish knowing agents (other than those with pre-existing insurance or a trade union or association) may well not be able to litigate other than as litigant in person.

6.105 Advice to agents on claiming compensation includes:

1. Do not bring a claim until all commission due is paid, as often the first action a principal will take when presented with a claim is to hold back money legitimately due. Collect all commission owed before mentioning a compensation claim.

2. Make sure a claim is made within the 12-month period after termination and in writing.

3. Do not assume there is an absolute entitlement to a payment on termination – many agents think this is the case. Take legal advice, and refer to Chapter 5 above.

4. Do not resign. Rights can be lost by so doing.

5. Avoid obvious breaches of the agency contract as otherwise the principal may be able to avoid payment of compensation/indemnity.

6. Do not accept any small sum in full and final settlement unless you are sure that it is acceptable.

7. Do not sign any document without legal advice.

8. Do not assume agency agreements are not legally binding just because the agent never signed them. Expressly reject them in writing and keep copies of letters. Also reject any change to an area product range or commission rate as otherwise it may be accepted by default.

9. Check the contract every time a change is proposed – such as the appointment of a sub-agent. It may be prohibited.

10. Do not accept the principal's first offer but only litigate where there is enough money at stake to make the trouble and expense worthwhile. If the case is unsuccessful all the agent's personal assets could be lost. It would not be unusual in a High Court litigation case for the other side to accumulate costs of up to £300,000 and more, and therefore litigation should not be entered into lightly. Obtain estimates of legal

costs and ensure regular bills are sent out, and consider the question of costs against likely damages recoverable at every stage. Never litigate on principle.

11   Consider all 'without prejudice' offers carefully. It is better to accept eight months' commission after paying for a few solicitors' letters than spending two years getting a case to court, paying lawyers every month in that period and then finding the court awards less because the judge did not understand the Regulations properly. In *Barrett McKenzie v Escada* [2001] ECC 50 the agent rejected a 15-months' commission Part 36 offer. He then won less than that at trial and thus because of how Part 36 of the Civil Procedure Rules 1998 works had to pay both side's legal costs. He ended up without a penny and indeed owing more than he won. In the Court of Appeal interim decision in *Rossetti Marketing Ltd v Diamond* [2012] EWCA Civ 1021 (above) an interim costs payment of £300k against the principal was overturned and the court intimated there had been an earlier Part 36 offer.

12   Where several agents of the same principal have their contracts terminated, it can be sensible to pool resources and instruct one solicitor, assuming there are no conflicts of interest. It may even be possible to include both claims on the same summons, though this may be challenged by the defendant.

Reducing compensation – principals

6.106   The following guidelines help principals avoid claims:

1.   Draft contracts well so that there are a number of possible substantial breaches of contract of which the agent can be accused and include an indemnity clause (capped at a year's commission over the last five years but not necessarily as high as a year's commission) but only if the Regulations apply and this is a situation under the Regulations which entitles the agent to claim.

2.   Consider using distributors or employees rather than agents.

3.   Cut down the product range before a termination (ensuring the contract allows for this) so the agent's commission becomes very little and no one would buy the agency. Reducing the territorial scope by agreement as in *Scottish Power Energy Retail Ltd v Taskforce Contracts Ltd* [2008] ScotCS CSOH 110 and *Tony Vick v Vogle-Gapes Ltd* [2006] EWHC 1579 may also assist the principal but stopping short of termination. Reducing it to 10% of the original area, however, may be regarded as 'constructive termination' entitling the agent to terminate for breach and make a claim.

4.   Keep full records of what the turnover on the area was before the agent started and any assistance or customers given to the agent by the

principal although that will not at the end of the day help in reducing compensation it may have a practical effect in persuading an agent to accept less.

5. Do not mention compensation to the agent.

6. Persuade the agent to resign rather than give him notice of termination. In most cases there is no compensation on resignation and sack agents when profits are low in times of recession not at the top of market cycles

7. Keep good records and send regular notices to a non-performing agent. Do not accept and waive major breaches of contract by the agent.

8. Give the legal notice period required to be given and pay all commission up to the date of termination and a reasonable period thereafter as required by the Regulations.

9. Wait for the agent to make a claim. He may never do so. There is no obligation to pay anything unless he makes a claim within 12 months of termination (regulation 17(9)).

10. If he makes a claim, either do not reply or 'fob him off' in reply – not a particularly good practice or very moral but often successful as the agent cannot afford litigation in many cases particularly under the litigation changes described above. Many principals delay in replying to letters, though in practice it is normally better and cheaper to settle quickly.

11. Where the principal is itself an agent, there may be a claim against the principal's own principal.

12. If the principal has legal expenses insurance which may cover the costs speak to the insurers before taking any action.

13. If correspondence with the agent is not resulting in a quick solution just wait for the agent to sue. Often, he will not.

14. If a court claim arrives note all deadlines and take legal advice.

15. Consider making a Part 36 offer or other without prejudice offer in a sum advised by the principal's solicitors. This means that if the agent is awarded less at trial there are significant cost disadvantages.

16. When negotiating or fighting a claim, try to show:

    (a) the Regulations do not apply – see Chapter 1 – on the grounds of secondary activities, no continuing authority to negotiate, activities outside the UK, etc;

    (b) there were no substantial benefits for the principal so no compensation or indemnity is payable/the agency has no resale value going forward on the *Lonsdale* principles;

    (c) the agent was in substantial breach of contract such as failing to make a contractual required target sum so no compensation or indemnity is payable and that this justifies immediate termination – this is one reason why having detailed duties imposed on the agent in the contract is useful such as to visit outlets regularly – some principals require an agent to use a tracking phone app for monitoring sales calls (eg www.salesforce.com). See also *Spectrum Agencies v Crocs Europe BV* [2012] EWCA Civ 1400 (CA) in Chapter 5;

(d) the agent had substantial expenses which should be taken off his commission in calculating the sum;

(e) the obligation to mitigate loss (not clear this applies however after *Lonsdale*) and allowance for accelerated receipt;

(f) poor continuing receipts after the agent left, or the agent took customers with him;

(g) the worst period for commission receipts – in other words for compensation when no period for averaging is given, unlike the indemnity, and seek to illustrate that the future commission the agent would have earned had the contract carried on would not have been much. Some principals wait until recessions when agents are earning much less and terminate agency contracts then as it is cheaper to do so as the compensation payment will be less.

17. Discount the sum reached on the above to take account that the agent is being saved litigation. Normally, settlements at the door of the court are a lot higher than early on after a few letters have been exchanged.

Other contract provisions – indemnity or compensation

6.107 Some contract provisions have been examined in the section above. In other cases, the parties may provide that an indemnity is payable. As seen above if the parties in the UK want an indemnity to be payable rather than compensation, then they need to provide for it in their contract.

It may be permissible to say that an indemnity will apply unless the sum assessed for compensation is less, in which case that will apply.

6.108 The first indemnity decision *Duncan Moore v Piretta* discussed under the indemnity section above resulted in the sum calculated for the indemnity being reduced when the final stage of calculation of application of the one-year cap was completed. This perhaps shows the merits of the indemnity over compensation.

Restrictive covenants and agency

6.109 Regulation 20 of the Regulations provides that a restraint of trade clause is valid only if it is in writing and 'relates to the geographical area or the group of customers and the geographical area entrusted to the commercial agent and to the kind of goods covered by his agency under the contract'. It must not last for more than two years after termination of the agency contract. Nothing in the Regulations affects any rules of law which impose restrictions on restraint of trade clauses. This means in some cases a period of two years may be regarded by the court as void if it is unreasonable in all the circumstances under English restraint of trade law.

6.110   Mention was made above of the effect such a clause can have on compensation claims. If the agent cannot work, his claim may be higher – but only if compensation is assessed based on an obligation to mitigate loss and proof of the loss suffered, which is not apparently the case under French law on which the Agency Directive's compensation provisions are based.

6.111   In general, however, the question as to what restrictions should be imposed on the agent during and after the agency agreement is a commercial issue. During the term it would be expected that a restrictive covenant be imposed. Indeed, it is arguable that an agent may be in breach of his duty of good faith if he takes on a competing agency. This is harder to maintain than enforcement of a clear clause. Once the contract is over, in many cases two years may be too long or unnecessary and a shorter period may be substituted such as one year or six months or even three months. In *Tigana* it was pointed out that a post-termination restriction which could stop the agent earning money after termination could go to extend the compensation to which the agent would be entitled; thus, only include one with care and after considering that potential disadvantage. In sales of a business the sellers expect to be subject to such restrictions but in agreeing to take on agency it is possible a buyer would pay less because of a long post-termination restrictive covenant. In *Lonsdale* the Winemakers Federation of Australia were allowed to intervene and it was established that if a wine agent or any agent took all the customers with him then he did not receive compensation as the asset of the business/the goodwill etc had gone with the agent and nothing of value was left. Chapter 3 looked at competition law and agency contracts.

6.112   In *BCM Group Plc v Visualmark Ltd* [2006] EWHC 1831 the contract provided:

> 'Within a period of two years thereafter (Visualmark) will not thereafter canvass, approach or solicit the custom of (in respect of any business which competes for the business of (BCM Group) as at the date of such termination) any person firm or company who has, during the period of one year prior to termination been a customer of (BCM Group).'

The court held this was too wide as it extended to customers with whom the agent had had no contact. The court also said that despite the two-year period being permitted in the Regulations and being acceptable here, in some agency cases two years may be too long which is useful to bear in mind when drafting agency agreements. Two years also stops an agent working and is probably unnecessary for most principals. Six months may be more common and fair.

6.113   In *One Money Mail Ltd v (1) Ria Financial Services (2) Sebastian Wasilewski* [2015] EWCA Civ 1084 the Court of Appeal looked at restrictive covenants in an agency contract. Mr Wasilewski was appointed as agent by One Money Mail (OMM). OMM specialised in payment services for Polish workers. The case was not therefore about compensation under the Regulations as services not goods were being marketed. Even so, it is useful as an illustration of how the courts decide issues of non-competition clauses in agency contracts. At first instance the court held that restrictions on the agent were in restraint of trade.

The Court of Appeal disagreed and relied upon the case of *Esso Petroleum Co Ltd v Harper's Garage (Stourport) Ltd* [1968] AC 269. Most of the breaches of contract by acting for a competing company by the agent were during the term of the agency contract, including signature of an agency agreement with a company known as Ria, but there was also a six-month termination clause applying within a five-mile radius of the area of Herefordshire where the parties operated as well in the original agency agreement which was also breached. The Court of Appeal held the restrictions were valid and not in restraint of trade. Given that the Regulations (which did not apply in this case) allow a two-year post-termination restriction, the court's conclusion is not surprising. However, the agent was by this time bankrupt.

Litigating agency claims

6.114   This book concentrates on the Regulations and does not propose to cover in detail general principles of litigation. In most cases advice should be sought from solicitors with experience of litigation and the Regulations. Solicitors will be aware of the rules of litigation in general such as when to bring a claim in the High Court as opposed to the county court and what is the effect of a without prejudice offer. If in doubt, solicitors should take advice from counsel.

Pre-action correspondence

6.115   In most agency cases correspondence between principal and agent or their solicitors is all that takes place before a settlement is reached. This would normally be along the lines of the letters given at the end of this book. Often one letter setting out the agent's full rights is sent at the same time as a 'without prejudice' letter settling or offering to settle for a particular sum. Sometimes a telephone call between lawyers or even contact direct between clients can hurry a settlement and avoid the need to litigate. Be aware of the requirement for correspondence before litigating under pre-action protocol rules where applicable. A list of the protocols is at https://www.justice.gov.uk/courts/procedure-rules/civil/protocol. Claiming from a sole trader principal (although these are rare) may mean the pre-action debt protocol applies.

Where to litigate

6.116   Eventually it may become clear that litigation is required. First it should be checked whether the contract provides for disputes to go to arbitration or through the courts. In one case in which the author advised the contract provided for arbitration which the agent was glad to discover. However, on further enquiry a £1,000 registration fee with the arbitration body was required as opposed to a court summons fee which for smaller cases can be lower (although in 2015 court costs rose considerably – £10k for £200k+ claims for example). In other cases, the parties may agree to submit to non-binding mediation. The writer has settled a number of agency disputes through mediation using the mediation body Centre of Effective Dispute Resolution (CEDR) and other mediators.

6.117   For claims over £50,000 the High Court will usually be used. However, this is a very brief summary of the relevant rules and legal advice should be sought. The county court will be cheaper and may be faster. There may be more likelihood of a judge with an understanding of EU law in the High Court.

6.118   The stages of litigation are not set out here. Often counsel is used to draft the particulars of claim in agency cases and sometimes letters before action, although in practice most settle, and there may therefore be no advantage in involving counsel at an early stage and incurring the costs of so doing. For solicitors without experience of the Regulations, however, a counsel's opinion on the merits of the case will assist at an early stage. Indeed, the writer (a solicitor) often advises other solicitors' firms on agency law – disputes and contracts and other similar matters.

Counterclaims

6.119   Defendants may like to consider a counterclaim against the agent. This is common. Sometimes it is justified – such as where the agent has samples or other property of the principal which he is refusing to hand back or owes money on his sample account to the principal. In other cases, it is more spurious and designed to scare the agent into giving up his case or accepting a smaller sum in settlement. Examples include principals who make out a case that the agent had been handling competing products during the agency when he had not, or that his failure to maximise sales was a breach of contract or that the agent defamed the principal (sometimes true, sometimes invented). In *Rossetti Marketing Ltd v (1) Diamond Sofa Company, (2) Solutions Marketing Ltd* [2012] EWCA Civ 1021 (see Chapter 2) the agent was allegedly in breach of contract in operating two declared potentially competitive agencies and the principal had a potential counter-claim against the agent, the Court of Appeal said. It appears that case settled after the interim decision however.

Offers and settlements

6.120   If a 'without prejudice' offer is made, all the conditions required should be set out and a time limit placed on it. It may be without prejudice save as to costs.

An example of a settlement 'Consent Order' is given in Appendix 4 of this book.

6.121   Advice on settling claims:

1.   The principal may want the matter kept confidential; though in practice this can be hard to enforce.

2.   There may be a deadline for payment of the money.

3.   The sum to be paid should be clear. Do not say eight months' commission, for example, because often the greatest disputes are over what is an average month's commission. State the precise sum.

4.   If commission is due on orders before and after termination specify this too. In many cases the principal and agent do not want to wait until all orders are received, and will settle on one sum they can accept even if later orders come in.

5.   Deal with return of any property of either party held by the other.

6.   State the sum is in full and final settlement. There is an example of a consent order following litigation in the county court (see Appendix 4). Sometimes principals have offered a sum to an agent on termination. He has taken it and then sued for more.

7.   The settlement agreement itself should not be 'without prejudice' and must be legally binding. Both parties should sign and date it. If there is litigation then the consent order should be stamped by the court. Always read the latest court rules and forms on consent orders and the like (e.g. Chancery Guide at https://www.judiciary.uk/wp-content/uploads/2016/02/chancery-guide-feb-2016.pdf gives guidance on orders and their drafting (page 96 gives the format for a Tomlin order), although many agency claims are brought in the Queen's Bench Division of the High Court (if not the county court)).

8.   Deal with VAT. Agents might insist VAT is paid on the sum concerned in case later the HMRC VAT inspectors think it should have been paid. It should not cost the principal any more as he can claim back the VAT. In practice most agents agree to be indemnified for the VAT by the principal if later it is assessed as due. The distinction appears to be that payment of commission and for services etc is VATable whereas compensation won in court is not normally so. However, in the *Duncan Moore v Piretta* case (mentioned previously) VAT was paid on the whole sum but not on the interest. It is more common that instead the principal gives a written indemnity to pay VAT if subsequently assessed on presentation of a VAT

invoice. Commission that is due is subject to VAT of course, so it is not always simple to work out what elements of a negotiated settle carry VAT and which do not. Also, some agents are not registered for VAT so when they win a case and win some solicitors' costs they also claim the VAT they paid, whereas if the agent were registered for VAT the agent then may claim from the losing defendant just the legal fees awarded but not the VAT upon them (to avoid double recovery of VAT).

9.   Address any interest due to the agent and whether each side bears their legal costs. If commission is paid late statutory interest under the Late Payment of Commercial Debts (Interest) Act 1998 may be payable at base rate plus 8%. If there have just been a few letters, normally both sides will bear their own costs. If the agent has taken the case as far as witness statements and setting the matter down for a trial, then the agent normally, quite rightly, demands payment of his costs. Generally, it is better at least for smaller agency claims if the figure for these costs can be agreed, rather than the bill going to taxation which can be a lengthy procedure. In some cases, agents have their costs paid for by their trade association, but even there it is on the basis that the association's lawyers will then recover costs from the principal so it does not mean the principal will then avoid having to pay the agent's costs.

10.   Deal with any other remaining issues between the parties. They might want to agree a statement to be issued to customers or there might be assistance the agent must give to a new agent (unlikely if litigation has just finished).

11.   Where the principal is abroad then issues such as the currency of payment should be ascertained.

If the matter is not settled early then the solicitors will need to ensure they proceed beyond issuing to the proceedings, defence, counterclaim reply etc to disclosure.

Disclosure

6.122   Many agents are bad at keeping records. Some are excellent. Some cannot even produce copies of commission statements over the years or their invoices. Normally one or other side will have clear details though of the commission paid. A lot of documents will be electronic and the parties will need to follow the usual litigation rules in that regard and indeed often need to agree 'search terms'. The following documents should be found:

1.   The agency agreement or letter of appointment.

2.   All letters over the years varying it such as reductions to commission rates, areas, exclusivity etc.

3.   Correspondence about poor performance or target figures. Make sure all electronic disclosure rules are followed and tell the agent or principal

early on that they must not destroy any emails which may be relevant in litigation even if part of their regular document destruction policies. There is a legal duty to preserve evidence once litigation is in prospect. Some evidence of performance may indeed be held in apps and the cloud.

4. Sales manuals – they may contain contractual statements.

5. Details of turnover on the agent's area when he was appointed.

6. Details of customers 'given' to the agent and any valuation reports undertaken so far.

7. Details of those customers the agent has brought in.

8. Volumes of business with individual customers and how they have grown over the years.

9. Contrasts on commission and turnover figures with other agents in other areas – perhaps which illustrate how badly an agent was doing.

10. Evidence of breaches of contract of the agent – such as publicity over his appointment with a competitor.

11. Correspondence about the agent attending trade fairs or failing to do so or otherwise performing the contract, such as sheets completed after visits. Most of this correspondence is in e-mails these days so always ask to see those.

12. Complaints from customers, whether about principal or agent.

13. Complaints by agent to principal about defective products, failures to pay commission when due etc.

14. Full details of the agent's expenses incurred in relation to this part of the business and his accounts generally. Asking to see his tax returns can be illuminating and lead to disputes the agent perhaps having claims more than he ought for expenses on accountants' advice and later wanting to back-track in the settlement negotiations

15. Information on whether the agency activities are secondary or not. Is the agent also a distributor of goods etc and how has this changed over time?

16. Information on the agent's current financial position – out of work, new agencies, lower income in new employment.

17. Details of the principal's profits from the area; how a new agent is doing there; what customers have migrated after the agent left.

18. The principal's annual reports and accounts.

19. Details of any common law damages suffered through a termination in breach of contract.

No list can be entirely comprehensive and each case will require different documents. In some cases, most of the records will be held on computer. In others the parties are lucky if there are six documents – a few commission statements and virtually no correspondence and certainly no written contract.

Witness statements

6.123 Normally the agent himself will be the main witness and his contact at the principal the other. If he is accused of bad faith, he may need customers as witnesses to support his position. If the agent is, as in one case, over 80, medical evidence may be needed as to his fitness to carry on. Agents' estates can also claim if the agent has died, in which case the spouse or others with knowledge of the agent's activities may be needed as witnesses. The Manufacturers' Agents' Association produces a card that members can place with their will to notify their heirs of the potential claim.

Trial

6.124 Most cases settle. However, if the matter proceeds to a trial stage it is always worth trying to achieve a last minute settlement. If not, then the matter will proceed before a judge in the normal way. The agency cases which have led to a trial illustrate how different the issues are. They range from a decision about whether the Regulations apply at all, to whether a penalty clause is enforceable, and to whether an agent can retain possession of goods worth £300,000 to set off against his claim to an agent claiming an indemnity specified in his contract and all the the cases covered in this book. Litigation is a rich person's game and even in 'sure fire winner' cases can come with nasty surprises. Principals and agents are usually better off settling even on terms they do not much like than running the risks of a trial.

Further information

6.125 Details for mediation of disputes can be found on the website of the Centre of Effective Dispute Resolution – CEDR – at www.cedr.com.

International Dispute Resolution Centre
70 Fleet Street
London
EC4Y 1EU
United Kingdom
Tel +44 (0)20 7536 6000
www.cedr.com
E-mail info@cedr.co.uk

Details of virtually all the judgments to date are on the Fox Williams website – http://www.agentlaw.co.uk.

The Manufacturers' Agents' Association represents many agents – http://www.themaa.co.uk/.

Roderick Munday *Agency: Law and Principles* (2016, 3rd edn, OUP)

Fergus Randolph and Jonathan Davey *The European Law of Commercial Agency* (2010, 3rd edn, Hart Publishing/Bloomsbury Professional) summarises earlier cases.

See also Jeremy Scholes and Severine Saintier *Commercial Agents and the Law* (2020, 2nd edn, Lloyd's Commercial Law Library, published by Informa Law for Routledge).

Corporate Briefing newsletter provides details of commercial agency cases from time to time – http://www.singlelaw.com/corporate-briefing.

The writer's firm litigates cases for principals and agents – www.singlelaw.com.

Chapter 7

Valuations of Commercial Agents

This chapter is written by Charles Lazarevic of Vero Consulting Ltd.

> 'I would agree that prima facie the value of the agency should be fixed by reference to its net earnings because, as a matter of common sense, that is what will matter to the hypothetical purchaser. Furthermore, in the case of an agent who has more than one agency, the costs must be fairly attributed to each. He cannot simply say, as Mr Lonsdale did in this case, that the marginal cost of the Elmdale agency was little or nothing because he had to see the same customers and go to the same exhibitions for Wendel.'

Lonsdale (t/a Lonsdale Agencies) v Howard & Hallam Ltd [2007] UKHL 32 [29]

7.1   In his speech in the *Lonsdale* decision, Lord Hoffmann set out the interpretation of the Regulations which the UK courts should apply and explained that compensation should be calculated as the amount which a hypothetical purchaser would be willing to pay 'to have been able to take over the agency and … stand in the shoes of the agent' ([2007] UKHL 32 [12]). He also affirmed that a commercial agent is entitled to be compensated for the value of his agency as at termination, on the assumption it is an assignable asset, even if it is not assignable, which is why he uses the term 'hypothetical purchaser'.

7.2   The author has been appointed by principals and agents on many occasions, and occasionally jointly by both parties, to assist in determining the level of compensation due under regulation 17(3).

Commission under Regulation 8

7.3   If the agent is entitled to commission under Regulation 8, occasionally an accountant may be used to quantify the amount due. It may take some considerable time to quantify the entitlement as it depends on knowing which contracts will come to fruition.

7.4   It should be remembered that commission payable under Regulation 8 may have an impact on the quantification of the compensation under Regulation 17, as discussed below as the hypothetical purchaser would not receive the commission on the pipeline sales that were payable to the terminated agent.

How compensation under Regulation 17 should be calculated

7.5   Lord Hoffmann's speech in the *Lonsdale* decision explained that the basis for quantifying compensation should be (at [2007] UKHL 32 [12]):

> 'Like any other exercise in valuation, this requires one to say what could reasonably have been obtained, at the date of termination, for the rights which the agent had been enjoying. For this purpose it is obviously necessary to assume that the agency would have continued and the hypothetical purchaser would have been able properly to perform the agency contract'

He went on to describe the assumptions one should make in setting the compensation to be (at [2007] UKHL 32 [21]):

> '.. the amount which the agent could reasonably expect for the right to stand in his shoes, continue to perform the duties of the agency and receive the commission which he would have received.'

In essence, Lord Hoffmann explained that the exercise to be performed is that of a business valuation.

Valuation methodologies

7.6   Lord Hoffmann said that (at [2007] UKHL 32 [35]):

> 'I do not see how, if the matter goes to court, the judge can decide the case without some information about the standard methodology for the valuation of such businesses.'

It is impossible to describe the standard methodologies within a single short chapter. There are many textbooks and articles on that subject alone. What follows is no more than a summary. The common approaches that can be taken are:

1   **Net assets** – Where a business relies on fixed assets to generate its income then it is common practice in many industries to value businesses based on the value of those fixed assets. A common example being investment property businesses;

2   **Multiple of earnings** – Businesses are often valued by reference to their net earnings. The theory being that comparable businesses will have values proportional to their net earnings (for example, if it is known that

one business sold for four times its net earnings then it may be possible to multiply a comparable business's net earnings by four to arrive at an estimate for its value); and

3   **Discounted cash flow** – When the net earnings of a business being valued are expected to increase or fluctuate considerably, it is possible to perform a more complex valuation which takes these changes into account, such as a discounted cash flow valuation. In view of the large number of figures involved, these calculations are usually performed using spreadsheets. This calculation requires the estimation of an appropriate discount rate. For businesses with established cash flows where comparable businesses can be identified, this method can serve as a useful crosscheck for valuations performed on other bases.

Some industries also have their own rule-of-thumb methods of valuation. The author has not found these to be the useful in the valuation of commercial agencies.

7.7   The net assets method is not an appropriate method for valuing agency because it is not a business that is generally reliant on income generating assets. Furthermore, in his speech, Lord Hoffmann explained that the valuation of commercial agencies for the purposes of calculating compensation under the Regulations should be *'fixed by reference to its net earnings'* suggesting that either the multiple of earnings or discounted cash flow method would be appropriate.

7.8   Where sufficient, reliable evidence is available it is useful to value the business using both the multiple of earnings and the discounted cashflow method as a cross check. If they produce widely different results, the differences between these need to be investigated in order to see how these should impact on the valuation. While valuers generally will provide a range of valuations to take account of various uncertainties, an expert valuation under these Regulations is generally required to provide a single valuation figure.

7.9   It will be clear from this summary that valuations of this type involve an element of judgement, and that this judgement would be applied slightly differently by different experts.

Multiples

7.10   As pointed out by Lord Hoffmann, agencies are generally not bought and sold, so valuations of agencies in accordance with Regulation 17 tend to be hypothetical. The idea behind looking for comparable business sales is that two companies with the same growth prospects, similar profitability and similar debt levels (relative to profits) should be sold at a similar multiple of earnings. In order to find the nearest relevant comparable transactions just prior to the date of termination, it is usual to look for equivalent businesses that were purchased or sold during the two years prior to termination. This is particularly difficult in this area, as Lord Hoffmann himself recognises that these businesses are not traded. Agencies tend to be small private companies and there is often limited information on the price paid for equivalent businesses.

7.11 Identifying comparable business sales requires access to databases of historical information as well as considerable skill and judgement in selecting the appropriate transactions, while rejecting others. One generally looks for business sales from the same or similar industry sector in order to reflect the same risk profile. Differences in multiples should ultimately reflect differences in growth or risk. Classified advertisements are generally not a very good guide as they generally contain very limited financial information on the business or its trading history, and will only present asking prices rather than the prices eventually agreed.

7.12 One should try to include only transactions where one is able to obtain information about the value of the transaction, the company's trading history and balance sheets, and a reasonable degree of further details about the business's financial affairs.

7.13 If there are no transactions in equivalent small private businesses, one is forced to look at transactions involving much larger businesses or even listed companies, which then require additional corrections to take account of the lower multiples commanded by smaller businesses due to their additional risk profile.

Discount rate

7.14 The value of a business arises from the value of the future benefits it brings, usually in the form of future cash flows from its trading activities. In order to arrive at a single figure for the value of all the future receipts, these cash flows need to be adjusted or weighted for the time value of money and the business risk that the amount received will not be what is expected.

7.15 These weightings are called the discount rate and these are chosen to reflect these two factors based on this risk (the higher the risk the higher the discount rate) and this is used to discount all forecast future cash flows to calculate the valuation.

7.16 This requires the estimation of an appropriate discount rate. The discount rate reflects the return on investment that a hypothetical purchaser would require.

Regulation 8

7.17　If the agent is entitled to commission under Regulation 8, it is unlikely that an accountant will be required to quantify the amount due. Also, it may take some considerable time to quantify the entitlement as it depends on knowing which contracts would come to fruition.

7.18　It should be remembered that commission payable under Regulation 8 may have an impact on the quantification of the compensation under Regulation 17, as discussed below. Essentially the terminated agent is entitled to receive the commission that otherwise would have been payable in the normal course of events after the termination date. The hypothetical purchaser would recognise that he will not receive commission in the period immediately following the termination date attributable to the efforts of the terminated agent, possibly leading to a reduction in the valuation under Regulation 17(3).

Indemnity or compensation

7.19　As has already been stated, the Regulations allow for the damages to be awarded on either the indemnity or compensation basis. The quantification of the amount due on the indemnity basis should be more straightforward as the calculation is based on a number of clearly identifiable factors.

7.20　It is the author's understanding that the customers inherited from the principal or an earlier agent are excluded from claims under the indemnity principle (unless the agent has increased the business from those customers) but not for compensation claims. The quantification based on the *Lonsdale* decision does not require earnings from inherited customers to be excluded. This point is overlooked at the principal's peril. This may lead more agency agreements on the basis of compensation to require new agents to pay the principal for any customers they will inherit on a similar basis as any claims they may make on termination.

The *Lonsdale* rules

7.21　The *Lonsdale* approach involves considering the present value of future returns by reference to the price that someone would pay for the income stream which the agency would have generated net of costs (effectively, the potential profit or net income). This is often calculated by reference to the past pattern of commissions and costs incurred in generating them using management accounts and other information including information from the principal and agent.

7.22　There is often a considerable difference of opinion between the parties on the estimate of costs that a hypothetical purchaser would need to incur to maintain the agency, a matter which affects the net earnings for the valuation. While this should be relatively straightforward where there is a single agency (as there should be sufficient historical records to assist in this exercise), where an agency acts for several principals there will be an issue concerning how costs are allocated and apportioned between the subject agency and its other agencies.

7.23   In the author's view the principal and his advisors are often at a disadvantage in quantifying these sums as they will not have sufficient information concerning the agent's activities and the costs incurred in servicing the agency over the years. In other words the agent is likely to have the advantage of presenting most of the evidence that will be used in the quantification.

Allocation of costs

7.24   *Lonsdale* said: 'in the case of an agent who has more than one agency, the costs must be fairly attributed to each' ([2007] UKHL 32 [29]).

In the author's experience quantifying the compensation on the *Lonsdale* basis in multiple agency cases is one of the most contentious areas as there may be arguments over the method of allocating and apportioning costs across the various agencies. The agent's evidence will often be the main source as the principal is unlikely to have received this information during the relationship. For example, does the agent offer several principal's products when he visits some, or even most, of his customers? Some products may be much more expensive and involve much less sales effort, and so it would not be appropriate to apportion costs associated with visiting these customers on the basis of turnover. It may be that the correct allocation cannot be agreed and can only be determined following oral evidence under cross-examination in court. In order to assist in any negotiations, the expert should set out and show the impact on the valuation of the different possible bases of allocating expenses using the disputed evidence from the agent and principal, as well as showing the different approaches that the court could take on the overall allocation based on the *Lonsdale* decision.

7.25   For those costs which could not be directly attributed to a particular agency, either because records were unavailable or because they represented overheads shared by a number of agencies, the hypothetical purchaser would need to estimate the extent to which they were likely to have related to the agency As a practical suggestion, in the absence of compelling evidence to the contrary, it might be appropriate to apportion other overheads equally between the agent's various principals. In other words, each agency would bear it proportion of the other overheads, although this might be a little harsh on new agencies in the early stages of development where little commission had been generated following considerable effort.

7.26   The valuer should also consider whether some categories of cost have been omitted. For example, a sole trader or a partner's own or family member's time may not have been included or fully costed in the accounts. This is likely to be an area that the principal will explore in some detail as it could lead to a reduction in the earnings figure ultimately used in the valuation.

Issues frequently arising in commercial agency valuations

Type of customers and evidence in customer files

7.27   If the customer base comprises of a wide range of long term customers in a variety of business sectors, this could be said to reduce the risk that sales would be lost and commission income reduced due to the loss of a few customers. If the agency relies on a small number of customers, it could be argued that this is a significant risk factor that should be taken into account in the valuation. If the commercial income fluctuates significantly from year to year, this may suggest an increased risk that should be reflected in the valuation. The agent's customer files may be a useful source of information regarding these factors as will be the manner in which the agency was conducted, the effort required to secure orders and the cost of achieving the level of agency business.

7.28   The files might also help establish the technical level of expertise required to sell the product and the nature of the relationship. This could have a bearing on whether it would be usual to have a restrictive covenant in any hypothetical sale agreement. If not, this could depress the value of the agency considerably.

7.29   Sometimes the records concerning the level of skill and amount of effort required to secure business for the principal will be very limited, particularly where customer files have been poorly maintained or are no longer available. Some agents do not prepare formal visit reports and would only make a note if something substantive happened. Sometimes the only source will be the evidence from the agent himself. It will be very evident to both parties that the basis on which the agent's costs are allocated and apportioned between the various principals will have a very significant bearing on the hypothetical valuation.

7.30   There is no hard and fast rule regarding the level of investigation required for the purposes of establishing the costs of servicing the businesses. It has been argued that it would be unusual to go into considerable detail in a valuation in some cases and not in others. The author has been involved in a number of cases where very detailed investigations have been undertaken on such documents as were available, to arrive at the actual figures attributable to each agency even down to analysing mobile phone records and estimating travel times and waiting times to see individual customers.

Restrictive covenants

7.31   If the agency agreement has restrictive covenants on agents, this may enhance the valuation, as it would suggest the outgoing agent would be assumed to leave all his customers behind. However, if the outgoing agent has a close relationship with some or all his customers, this would suggest they would stay with the agent and move to any new principal. The court could assume that a hypothetical purchaser would obtain a restriction covenant, even if it is not expressly stated in the agency agreement. This would have less significance where the principal's goods are unique or have only few competitors, rather than being generic.

Also, an exclusive agency is likely to be more valuable than one where other agents and the principal are entitled to approach directly.

Level of skill and experience required

7.32   The hypothetical purchase would consider the cost of employing staff with the requisite level of skill and experience in order to continue to service the agency. The agent is likely to suggest that the agency business can be conducted with less expensive staff, whilst the principal will point to the considerable skill and experience required to ensure that the customers are retained and the business continues to grow. To some degree this will require knowledge of the market place and industry at the relevant date, information that may not be readily available to the principal.

Office costs

7.33   Office costs will need to be estimated for operating the agency. The author has been involved in valuations where there have been disputes over the allocation and apportionment of rent and rates, travel costs, car expenses, telephone, entertaining, printing, postage and stationery, legal and professional fees, directors' remuneration, repairs and maintenance.

7.34   This raises the question of whether it is reasonable to attribute various characteristics to the hypothetical purchaser, such as whether an existing administration function exists that could easily absorb the additional work required to service one extra agency at minimal cost. Also, the skills required of staff and family members (who may provide their time at a reduced cost, or sometimes at an inflated cost when considering the work undertaken) should be quantified at normal market rates in the valuation.

7.35   In his speech, Lord Hoffmann refers to His Honour Judge Harris's judgment where he recognised that one should consider the probable circumstances of a potential purchaser when conducting the valuation when he said that *'likely buyers would be men of modest means'* ([2007] UKHL 32 [32]).

The hypothetical purchaser's circumstances might dictate that he is able to achieve cost savings not available to others in the market, or he might face costs which are peculiar to him and which would then devalue the business from his perspective. It will be necessary to consider the characteristics of the probable hypothetical purchaser, depending on the sector in question. A hypothetical purchaser with no existing agencies would need to incur more costs in servicing the agency that someone with several existing agencies. A hypothetical purchaser would consider the marginal costs it would incur, together with the opportunity costs associated with the use of existing personnel and assets when considering how much they would be willing to pay to acquire the agency.

7.36   For example, agents visiting the major retailers are more likely to represent several principals selling a variety of products to the retail chains. However, in the author's view a hypothetical purchaser is unlikely to pass all potential cost savings he might enjoy on to the vendor of the business. The value of a business to a given hypothetical purchaser is not therefore necessarily the same as the amount that a hypothetical purchaser would be willing to pay.

Net assets retained

7.37   Assuming that the agency was wound down rather than sold, the agent would have retained various fixed assets, the working capital released and possibly other assets. They should be valued and deducted from the valuation as these are normally passed to the purchaser on sale.

Worked example 1:

7.38   This first example is a common situation. An individual operates as a one-man business from home. He receives a steady level of income from his agency commission, after deducting his business expenses that is equivalent to the salary he could expect to earn in an equivalent role as an employee. There is little prospect of growth in earnings beyond the normal level of inflation.

This is very similar to the *Lonsdale* situation. Quoting His Honour Judge Harris in paragraph [33] of the *Lonsdale* judgment:

> 'This was an agency producing a modest and falling income in a steadily deteriorating environment. There is no evidence that anyone would have paid anything to buy it...I am strongly tempted to find that no damage has been established...But perhaps that conclusion, though I regard it as logical, is a little over rigorous given that the defendant has already made a payment. Doing the best I can, I find that the appropriate figure for compensation is one of £5,000.'

On the basis that the individual could obtain employment at a similar level of income without incurred any significant costs, one would place only a nominal value on the agency of perhaps no more than £5,000, following Lord Hoffmann's example *in Lonsdale.*

Worked example 2:

7.39 A group of four individuals with engineering backgrounds operated together as commercial agents representing three principals. They operated fairly autonomously, covering different regions of the country from their homes. The most senior individual was the managing director who maintained a small office at his home. They had helped one principal to design and market a successful product to their existing customer base. When they visited their customers they offered products from all three principals as the products were complementary and customers generally purchased all three principals' products. Their total commission income was £500,000 and this arose from a broad range of customers, although the terminated agency represented two thirds of the commission income. Their total costs excluding salaries were £150,000. The remaining income was paid as salaries in the following proportions: £150,000, £125,000, £45,000, £30,000. The agency had had working capital of £100,000 tied up in the business and £50,000 had been released following the termination of the agency. There is evidence that individuals with an engineering background could be employed to carry out the managing director's tasks for £45,000 and the remaining three employees could be replaced at an annual salary costs £30,000 each. No payment was due under Regulation 8.

As the product was highly technical it would be reasonable to assume that it would be difficult for the agency to offer competing products and it was also reasonable to assume that a non-complete clause would be offered to the hypothetical purchaser. As the business had a wide range of customers, this was not regarded as a risk factor. Following research of the purchase and sale of similar businesses, a pre-tax earnings multiple of 4 was considered reasonable.

It could be argued that the marginal cost of servicing this agency was negligible, as the same customers had to be visited on behalf of the remaining two principals, or alternatively it could be argued that the costs should be shared equally by all three agencies. It could equally be argued that as this agency represented two third of the commission income, two thirds of the effort went into servicing this principal. In the *Berry v Laytons* case, Mrs Justice Sharpe decided in very similar circumstances that the fair allocation of costs on the *Lonsdale* basis would be 50% of £285,000 (150,000 + 45,000 +3 × 30,000). This means that the net earnings lost as a result of the termination were £48,333 (two thirds of 500,000, less 285,000). Applying a pre-tax multiple might be 4, gives a valuation of £193,333. From this figure should be deducted the working capital released of £50,000 to arrive at a compensation claim of £143,333.

Had there been a payment under Regulation 8, this might have had an impact on the quantification of the compensation due under Regulation 17(3).

Practical points

7.40   The above discussion shows that agencies will be less valuable after they lose a major customer in a contracting sector or in an economic downturn. Principals will be liable to compensate an agent on termination for business that the principal himself may have generated or passed on from a previous agent and it makes little difference whether the relationship had existed for a long or short time. This would not be the case on an indemnity basis. This is often overlooked by principals when entering into agency arrangements. Principals should consider whether new agency agreements on the basis of compensation, should pay for inherited customers.

7.41   Some principals do not question how the agent has conducted his business or what his operating costs are until he receives a claim for compensation. This means that if the agency is terminated and compensation payable under Regulation 17, the principal will be severally hampered in the negotiations due to this lack of understanding. Experiences suggests that principals should ensure that they include a requirement for their agents to file regular marketing and visit reports on their activities, including details of time and costs incurred, the level of skill, experience and remuneration of all staff assigned to deal with the principal's business, and all other costs of servicing the agency and overheads.

7.42   The valuation of any business is always somewhat subjective and so it is not unusual to have different experts presenting widely differing views on the value of an agency. If the experts adopt a sensible approach aimed at assisting the parties to reach a fair settlement, it should be possible to set out the reasons why they have taken different positions on various matters and assist the parties to decide on an acceptable settlement.

Charles Lazarevic, Vero Consulting Ltd

Chapter 8

Foreign agency arrangements

8.1 This chapter looks at issues which arise where the agent is abroad. It cannot provide legal advice on the laws which apply in over 100 countries of the world however, and it remains crucial to obtain legal advice from local lawyers. Even within the EU, where in theory commercial agency law for agents selling goods (but not services), is harmonised there are material differences. As seen in earlier chapters Member States were even given the option of choosing an indemnity payment of a maximum of a year's commission on termination or a compensation payment without such maximum cap. Some countries such as most states of the USA have no compensation system for agents, as was the case in the UK until 1994. What counts in such countries is whether the agreement between the parties has been followed and if the notice period specified in the contract has been given. Other countries provide compensation to agents selling services as well as goods and even to distributors. Many will not respect choice of law and jurisdiction clauses and award compensation even in cases where the English courts would not do so. However, there is then the issue of whether that foreign judgment can be enforced against the UK principal if that principal has no assets in the relevant jurisdiction. Within the EU the Rome I 593/2008 (choice of law in contractual matter), Rome II 864/2007 (choice of law in non contractual matters) and Brussels Regulation 1215/2012 (jurisdiction) all play a part in determining the legal position. The position in relation to UK Brexit always needs to be considered, including transitional arrangements concerning the Rome and Brussels Regulations addressed in article 66 of the EU/UK Withdrawal Agreement.

List of issues

8.2 Below is a list of relevant questions when dealing with a foreign agency arrangement:

- Which country's law will apply? Make sure the contract includes this.

- Which jurisdiction will hear disputes? The contract again should specify this.

- Where will the agent carry out his or her duties?

- Will the duties spread across UK/EU and non-EU countries or across some countries where compensation is paid to agents on termination of their agency and others where it does not? Would it be better to have two separate agreements in such a case?

- Does the local law require the agency agreement be registered with a state body?

- Does the local law require that local law be specified in the agreement?

- Does the local law require that only a form of agency document/contract be used specified by those laws? Some states have this. In such a case it may still be possible to use an English model contract but that is not always the case.

- Even if English law is specified have local lawyers look at the agreement in case there are provisions locally which may prevail. In practice agents bring compensation claims in their home jurisdiction even if the agreement says otherwise. Sometimes local courts look favourably on the local agent and will ignore the choice of law and jurisdiction in the agreement. There may be no mutual recognition of choice of law and jurisdiction between the two countries involved in any event.

- Will the agreement be in English?

- Will the agreement contain a clause stating that if there is a conflict between different language versions which version will prevail?

Law and jurisdiction

8.3   English principals appointing agents abroad will usually choose to specify that English law and jurisdiction apply. The Brussels Regulation 1215/2012 (and for court proceedings begun before 10 January 2015 the predecessor Regulation 44/2001) provides that in the EU this choice of jurisdiction will be respected (the position after Brexit after the initial transition period needs to be considered) and in addition other states have reciprocal arrangements with the UK on such matters. Reference should be made to conflict of law textbooks if a difficult issue on jurisdiction does arise in practice. Be very careful if proceedings are launched not to have taken any step which suggests you or your client have accepted jurisdiction of the court concerned. Take legal advice in cases of doubt. For example, it may be necessary to state expressly that jurisdiction of the foreign court is not accepted so ensuring later that any adverse judgment is harder to have enforced against the party disputing jurisdiction.

8.4   Solicitors Fox Williams have given the following guidance on the changes brought about by the Brussels Regulations 1215/2012 in force 10 January 2015:

'Exclusive Jurisdiction Clauses – The New Trump Card

When negotiating an international agency or a distributorship agreement, you should think carefully about the country in which you want any disputes arising out of or in connection with the agreement to be resolved, if that eventuality should ever arise and then draft the clause which will provide this outcome (the "exclusive jurisdiction clause"). This might not seem like an important consideration when all is rosy at the outset, but it could save a lot of uncertainty and, therefore, costs if and when things do go wrong further down the line.

Indeed, if you are already party to a distributorship or agency agreement and are thinking about issuing court proceedings, you will need to check your agreement to see whether it contains an exclusive jurisdiction clause in favour of an EU member state court. If it does, you should only issue proceedings in that member state's court. To do otherwise is likely to be a futile endeavour, especially if your opponent plays its exclusive jurisdiction trump card.

This is especially so given the recent changes to the EU jurisdictional rules in commercial matters, which apply to court proceedings commenced from 10 January 2015 (the "recast Brussels Regulation"). Even if you do not think that you will become involved in litigation, the recast Brussels Regulation sends a clear message to all that exclusive jurisdiction clauses are the new trump card.

Exclusive jurisdiction clauses: prevention IS better than cure

The recast Brussels Regulation addresses the problems that can arise from the concept of the court in which proceedings are commenced first (that is, the "first seised").

Previously priority was given to the court first seised, meaning that a principal or agent could issue proceedings in its chosen court (for example, the Italian courts) even if to do so was in breach of an exclusive jurisdiction clause in an agency or distributorship agreement in favour of the English court. As a result, if the defendant to the proceedings did not want to litigate the dispute in Italy, it would have to incur costs challenging the jurisdiction of the Italian court (and succeed) before the dispute could be litigated in the correct forum (that is, the English court). This process could take many months.

The recast Brussels Regulation prevents litigation being commenced other than in the court in which proceedings are supposed to be commenced. It follows that where there is an exclusive jurisdiction clause in favour of an EU member state court (for example, the English court), proceedings should be commenced in the English court. If they are not, as in the above example, the Italian court would have to stay its proceedings until the English court declared that it had no jurisdiction (which would be unlikely, given the exclusive jurisdiction clause).

Goodbye to painstaking service out rules

The recast Brussels Regulation has also relaxed the rules around service of proceedings on defendants who are domiciled outside of the EU.

Where there is an English jurisdiction clause, the claimant will no longer require the court's permission to serve proceedings on a defendant outside of the EU regardless of where the other party is domiciled. This should make the process of serving the claim form on a defendant domiciled out of the EU much quicker and cheaper.

Victory shall be yours – enforcing a member state judgment elsewhere in the EU

The recast Brussels Regulation has scrapped the process of "exequatur" where, before a judgment of an EU member state court could be enforced in another EU member state, it first had to be declared enforceable or registered in the court of that other member state. Again, the removal of this hurdle should make the enforcement of a judgment from one member state in another member state quicker and cheaper.

Exclusive jurisdiction? More mumbo jumbo from the lawyers? An understandable but wrong question when a principal or a supplier appoints an agent or distributor in another country – not least as a way of limiting exposure on termination.'

Rebecca Richardson, Fox Williams
Reproduced with permission

The above was of course before UK Brexit, so always do take advice, particularly once the UK's Brexit arrangements after the initial transition period are clearer.

8.5   Reference should also be made to the decision of the Court of Appeal in *Lawlor v Sandvik Mining and Construction Mobile Crushers and Screens Ltd* [2013] EWCA Civ 365 on choice of law which is considered in Chapter 1. The agent had no written contract and would have won more compensation under English law, but the court found that Spanish law applied applying the Rome Convention (as the agreement pre-dated the Rome Regulation).

Public policy and compensation

8.6   Be aware that even if English law and jurisdiction is specified this will not always prevail. Some jurisdictional issues were discussed in Chapter 1 in particular the application of the Commercial Agents (Council Directive) Regulations 1993 to which reference should be made. In *Ingmar GB Ltd v Eaton Leonard Inc* [2001] Eu LR 756 (High Court, 31 July 2001) (also see earlier cases on jurisdiction ECJ 9 November 2000 (TLR, 16 November 2000), Case No C-381/98) (earlier decision (1999) Tr LR 327, 31 July 1998, CA) the European Court of Justice held that an agency agreement which is subject to the laws of a US state, will still provide an agent with EU compensation as it is a matter of public policy that agents are so compensated when the agent's duties were in the EU. Advisers need to ensure they tell their US and other foreign clients that even if foreign law is specified particularly that of a state without compensation for agents, an agent still may have protection under the Agency Directive or indeed other states

Case example – *Fern Computer Consultancy v Intergraph Cadworx & Analysis Solutions Inc* [2014] EWHC 2908

8.7   In this case the High Court held that a contract exclusively subject to Texan law and jurisdiction did not meet the hurdles for service of the legal proceedings outside the jurisdiction as pleaded relating to a claim under the Regulations, although the court did allow a claim in tort to be argued further in due course saying:

'**Conclusion**

I therefore conclude that:

(a)   Fern has not established that a claim under the Regulations can be brought within any of the currently proposed gateways [the rules allowing service abroad];

(b)   had it been able to invoke one of those gateways, Fern has a case for invoking the Regulations which raises a serious question to be tried and which passes that aspect of the requirements for service out of the jurisdiction;

(c)   the courts of England and Wales would be a proper place to bring such a claim;

(d)   permission to serve a claim for unpaid commission out of the jurisdiction should not have been granted.

In normal circumstances that would lead to an order setting aside the order granting permission to serve out of jurisdiction. That is the order that should be made at this stage in relation to the claim for unpaid commission. However, in relation to the claim under the Regulations the position is different. As I have indicated above, Fern wishes to advance an alternative case based on tort should it fail on the three gateways that it has hitherto relied on. That point was not argued at the hearing before me because Mr Dhillon, while accepting that a claim under the Regulations could be treated as a claim in tort, nonetheless had points that he wished to take against success on that Gateway and which he could not advance because he had not brought relevant authorities to court.

The point could therefore not be argued, and it would be unfair on Intergraph to fail to give it a proper opportunity to argue the point if it is to be advanced by Fern. Rather than requiring Fern to start all over again, which I am sure it would wish to do if necessary, the more convenient course may be to give an opportunity to amend and, having done so, to have the tort point argued in full. It may also be that there should be some submissions on gateway 20 (see above). I shall therefore give the parties an opportunity to make submissions on the appropriateness of that course and, it is adopted, restore the matter for further argument. If I am satisfied that the proper course is not to allow Fern to argue for further gateways then the correct order will be one which does indeed set aside the order permitting service out of the jurisdiction on both claims'.

The jurisdiction clause in the contract provided as follows:

'THIS AGREEMENT SHALL IN ALL RESPECTS BE INTERPRETED AND CONSTRUED IN ACCORDANCE WITH AND GOVERNED BY THE LAWS

OF THE STATE OF TEXAS USA (EXCLUDING ITS CHOICE OF LAW PROVISIONS) REGARDLESS OF THE PLACE OF ITS EXECUTION OR PERFORMANCE. For the benefit of [Intergraph], [Fern] hereby irrevocably agrees that any legal action, suit or proceeding arising out of or relating to this Agreement shall be brought in the courts of the State of Texas sitting in Houston, Harris County, Texas, or in the United States District Court for the Southern District of Texas. By the execution and delivery of this agreement, [Fern] hereby irrevocably consents and submits to the exclusive jurisdiction of such courts in any such action, suit or proceeding. [Fern] irrevocably waives any objection which it may now or hereafter have to the laying of venue for any action, suit or proceeding arising out of or relating to this Agreement in the courts of the State of Texas sitting in Houston, Harris County, Texas, or in the United States District Court for the Southern District of Texas, and irrevocably waives any claim that any such action, suit or proceeding brought in any such court has been brought in an inconvenient forum.'

The case was due to be heard in Texas in 2015 but is probably settled as there appear to be no detail of it after the 2014 decision above.

Case example – *Agro Foreign Trade & Agency Ltd v Petersime NV* (Case C-507/15)

8.8   In this case the principal was in Belgium (in the EU) and the agent in Turkey, Turkey having an association agreement with the EU. The contract was subject to Belgian law. Belgian law protects agents under its provisions in Belgium (not Turkey). The agent did not have its main business address, offices nor work in Belgium. The Court of Justice of the EU (CJEU) held it was perfectly proper for Belgian law to limit its protection for agents only to those agents operating in Belgium.

8.9   In Spain agents marketing services are protected. The Agency Directive only protects agents marketing goods as does English law. The Directive was not 'maximum' harmonisation so member states may have stricter laws unlike some other directives. So the starting point for a principal, at least until the end of the Brexit transition period and unless and until the UK no longer has similar rules in place, fending off a claim in Spain would be that the contract provides English law and jurisdiction and that the Rome I Regulation (593/2008) respects a choice of law as does the Brussels regulation 1215/2012 (and for court proceedings begun before 10 January 2015 the predecessor Brussels Regulation 44/2001) which both apply in Spain. Rome I in force in the UK since December 2009 provides:

'3. Freedom of choice

1.   A contract shall be governed by the law chosen by the parties. The choice shall be made expressly or clearly demonstrated by the terms of the contract or the circumstances of the case. By their choice the parties can select the law applicable to the whole or to part only of the contract.'

If there is no written agency contract, then under Rome I for services (all agencies are services contracts) under article 4.1(b):

> '(b)   a contract for the provision of services shall be governed by the law of the country where the service provider has his habitual residence;'

This means where the agent is based abroad and there is no written contract the law is that of where the agent is situated. Rome I on employment contracts is also worth considering (again subject to any Brexit effects) although most agents are not employees:

'*Article 8* Individual employment contracts

1. An individual employment contract shall be governed by the law chosen by the parties in accordance with Article 3. Such a choice of law may not, however, have the result of depriving the employee of the protection afforded to him by provisions that cannot be derogated from by agreement under the law that, in the absence of choice, would have been applicable pursuant to paragraphs 2, 3 and 4 of this Article.

2. To the extent that the law applicable to the individual employment contract has not been chosen by the parties, the contract shall be governed by the law of the country in which or, failing that, from which the employee habitually carries out his work in performance of the contract. The country where the work is habitually carried out shall not be deemed to have changed if he is temporarily employed in another country.

3. Where the law applicable cannot be determined pursuant to paragraph 2, the contract shall be governed by the law of the country where the place of business through which the employee was engaged is situated.

4. Where it appears from the circumstances as a whole that the contract is more closely connected with a country other than that indicated in paragraphs 2 or 3, the law of that other country shall apply.'

There are also some mandatory overriding provisions in article 9 which some member states might use to impose their own national agency law.

8.10   It is also possible as seen in one case where the contract and arbitration under it was expressly stated to be under Canadian laws that the court would see the compensation claim as separate from a claim for breach of contract. This is one reason why since the Rome II regulation (864/2007) came into force on choice of law in non contractual matters some lawyers have changed their jurisdiction clauses to refer to disputes 'in contract and in tort' so they are expressing a choice relating to tortuous claims as well as contractual claim. Even so there are sufficient 'get outs' under international conflict of laws rules and some states in the world favouring their nationals or simply not recognising rights such as compensation for agents that it is always wise to seek legal advice before entering into and terminating a foreign agency agreement.

Case example – *Unamar* (Case C-184/12)

8.11 In *United Antwerp Maritime Agencies (Unamar) NV Navigation Maritime Bulgare* Case C-184/12 – the *Unamar* case, the CJEU held that even though an agency agreement was under Hungarian law which provided no compensation (just like English and EU law) on termination of an agency agreement where the agent marketed services rather than goods, and although the case should be heard in Hungary, Belgian rights to compensation for agents were payable.

This was the question referred to the CJEU:

'Having regard, not least, to the classification under Belgian law of the provisions at issue in this case (Articles 18, 20 and 21 of the [Law on] commercial agency contracts) as special mandatory rules of law within the terms of Article 7(2) of the Rome Convention, must Articles 3 and 7(2) of the Rome Convention, read, as appropriate, in conjunction with [Directive 86/653], be interpreted as meaning that special mandatory rules of law of the forum that offer wider protection than the minimum laid down by [Directive 86/653] may be applied to the contract, even if it appears that the law applicable to the contract is the law of another Member State of the European Union in which the minimum protection provided by [Directive 86/653] has also been implemented?'

The court concluded:

'Articles 3 and 7(2) of the Convention on the law applicable to contractual obligations opened for signature in Rome on 19 June 1980 must be interpreted as meaning that the law of a Member State of the European Union which meets the minimum protection requirements laid down by Council Directive 86/653/EEC of 18 December 1986 on the coordination of the laws of the Member States relating to self-employed commercial agents and which has been chosen by the parties to a commercial agency contract may be rejected by the court of another Member State before which the case has been brought in favour of the law of the forum, owing to the mandatory nature, in the legal order of that Member State, of the rules governing the situation of self-employed commercial agents, only if the court before which the case has been brought finds, on the basis of a detailed assessment, that, in the course of that transposition, the legislature of the State of the forum held it to be crucial, in the legal order concerned, to grant the commercial agent protection going beyond that provided for by that directive, taking account in that regard of the nature and of the objective of such mandatory provisions.'

This is unfortunate as it leads to distortions in what should be a single market and brings less certainty to businesses.

In describing earlier case law, the court said:

'36 The Court has already had occasion to hold that Directive 86/653 aims to coordinate the laws of the Member States as regards the legal relationship between the parties to a commercial agency contract (Case C-215/97 *Bellone* [1998] ECR I-2191, paragraph 10; Case C-465/04 *Honyvem Informazioni Commerciali* [2006] ECR I-2879, paragraph 18; and Case C-348/07 *Semen* [2009] ECR I-2341, paragraph 14).

37   It is apparent from the second recital in the preamble to the Directive that the harmonising measures laid down by the Directive are intended, inter alia, to eliminate restrictions on the carrying-on of the activities of commercial agents, to make the conditions of competition within the Community uniform and to increase the security of commercial transactions (Case C-381/98 *Ingmar GB* [2000] ECR I-9305, paragraph 23).

38   It is also clear from settled case-law that, inter alia, national provisions subjecting the validity of an agency contract to a condition of entry in the register provided for that purpose are capable of significantly hindering the conclusion and operation of agency contracts between parties in different Member States and therefore from that point of view are contrary to the aims of Directive 86/653 (see, to that effect, *Bellone*, paragraph 17).'

The above at least does remind countries that adverse requirements such as compulsory registers of agents are not lawful.

Protecting agents in non-compensation states

8.12   Is it possible when acting for agents who operate outside the EEA and outside any countries with compensation for agents, to give them protection by way of compensation? Under English law, as long as a sum for compensation does not amount to a 'penalty clause' (in which case it would be void) there is no reason why an agent appointed for say, the state of New York could not have a contractual provision which states that when his contract is terminated he will be paid compensation as if the 1993 Regulations applied or some other sum.

8.13   Another way to protect an agent could simply be to have a long compulsory notice period and if that is not then served on termination the agent's damages for breach of contract could in effect amount to compensation.

Export control

8.14   Some products will be subject to UK export control legislation such as military products. Others may be caught if the regime is sensitive such as exports to North Korea. The UK principal should always check if the products can be exported whether via an agent or otherwise to a particular state before appointing the foreign agent. Further information on UK export control is at https://www.gov.uk/business-and-industry/export-controls.

8.15   Some products such as computer software even where being bought and sold in the UK may still be subject to US export control legislation. Those rules should also be checked. Many software distribution and licensing contracts in the UK under English law include a US export control law clause.

Foreign agents – information

8.16   It is best to seek local law advice abroad from lawyers who know about their national agency legislation. Directories such as *Chambers and Partners Global Directory* – see https://chambers.com/ – give details of foreign lawyers who are expert in other fields. The Department for Business, Energy and Industrial Strategy may be able to provide some assistance or local embassies or consulates in the state concerned.

8.17   *Appointing Commercial Agents in Europe* was a book published in 1996, still available in 2020 on Amazon, written by lawyers in some EU states with chapters on local law covering UK, Austria, Belgium, Denmark, Finland, France, Germany, Greece, Ireland, Italy, Luxembourg, Netherlands, Portugal, Spain and Sweden. Issues addressed and also which should be addressed by anyone seeking local law advice include:

- who is an agent?

- how is agent defined?

- what is the difference between agent and distributor in that jurisdiction?

- duties of agents;

- remuneration;

- liability of principal for agent's acts;

- product liability issues;

- compensation;

- dispute resolution;

- competition law and agency;

- sub-agents.

However, check the latest position by taking local law advice.

Practical issues with foreign agents

8.18   Many businesses are caught out by not assessing their foreign agents properly. It is wise to follow up references, visit the agents in person and at their premises abroad and test and check their local knowledge. They may not know the whole of the territory so it can be more sensible to appoint them for a part of their region rather than giving them immediate exclusive rights to the whole area. Check if their knowledge of English is sufficient for the relationship to be workable and ensure a contract is signed with them ideally checked by local lawyers, before they start work. Ensure the contract specifies they are not allowed to register the trade marks of the principal in their local country as their own, nor register them as Internet domain names. If they do, termination can be harder as the names then need to be transferred back to the principal.

Agent or distributor?

8.19   Businesses who are based abroad are often faced with the decision as to whether to appoint an agent or a distributor. Chapter 1 also looked at issues over definition of 'agent'. Agents are closely controlled. They must normally market the products at the prices and on the terms of business of the supplier. The supplier sells the goods to customers. The agent never owns them.

8.20   Distributors have more power and also take more risks. They buy the goods and resell them. Although they may have bought them on a sale or return basis in many cases, they take the risk that the goods may never be resold. They hold stocks of products. They must be free to resell the goods at the prices and on the terms of business that they wish. If not, then there is a serious breach of UK and EU competition law.

8.21   In deciding whether a particular relationship is one of agency or distribution the title which the parties give to it is not decisive. Many an agent has been called a distributor or dealer or franchisee. The important legal test is whether the agent buys the goods and resells them or is the contract of sale between the supplier and the customer? It is important to know the difference between these two methods of operation because agents have strong legal protection in many states, not just the EU, although in some countries such as Belgian distributors have protection on termination as well. Consideration was given in Chapter 1 to the distinction and those arrangements which appear to be a hybrid of both agency and distribution.

- Does the 'agent' buy the goods and resell them? If so – distributor.

- Who takes the bad debt risk on the transaction? Normally agents do not but distributors do.

- Does the supplier determine the price the goods are sold to the customer?

- Is the 'agent' paid in commission? Commission normally indicates an agency relationship though agents paid a retainer may still be 'agents' rather than distributors.

- What do the parties call each other in the contract? This is not decisive, but it does indicate what relationship is envisaged.

Summary of agency agreement contents

1   Appointment

8.22   The contract should state if the agent is given:

- An exclusive territory.

- An exclusive group of customers.

- Protection from other agents but the principal (person appointing the agent) can compete – this is what is known as a 'sole' agency rather than an exclusive one. In practice it is much better to add 'The principal shall not compete with the agent in the territory nor appoint other agents there' or 'the principal shall not appoint other agents in the territory but may make sales in the territory itself' so that the parties are clear as to exactly what is meant by 'sole' or 'exclusive'. Many people use the terms incorrectly hence an explanation is wise.

Particularly where a foreign agent is appointed language difficulties can lead to many kinds of misunderstanding. To attempt to 'fudge' a controversial issue to avoid disputes before the contract is signed, by vague wording in the agreement is a recipe for legal disaster later.

Just as important as making it clear if the agent has an exclusive territory or not is the issue of whether the agent is paid commission on all orders in his territory – which effectively makes him exclusive for all practical purposes – see commission section below.

2 Duration and notice

8.23 Some agents are appointed for no fixed period and these are indefinite agency agreements. The parties can terminate the agreement by giving written notice to each other, but otherwise the agreement carries on. As seen earlier in this book, in the UK and in the European Economic Area (EEA) an agent is entitled to one month's notice of termination in the first year, two in the second and three in the third and subsequent years, although the EU Agency Directive allows EU Member States to choose longer periods if they wish and if the agency agreement provides for a longer period then that will prevail. If an agreement within the Directive provides for a shorter period however, to terminate an indefinite contract, then that shorter period will be invalid. That is why it is crucial to know in a particular case whether the Directive applies or not.

If instead the agent is appointed for a fixed term, such as one year, then the contract will expire at the end of that period, but if the business relationship in practice continues then the agreement becomes an indefinite contract which can be terminated on the notice periods set out above.

There may be additional circumstances in which the contract can be terminated specified in the agreement – such as where the agent reaches retirement age which may be 65 years or whatever is specified in the agreement. There is no automatic right to terminate on retirement age being reached in the relevant country. Termination in particular for breach, and compensation which may be payable on termination, is addressed elsewhere in this book.

3   *Duties*

8.24   The most important clause is that setting out what the parties will do. It will normally be a comprehensive clause. Below is an example of the duties set out in an agency agreement, though obviously what the agent's duties are depends on the industry and practice concerned. It is particularly important with foreign agents to set out their duties very clearly as their expectations and understandings may not be clear.

The Agent shall use its best endeavours to promote and market the Products to existing and prospective customers in the Territory.

The Agent shall:

(a)   make such personal visits to existing and potential customers as are necessary to promote and sell the Products;

(b)   advertise and distribute publicity material concerning the Products in the Territory, subject to obtaining prior approval in writing from the Principal on the form and extent of such advertising and publicity materials;

(c)   attend relevant trade exhibitions or other sales outlets in the Territory, comprising at least two such exhibitions in each calendar year;

(d)   promptly refer enquiries concerning the Products from customers and prospective customers outside the Territory to the Principal;

(e)   maintain a list of customers and potential customers for the Products in the Territory and on request from the Principal from time to time supply a copy of the list, which list is proprietary information and trade secrets of the Principal;

(f)   from time to time keep the Principal fully informed of the Agent's promotional and marketing activities in respect of the Products and within 30 days after the end of each calendar quarter provide the Principal with a detailed report of those activities or even more often notify the Principal such as notification of weekly sales calls or even online tracking via applications such as www.salesforce.com via mobile telephones and the like subject to consent of the Agent to ensure compliance with local data protection legislation; and

(g)   from time to time keep the Principal informed of market conditions for the Products in the Territory and the activities and products of the Principal's competitors in the Territory.

The Agent shall act at all times in good faith towards the Principal and not let its own personal interest conflict with the duties owed to the Principal under this Agreement nor under the general law.

The Agent shall comply with all reasonable instructions given by the Principal concerning the sale and promotion of the Products.

The law in relation to the duties of agent and principal is set out in the EU Agency Directive and the UK Regulations in limited fashion. The agent must act in good faith towards the principal. For agencies outside the UK/EU the parties can agree those duties. However, whatever the law which applies the parties can agree the detailed duties with the agent.

4 Targets

8.25   Most important of all for those wanting agents to maintain a specific level of sales is the right to impose target figures on the agent which the agent must meet. The wording is very important. If the contract states the agent must aim to meet the target and he tries but fails, then there is no breach of contract on the agent's part. If instead the agency agreement requires the agent to meet the targets and if he does not his contract is terminated or his exclusive agreement becomes non-exclusive, then the position is different. The agent may be in breach of contract and possibly can even be dismissed without payment of any compensation.

5 Commission

8.26   Most agents are paid a percentage commission on the sales they generate or on any order emanating from their territory. The law in the EU is set out in the Agency Directive as already seen and in the UK in the Regulations. This requires that the agent be paid commission on all orders from his exclusive territory (although EU Member States can provide for payment of commission on all orders even from non-exclusive territories). Therefore, principals need to check the relevant EU State's law rather than assuming that laws will be the same throughout the EU. The Directive provides that the agent is entitled to commission on:

(1)   All orders received up to the date of commission.

(2)   Commission on orders received after that where found through the agent's efforts, for a reasonable period. Often contracts seek to specify what such a period might be, such as three months. This is entirely separate from and in addition to any compensation or indemnity payment to which the agent may be entitled after termination.

(3)   Commission on all orders from the agent's exclusive territory – though the contract may vary this.

The Directive and UK Regulations also provide that the agent's right to commission is extinguished (lost) where the customer later reneges on payment (except where the principal is to blame).

Example

8.27   Company Y sells to Company X. Agent Z arranged the sale. X then refuses to pay as the goods are faulty. Y is to blame so Z is still entitled to commission. If instead X went into liquidation or just refused to pay, then Z can be made to repay commission he has had or Y can withhold the commission from him as Y was not to blame for the transaction not proceeding. Nothing in the Directive requires any company/principal to accept any order put forward to him by the agent. This remains a matter for discretion on the part of the principal. The principal in the EEA however must keep the agent informed of the likely volume of orders, in particular if the volume will be less than the agent would have expected. This is a requirement of the Agency Directive.

Issues to consider in agreements – commission

8.28

- Will the agent be paid before the customer pays the principal? The Directive requires that the agent be paid at the latest when the customer has executed their part of the transaction. It is not clear if this means when the customer pays or when the goods are shipped to the customer. Many principals pay when the goods are shipped.

- Will the agent have to repay commission where the customer does not pay the principal and if so after what period?

- Will the agent be paid a fixed retainer and any money for expenses, including advertising? Check whether under the laws of the country concerned the nature of the relationship is in reality one of employee and employer or whether the agent is self-employed.

- What is the commission levied on? Define net sales. Deal with bad debts.

- If the agent is taken on to replace a departing agent is the commission to be shared with the old agent for a period?

- Is there a reduced level of commission of certain house accounts serviced by head office of the principal and customer?

- Does the principal reserve the right to designate accounts house accounts later, for example if a small store becomes part of a bigger chain which is already a house account or if a customer refuses to deal through the agent?

- What is the commission rate and when can the rate be varied, for example when there are special deals offered to customers?

Restrictive covenants

8.29 The Agency Directive permits a restriction on the agent for up to two years after termination of the agreement. This could prevent the agent for the range of products or area with which he was involved engaging in competition with the principal. In Chapter 6, consideration was given to this. The case law makes it clear that a two- year post-termination restrictive covenant may in some particular cases be too long for a restriction to be valid, notwithstanding the Regulations/Directive permitting such length of restriction – see *BCM Group Plc v Visualmark Ltd* [2006] EWHC 1831. During the period of the agency the principal may want to restrict the agent from carrying any competing agencies and perhaps even from taking on too many other agencies. Some agents handle six agencies or more and this can result in some agents not devoting sufficient efforts to a particular agency. Also in assessing how the agent has built up a customer base for the duration of the agency, in particular in looking at what compensation under the Agency Directive may be payable on termination, the principal will find it useful to know what level of sales was being achieved when the agent was appointed and what other sources of income the agent has from other agencies.

Other clauses

8.30   This very brief summary of agency clauses does not address many of the other clauses which would be included. For example, there may be clauses protecting the confidential information and intellectual property of each party. A restriction on the agent registering in his own name (whether at a local 'Companies House', trade mark register or domain name registry or otherwise) the principal's trade name in the country concerned is sensible. For foreign agents, where a translation of the agreement will be arranged, state which version will prevail if a conflict between the clauses arises.

8.31   There will be general clauses at the end of the agreement dealing with issues such as choice of law and whether disputes go to court or formal arbitration etc.

8.32   Most of those appointing an agent or distributor hope nothing will ever go wrong with the relationship. However, all those with experience of managing agents and distributors know that over time it is inevitable, whatever good practices are operated, that things will go wrong. Common disputes include:

• agent failing to meet minimum sales targets;

• distributor not meeting minimum purchase requirements in his exclusive territory;

• agent or distributor losing interest in the agency/distributorship because of other activities in which they are engaged;

• customer complaints about agent or distributor;

• failure to perform provisions of the contract;

• agent or distributor setting up in competition;

- agent or distributor registering principal/supplier trade mark in its own name after termination;

- appointment of sub-agent without consent;

- disputes over payment – distributor failing to pay or commission disputes with agent such as over orders procured by other agents or two agents together.

Although a well drawn contract can ensure that the legal position of those appointing the agent or distributor is secured no steps can be taken which will entirely eliminate the risk of a dispute arising.

Monitoring

8.33   Do not put the contract away after signature and never refer to it again. If there is a failure to enforce a provision, then the agent/distributor may be entitled in law to treat this as a 'waiver' of a breach of contract. It is particularly important to monitor foreign agency arrangements.

Example

8.34   Señor Juan was appointed as exclusive Spanish agent by the UK Beans Company Ltd in 2002 under a short letter of appointment. He was given annual sales targets. However, no mention has been made of the targets since and Señor Juan each year has failed to meet the target in his original contract. Beans has never complained about this. It is likely that the breach of contract is waived. As it is a short letter of appointment there is no standard clause called 'waiver' which would be present in many agency or distribution agreements stating that any failure to enforce a right is not to be taken as a waiver of that right. When Beans comes to take legal action, it finds it has lost its legal rights.

Regular visits to the agent or distributor abroad can also ensure that the UK supplier is aware of how the agency or distributorship is operating. Many companies will have a check list they have drawn up to monitor the agent or distributor. Agents generally are controlled much more closely than distributors but even distributors can be set targets and their performance regularly considered. Targets are not the only area to monitor. Check:

- financial performance against targets;

- quality of customers found – ie do they always pay on time; are they big companies; are they disreputable; do they become bad debtors?

- effort the agent puts in – in some industries or over certain time periods the sales may drop off, but this may be due to an industry recession, poor quality products of the supplier or some other extraneous reason;

- whether the agent/distributor is distracted with other activities such as sale of third parties' products;

- advertising in the territory – many UK exporters want to vet local advertising in advance;

- levels of customer service in the territory, whether distributor handles complaints/guarantee work well etc.

Resolving disputes

8.35 Exporters should avoid going to court whenever they can. They should also avoid formal arbitration. Most commercial contracts will state whether disputes go to court or arbitration. Arbitration is often very formal with both parties appointing lawyers so do not assume it will be cheaper or quicker. Indeed, some agency contracts providing for arbitration have ended up in court after the expensive arbitration proceedings were over – see *Alan Ramsey Sales and Marketing Limited v Typhoo Tea Ltd* [2016] EWHC 486 (Comm) where one party appealed to the Commercial Court after the arbitration decision under section 1(2) of the Arbitration Act 1979. Sometimes it is worth trying mediation first. This is non-binding unless an agreement is reached and can be quick and an easy means of settling disputes. In practice most disputes are resolved by some form of mediation even if simply this involves without prejudice discussions with lawyers or senior directors of the companies concerned. If mediation does not work then either a court action is started or the case goes to arbitration.

8.36 With foreign agents or dealers, it can be sensible to suggest arbitration in a neutral country such as Sweden or Switzerland, but this can be very expensive indeed. Most UK exporters will prefer to include a clause stating:

> 'This Agreement is subject to English law and the parties agree to submit to the exclusive jurisdiction of the English courts in relation to any dispute hereunder.'

Those in Scotland will want Scottish law instead. There is no such thing as UK law. Even where this is specified local laws protecting agents or distributors may apply because some countries will not respect the choice of law in these matters. Some states such as some in the Middle East require that distribution and agency agreements are subject to local law before the contracts and the appointments are registered and approved. The Regulations apply in Great Britain. Northern Ireland has its own almost identical set of regulations.

Breach of contract

8.37 When will there be a breach of the agency or distribution agreement? In most cases this will be clear from the terms of the written contract. The contract may provide that the agent, for example, must not handle competing products and yet he does. Or the distributor may advertise outside his territory when he is prohibited from doing this. The UK exporter should notify the distributor in writing of the breach of contract. Most contracts allow a period in which a breach which can be remedied is put right before the drastic step of termination of the agreement arises.

8.38 Not all breaches can be remedied. For example, if confidential information has been disclosed it cannot be undisclosed. In such cases an immediate termination is allowed where the contract provides for this. Sometimes there is just a right to terminate for a material breach of contract and not any breach. It all depends on what the contract says. If there is no written contract then if English law applies, the rule is that breach of a fundamental condition of the contract entitles the other party to terminate and breach of a minor clause or warranty does not. For breach of warranty a claim for damages can be started but no termination. In practice most contracts include a right to terminate for breach.

8.39 The most important point is to ensure that the contract's provisions are followed to the letter. However, take legal advice first. In certain cases, there may be a dispute about which party's contract applies. For example, the supplier may have sent his contract to the distributor and the distributor may have sent his to the supplier and neither signed the other. Following the terms of termination in one contract may be tantamount to accepting that those terms apply so seek advice first.

Notices of termination

8.40 In practice sometimes notices of termination are very badly drafted. It is not always clear if notice was given and on what date or there is simply a telephone call. As it is crucial in law to give notice correctly this is an issue all those using agents and distributors must get right. The following might comprise adequate notice:

Dear [Agent]

I refer to our agency agreement dated [   ] 2015. It has come to our attention that you have begun to handle products of our competitor [   ] which is flagrant breach of clause [   ] of our agreement, which prohibits you from handling competing products.

This letter is formal notice of termination of our agreement forthwith under clause [   ] of the agreement which entitles us to terminate immediately for irremediable breaches of this type.

Kindly return all company property to us immediately in accordance with clause [   ] and cease acting as our agent from today's date. We reserve our legal rights in relation to any breaches of contract by you. Your agency terminates with effect from the date at the top of this letter. Acknowledge receipt of this letter.

Yours sincerely,

Obviously, it is crucial that before matters reach this stage the agent or distributor has (for breaches which can be remedied) been given an opportunity to put the breach right. However, even that is a difficult issue as there may be no compensation payable but only where the agent's breach is such that it is irremediable and justifies termination forthwith, hence the letter above refers to termination forthwith. It is sensible to have warning letters on file to show the court that the agent or distributor has been treated reasonably, particularly for agents who are more akin to employees than distributors. The letter above reserves rights and this includes a right to sue the agent for damages. For example, often an agent whose contract is terminated will bring a claim for compensation and the principal who has appointed the agent may be able to sue the agent back for damages under a counterclaim.

Further information

8.41   UK Export Control – https://www.gov.uk/business-and-industry/export-controls

www.chambers.com gives details of foreign lawyers.

Corporate Briefing newsletter covers international legal issues – www.chambersandpartners.com

Appendix 1

UK commercial agency laws and materials

Appl.1

Commercial Agents (Council Directive) Regulations 1993 (SI 1993/3053)

[NOTE: consolidated to include Commercial Agents (Council Directive) (Amendment) Regulations (1993 SI 1993/3173) amending regulation 18 and The Commercial Agents (Council Directive) (Amendment) Regulations 1998 (SI 1998/2868) amending regulation 1(3)]

The Secretary of State, being a Minister designated for the purposes of section 2(2) of the European Communities Act 1972 in relation to measures relating to relations between commercial agents and their principals, in the exercise of the powers conferred by him by that section, hereby makes the following Regulations

PART I
GENERAL

1 Citation, commencement and applicable law
   (1) These Regulations may be cited as the Commercial Agents (Council Directive) Regulations 1993 and shall come into force on 1 January 1994.
   (2) These Regulations govern the relations between commercial agents and their principals and, subject to paragraph (3), apply in relation to the activities of commercial agents in Great Britain.
   [(3) A court or tribunal shall:
        (a) apply the law of the other Member State concerned in place of regulations 3 to 22 where the parties have agreed that the agency contract is to be governed by the law of that Member State;

229

(b)   (whether or not it would otherwise be required to do so) apply these regulations where the law of another Member State corresponding to these regulations enables the parties to agree that the agency contract is to be governed by the law of a different Member State and the parties have agreed that it is to be governed by the law of England and Wales or Scotland.]

[NOTE: 1(3) as above replaced the earlier version of 1(3) by The Commercial Agents (Council Directive) (Amendment) Regulations 1998 (SI 1998/2868)]

[The following was removed in 1998 from the regulations: *(3) Regulations 3 to 22 do not apply where the parties have agreed that the agency contract is to be governed by the law of another Member State.*]

---

2   Interpretation, application and extent

(1)   In these Regulations—

'commercial agent' means a self-employed intermediary who has continuing authority to negotiate the sale or purchase of goods on behalf of another person (the 'principal'), or to negotiate and conclude the sale or purchase of goods on behalf of and in the name of that principal; but shall be understood as not including in particular:

(i)   a person who, in his capacity as an officer of a company or association, is empowered to enter into commitments binding on that company or association;

(ii)   a partner who is lawfully authorised to enter into commitments binding on his partners;

(iii)   a person who acts as an insolvency practitioner (as that expression is defined in section 388 of the Insolvency Act 1986) or the equivalent in any other jurisdiction;

'commission' means any part of the remuneration of a commercial agent which varies with the number or value of business transactions;

['EEA Agreement' means the Agreement on the European Economic Area signed at Oporto on 2nd May 1992 as adjusted by the Protocol signed at Brussels on 17th March 1993;]

[NOTE: Above definition of EEA Agreement added by The Commercial Agents (Council Directive) (Amendment) Regulations 1998 (SI 1998/2868)]

'Member State' includes a State which is a contracting party to the EEA Agreement

'restraint of trade clause' means an agreement restricting the business activities of a commercial agent following termination of the agency contract.

(2) These Regulations do not apply to—
    (a) commercial agents whose activities are unpaid;
    (b) commercial agents when they operate on commodity exchanges or in the commodity market;
    (c) the Crown Agents for Overseas Governments and Administrations, as set up under the Crown Agents Act 1979, or its subsidiaries.

(3) The provisions of the Schedule to these Regulations have effect for the purpose of determining the persons whose activities as commercial agents are to be considered secondary.

(4) These Regulations shall not apply to the persons referred to in paragraph (3) above.

(5) These Regulations do not extend to Northern Ireland.

PART II
RIGHTS AND OBLIGATIONS

3 Duties of a commercial agent to his principal

(1) In performing his activities a commercial agent must look after the interests of his principal and act dutifully and in good faith.

(2) In particular, a commercial agent must—
    (a) make proper efforts to negotiate and, where appropriate, conclude the transactions he is instructed to take care of;
    (b) communicate to his principal all the necessary information available to him;
    (c) comply with reasonable instructions given by his principal.

4 Duties of a principal to his commercial agent

(1) In his relations with his commercial agent a principal must act dutifully and in good faith.

(2) In particular, a principal must—
    (a) provide his commercial agent with the necessary documentation relating to the goods concerned;
    (b) obtain for his commercial agent the information necessary for the performance of the agency contract, and in particular notify his commercial agent within a reasonable period once he anticipates that the volume of commercial transactions will be significantly lower than that which the commercial agent could normally have expected.

(3) A principal shall, in addition, inform his commercial agent within a reasonable period of his acceptance or refusal of, and of any non-execution by him of, a commercial transaction which the commercial agent has procured for him.

5   Prohibition on derogation from regulations 3 and 4 and consequence of breach

(1)   The parties may not derogate from regulations 3 and 4 above.

(2)   The law applicable to the contract shall govern the consequence of breach of the rights and obligations under regulations 3 and 4 above.

PART III
REMUNERATION

6   Form and amount of remuneration in absence of agreement

(1)   In the absence of any agreement as to remuneration between the parties, a commercial agent shall be entitled to the remuneration that commercial agents appointed for the goods forming the subject of his agency contract are customarily allowed in the place where he carries on his activities and, if there is no such customary practice, a commercial agent shall be entitled to reasonable remuneration taking into account all the aspects of the transaction.

(2)   This regulation is without prejudice to the application of any enactment or rule of law concerning the level of remuneration.

(3)   Where a commercial agent is not remunerated (wholly or in part) by commission, regulations 7 to 12 below shall not apply.

7   Entitlement to commission on transactions concluded during agency contract

(1)   A commercial agent shall be entitled to commission on commercial transactions concluded during the period covered by the agency contract—

   (a)   where the transaction has been concluded as a result of his action; or

   (b)   where the transaction is concluded with a third party whom he has previously acquired as a customer for transactions of the same kind.

(2)   A commercial agent shall also be entitled to commission on transactions concluded during the period covered by the agency contract where he has an exclusive right to a specific geographical area or to a specific group of customers and where the transaction has been entered into with a customer belonging to that area or group.

8   Entitlement to commission on transactions concluded after agency contract has terminated

Subject to regulation 9 below, a commercial agent shall be entitled to commission on commercial transactions concluded after the agency contract has terminated if—

   (a)   the transaction is mainly attributable to his efforts during the period covered by the agency contract and if the transaction was entered into within a reasonable period after that contract terminated; or

   (b)   in accordance with the conditions mentioned in regulation 7 above, the order of the third party reached the principal or the commercial agent before the agency contract terminated.

9   Apportionment of commission between new and previous commercial agents

   (1)   A commercial agent shall not be entitled to the commission referred to in regulation 7 above if that commission is payable, by virtue of regulation 8 above, to the previous commercial agent, unless it is equitable because of the circumstances for the commission to be shared between the commercial agents.

   (2)   The principal shall be liable for any sum due under paragraph (1) above to the person entitled to it in accordance with that paragraph, and any sum which the other commercial agent receives to which he is not entitled shall be refunded to the principal.

10   When commission due and date for payment

   (1)   Commission shall become due as soon as, and to the extent that, one of the following circumstances occurs—

      (a)   the principal has executed the transaction; or

      (b)   the principal should, according to his agreement with the third party, have executed the transaction; or

      (c)   the third party has executed the transaction.

   (2)   Commission shall become due at the latest when the third party has executed his part of the transaction or should have done so if the principal had executed his part of the transaction, as he should have.

   (3)   The commission shall be paid not later than on the last day of the month following the quarter in which it became due, and, for the purposes of these Regulations, unless otherwise agreed between the parties, the first quarter period shall run from the date the agency contract takes effect, and subsequent periods shall run from that date in the third month thereafter or the beginning of the fourth month, whichever is the sooner.

   (4)   Any agreement to derogate from paragraphs (2) and (3) above to the detriment of the commercial agent shall be void.

11   Extinction of right to commission

   (1)   The right to commission can be extinguished only if and to the extent that—

      (a)   it is established that the contract between the third party and the principal will not be executed; and

      (b)   that fact is due to a reason for which the principal is not to blame.

(2)   Any commission which the commercial agent has already received shall be refunded if the right to it is extinguished.

(3)   Any agreement to derogate from paragraph (1) above to the detriment of the commercial agent shall be void.

12   Periodic supply of information as to commission due and right of inspection of principal's books

(1)   The principal shall supply his commercial agent with a statement of the commission due, not later than the last day of the month following the quarter in which the commission has become due, and such statement shall set out the main components used in calculating the amount of the commission.

(2)   A commercial agent shall be entitled to demand that he be provided with all the information (and in particular an extract from the books) which is available to his principal and which he needs in order to check the amount of the commission due to him.

(3)   Any agreement to derogate from paragraphs (1) and (2) above shall be void.

(4)   Nothing in this regulation shall remove or restrict the effect of, or prevent reliance upon, any enactment or rule of law which recognises the right of an agent to inspect the books of a principal.

PART IV
CONCLUSION AND TERMINATION OF THE AGENCY CONTRACT

13   Right to signed written statement of terms of agency contract

(1)   The commercial agent and principal shall each be entitled to receive from the other, on request, a signed written document setting out the terms of the agency contract including any terms subsequently agreed.

(2)   Any purported waiver of the right referred to in paragraph (1) above shall be void.

14   Conversion of agency contract after expiry of fixed period

An agency contract for a fixed period which continues to be performed by both parties after that period has expired shall be deemed to be converted into an agency contract for an indefinite period.

15   Minimum periods of notice for termination of agency contract

(1)   Where an agency contract is concluded for an indefinite period either party may terminate it by notice.

(2)   The period of notice shall be—

  (a)   1 month for the first year of the contract;
  (b)   2 months for the second year commenced;
  (c)   3 months for the third year commenced and for the subsequent years;

and the parties may not agree on any shorter periods of notice.

(3)   If the parties agree on longer periods than those laid down in paragraph (2) above, the period of notice to be observed by the principal must not be shorter than that to be observed by the commercial agent.

(4)   Unless otherwise agreed by the parties, the end of the period of notice must coincide with the end of a calendar month.

(5)   The provisions of this regulation shall also apply to an agency contract for a fixed period where it is converted under regulation 14 above into an agency contract for an indefinite period subject to the proviso that the earlier fixed period must be taken into account in the calculation of the period of notice.

16   Savings with regard to immediate termination

These Regulations shall not affect the application of any enactment or rule of law which provides for the immediate termination of the agency contract—

(a)   because of the failure of one party to carry out all or part of his obligations under that contract; or

(b)   where exceptional circumstances arise.

17   Entitlement of commercial agent to indemnity or compensation on termination of agency contract

(1)   This regulation has effect for the purpose of ensuring that the commercial agent is, after termination of the agency contract, indemnified in accordance with paragraphs (3) to (5) below or compensated for damage in accordance with paragraphs (6) and (7) below.

(2)   Except where the agency contract otherwise provides, the commercial agent shall be entitled to be compensated rather than indemnified.

[NOTE: contract substituted in (2) for typographical error 'contact' by The Commercial Agents (Council Directive) (Amendment) Regulations 1998 (SI 1998/2868)]

---

(3)   Subject to paragraph (9) and to regulation 18 below, the commercial agent shall be entitled to an indemnity if and to the extent that—

(a)   he has brought the principal new customers or has significantly increased the volume of business with existing customers and the principal continues to derive substantial benefits from the business with such customers; and

(b)   the payment of this indemnity is equitable having regard to all the circumstances and, in particular, the commission lost by the commercial agent on the business transacted with such customers.

(4)   The amount of the indemnity shall not exceed a figure equivalent to an indemnity for one year calculated from the commercial

agent's average annual remuneration over the preceding five years and if the contract goes back less than five years the indemnity shall be calculated on the average for the period in question.

(5)   The grant of an indemnity as mentioned above shall not prevent the commercial agent from seeking damages.

(6)   Subject to paragraph (9) and to regulation 18 below, the commercial agent shall be entitled to compensation for the damage he suffers as a result of the termination of his relations with his principal.

(7)   For the purpose of these Regulations such damage shall be deemed to occur particularly when the termination takes place in either or both of the following circumstances, namely circumstances which—

   (a)   deprive the commercial agent of the commission which proper performance of the agency contract would have procured for him whilst providing his principal with substantial benefits linked to the activities of the commercial agent; or

   (b)   have not enabled the commercial agent to amortise the costs and expenses that he had incurred in the performance of the agency contract on the advice of his principal.

(8)   Entitlement to the indemnity or compensation for damage as provided for under paragraphs (2) to (7) above shall also arise where the agency contract is terminated as a result of the death of the commercial agent.

(9)   The commercial agent shall lose his entitlement to the indemnity or compensation for damage in the instances provided for in paragraphs (2) to (8) above if within one year following termination of his agency contract he has not notified his principal that he intends pursuing his entitlement.

18   Grounds for excluding payment of indemnity or compensation under regulation 17

The [indemnity or] compensation referred to in regulation 17 above shall not be payable to the commercial agent where—

   (a)   the principal has terminated the agency contract because of default attributable to the commercial agent which would justify immediate termination of the agency contract pursuant to regulation 16 above; or

   (b)   the commercial agent has himself terminated the agency contract, unless such termination is justified—

      (i)   by circumstances attributable to the principal, or

      (ii)   on grounds of the age, infirmity or illness of the commercial agent in consequence of which he cannot reasonably be required to continue his activities; or

   (c)   the commercial agent, with the agreement of his principal, assigns his rights and duties under the agency contract to another person.

[NOTE: Words in square brackets inserted by SI 1993/3173, reg 2]

19 Prohibition on derogation from regulations 17 and 18

The parties may not derogate from regulations 17 and 18 to the detriment of the commercial agent before the agency contract expires.

20 Restraint of trade clauses

(1) A restraint of trade clause shall be valid only if and to the extent that—

(a) it is concluded in writing; and

(b) it relates to the geographical area or the group of customers and the geographical area entrusted to the commercial agent and to the kind of goods covered by his agency under the contract.

(2) A restraint of trade clause shall be valid for not more than two years after termination of the agency contract.

(3) Nothing in this regulation shall affect any enactment or rule of law which imposes other restrictions on the validity or enforceability of restraint of trade clauses or which enables a court to reduce the obligations on the parties resulting from such clauses.

PART V
MISCELLANEOUS AND SUPPLEMENTAL

21 Disclosure of information

Nothing in these Regulations shall require information to be given where such disclosure would be contrary to public policy.

22 Service of notice etc

(1) Any notice, statement or other document to be given or supplied to a commercial agent or to be given or supplied to the principal under these Regulations may be so given or supplied:

(a) by delivering it to him;

(b) by leaving it at his proper address addressed to him by name;

(c) by sending it by post to him addressed either to his registered address or to the address of his registered or principal office;

or by any other means provided for in the agency contract.

(2) Any such notice, statement or document may—

(a) in the case of a body corporate, be given or served on the secretary or clerk of that body;

(b) in the case of a partnership, be given to or served on any partner or on any person having the control or management of the partnership business.

23 Transitional provisions

(1) Notwithstanding any provision in an agency contract made before 1 January 1994, these Regulations shall apply to that contract after that date and, accordingly any provision which is inconsistent with these Regulations shall have effect subject to them.

(2) Nothing in these Regulations shall affect the rights and liabilities of a commercial agent or a principal which have accrued before 1 January 1994.

SCHEDULE

Regulation 2(3)

1   The activities of a person as a commercial agent are to be considered secondary where it may reasonably be taken that the primary purpose of the arrangement with his principal is other than as set out in paragraph 2 below.

2   An arrangement falls within this paragraph if—

(a) the business of the principal is the sale, or as the case may be purchase, of goods of a particular kind; and

(b) the goods concerned are such that—

(i) transactions are normally individually negotiated and concluded on a commercial basis, and

(ii) procuring a transaction on one occasion is likely to lead to further transactions in those goods with that customer on future occasions, or to transactions in those goods with other customers in the same geographical area or among the same group of customers, and

that accordingly it is in the commercial interests of the principal in developing the market in those goods to appoint a representative to such customers with a view to the representative devoting effort, skill and expenditure from his own resources to that end.

3   The following are indications that an arrangement falls within paragraph 2 above, and the absence of any of them is an indication to the contrary—

(a) the principal is the manufacturer, importer or distributor of the goods;

(b) the goods are specifically identified with the principal in the market in question rather than, or to a greater extent than, with any other person;

(c) the agent devotes substantially the whole of his time to representative activities (whether for one principal or for a number of principals whose interests are not conflicting);

(d) the goods are not normally available in the market in question other than by means of the agent;

(e) the arrangement is described as one of commercial agency.

4   The following are indications that an arrangement does not fall within paragraph 2 above—

(a)   promotional material is supplied direct to potential customers;

(b)   persons are granted agencies without reference to existing agents in a particular area or in relation to a particular group;

(c)   customers normally select the goods for themselves and merely place their orders through the agent.

5   The activities of the following categories of persons are presumed, unless the contrary is established, not to fall within paragraph 2 above—

Mail order catalogue agents for consumer goods.

Consumer credit agents.

App1.2

Commercial Agents (Council Directive) Regulations (Northern Ireland) 1993 (SI 1993/483)

[NOTE: Consolidated to include the Commercial Agents (Council Directive) (Amendment) Regulations (Northern Ireland) 1999 (SI 1999/201) amending regulations 1(3) and 2(2)]

The Department of Economic Development, being a Department designated by the European Communities (Designation) Order 1989 for the purposes of section 2(2) of the European Communities Act 1972 in relation to measures relating to relations between commercial agents and their principals, in the exercise of the powers conferred on it by that section, hereby makes the following Regulations—

PART I

GENERAL

1   Citation, commencement and applicable law

(1)   These Regulations may be cited as the Commercial Agents (Council Directive) Regulations (Northern Ireland) 1993 and shall come into operation on 13 January 1994.

(2)   These Regulations govern the relations between commercial agents and their principals and, subject to paragraph (3) apply in relation to the activities of commercial agents in Northern Ireland.

[(3)   A court or tribunal shall—

(a)   apply the law of the other member State concerned in place of regulations 3 to 22 where the parties have agreed that the agency contract is to be governed by the law of that member State;

(b)   (whether or not it would otherwise be required to do so) apply these Regulations where the law of another member State corresponding to these Regulations enables the parties to agree that the agency contract is to be governed by the law of a different member State and the parties have agreed that it is to be governed by the law of Northern Ireland.]

[NOTE: 1(3) Substituted by the Commercial Agents (Council Directive) (Amendment) Regulations (Northern Ireland) 1999 (SI 1999/201), reg 3]
[The following was removed in 1999 from the regulations: *(3) Regulations 3 to 22 do not apply where the parties have agreed that the agency contract is to be governed by the law of a member State of the European Communities other than the United Kingdom.*]

2   Interpretation and application

(1)   The Interpretation Act (Northern Ireland) 1954 shall apply to these Regulations as it applies to a Measure of the Northern Ireland Assembly.

(2)   In these Regulations—

'commercial agent' means a self-employed intermediary who has continuing authority to negotiate the same or purchase of goods on behalf of another person (the 'principal'), or to negotiate and conclude the sale or purchase of goods on behalf of and in the name of that principal; but shall be understood as not including in particular:

   (i)   a person who, in his capacity as an officer of a company or association, is empowered to enter into commitments binding on that company or association;

   (ii)   a partner who is lawfully authorised to enter into commitments binding on his partners;

   (iii) a person who acts as an insolvency practitioner (as that expression is defined in Article 3 of the Insolvency (Northern Ireland) Order 1989) or the equivalent in any other jurisdiction;

'commission' means any part of the remuneration of a commercial agent which varies with the number or value of business transactions;

['EEA Agreement' means the Agreement on the European Economic Area signed at Oporto on 2nd May 1992 as adjusted by the Protocol signed at Brussels on 17th March 1993;]

['member State' includes a State which is a contracting party to the EEA Agreement;]

'restraint of trade clause' means an agreement restricting the business activities of a commercial agent following termination of the agency contract.

(3)   These Regulations do not apply to—

   (a)   commercial agents whose activities are unpaid;

   (b)   commercial agents when they operate on commodity exchanges or in the commodity market;

   (c)   the Crown Agents for Overseas Governments and Administrations, as set up under the Crown Agents Act 1979, or its subsidiaries.

(4)   The provisions of the Schedule have effect for the purpose of determining the persons whose activities as commercial agents are to be considered secondary.

(5)   These Regulations shall not apply to the persons referred to in paragraph (4).

(6)   Regulations 7 to 12 shall not apply where a commercial agent is not remunerated wholly or partly by commission.

[NOTE: Definitions in 2(2) inserted by the Commercial Agents (Council Directive) (Amendment) Regulations (Northern Ireland) 1999 (SI 1999/201), reg 4.]

PART II
RIGHTS AND OBLIGATIONS

3   Duties of a commercial agent to his principal

(1)   In performing his activities a commercial agent shall look after the interests of his principal and act dutifully and in good faith.

(2)   Without prejudice to the generality of paragraph (1), a commercial agent shall in particular—

    (a)   make proper efforts to negotiate and, where appropriate, conclude the transactions he is instructed to take care of;

    (b)   communicate to his principal all the necessary information available to him;

    (c)   comply with reasonable instructions given by his principal.

4   Duties of a principal to his commercial agent

(1)   In his relations with his commercial agent a principal shall act dutifully and in good faith.

(2)   Without prejudice to the generality of paragraph (1), a principal shall in particular—

    (a)   provide his commercial agent with the necessary documentation relating to the goods concerned;

    (b)   obtain for his commercial agent the information necessary for the performance of the agency contract, and in particular notify his commercial agent within a reasonable period once he anticipates that the volume of commercial transactions will be significantly lower than that which the commercial agent could normally have expected.

(3)   A principal shall, in addition, inform his commercial agent within a reasonable period of his acceptance or refusal of, and of any non-execution by him of, a commercial transaction which the commercial agent has procured for him.

5   Prohibition on derogation from regulations 3 and 4 and consequence of breach

(1)   The parties may not derogate from regulations 3 and 4.

(2)   The law applicable to the contract shall govern the consequences of breach of the rights and obligations under regulations 3 and 4.

PART III
REMUNERATION

6   Form and amount of remuneration in absence of agreement

(1)   In the absence of any agreement as to remuneration between the parties, a commercial agent shall be entitled to the remuneration that commercial agents appointed for the goods forming the subject of his agency contract are customarily allowed in the place where he carries on his activities and, if there is no such customary practice, a commercial agent shall be entitled to reasonable remuneration taking into account all the aspects of the transaction.

(2)   This regulation is without prejudice to the application of any enactment or rule of law concerning the level of remuneration.

7   Entitlement to commission on transactions concluded during agency contract

(1)   A commercial agent shall be entitled to commission on commercial transactions concluded during the period covered by the agency contract—

    (a)   where the transaction has been concluded as a result of his action; or

    (b)   where the transaction is concluded with a third party whom he has previously acquired as a customer for transactions of the same kind.

(2)   A commercial agent shall also be entitled to commission on transactions concluded during the period covered by the agency contract where he has an exclusive right to a specific geographical area or to a specific group of customers and where the transaction has been entered into with a customer belonging to that area or group.

8   Entitlement to commission on transactions concluded after agency contract has terminated

Subject to regulation 9 below, a commercial agent shall be entitled to commission on commercial transactions concluded after the agency contract has terminated if—

    (a)   the transaction is mainly attributable to his efforts during the period covered by the agency contract and if the transaction was entered into within a reasonable period after that contract terminated; or

    (b)   in accordance with the conditions mentioned in regulation 7, the order of the third party reached the principal or the commercial agent before the agency contract terminated.

9   Apportionment of commission between new and previous commercial agents

(1)   A commercial agent shall not be entitled to the commission referred to in regulation 7 if that commission is payable, by virtue of regulation 8, to the previous commercial agent, unless it is

equitable because of the circumstances for the commission to be shared between the commercial agents.

(2) The principal shall be liable for any sum due under paragraph (1) to the person entitled to it in accordance with that paragraph, and any sum which the other commercial agent receives to which he is not entitled shall be refunded to the principal.

10 When commission due and date for payment

(1) Commission shall become due as soon as, and to the extent that, one of the following circumstances occurs—

(a) the principal has executed the transaction; or

(b) the principal should, according to his agreement with the third party, have executed the transaction; or

(c) the third party has executed the transaction.

(2) Commission shall become due at the latest when the third party has executed his part of the transaction or should have done so if the principal had executed his part of the transaction, as he should have.

(3) The commission shall be paid not later than on the last day of the month following the quarter in which it became due, and, for the purposes of these Regulations, unless otherwise agreed between the parties, the first quarter period shall run from the date the agency contract takes effect, and subsequent periods shall run from that date in the third month thereafter or the beginning of the fourth month, whichever is the sooner.

(4) Any agreement to derogate from paragraphs (2) and (3) to the detriment of the commercial agent shall be void.

11 Extinction of right to commission

(1) The right to commission can be extinguished only if and to the extent that—

(a) it is established that the contract between the third party and the principal will not be executed; and

(b) that fact is due to a reason for which the principal is not to blame.

(2) Any commission which the commercial agent has already received shall be refunded if the right to it is extinguished.

(3) Any agreement to derogate from paragraph (1) to the detriment of the commercial agent shall be void.

12 Periodic supply of information as to commission due and right of inspection of principal's books

(1) The principal shall supply his commercial agent with a statement of the commission due, not later than the last day of the month following the quarter in which the commission has become due, and such statement shall set out the main components used in calculating the amount of the commission.

(2) A commercial agent shall be entitled to demand that he be provided with all the information (and in particular an extract from the books) which is available to his principal and which he needs in order to check the amount of the commission due to him.

(3) Any agreement to derogate from paragraphs (1) and (2) shall be void.

(4) Nothing in this regulation shall remove or restrict the effect of, or prevent reliance upon, any enactment of rule of law which recognises the right of an agent to inspect the books of a principal.

PART IV

CONCLUSION AND TERMINATION OF THE AGENCY CONTRACT

13 Right to signed written statement of terms of agency contract

(1) The commercial agent and principal shall each be entitled to receive from the other, on request, a signed written document setting out the terms of the agency contract including any terms subsequently agreed.

(2) Any purported waiver of the right referred to in paragraph (1) shall be void.

14 Conversion of agency contract after expiry of fixed period

An agency contract for a fixed period which continues to be performed by both parties after that period has expired shall be deemed to be converted into an agency contract for an indefinite period.

15 Minimum periods of notice for termination of agency contract

(1) Where an agency contract is concluded for an indefinite period either party may terminate it by notice.

(2) The period of notice shall be—
 (a) 1 month for the first year of the contract;
 (b) 2 months for the second year commenced;
 (c) 3 months for the third year commenced and for the subsequent years;
 and the parties may not agree on any shorter periods of notice.

(3) If the parties agree on longer periods than those laid down in paragraph (2), the period of notice to be observed by the principal shall not be shorter than that to be observed by the commercial agent.

(4) Unless otherwise agreed by the parties, the end of the period of notice shall coincide with the end of a calendar month.

(5) Subject to paragraph (6) the provisions of this regulation shall also apply to an agency contract for a fixed period where it is converted under regulation 14 into an agency contract for an indefinite period.

(6) The earlier fixed period shall be taken into account in the calculation of the period of notice.

16 Savings with regard to immediate termination

These Regulations shall not affect the application of any enactment or rule of law which provides for the immediate termination of the agency contract—

(a) because of the failure of one party to carry out all or part of his obligation under that contract; or

(b) where exceptional circumstances arise.

17 Entitlement of commercial agent to indemnity or compensation on termination of agency contract

(1) This regulation has effect for the purpose of ensuring that the commercial agent is, after termination of the agency contract, indemnified in accordance with paragraphs (3) to (5) or compensated for damage in accordance with paragraphs (6) and (7).

(2) Except where the agency contract otherwise provides, the commercial agent shall be entitled to be compensated rather than indemnified.

(3) Subject to paragraph (9) and regulation 18, the commercial agent shall be entitled to an indemnity if and to the extent that—

(a) he has brought the principal new customers or has significantly increased the volume of business with existing customers and the principal continues to derive substantial benefits from the business with such customers; and

(b) the payment of this indemnity is equitable having regard to all the circumstances and, in particular, the commission lost by the commercial agent on the business transacted with such customers.

(4) The amount of the indemnity shall not exceed a figure equivalent to an indemnity for one year calculated from the commercial agent's average annual remuneration over the preceding five years and if the contract goes back less than five years the indemnity shall be calculated on the average for the period in question.

(5) The grant of an indemnity shall not prevent the commercial agent from seeking damages.

(6) Subject to paragraph (9) and regulation 18, the commercial agent shall be entitled to compensation for the damage he suffers as a result of the termination of his relations with his principal.

(7) For the purpose of these Regulations such damage shall be deemed to occur particularly when the termination takes place in either or both of the following circumstances, namely circumstances which—

(a) deprive the commercial agent of the commission which proper performance of the agency contract would have procured for him whilst providing his principal with substantial benefits linked to the activities of the commercial agent; or

(b) have not enabled the commercial agent to amortise the costs and expenses that he had incurred in the performance of the agency contract on the advice of his principal.

(8) Entitlement to the indemnity or compensation for damage as provided for under paragraphs (2) to (7) shall also arise where the
agency contract is terminated as a result of the death of the commercial agent.

(9) The commercial agent shall lose his entitlement to the indemnity
or compensation for damage in the instances provided for in paragraphs (2) to (8) if within one year following termination of his
agency contract he has not notified his principal that he intends
pursuing his entitlement.

18 Grounds for excluding payment of indemnity or compensation under regulation 17

The indemnity or compensation referred to in regulation 17 shall not be
payable to the commercial agent where—

(a) the principal has terminated the agency contract because of default
attributable to the commercial agent which would justify immediate termination of the agency contract pursuant to regulation 16
above; or

(b) the commercial agent has himself terminated the agency contract,
unless such termination is justified—
  (i) by circumstances attributable to the principal, or
  (ii) on grounds of the age, infirmity or illness of the commercial agent in consequence of which he cannot reasonably be
required to continue his activities; or

(c) the commercial agent, with the agreement of his principal, assigns
his rights and duties under the agency contract to another person.

19 Prohibition on derogation from regulations 17 and 18

The parties may not derogate from regulations 17 and 18 to the detriment
of the commercial agent before the agency contract expires.

20 Restraint of trade clauses

(1) A restraint of trade clause shall be valid only if and to the extent
that—
  (a) it is concluded in writing; and
  (b) it relates to the geographical area or the group of customers
and the geographical area entrusted to the commercial agent
and to the kind of goods covered by his agency under the
contract.

(2) A restraint of trade clause shall be valid for not more than two years
after termination of the agency contract.

(3) Nothing in this regulation shall affect any enactment or rule of law
which imposes other restrictions on the validity or enforceability
of restraint of trade clauses or which enables a court to reduce the
obligations on the parties resulting from such clauses.

PART V
MISCELLANEOUS AND SUPPLEMENTAL

21 Disclosure of information

Nothing in these Regulations shall require information to be given where such disclosure would be contrary to public policy.

22 Service of notice etc

(1) Any notice, statement or other document to be given or supplied to a commercial agent or to be given or supplied to the principal under these Regulations may be so given or supplied—
  (a) by delivering it to him;
  (b) by leaving it at his usual address addressed to him by name;
  (c) by sending it by post to him addressed either to his usual or last known address or to the address of his principal place of business,

  or by any other means provided for in the agency contract.

(2) Any such notice, statement or document may—
  (a) in the case of a body corporate, be given or served on the secretary or clerk of that body;
  (b) in the case of a partnership, be given to or served on any partner or any person having the control or management of the partnership business.

23 Transitional provisions

(1) Notwithstanding any provision in an agency contract made before 13 January 1994, these Regulations shall apply to that contract after that date and, accordingly any provision which is inconsistent with these Regulations shall have effect subject to them.

(2) Nothing in these Regulations shall affect the rights and liabilities of a commercial agent or a principal which have accrued before 13 January 1994.

SCHEDULE

Regulation 2(4)

1 The activities of a person as a commercial agent are to be considered secondary where it may reasonably be taken that the primary purpose of the arrangement with his principal is other than as set out in paragraph 2.

2 An arrangement falls within this paragraph if—
  (a) the business of the principal is the sale, or as the case may be, purchase of goods of a particular kind, and
  (b) the goods concerned are such that—
    (i) transactions are normally individually negotiated and concluded on a commercial basis; and
    (ii) procuring a transaction on one occasion is likely to lead to further transactions in those goods with that customer on

future occasions, or to transactions in those goods with other customers in the same geographical area or among the same group of customers, and

that accordingly it is in the commercial interests of the principal in developing the market in those goods to appoint a representative to such customers with a view to the representative devoting effort, skill and expenditure from his own resources to that end.

3   The following are indications that an arrangement falls within paragraph 2, and the absence of any of them is an indication to the contrary—

(a)   the principal is the manufacturer, importer or distributor of the goods;

(b)   the goods are specifically identified with the principal in the market in question rather than, or to a greater extent than, with any other person;

(c)   the agent devotes substantially the whole of his time to representative activities (whether for one principal or for a number of principals whose interests are not conflicting);

(d)   the goods are not normally available in the market in question other than by means of the agent; and

(e)   the arrangement is described as one of commercial agency.

4   The following are indications that an arrangement does not fall within paragraph 2—

(a)   promotional material is supplied direct to potential customers;

(b)   persons are granted agencies without reference to existing agents in a particular area or in relation to a particular group; and

(c)   customers normally select the goods for themselves and merely place their orders through the agent.

5   The activities of the following categories of persons are presumed, unless the contrary is established, not to fall within paragraph 2—

(a)   mail order catalogue agents for consumer goods; and

(b)   consumer credit agents.

App1.3

Department of Trade and Industry Guidance Notes on the Commercial Agents (Council Directive) Regulations 1993[1] (September 1994)

[Note: as at 2010 these are archived on the National Archives web site but have not been replaced and remain useful guidance]

The Commercial Agents (Council Directive) Regulations 1993 (SI 1993/3053 as amended by SI 1993/3173)

---

1   Reproduced with kind permission of the Department of Trade and Industry.

PART I
(A) HISTORICAL BACKGROUND TO THE DIRECTIVE

The main purposes of the Directive were to harmonise the laws of Member States, which the Council of Ministers considered detrimental to the functioning of the Single Market, and to strengthen the position of the commercial agent in relation to his principal.

Independent commercial agents can be in a weak position when dealing with their principals, although it is acknowledged that this is not always the case. Agents have found difficulty obtaining written contracts and access to all the information they need to verify that they were being paid the correct amount of commission, and some have suffered financially because their commission has not been paid promptly and because their contracts were terminated with little or no notice.

(B) PREAMBLE TO THE DIRECTIVE

The preamble to the Directive includes the following recitals which are at the heart of the thinking behind the need for the Directive—

Whereas the differences in national laws concerning commercial representation substantially affect the conditions of competition and the carrying-on of that activity within the Community and are detrimental both to the protection available to commercial agents vis-à-vis their principals and to the security of commercial transactions; whereas moreover those differences are such as to inhibit substantially the conclusion and operation of commercial representation contracts where principal and commercial agent are established in different Member States.

Whereas trade in goods between Member States should be carried on under conditions which are similar to those of a single market, and this necessitates approximation of the legal systems of the Member States to the extent required for the proper functioning of the common market; whereas in this regard the rules concerning conflict of laws do not, in the matter of commercial representation, remove the inconsistencies referred to above, nor would they even if they were made uniform, and accordingly the proposed harmonisation is necessary notwithstanding the existence of those rules.

(C) IMPLEMENTATION OF THE DIRECTIVE

The Directive has been implemented as regards the law of England and Wales, and Scotland by Statutory Instrument No 1993/3053 as amended by Statutory Instrument No 1993/3173. Separate implementing provision is made in relation to Northern Ireland by the Commercial Agents (Council Directive) Regulations (Northern Ireland) 1993 (Statutory Rules for Northern Ireland No 1993/483).

(D) PURPOSE OF THE GUIDANCE NOTES

The purpose of these notes is to assist commercial agents, principals, and their legal advisers to understand the effect of the Commercial Agents (Council Directive) Regulations 1993 by explaining why particular options for implementing the Directive were chosen and by setting out the Department's view on a number of points of difficulty. It must be emphasised that the Department's view is no more than that. As with other Community legislation, the Directive has to be interpreted uniformly throughout the Community and ultimately only the European Court can do that.

The guidance notes are in two parts. Part I continues by setting out, by regulation, the Department's general interpretation of the intention behind the Directive and hence the Regulations. Part II deals with other more specific and general points which arise during the consultation.

The notes deal only with those provisions which are novel or about which, during consultation, specific queries were raised. **IN THAT CONNECTION IT SHOULD BE NOTED THAT THE TEXT OF REGULATIONS 5, 13, 14, 15, 18, 19, 21, 22 AND 23 IS NOT PRINTED, NOR DO THESE NOTES CONTAIN ANY SPECIFIC COMMENT ON THEM**. Further issues on particular provisions may arise in the future, and the contact point is—

> Barrie Stevenson
> Consumer and Competition Policy Directorate
> Department of Trade and Industry
> 1 Victoria Street
> London SW1H 0ET
> Tel: 020 7215 0319
> E-mail: Barrie.Stevenson@dti.gsi.gov.uk

The Department has taken the view that, for the most part, the substantive provisions of the Directive leave the Member States with little or no discretion as to implementation of the Directive in national law and therefore, the wording of the Regulations follows that of the Directive very closely.

(E) DETAILS OF THE REGULATIONS AND THE DEPARTMENT'S INTERPRETATION

Regulation 1

1   (1)   These Regulations may be cited as the Commercial Agents (Council Directive) Regulations 1993 and shall come into force on 1 January 1994.

     (2)   These Regulations govern the relations between commercial agents and their principals and, subject to paragraph (3), apply in relation to the activities of commercial agents in Great Britain.

     (3)   Regulations 3 to 22 do not apply where the parties have agreed that the agency contract is to be governed by the law of another Member State.

Interpretation

This Regulation sets out the circumstances in which the Regulations will apply to an agency contract. If the agent carries out his activities as a commercial agent in Great Britain, then the Regulations will apply unless the parties expressly choose the law of another Member State as the law which is to apply to the agency contract. If the law of a non-EU country is chosen then the provisions of the Regulations are intended to override that choice of law in so far as any of the activities of the commercial agent are carried out in Great Britain.

Regulation 1(2) provides that the Regulations govern relations between commercial agents and their principals and apply in relation to the activities of commercial agents in Great Britain (whether or not the agent is physically based in Great Britain).

The provisions of the Regulations, where the agent carries on his activities outside Great Britain, do not, however, prevent the parties from choosing the law of a part of Great Britain (for example the law of England and Wales) and incorporating in the agency agreement some or all of the provisions of the Regulations which the parties might wish to agree should apply as though the agents activities were, in fact, to be carried on in Great Britain. However, in such a case, if litigation arises, the court hearing the action may or may not—

(i)   uphold the choice of law, and

(ii)   accept the validity of such incorporation.

The state of the law of the other Member States relating to commercial agents will depend, in part, on the manner in which the Directive has been implemented in those States, and advice as to the relevant foreign law (both within the EU and outside) should be sought in appropriate cases.

Some examples appear in the Annex to these notes which are intended to show the application (or otherwise) of the Regulations where the principal is based in one country and his agent performs his activities in another.

The Regulations apply to Great Britain (regulation 2(5)). The Directive has been implemented separately in relation to Northern Ireland by the Commercial Agents (Council Directive) Regulations (Northern Ireland) 1993 (Statutory Rules for Northern Ireland No 1993/483).

Regulation 2

(Articles 1 and 2 of the Directive)

2   (1)   In these Regulations—

'commercial agent' means a self-employed intermediary who has continuing authority to negotiate the sale or purchase of goods on behalf of another person (the 'principal'), or to negotiate and conclude the sale or purchase of goods on behalf of and in the name of that principal; but shall be understood as not including in particular—

(i)   a person who, in his capacity as an officer of a company or association, is empowered to enter into commitments binding on that company or association;

(ii)   a partner who is lawfully authorised to enter into commitments binding on his partners;

(iii) a person who acts as an insolvency practitioner (as that expression is defined in s 388 of the Insolvency Act 1986) or the equivalent in any other jurisdiction;

'commission' means any part of the remuneration of a commercial agent which varies with the number or value of business transactions; 'restraint of trade clause' means an agreement restricting the business activities of a commercial agent following termination of the agency contract.

(2) These Regulations do not apply to—
   (a) commercial agents whose activities are unpaid;
   (b) commercial agents when they operate on commodity exchanges or in the commodity market;
   (c) the Crown Agents for Overseas Governments and Administrations, as set up under the Crown Agents Act 1979, or its subsidiaries.

(3) The provisions of the Schedule to these Regulations have effect for the purposes of determining the persons whose activities as commercial agents are to be considered secondary.

(4) These Regulations shall not apply to the persons referred to in paragraph (3) above.

(5) These Regulations do not extend to Northern Ireland.

Interpretation

The Regulation sets out the definitions of the terms used within the Regulations and also excludes those agents where the activities are considered secondary.

The expression 'self-employed' is derived from articles 52 and 57 [now articles 43 and 47] of the Treaty of Rome (which deal with freedom of establishment and freedom to provide services) and is consistent with Community law, to be understood as including, for example, companies as well as self-employed individuals.

If an agent is appointed for a specified number of transactions, then he would be excluded from the scope of the Regulations, owing to his lack of continuing authority.

'Goods' clearly has to be interpreted in accordance with the EC Treaty and, for that reason, the Regulations do not define the word. However, it is considered that the definition of 'goods' in s 61(1) of the Sale of Goods Act 1979 as including, inter alia, all personal chattels other than things in action (eg shares) and money, may offer a reasonable guide, without necessarily being absolutely co-extensive with the Directive meaning.

Interpretation of the term 'secondary activities' and the provisions of the Schedule to the Regulations are dealt with later in these notes.

Some agents only effect introductions between their principals and third parties. The question arises as to whether such agents are commercial agents for the purposes of the Regulations. Such agents are sometimes known as 'canvassing' or 'introducing' agents. As such, they generally lack the power to bind their principals and are not really agents in the true sense of the word. However, to the extent that such an agent 'has continuing authority to negotiate the sale or purchase of goods' on behalf of his principal, even though, as a matter of fact, he merely effects introductions, it seems that he would fall within the definition of 'commercial agent' in regulation 2(1). It is clear that an 'introducing' agent who lacks such authority falls outside the scope of the definition of 'commercial agent'. It may be that the courts would give a wide interpretation to the word 'negotiate' and that, as a result, 'introducing' agents will, in general, have the benefit of the Regulations.

It is thought that the Regulations do apply to *del credere* agents who exhibit the characteristics set out in definition of 'commercial agent'. The Department does not consider that the additional features of a *del credere* agency causes the agent to fall outside the definition. Questions can, however, arise as to whether a person is an agent at all who, in consideration of extra remuneration, guarantees to his principal that third parties with whom he enters into contracts on behalf of the principal will duly pay any sums becoming due under those contracts (and thus appears to be a *del credere* agent), or, whether that person is really acting on his own account.

Regulation 2(2)(b) provides that the Regulations do not apply to commercial agents when they op erate on commodity exchanges or in the commodity market. A 'commodity' is any tangible good. So called 'commodity exchanges' deal in such goods and, to a large extent, in commodity 'futures' ie the right to buy or sell a particular commodity at a particular price at a particular time in the future, hence eg 'coffee futures'.

Regulation 3
(Article 3 of the Directive)

3   (1)   In performing his activities a commercial agent must look after the interests of his principal and act dutifully and in good faith.
    (2)   In particular, a commercial agent must—
        (a)   make proper effects to negotiate and, where appropriate, conclude the transactions he is instructed to take care of;
        (b)   communicate to his principal all the necessary information available to him;
        (c)   comply with reasonable instructions given by his principal.

Interpretation

This Regulation sets out the duties which the agent owes to the principal and, in effect, restates the duties owed at common law by an agent to his principal.

It is not certain how an agent's duty to 'communicate to his principal all the necessary information available to him' is to be fulfilled where an agent is acting for several principals. However, parties to contracts of commercial agency will doubtless wish to explore the possibility of agreeing on express terms to cover that situation.

Regulation 4
(Article 4 of the Directive)

4   (1)   In his relations with his commercial agent a principal must act dutifully and in good faith.

(2)   In particular, a principal must—
  (a)   provide his commercial agent with the necessary documentation relating to the goods concerned;
  (b)   obtain for his commercial agent the information necessary for the performance of the agency contract, and in particular notify his commercial agent within a reasonable period once he anticipates that the volume of commercial transactions will be significantly lower than that which the commercial agent could normally have expected.
(3)   A principal shall, in addition, inform his commercial agent within a reasonable period of his acceptance or refusal of, and of any non-execution by him of, a commercial transaction which the commercial agent has procured for him.

Interpretation

This Regulation deals with the principal's duties to the commercial agent. It is thought that these duties merely amplify the position at common law.

A principal is required to inform his commercial agent accordingly once the principal knows that business will decrease significantly or where an order will not be concluded.

Regulation 6
(Article 6 of the Directive)

6   (1)   In the absence of any agreement as to remuneration between the parties, a commercial agent shall be entitled to the remuneration that commercial agents appointed for the goods forming the subject of his agency contract are customarily allowed in the place where he carries on his activities and, if there is no such customary practice, a commercial agent shall be entitled to reasonable remuneration taking into account all the aspects of the transaction.
      (2)   This Regulation is without prejudice to the application of any enactment or rule of law concerning the level of remuneration.
      (3)   Where a commercial agent is not remunerated (wholly or in part) by commission, regulations 7 to 12 shall not apply.

Interpretation

This Regulation is applicable only where the parties have not agreed on the remuneration payable by the principal to the agent. In the event of a dispute as to the remuneration payable, the court would be likely to have regard to custom in the commercial area concerned. Should there be no identifiable custom in the area concerned, then it is considered that the agent would be entitled to a reasonable amount of remuneration. The position under the Regulations is thought to be similar to the position at common law.

It should be noted that where the commercial agent is not remunerated (wholly or in part) by commission, regulations 7–12 do not apply.

Regulation 7
(Article 7 of the Directive)

7   (1)   A commercial agent shall be entitled to commission on transactions concluded during the period covered by the agency contract—

    (a)   where the transaction has been concluded as a result of his action; or

    (b)   where the transaction is concluded with a third party whom he has previously acquired as a customer for transactions of the same kind.

    (2)   A commercial agent shall also be entitled to commission on transactions concluded during the period covered by the agency contract where he has an exclusive right to a specific geographical area or to a specific group of customers and where the transaction has been entered into with a customer belonging to that area or group.

Interpretation

This Regulation sets out the circumstances in which the agent may be considered to have earned his commission, and in that connection the view is taken that a transaction is 'concluded' when the principal and the third party have entered into a contract. The provisions of (2) include so called 'House Accounts' held by the principal ie where the principal deals directly with the third party although the agent has the rights to that area.

Regulation 8
(Article 8 of the Directive)

Subject to regulation 9 below, a commercial agent shall be entitled to commission on commercial transactions concluded after the agency contract has terminated if—

    (a)   the transaction is mainly attributable to his efforts during the period covered by the agency contract and if the transaction was entered into within a reasonable period after the contract terminated; or

    (b)   in accordance with the conditions mentioned in paragraph 7 above, the order of the third party reached the principal or commercial agent before the agency contract terminated.

Interpretation

This Regulation sets out when the agent is entitled to commission on commercial transactions concluded after the agency contract has come to an end. In particular where the transaction, was mainly a result of the agent's efforts during the contract and the transaction was entered into within a reasonable period after the end of the agency contract.

The principal and agent may attempt to define 'reasonable period' in their agreement. However, in the event of a dispute, despite any such definition, the matter would be ultimately for the decision of the court.

If the order was placed with the principal or agent before the termination of the agency contract, but the contract was not concluded until afterwards, then the principal would still be liable to pay commission.

Regulation 9
(Article 9 of the Directive)

9 (1) A commercial agent shall not be entitled to the commission referred to in regulation 7 above if that commission is payable, by virtue of regulation 8 above, to the previous commercial agent, unless it is equitable because of the circumstances for the commission to be shared between the commercial agents.

(2) The principal shall be liable for any sum due under paragraph (1) above to the person entitled to it in accordance with that paragraph, and any sum which the other commercial agent receives to which he is not entitled shall be refunded to the principal.

Interpretation
This Regulation deals with the apportionment of commission between a new agent and his predecessor for the same transaction.

The new agent is not entitled to commission if it is payable to the previous agent unless it is equitable because of the circumstances, for the commission to be shared between them.

It is the principal's duty to pay commission owing to agents and where commission is paid inadvertently to one agent which was in fact owed to the other, the agent must repay it or the principal reclaim it. In either circumstance the agent entitled to the commission should receive it.

Regulation 10
(Article 10 of the Directive)

10 (1) Commission shall become due as soon as, and to the extent that, one of the following circumstances occurs—
    (a) the principal has executed the transaction; or
    (b) the principal should, according to his agreement with the third party, have executed the transaction; or
    (c) the third party has executed the transaction.

(2) Commission shall become due at the latest when the third party has executed his part of the transaction or should have done so if the principal had executed his part of the transaction, as he should have.

(3) The commission shall be paid not later than on the last day of the month following the quarter in which it became due, and, for the purposes of these Regulations, unless otherwise agreed between the parties, the first quarter period shall run from the date the agency contract takes effect, and subsequent periods shall run from that date in the third month thereafter or the beginning of the fourth month, whichever is the sooner.

(4) Any agreement to derogate from paragraphs (2) and (3) above to the detriment of the commercial agent shall be void.

Interpretation

This Regulation sets out when the commission to be paid to an agent becomes due and when it should be paid. A transaction may be considered to be 'executed' in any of the following circumstances—

(i)   when the principal has accepted or delivered the goods;
(ii) when the principal should have accepted or delivered the goods;
(iii) when the third party accepts or delivers the goods; or
(iv) when the third party pays for the goods.

It is for the two parties to agree within the terms of the contract which of these circumstances will make the commission become due. Paragraph 2 of the Regulation provides for the latest date that the commission can become due.

It is not unusual for goods to be delivered by instalments. If the agency contract does not make specific provision for the matter, the question as to when commission is due would seem to depend upon the precise nature of the sale or purchase transaction. Where each instalment delivery is the subject of a separate contract, it seems likely that a separate commission payment will be due as each separate delivery is made, or should have been made. Where a single contract applies to a number of instalment deliveries, the position is somewhat less clear. However, in view of the words 'to the extent that' in regulation 10(1) the agent may be entitled to the commission which is attributable to each particular instalment delivery.

It should be noted that paragraph (4) of regulation 10 renders void any agreement to derogate to the detriment of the commercial agent from paragraph (2) and (3) of the Regulation.

Regulation 11

(Article 11 of the Directive)

11   (1)   The right to commission can be extinguished only if and to the extent that—

   (a)   it is established that the contract between the third party and the principal will not be executed; and

   (b)   that fact is due to a reason for which the principal is not to blame.

   (2)   Any commission which the commercial agent has already received shall be refunded if the right to it is extinguished.

   (3)   Any agreement to derogate from paragraph (1) above to the detriment of the commercial agent shall be void.

Interpretation

The Regulation outlines the circumstances when the agent's right to commission is forfeited. Should a contract not be executed the principal must not be at fault for the entitlement to commission to be extinguished. Any commission already paid by the principal under these circumstances would be refunded.

Regulation 12
(Article 12 of the Directive)

12   (1)   The principal shall supply his commercial agent with a statement of the commission due, not later than the last day of the month following the quarter in which the commission has become due, and such statement shall set out the main components used in calculating the amount of commission.

(2)   A commercial agent shall be entitled to demand that he be provided with the information (and in particular an extract from the books) which is available to his principal and which he needs in order to check the amount of commission due to him.

(3)   Any agreement to derogate from paragraphs (1) and (2) above shall be void.

(4)   Nothing in this Regulation shall remove or restrict the effect of, or prevent reliance upon, any enactment or rule of law which recognises the right of an agent to inspect the books of the principal.

Interpretation
The Regulation sets out the principal's obligation to provide the agent with a statement or commission due and must set out the main components in calculating the commission. It also requires the principal to provide the agent with all necessary information, including extracts from his (the principal's) books, to check the commission due, should the agent request such information. NB the principal is only required to provide relevant extracts and not his full books.

Regulation 16
(Article 16 of the Directive)

16   These Regulations shall not affect the application of any enactment or rule of law which provides for the immediate termination of the agency contract—

(a)   because of the failure of one party to carry out all or part of his obligations under that contract; or

(b)   where exceptional circumstances arise.

Interpretation
This Regulation preserves the common law and statutory rules of jurisdictions within Great Britain which provide for the immediate termination of an agency contract on the basis of the two matters set out in subparagraphs (a) and (b) of the Regulation. It is thought that the expression 'exceptional circumstances' in paragraph (b) would include matters falling within the doctrine of frustration.

Regulation 17
(Article 17 of the Directive)

17   (1)   This Regulation has effect for the purpose of ensuring that the commercial agent is, after termination of the agency contract,

indemnified in accordance with paragraphs (3) to (5) below or compensated for damage in accordance with paragraphs (6) and (7) below.

(2) Except where the agency contract otherwise provides, the commercial agent shall be entitled to be compensated rather than indemnified.

(3) Subject to paragraph (9) below and to regulation 18 below, the commercial agent shall be entitled to an indemnity if and to the extent that—

(a) he has brought the principal new customers or has significantly increased the volume of business from existing customers and the principal continues to derive substantial benefits from the business with such customers; and

(b) the payment of this indemnity is equitable having regard to all the circumstances and, in particular, the commission lost by the commercial agent on the business transacted with such customers.

(4) The amount of the indemnity shall not exceed a figure equivalent to an indemnity for one year calculated from the commercial agent's average annual remuneration over the preceding five years and if the contract goes back less than five years the indemnity shall be calculated on the average for the period in question.

(5) The granting of an indemnity as mentioned above shall not prevent the commercial agent from seeking damages.

(6) Subject to paragraph (9) and regulation 18 below, the commercial agent shall be entitled to compensation for the damage he suffers as a result of the termination of his relations with his principal.

(7) For the purposes of these Regulations such damage shall be deemed to occur particularly when the termination takes place in either or both of the following circumstances, namely circumstances which—

(a) deprive the commercial agent of the commission which proper performance of the agency contract would have procured for him whilst providing his principal with substantial benefits linked to the activities of the commercial agent; or

(b) have not enabled the commercial agent to amortise the costs and expenses that he had incurred in the performance of the agency contract on the advice of his principal.

(8) Entitlement to the indemnity or compensation for damage as provided for under paragraphs (2) to (7) above shall also arise where the agency contract is terminated as a result of the death of the commercial agent.

(9) The commercial agent shall lose his entitlement to the indemnity or compensation for damage in the instances provided for in paragraphs (2) to (8) above if within one year following termination of his agency contract he has not notified his principal that he intends pursuing his entitlement.

Interpretation

The Regulation deals with entitlement to indemnity/compensation upon termination of the agency contract. It is for the two parties to choose which of these options they would wish to include in their contract with the backstop of compensation should no choice be indicated. There is however, nothing to preclude the two parties from agreeing to use the compensation provisions in some cases and indemnity ones in others when terminating a particular contract. The indemnity/compensation is only payable where the principal will continue to benefit from the business that the agent has brought to the principal.

It should be noted that although having fixed term contracts or giving correct periods of notice (see regulation 15) could potentially reduce the level of indemnity/compensation it would not necessarily exclude it. The issue of whether compensation is payable on the expiry of a fixed term contract or where the contractural notice period in an indefinite term contract has been given is a matter for the courts to decide.

It is thought that in view of the terms of regulation 19 it would be possible for the two parties to derogate from this provision after the termination of the agency contract.

The word 'indemnity' has a rather more limited meaning than that which it normally bears in English law in that it—

(i)   appears to fall short of a complete making good of the loss suffered by the principal; and

(ii)   does not necessarily arise in relation to loss caused by the principal.

Its more limited nature may be inferred from regulation 17(5) which contemplates the possibility of the agent wishing to seek damages. The amount of the indemnity is, in any event, limited by regulation 17(4). The indemnity might appropriately be reviewed as approximating to a form of liquidated damages.

It remains to be seen how courts in Great Britain would assess amounts of compensation/indemnity, and the Department feels unable, at this stage, to offer any guidance as to the approach likely to be adopted.

Article 17.6 of the Directive requires the Commission to submit to the Council, by the end of 1994, a report on the implementation of article 17 (indemnity/compensation) and, if necessary to submit to the Council proposals for amendments.

As the meaning of 'substantial' in regulation 17(3)(a), it is thought that word would be interpreted as meaning 'material' or 'nor insignificant' having regard to the history of dealings between the principal and the agents and other relevant circumstances.

'Equitable' in regulation 17(3)(b) probably means 'just' or 'fair' rather than necessarily based on the doctrines or principles of equity — the latter, if they exist at all in the law of every Member State, being bound to vary from State to State.

Regulation 20

(Article 20 of the Directive)

20   (1)   A restraint of trade clause shall be valid only if and to the extent that—

    (a)   it is concluded in writing; and

    (b)   it relates to the geographical area or the group of customers and the geographical area entrusted to the commercial agent and to the kind of goods covered by his agency under the contract.

(2)   A restraint of trade clause shall be valid for not more than two years after the termination of the agency contract.

(3)   Nothing in this Regulation shall effect any enactment or rule of law which imposes other restrictions on the validity or enforceability of restraint of trade clauses or which enables a court to reduce the obligations on the parties resulting from such clauses.

Interpretation

A 'restraint of trade clause' is any agreement which restricts the business activities of a commercial agent following termination of the agency contract (see the definition in regulation 2).

The restraint of trade provisions only extend to the kind of goods that were covered in his contract. It is thought that the provisions would not extend to goods of a similar nature aimed at different types of purchasers.

THE SCHEDULE

1   The activities of a person as a commercial agent are to be considered secondary where it may reasonably be taken that the primary purpose of the arrangement with his principal is other than set out in paragraph 2 below.

2   An arrangement falls within this paragraph if—

    (a)   the business of the principal is the sale, or as the case may be purchase, of goods of a particular kind; and

    (b)   the goods concerned are such that—

        (i)   transactions are normally individually negotiated and concluded on a commercial basis, and

        (ii)   procuring a transaction on one occasion is likely to lead to further transactions in those goods with that customer on future occasions, or to transactions in those goods with other customers in the same geographical area or among the same group of customers, and

    that accordingly it is in the commercial interests of the principal in developing the market in those goods to appoint a representative to such customers with a view to the representative devoting effort, skill and expenditure from its own resources to that end.

3   The following are indications that an arrangement falls within paragraph 2 above, and the absence of any of them is an indication to the contrary—

    (a)   the principal is the manufacturer, importer or distributor of the goods;

    (b)   the goods are specifically identified with the principal in the market in question rather than, or to the greater extent than, with any other person;

     (c)   the agent devotes substantially the whole of his time to representative activities (whether for one principal or a number of principals whose interests are not conflicting);

     (d)   the goods are not normally available in the market in question other than by means of the agent;

     (e)   the arrangement is described as one of commercial agency.

4   The following are indications that an arrangement does not fall within paragraph 2 above—

     (a)   promotional material is supplied direct to potential customers;

     (b)   persons are granted agencies without reference to existing agents in a particular area or in relation to a particular group;

     (c)   customers normally select the goods for themselves and merely place their orders through the agent.

5   The activities of the following categories of persons are presumed, unless the contrary is established, not to fall within paragraph 2 above—

Mail order catalogue agents for consumer goods.

Consumer credit agents.

Interpretation

The Schedule sets out the criteria for determining the persons whose activities as commercial agents are considered secondary under UK law and are excluded from the provisions of the Regulations by virtue of regulation 2(3).

The first test is to determine whether or not a contract comes under the provisions of the Regulations. The determining factor is whether the agent is required to keep, as his own property, a considerable stock of the product.

The comparison to be made is between the agent's activities as a commercial agent and his other activities and not the relationship with the principal.

It is not possible to say which of the provisions in paragraphs 3 and 4 take priority and this will have to be determined on a case by case basis taking into account the exact nature of the agency contract.

PART II

(A) ANSWERS TO SPECIFIC QUESTIONS RAISED DURING THE
CONSULTATION EXERCISE

Q   **CAN THE PRINCIPLE OF SET-OFF CONTINUE TO APPLY?**

A   The Regulations do not mention set-off. It is thought that set-off will remain available to the principal, his agent and third parties in accordance with the rules of common law.

Q   **IF A PRINCIPAL EMPLOYS AN AGENT TO ACT FOR HIM IN A NUMBER OF DIFFERENT MEMBER STATES, COULD THERE BE ONE AGENCY CONTRACT GOVERNING THE RELATIONSHIP?**

A   This would be possible subject to the comments concerning the applicability of English law to contracts outside the UK.

Q REGULATION 17(8) EXPRESSLY ALLOWS INDEMNITY OR COMPENSATION WHERE THE AGENCY CONTRACT IS TERMINATED AS A RESULT OF THE COMMERCIAL AGENT'S DEATH. IS THE POSITION THE SAME IF THE COMMERCIAL AGENT (BEING A COMPANY) GOES INTO LIQUIDATION?

A Where the principal or agent is a company, at common law the actual authority of the principal or agent will be determined by its winding up or dissolution. It should be noted that where the authority is irrevocable it will not be determined by such events.

Q CAN AN AGE LIMIT BE FIXED FOR A COMMERCIAL AGENT?

A It is thought it can. Fixed contracts are permitted and if, for example, a 40-year-old agent is appointed 'until he is 60' this is equivalent to a fixed contract for 20 years or until death.

Q TO WHAT EXTENT CAN THE REGULATIONS BE DEROGATED FROM?

A There are three different types of Regulation within the Regulations: those which cannot be derogated from; those which cannot be derogated from to the detriment of the agent; and those which make no mention of derogation.

It can be argued that where regulations mean there to be no derogation, they say so. It can also be said that if nothing is said it is to be inferred that it can be derogated from. If this is so then, for example, the agency contract could express the agent's entitlement to commission as arising where the transaction is 'wholly' as a result of his action.

The Department's conclusion on this, although not a firm one, is that the terms of the agency contract can vary the events upon which the agent becomes entitled to commission, although they could not do so to an extent that it excludes the right altogether since this would conflict with regulation 11(1).

Q ARE SUB-AGENCY AGREEMENTS COVERED BY THE REGULATIONS?

A Whilst the position is not clear, the Regulations are, in principle, capable of covering sub-agency agreements.

Q IS IT POSSIBLE TO INCLUDE A LIQUIDATED DAMAGES PROVISION WITHIN THE CONTRACT?

A Liquidated damages is a provision within a contract where one party agrees to pay to the other a specified sum of money in the event of a breach of contract.

Such clauses may be permissible provided that they represent a genuine pre-estimate of damage.

Although one object of the clause will be to limit the principal's liability, it may not be a pure limitation clause in that it forms a compromise between the parties and is intended to be enforceable whether the actual loss is greater or less than the sum agreed. Nevertheless, as against the principal, such provisions risk attack by the agent as void by virtue of regulation 19.

Q   ARE THE REGULATIONS RETROSPECTIVE?

A   Only in the sense that they apply to all contracts as from 1 January 1994 and it is inevitable that in some respects account will have to be taken of what occurred before 1994. The Regulations do not, however, apply so as to affect the rights and liabilities of either the principal or agent if they have accrued before 1994.

Q   DO THE REGULATIONS APPLY TO AGENTS WHO SELL CHRISTMAS HAMPERS?

A   It is believed that the activities of such agents would be likely to be held as secondary, thus rendering the agents (by virtue of regulation 2(4)) outside the scope of the Regulations.

ANNEX
(A) EXAMPLES ON THE APPLICATION OF REGULATION 1

1   Principal in Great Britain, agent's activities in France (EU Member State)

The Regulations do not apply, since the agent's activities are in France and therefore are not in Great Britain (see regulation 1(2)). However, if the parties choose English law to govern the contract between them, it is suggested that the contract could provide for the provisions of the Regulations to apply to the relations between them as though the agent's activities were in Great Britain. Although the agent is in France, if the parties choose English law to govern the agency contract, the provisions of French law implementing the Directive would not apply (unless those provisions are held to be 'mandatory rules' (see article 3 of the Rome Convention on the law applicable to contractual obligations)).

2   Principal in Great Britain, agent's activities in Australia (non-EU Member State)

The Regulations do not apply, given that the agent's activities are in Australia and therefore not in Great Britain. However, again, it is thought that, as in the first example above, the parties could specifically adopt the provisions of the Regulations by contractual provision to that effect. Any 'mandatory rules' of the relevant Australian State(s) would need to be considered in case they were capable of over-riding any provisions of the contract.

3   Principal in France, agent's activities in Great Britain

In the absence of an express choice of French law, the Regulations would apply, given that the agent's activities are in Great Britain. If the parties choose French law, the Regulations would not apply (see regulation 1(3)), and the agent would have the protection of the Directive as implemented in French law.

4   Principal in USA, agent's activities in Great Britain

If the law of a part of Great Britain is chosen by the parties to govern the agency contract, it is concluded that the Regulations will apply.

However, if the law of a State of the US is chosen, no doubt an exclusive jurisdiction clause in favour of the courts of that State would also be included in the agency contract, on the basis of which a court in Great Britain may well decline jurisdiction. In the absence of such a clause, or if a court in Great Britain nevertheless accepts jurisdiction, the court may take the view (perhaps after making an article 177 reference to the European Court) that the Regulations constitute mandatory rules of the law of a part of Great Britain and that the Regulations should, accordingly, apply, the intention of the Directive being to afford certain protections to commercial agents operating within the European Union (but possibly only where the principal is also established within the European Union. Thus an agent in such circumstances would be unwise to assume that, despite operating in Great Britain, the Regulations would apply.

Appendix 2

European Community materials

Council Directive of 18 December 1986 (86/653) on the coordination of the laws of the Member States relating to self-employed commercial agents

The Council of the European Communities

Having regard to the Treaty establishing the European Economic Community, and in particular articles 57(2) and 100 thereof,

Having regard to the proposal from the Commission,

Having regard to the opinion of the European Parliament,

Having regard to the opinion of the Economic and Social Committee,

Whereas the restrictions on the freedom of establishment and the freedom to provide services in respect of activities of intermediaries in commerce, industry and small craft industries were abolished by Directive 64/224EEC (OJ 1964, 56/869).

Whereas the differences in national laws concerning commercial representation substantially affect the conditions of competition and the carrying-on of that activity within the Community and are detrimental both to the protection available to commercial agents vis-à-vis their principals and to the security of commercial transactions; whereas moreover those differences are such as to inhibit substantially the conclusion and operation of commercial representation contracts where principal and commercial agent are established in different Member States;

Whereas trade in goods between Member States should be carried on under conditions which are similar to those of a single market, and this necessitates approximation of the legal systems of the Member States to the extent required for the proper functioning of the common market; whereas in this regard the rules concerning conflict of laws do not, in the matter of commercial representation, remove the inconsistencies referred to above, nor would they even if they were made uniform, and accordingly the proposed harmonisation is necessary notwithstanding the existence of those rules;

Whereas in this regard the legal relationship between commercial agent and principal must be given priority;

Whereas it is appropriate to be guided by the principles of article 117 of the Treaty and to maintain improvements already made, when harmonising the laws of the Member States relating to commercial agents;

Whereas additional transitional periods should be allowed for certain Member States which have to make a particular effort to adapt their regulations, especially those concerning indemnity for termination of contract between the principal and the commercial agent, to the requirements of this Directive,

HAS ADOPTED THIS DIRECTIVE:

CHAPTER I — SCOPE

Article 1

1. The harmonisation measures prescribed by this Directive shall apply to the laws, regulations and administrative provisions of the Member States governing the relations between commercial agents and their principals.

2. For the purposes of this Directive, 'commercial agent' shall mean a self-employed intermediary who has continuing authority to negotiate the sale or the purchase of goods on behalf of another person, hereinafter called the 'principal', or to negotiate and conclude such transactions on behalf of and in the name of that principal.

3. A commercial agent shall be understood within the meaning of this Directive as not including in particular:
   — a person who, in his capacity as an officer, is empowered to enter into commitments binding on a company or association,
   — a partner who is lawfully authorised to enter into commitments binding on his partners,
   — a receiver, a receiver and manager, a liquidator or a trustee in bankruptcy.

Article 2

1. This Directive shall not apply to:
   — commercial agents whose activities are unpaid,
   — commercial agents when they operate on commodity exchanges or in the commodity market, or
   — the body known as the Crown Agents for Overseas Governments and Administrations, as set-up under the Crown Agents Act 1979 in the UK, or its subsidiaries.

2. Each of the Member States shall have the right to provide that the Directive shall not apply to those persons whose activities as commercial agents are considered secondary by the law of that Member State.

CHAPTER II — RIGHTS AND OBLIGATIONS

Article 3

1.   In performing his activities a commercial agent must look after his principal's interests and act dutifully and in good faith.
2.   In particular, a commercial agent must:
     (a)   make proper efforts to negotiate and, where appropriate, conclude the transactions he is instructed to take care of;
     (b)   communicate to his principal all the necessary information available to him;
     (c)   comply with reasonable instructions given by his principal.

Article 4

1.   In his relations with his commercial agent a principal must act dutifully and in good faith.
2.   A principal must in particular:
     (a)   provide his commercial agent with the necessary documentation relating to the goods concerned;
     (b)   obtain for his commercial agent the information necessary for the performance of the agency contract, and in particular notify the commercial agent within a reasonable period once he anticipates that the volume of commercial transactions will be significantly lower than that which the commercial agent could normally have expected.
3.   A principal must, in addition, inform the commercial agent within a reasonable period of his acceptance, refusal, and of any non-execution of a commercial transaction which the commercial agent has procured for the principal.

Article 5

The parties may not derogate from the provisions of articles 3 and 4.

CHAPTER III — REMUNERATION

Article 6

1.   In the absence of any agreement on this matter between the parties, and without prejudice to the application of the compulsory provisions of the Member States concerning the level of remuneration, a commercial agent shall be entitled to the remuneration that commercial agents appointed for the goods forming the subject of his agency contract are customarily allowed in the place where he carries on his activities. If there is no such customary practice a commercial agent shall be entitled to reasonable remuneration taking into account all the aspects of the transaction.
2.   Any part of the remuneration which varies with the number or value of business transactions shall be deemed to be commission within the meaning of this Directive.

3.   Articles 7 to 12 shall not apply if the commercial agent is not remuner-
     ated wholly or in part by commission.

Article 7

1.   A commercial agent shall be entitled to commission on commercial
     transactions concluded during the period covered by the agency con-
     tract:
     (a)   where the transaction has been concluded as a result of his action;
           or
     (b)   where the transaction is concluded with a third party whom he has
           previously acquired as a customer for transactions of the same kind.
2.   A commercial agent shall also be entitled to commission on transactions
     concluded during the period covered by the agency contract:
     —   either where he is entrusted with a specific geographical area or
           group of customers,
     —   or where he has an exclusive right to a specific geographical area
           or group of customers,
     and where the transaction has been entered into with a customer
           belonging to that area or group.
     Member States shall include in their legislation one of the possibilities
     referred to in the above two indents.

Article 8

A commercial agent shall be entitled to commission on commercial
transactions concluded after the agency contract has terminated:
(a)   if the transaction is mainly attributable to the commercial agent's efforts
      during the period covered by the agency contract and if the transaction
      was entered into within a reasonable period after that contract termi-
      nated; or
(b)   if, in accordance with the conditions mentioned in article 7, the order
      of the third party reached the principal or the commercial agent before
      the agency contract terminated.

Article 9

A commercial agent shall not be entitled to the commission referred to in
article 7, if that commission is payable, pursuant to article 8, to the previous
commercial agent, unless it is equitable because of the circumstances for the
commission to be shared between the commercial agents.

Article 10

1.   The commission shall become due as soon as and to the extent that one
     of the following circumstances obtains:
     (a)   the principal has executed the transaction; or
     (b)   the principal should, according to his agreement with the third
           party, have executed the transaction; or
     (c)   the third party has executed the transaction.

2. The commission shall become due at the latest when the third party has executed his part of the transaction or should have done so if the principal had executed his part of the transaction, as he should have.
3. The commission shall be paid not later than on the last day of the month following the quarter in which it became due.
4. Agreements to derogate from paragraphs 2 and 3 to the detriment of the commercial agent shall not be permitted.

Article 11
1. The right to commission can be extinguished only if and to the extent that:
    —   it is established that the contract between the third party and the principal will not be executed, and
    —   that fact is due to a reason for which the principal is not to blame.
2. Any commission which the commercial agent has already received shall be refunded if the right to it is extinguished.
3. Agreements to derogate from paragraph 1 to the detriment of the commercial agent shall not be permitted.

Article 12
1. The principal shall supply his commercial agent with a statement of the commission due, not later than the last day of the month following the quarter in which the commission has become due. This statement shall set out the main components used in calculating the amount of commission.
2. A commercial agent shall be entitled to demand that he be provided with all the information, and in particular an extract from the books, which is available to his principal and which he needs in order to check the amount of the commission due to him.
3. Agreements to derogate from paragraphs 1 and 2 to the detriment of the commercial agent shall not be permitted.
4. This Directive shall not conflict with the internal provisions of Member States which recognise the right of a commercial agent to inspect a principal's books.

CHAPTER IV — CONCLUSION AND TERMINATION OF THE AGENCY CONTRACT

Article 13
1. Each party shall be entitled to receive from the other on request a signed written document setting out the terms of the agency contract including any terms subsequently agreed. Waiver of this right shall not be permitted.
2. Notwithstanding paragraph 1 a Member State may provide that an agency contract shall not be valid unless evidenced in writing.

Article 14
An agency contract for a fixed period which continues to be performed by both parties after that period has expired shall be deemed to be converted into an agency contract for an indefinite period.

Article 15
1.   Where an agency contract is concluded for an indefinite period either party may terminate it by notice.
2.   The period of notice shall be one month for the first year of the contract, two months for the second year commenced, and three months for the third year commenced and subsequent years. The parties may not agree on shorter periods of notice.
3.   Member States may fix the period of notice at four months for the fourth year of the contract, five months for the fifth year and six months for the sixth and subsequent years. They may decide that the parties may not agree to shorter periods.
4.   If the parties agree on longer periods than those laid down in paragraphs 2 and 3, the period of notice to be observed by the principal must not be shorter than that to be observed by the commercial agent.
5.   Unless otherwise agreed by the parties, the end of the period of notice must coincide with the end of a calendar month.
6.   The provisions of this article shall apply to an agency contract for a fixed period where it is converted under article 14 into an agency contract for an indefinite period, subject to the proviso that the earlier fixed period must be taken into account in the calculation of the period of notice.

Article 16
Nothing in this Directive shall affect the application of the law of the Member States where the latter provides for the immediate termination of the agency contract:
(a)   because of the failure of one party to carry out all or part of his obligations;
(b)   where exceptional circumstances arise.

Article 17
1.   Member States shall take the measures necessary to ensure that the commercial agent is, after termination of the agency contract, indemnified in accordance with paragraph 2 or compensated for damage in accordance with paragraph 3.
2.   (a)   The commercial agent shall be entitled to an indemnity if and to the extent that:
— he has brought the principal new customers or has significantly increased the volume of business with existing customers and the principal continues to derive substantial benefits from the business with such customers, and
— the payment of this indemnity is equitable having regard to all the circumstances and, in particular, the commission lost by the commercial agent on the business transacted

with such customers. Member States may provide for such circumstances also to include the application or otherwise of a restraint of trade clause, within the meaning of article 20;

(b) The amount of the indemnity may not exceed a figure equivalent to an indemnity for one year calculated from the commercial agent's average annual remuneration over the preceding five years and if the contract goes back less than five years the indemnity shall be calculated on the average for the period in question;

(c) the grant for such an indemnity shall not prevent the commercial agent from seeking damages.

3. The commercial agent shall be entitled to compensation for the damage he suffers as a result of the termination of his relations with the principal. Such damage shall be deemed to occur particularly when the termination takes place in circumstances:

— depriving the commercial agent of the commission which proper performance of the agency contract would have procured him whilst providing the principal with substantial benefits linked to the commercial agent's activities,

— and/or which have not enabled the commercial agent to amortise the costs and expenses that he had incurred for the performance of the agency contract on the principal's advice.

4. Entitlement to the indemnity as provided for in paragraph 2 or to compensation for damage as provided for under paragraph 3, shall also arise where the agency contract is terminated as a result of the commercial agent's death.

5. The commercial agent shall lose his entitlement to the indemnity in the instances provided for in paragraph 2 or to compensation for damage in the instances provided for in paragraph 3, if within one year following termination of the contract he has not notified the principal that he intends pursuing his entitlement.

6. The Commission shall submit to the Council, within eight years following the date of notification of this Directive, a report on the implementation of this Article, and shall if necessary submit to it proposals for amendments.

Article 18

The indemnity or compensation referred to in article 17 shall not be payable:

(a) where the principal has terminated the agency contract because of default attributable to the commercial agent which would justify immediate termination of the agency contract under national law;

(b) where the commercial agent has terminated the agency contract unless such termination is justified by circumstances attributable to the principal or on grounds of age, infirmity or illness of the commercial agent in consequence of which he cannot reasonably be required to continue his activities;

(c) where, with the agreement of the principal, the commercial agent assigns his rights and duties under the agency contract to another person.

Article 19

The parties may not derogate from articles 17 and 18 to the detriment of the commercial agent before the agency contract expires.

Article 20

1. For the purposes of this Directive, an agreement restricting the business activities of a commercial agent following termination of the agency contract is hereinafter referred to as a restraint of trade clause.
2. A restraint of trade clause shall be valid only if and to the extent that:
    (a) it is concluded in writing; and
    (b) it relates to the geographical area or the group of customers and the geographical area entrusted to the commercial agent and to the kind of goods covered by his agency under the contract.
3. A restraint of trade clause shall be valid for not more than two years after termination of the agency contract.
4. This article shall not affect provisions of national law which impose other restrictions on the validity or enforceability of restraint of trade clauses or which enable the courts to reduce the obligations on the parties resulting from such an agreement.

CHAPTER V — GENERAL AND FINAL PROVISION

Article 21

Nothing in this Directive shall require a Member State to provide for the disclosure of information where such disclosure would be contrary to public policy.

Article 22

1. Member States shall bring into force the provisions necessary to comply with this Directive before 1 January 1990. They shall forthwith inform the Commission thereof. Such provisions shall apply at least to contracts concluded after their entry into force. They shall apply to contracts in operation by 1 January 1994 at the latest.
2. As from the notification of this Directive, Member States shall communicate to the Commission the main laws, regulations and administrative provisions which they adopt in the field governed by this Directive.
3. However, with regard to Ireland and the United Kingdom, 1 January 1990 referred to in paragraph 1 shall be replaced by 1 January 1994.
    With regard to Italy, 1 January 1990 shall be replaced by 1 January 1993 in the case of the obligations deriving from article 17.

Article 23

This Directive is addressed to the Member States.

Done at Brussels, December 18, 1986.

App2.2

Report on the application of article 17 of Council Directive on the coordination of the laws of the Member States relating to self-employed commercial agents (86/653/EEC)

(Doc. Com (96) 354 final, 23.07.1998)

This Report is made under article 17(6) of Council Directive on the co-ordination of the laws of the Member States relating to Self-Employed Commercial Agents 86/653/EEC. Article 17 of Directive requires Member States to take the measures necessary to ensure that the commercial agent is, after termination of the agency contract, indemnified or compensated.

Article 17 represents a compromise between the Member States. It was therefore agreed that Member States should have the choice between the indemnity system and the compensation system and that the Commission would undertake a report to the Council on the practical consequences of the different solutions.

This report is made on the basis of responses to a questionnaire which was sent out, inter alia, to organisations representing agents and principals, chambers of commerce and federations of industry and legal practitioners specialising in agency law. The authorities of Member States were also invited to contribute with their views and experience.

THE TWO SYSTEMS

1.   The indemnity system

Under the indemnity system, the agent is entitled, after cessation of the contract, to payment of an indemnity if and to the extent that he has brought new customers to the principal or has significantly increased the volume of business with existing customers and the principal continues to derive substantial benefits from such customers after the cessation of the contract. The payment of the indemnity must be equitable having regard to all the circumstances and, in particular, the commission lost by the commercial agent on the business transacted with such customers. Finally, the Directive provides a ceiling on the level of indemnity of one year calculated from the agent's average annual remuneration over the preceding five years and if the contract goes back less than five years the maximum is to be calculated on the average for the period in question.

The indemnity represents the continuing benefits to the principal due to the efforts of the agent. The agent, however, will only have received commission during the duration of the contract, which will not typically reflect the value of the goodwill generated for the principal. It is for this reason that the payment of a goodwill indemnity is commercially justified. An indemnity will only be payable if the agent has brought to the principal new customers or increased business with existing customers. If no goodwill has been generated or there is a group of customers whom the principal can derive no benefit from, no indemnity need be paid. Therefore, a principal should not be forced to pay an unreasonable amount of indemnity.

The indemnity system was modelled on article 89b of the German Commercial Code which had provided for the payment of a goodwill indemnity since 1953 and concerning which a large body of case-law has developed regarding its calculation. This case-law and practice should provide invaluable assistance to the Courts of other Member States when seeking to interpret the provisions of article 17(2) of the Directive.

First it is necessary to ascertain whether an agent has a right to an indemnity having regard to the circumstances in which the agency contract was terminated. An indemnity is payable on termination of the contract except where one of the circumstances in article 18 of the Directive applies. Clearly, the indemnity is payable on the end of a fixed term contract and in principle, an indemnity or limited indemnity is payable on the bankruptcy of the principal.

Secondly, the conditions set out in article 17(2)(a) of the Directive have to be met, namely that either the agent has brought new customers or has substantially increased the volume of business with existing customers. As regards the volume of business with old customers, the German courts look to see if the increase in volume is such that it can be considered to be economically equivalent to the acquisition of a new customer. In relation to new customers, the addition of one new customer is sufficient. However, new customers from outside his territory for which the agent is not entitled to commission are excluded as there is no loss of commission for which the agent needs to be compensated. The agent must have acquired the new client and in this respect the instrumentality of the agent is crucial. A small level of involvement is sufficient and it is enough that the agent has merely contributed to bringing the new customer. However, the agent must have played an active role and therefore the existence of a new customer who falls within the territorial scope of an exclusive agency agreement will not automatically suffice.

Thirdly, the principal must continue after the end of the agency contract to derive substantial benefits with such customers. This is presumed to be the case even if the principal sells his business or client list if it can be shown that the purchaser will use the client base. If the agent continues to meet the needs of the same clients for the same products, but for a different principal, the agent is prevented from seeking an indemnity. It is also possible for the court to consider a fall in the turnover of the principal's business. Fourthly the payment of an indemnity must be equitable.

As to the actual calculation of the indemnity, it is undertaken in the following way:

Stage 1

(a) The first stage in line with the second indent of article 17(2)(a) is to ascertain the number of new customers and the increased volume of business with existing customers. Having identified such customers the gross commission on them is calculated for the last 12 months of the agency contract. Fixed remuneration can be included if it can be considered to be remuneration for new customers. Special circumstances may justify departing from this, for example, where there is a long start up period.

(b)   An estimate is then made as to the likely future duration of the advantages to the principal deriving from business with the new customers and such old customers with whom the business has been significantly increased (intensified customers) which is calculated in terms of years. The aim is to predict the likely length of time the business with the new and intensified customers will last. This will involve considering the market situation at time of termination and the sector concerned. The fact that sales drop after termination of the contract does not automatically lead to a corresponding reduction in the level of indemnity as sales may decline due to lowering in quality of goods or competition. The usual period is two to three years, but can be as much as five years.

(c)   The next factor to consider is the rate of migration. It is acknowledged that over time customers will be lost as customers naturally move away. The rate of migration is calculated as a percentage of commission on a per annum basis and is taken from the particular experience of the agency in question. This clearly varies, but in one case the Bundesgerichtshof held that the rate of migration was 38%.

(d)   The figure is then reduced in order to calculate the present value taking into account that there is an accelerated receipt of income. Such a calculation based on average interest rates is a concept found in other jurisdictions.

Stage 2

It is at this stage that the question of equity is considered as set out in article 17(2)(a) second indent of the Directive. The figure is rarely adjusted for reasons of equity in practice. The following factors are taken into account:

—   Whether the agent is retained by other principals;
—   The fault of the agent;
—   The level of remuneration of the agent. For example, did the principal recently reduce the rate of commission eg because he felt that agent's earnings were becoming too high or pay to the agent a large amount of commission on contracts with customers which the agent did not introduce or had little to do with? Also, did the agent receive special compensation for keeping a consignment inventory, special bonuses for new clients, *del credere* commission, any special allowance for trade fairs or extra payments for sub-agents? Did he incur costs regarding loss of sub-agents?
—   Decrease in turnover of the principal;
—   Extent of the advantage to the principal;
—   Payment of pension contributions by the principal;
—   The existence of restraint of trade clauses. Clearly, a principal will be required to pay a higher indemnity for this.

Stage 3

The amount calculated under Stages 1 and 2 is then compared with the maximum under article 17(2)(b) of the Directive. This provision provides that the amount of the indemnity may not exceed a figure equivalent to remuneration for one year calculated from the commercial agent's average annual remuneration over the preceding five years and if the contract goes back less than five years the indemnity shall be calculated on the average for the period in question. The maximum is in fact therefore a final corrective, rather than as a method of calculating the indemnity.

In calculating the maximum, remuneration includes all forms of payment, not just commission and is based on all customers, not only new or intensified customers. If the sum under stages 1 and 2 is less than the maximum then this sum is awarded. If however, the sum exceeds the maximum, it is the maximum which is awarded. It is unusual for the maximum to be reached unless the agent has procured all or most of the customers.

An example of stages 1 to 3 is set out:

Commission on new customers and/or intensified customers over last 12 months of agency	50,000 ECUs

Anticipated duration of benefits is three years with 20% migration rate

Year 1 50,000 – 10,000 =	40,000 ECUs
Year 2 40,000 – 8,000 =	32,000 ECUs
Year 3 32,000 – 6,400 =	25,600 ECUs
Total lost commission	97,600 ECUs

Correction to present value say 10%. This figure being equal to the actual indemnity	87,840 ECUs

This figure might be adjusted for reasons of equity (stage 2 above)

A final correction must be made should the amount exceed the maximum under article 17(2)(b) of the Directive.

Article 17(2)(c) states that the grant of an indemnity shall not prevent the commercial agent from seeking damages. This provision governs the situation where the agent under national law is entitled to seek damages for breach of contract or failure to respect the notice period provided for under the Directive. Annex B attempts to identify these provisions.

It can thus be seen that the method of calculation of the indemnity is extremely precise and should lead to a predictable outcome. Principals should therefore be able to ascertain their risks in advance and to be able to enter into agency contracts with some degree of assurance. From the agent's perspective, clearer rights make it easier for the claim to be made and established.

2.   The compensation system

Under article 17(3) of the Directive, the agent is entitled to compensation for the damage he suffers as a result of the termination of his relations with his principal. Such damage is deemed to occur particularly when the termination takes place in circumstances:

—   depriving the agent of the commission which proper performance of the agency contract would have procured him whilst providing the principal with substantial benefits linked to the agent's activities.

—   and/or which have not enabled the agent to amortise the costs and expenses he had incurred for the performance of the agency contract on the principal's advice.

There is no maximum level of compensation.

The compensation system was based on French law, which dated from 1958 and whose aim was to compensate the agent for the loss he suffered as a result of the termination of the agency contract. As for the indemnity system in Germany, a body of case-law has developed in France concerning the right and level of compensation. Various judgments of the French courts have justified the payment of compensation on the ground that it represents the cost of purchasing the agency to the agent's successor or on the ground that it represents the time it takes for the agent to re-constitute the client base which he has been forcefully deprived of.

By judicial custom the level of compensation is fixed as the global sum of the last two years' commission or the sum of two years' commission calculated over the average of last three years of the agency contract which conforms with commercial practice. However, the courts retain a discretion to award a different level of compensation where the principal brings evidence that the agent's loss was in fact less, for example, because of the short duration of the contract or where, for example, the agent's loss is greater because of the agent's age or his length of service.

The indemnity is calculated on all remuneration, not just commission. It is based on the gross figure. No distinction is made between old and new customers and it includes special commission. There is no practice to reduce for professional costs. Finally, outstanding commissions must also be included in the calculation.

The indemnity represents that part of the market lost to the agent and his loss is fixed at that moment. Accordingly, future occurrences are not taken into account, such as the principal ceasing to trade, the agent continuing to work with the same clients or developments in the market place. Similarly, the agent is not required to mitigate his loss.

The Directive has brought about a greater interest in claiming damages for failure to respect the proper notice period. The amount awarded is the highest of the period not respected calculated on commission received for the last two years or the commission received during the identical period the previous year.

Further, more specific comments on the system in France can be found in Annex B.

Position in Member States

All Member States have implemented the Directive and a list of the laws is annexed to this Report as Annex A. With the exception of France, the UK and Ireland, Member States have incorporated the indemnity option into their national law. The UK has permitted the parties to choose the indemnity option, but if they fail to do so, the agent will be entitled to compensation. Ireland has failed to make any choice at all in its legislation and accordingly the Commission has opened article 169 proceedings. The Commission has also opened infraction proceedings against Italy for failure to implement article 17 of the Directive correctly. Further details can be found in Annex B concerning Irish and Italian law.

In most Member States there has yet to be any reported court decision, whilst in other Member States there are only a small number of cases. This is explained by the fact that the laws in most Member States are still very new and that these laws have only applied to all contracts in operation as from 1 January 1994. In addition, in France and Germany where there are cases, many agencies are not international in nature and the law follows long established traditions.

The second reason for the lack of reported cases is the tendency for the parties to settle cases before the court hearing. Agents are not always in the financial position to pursue their claims through the courts and therefore are forced to accept settlements. In addition, the uncertainty linked to court proceedings, invariably in a different jurisdiction deters agents from pursuing their claims through the courts.

The cases in Germany and France show a continuity with the existing jurisprudence in these countries. In Portugal, where the Directive represents a change to the previous situation the case-law shows an approach which is different to that of the German courts with an attempt by the judge to apply directly the principle of equity. In Italy, where there has only been one judgment under the new article 1751 of the Civil Code, the Viterbo Magistrate Court has ruled, that having regard to the lack of criteria for calculation of the indemnity in article 1751 of the Civil Code, it would apply the collective agreement. The collective agreement follows a system of calculation based on the duration of the agency and is not related to the number of new customers brought. Thus, it also takes a different approach to the German courts. However, this is a single judgment of the Italian courts and has yet to be confirmed. In Denmark, only three judgments have been reported. A fourth judgment is now subject to appeal. The reported cases reveal a tendency to take over and follow German jurisprudence. Having regard to the relative lack of jurisprudence and the nature of the subject matter, the Commission in its preparation for this Report sought to ascertain the practical as well as the legal situation. An outline of the legal and practical position is set out in more detail in Annex B.

There are no statistics available in any of the Member States. The International Union of Commercial Agents and Brokers have now started to collect data. This is a helpful development, as IUCAB should be able to collect a good level of data through its member organisations in Member States and

IUCAB has offered to present these statistics periodically to the Commission. The Portuguese authorities have also established a centralised method of collecting information from all courts on the nature and outcome of cases which involve EC law or the Lugano Convention, which of course, includes the Directive on Commercial Agents.

Business Practice

The Commission sought to ascertain whether, as a result of the Directive and in particular the right to an indemnity or compensation, there had been any change in business practice. The Commission also wanted to establish whether, as a result of the different options, distortions in competition had arisen. The lack of statistics makes it more difficult to reach conclusions in this regard.

Overall, the Commission found that there had not been any change in business practice. There was some evidence that principals were moving to distributorship contracts in France, Germany, Luxembourg and Belgium. This can be partially explained by the fact that on lawful termination of distributorship contracts no indemnity or compensation is payable or a reduced level. In the UK, Ireland and Sweden it was reported that principals were now considering much more carefully whether agency contracts were the most appropriate business arrangements and were therefore taking a much more cautious approach. However, principals were not always actually moving away from agency contracts.

In the UK there appears to have been a specific reaction. First prior to the coming into force of the UK Regulations implementing the Directive, principals terminated their agency contracts and on the whole renegotiated new contracts. There were, however, occasions where new agency contracts were not entered into or the agents were taken on as employees. This reflects the fundamental change brought about by the Directive to UK law and the fear of principals of the unknown. It is too soon to determine whether there will be a permanent shift away from agency contracts in the UK.

Under French law and practice, compensation awarded in the vast majority of cases amounts to two years commission which is twice the legal maximum provided for under the indemnity option. This clearly makes the appointment of an agent in France under French law a much more costly enterprise. This has led some principals when appointing an agent in France to seek to apply a law other than French law or to avoid entering into agency contracts altogether. There is no evidence of any widespread problems or distortions in trade as regards those Member States who have opted for the indemnity system and those who have opted for the compensation option.

Reactions of Principals and Agents

It can generally be said that agents have given a positive response to the Directive as it is considered to have increased their rights. This would be the case in Austria, Denmark, Finland, Ireland, Luxembourg, Sweden and the UK. French agents continue to feel positively about the system of compensation in France and do not wish for change.

The reaction of principals has been mixed. To some extent, principals are bound to feel negative about change as they now have to grant greater rights to agents. For other principals it is not that they are against paying an indemnity on termination, but rather there is a degree of discontent in that the system lacks clarity. French principals appear to support the compensation system and have not raised any objections regarding it.

There is no tendency amongst either agents or principals in the Member States who have implemented the indemnity option to favour anything other than the indemnity system. In the UK, where the parties are able to opt in favour of payment of an indemnity, no clear preference emerges although most contracts do not contain an indemnity provision. Principals are still unclear about what the differences between the two systems are. There is a certain level of interest in the indemnity amongst some principals because of the maximum limit, but other principals prefer the compensation option as agents must prove actual loss.

DIFFICULTIES

A number of difficulties have arisen in relation to article 17 of the Directive.

(1) Interpretation difficulties

Many commentators and lawyers have pointed to the imprecise and uncertain nature of article 17, which causes difficulty in trying to advise clients on the extent of an agent's rights on termination. This was reported in particular in Denmark, Ireland, Italy, Spain, Sweden and the UK.

a. Indemnity

As regards the indemnity option, there has been a tendency in some Member States to seek reliance on the maximum figure whereas under the German system, which influenced the Directive, the maximum has no bearing on the actual method of calculation of the indemnity. It is merely used at the end of the process as a final adjuster. In some Member States attempts are made to try and establish an equitable amount taking into account various different factors, which again is not the approach taken by the German courts. Denmark and Austria appear to follow the German model but in the case of Austria, the maximum limit is often reached, whereas in Germany it is very rarely reached except when all the customers have been brought by the commercial agent.

In Italy, it appears, at the moment, that the previous system continues to apply even though a new law was introduced. This has been re-enforced in the ruling in the Pretura Viterbo case in which the court held that the provision of article 1751 of the Italian Civil Code, which implements article 17(2) of the Directive, was so uncertain as to the method of calculation of the indemnity, it would apply the collective agreement. The method of calculation under the collective agreement does not correspond with the German model, but is based on the length of the contract, the level of commission and the percentages set out in the collective agreement. It therefore appears there is a divergence of approaches. However, there is of course still only a very limited jurisprudence of the courts of Member States concerning article 17 outside Germany.

b. Compensation

As regards the compensation option, clearly this has not presented problems of interpretation in France where pre-existing jurisprudence has continued to be applied. However, as regards the UK which applies the compensation option in default of the choice of the parties, there is a fundamental difference in approach. At this stage, there is no UK case-law but the parties in practice are attempting to apply common law principles. These common law principles are directly opposed to the well-established method of calculation of compensation in France. For example, the English system will take account of future developments after termination of the contract and this results in the need for the injured person to mitigate his loss. Whereas, under French law, events after the termination of the agency contract have no bearing on the compensation to be awarded. Under French law, the standard award is two years' commission which represents the value of the purchase of an agency or the period it will take the agent to re-establish his client base. It is difficult to see how the UK courts will reach this figure. This, no doubt, derives from the previous legal position in the UK, that agency contracts could be terminated on notice without any payment being due. This naturally has had consequences for business practices. There was no real concept of goodwill attaching to an agency to which the agent had a right to a share in. It is not possible to predict how the UK courts will interpret the Directive, but it seems likely that they will have regard to existing common law principles.

The same difficulties are likely to arise in Ireland if Ireland opts for the compensation option.

c. Consequences of uncertainty

The difficulties in interpretation have had an effect on the reactions of agents and principals to the Directive. For both it has entailed increased time being spent on negotiation since rights and levels of rights are not clearly established. This benefits neither party. It has also led to different amounts being awarded. Uncertainty and divergence also lead to a reluctance to create agencies and act as a barrier to principals to take on agents in other Member States. It is important that the Directive is uniformly interpreted and leads to predictable and clear results.

(2) Position of agents

The Directive has led to an improvement in the position of agents vis-à-vis their principals. Nevertheless it appears that agents are not always able to enforce their rights to the full because they lack the resources to take court action. This is a problem of a general nature and not specific to the Directive. Possible remedies lie outside the remit of this Report. However, it is the view of the Commission that clarification of the provisions of the Directive and methods of calculation will be of assistance to agents and make the enforcement of rights easier.

(3)   Choice of law

Finally, certain problems have been encountered with regard to choice of law clauses in contracts and attempts have been made to avoid the application of certain laws by choice of law clauses or jurisdiction clauses. The Directive does not lay down any rules concerning private international law. The parties are therefore free to choose the law which is to govern the agency contract, subject to the rules contained in the Rome Convention 1980 on the law applicable to contractual obligations. In the Commission's opinion articles 17 and 18 of the Directive are mandatory rules and accordingly, the courts of the Member States can apply the law of the forum in accordance with the 1980 Rome Convention and thereby ensure the application of the Directive. The 1968 Brussels Convention on jurisdiction and enforcement of judgments in civil and commercial matters will also assist in ensuring, that in so far as Community cases are concerned and the agent is carrying on his activities in the EC, that a court of a Member State will have jurisdiction. Accordingly, there does not appear to be any need to amend the Directive in this regard.

CONCLUSION

The Commission notes that the indemnity option has been chosen by the vast majority of Member States and that this has received the support of agents and principals in those Member States. The Directive provides for a ceiling on the level of indemnity, but does not give precise guidance for its method of calculation. A clear and precise method of calculation would lead to greater legal certainty, which would be of advantage to both parties. As regards the compensation option, which has been maintained by France, it does not appear to have caused problems for agents and principals in France. The level of compensation in France is generally much higher than the level of indemnity. The implementation in the UK whereby the parties have the choice of the system has led to uncertainty, particularly as neither of the two options is known to the British legal system.

At this stage, there is very little jurisprudence concerning the Directive. Having regard to the information received, it appears that there is a need for clarification of article 17. Any more further far-reaching conclusions are premature. The Commission considers that this Report, which gives detailed information, particularly concerning the method of calculation of the indemnity as it is carried out in Germany, provides further clarification of article 17 of the Directive and secondly, by so-doing should facilitate a more uniform interpretation of article 17 of the Directive.

ANNEX A

LIST OF MEMBER STATES' LAWS IMPLEMENTING THE DIRECTIVE ON COMMERCIAL AGENTS (86/653/EEC)

Expiry of implementation period: 31.12.89
(United Kingdom and Ireland: 31.12.93)
(Italy, concerning article 17: 31.12.92)

1. Belgium	Law of 13.4.1995 published in Moniteur Belge of 2.6.1995, p 15621 entry into force: 12.6.1995
2. Denmark	Law No 272 of 2.5.90 publication: Lovtidende A. 1990 p 922 entry into force: 4.5.90 application in contracts in operation: 1.1.92
3. Germany	Law of 23.10.89 publication: Bundesgesetzblatt 1989 I 1910 entry into force: 1.1.90 application to contracts in operation: 1.1.94
4. Greece	Presidential Decree No 219 of 18.5.1991 publication: OJ of the Greek government No 81 of 30.5.1991 and No 136 of 11.9.1991 as amended by Decrees No 249/93, 88/94 and 312/95. entry into force: 30.5.1991 application to contracts in operation: 1.1.94
5. Spain	Law 12/1992 of 27.5.1992 publication: BOE No 129 of 29.5.1992 entry into force: 19.6.1992 application to contracts in operation: 1.1.94
6. France	Law No 91-593 of 25.6.1991 publication: OJ of the French Republic 17.6.1991 p 8271 entry into force: 28.6.1992 Decree No 92-506 of 10.6.1992 Publication: OJ of the French Republic 12.6.1992 p 7720 entry into force: 1.1.1994 application to contracts in operation: 1.1.94
7. Ireland	Statutory Instrument: SI No 33 of 1994 of 21.2.1994 Entry into force: 1.1.1994 application to contracts in operation: 1.1.94
8. Italy	Legislative Decree No 303 of 10.9.1991 publication: Gazetta ufficiale no 57 of 20.9.1991 entry into force: 1.1.1993 application to contracts in operation: 1.1.94
9. Luxembourg	Law of 3 June 1994 publication: Memorial A-No 58 of 6.7.1994, p 1088 application to contracts in operation: 1.1.94

10. *Netherlands*   Law of 5.7.89
                    publication: Staatsblad 1989 no 312
                    entry into force: 1.11.89
                    application to contracts in operation: 1.1.94
                    Re-enacted by law No 374 of 1993 as articles 400–445 of
                    Title 7 of the Burgerlijk Wetboek
11. *Austria*   Federal Act of 11.2.1993
                    published in Federal Gazette 88
                    entry into force: 1.3.1993
                    application to contracts in operation: 1.1.1994
12. *Portugal*   Decree No 178/86 of 3.7.86
                    publication: Diário da República, I série, 1986, p 1575
                    entry into force: 2.8.86
                    application to contracts in operation: 2.8.86
                    amended by law No 118/93 of 13.4.93 published Diário da
                    República No 86 p 1818 of 13.4.93
                    application to contracts in operation: 1.1.94
13. *Finland*   Law No 417 of 8.5.1992
                    published in Gesetzblatt of 14.5.1992
                    entry into force: 1.11.1992
                    application to contracts in force: 1.1.1994
14. *Sweden*   Law No 351 of 2.5.1991
                    entry into force: 1.1.1992
                    application to contracts in force: 1.1.1994
15. *UK*   Statutory Instrument SI 1993 No 3053 of 7.12.9 and
                    SI 1993 No 3173 of 16.12.1993
                    entry into force: 1.1.94
                    application to contracts in operation: 1.1.1994
                    Northern Ireland:
                    Statutory Rules of Northern Ireland 1993 no 483 of 17.12.1993
                    entry into force: 13.1.1994
                    application to contracts in operation: 13.1.1994

ANNEX B

Belgium

The Law on Commercial Agent Contract only came into force on 12 June
1995. Accordingly, there are no cases decided by the courts on the new law.

Article 20 of the law introduced the right to a goodwill indemnity. Prior to
the new law, the right to a goodwill indemnity had been rejected by the main
decisions of the Belgian courts as goodwill was considered to attach to the
principal more than to the agent. Accordingly, the new law has brought about
an important change to the law.

The law contains no guidance as to how the indemnity is to be
calculated, but it is argued by most commentators that is for the judge to
determine the amount taking into account various factors such as level of

commission in last years of the contract, level of development of customers, extent to which principal will continue to derive benefits, duration of contractual relations, level of involvement of the principal, existence of a pension financed by the principal or whether the agent's contract with the principal is his sole agency. One author has specifically drawn on the German method of calculation.

Practising Belgian lawyers considered that regard would be had to the law on commercial representatives and to the German experience. Under the Law on Commercial Representatives of 3 July 1978, however, the indemnity is calculated on the basis of three months' wages for a commercial representative who has acted for the same principal for a period of one to five years. This period is increased by one month for each further five years.

Under article 18(3) of the Belgian law, it is possible to claim damages for lack of notice, which amounts to lost commission in accordance with method of calculation set out in this article.

Finally, under article 21 of the Belgian law, an agent who has a right to an indemnity can claim in addition damages for the harm actually suffered. It is not clear in what circumstances this is payable and whether entitlement to an indemnity automatically gives a right to seek damages. In the view of the Commission this latter interpretation would be contrary to article 17(1) of the Directive as the effect of such an interpretation would be that the two options would apply cumulatively.

Denmark

With the implementation of the Directive in Denmark and the introduction of the right to an indemnity under Section 25 of Law No 272 of 2 May 1990, a new right was granted which had not existed under the previous law.

To date, only three judgments have been reported. In *Lope Handel* the principal was ordered to pay losses for the failure to respect the contractual period of notice and to pay an indemnity of one year's commission on the new customers acquired for the principal by the agent. It was proved that the new customers were lost one year after termination of an agency contract. In *S&L*, the principal was ordered to pay an indemnity equivalent to the maximum. It was proved that practically all the customers were brought by the agent. In *Cramer*, the court found that a substantial number of customers were once-only customers with whom the principal could expect no further business. The principal was ordered to pay an indemnity amounting to DKK 150,000. For comparison the maximum would have been 400,000.

In practice it appears that agents seek the maximum amount and principals try to argue the figure down. At present, although there is no set picture, there is no tendency to pay the maximum figure. Calculations appear to follow the German model.

As for other Member States, no useful statistics are available.

Section 6 of the law implements article 17(2)(c) of the Directive and provides that if an agent or principal is in breach of his obligations to the other, the other is entitled to compensation for any damage caused thereby.

Germany

Article 89b of the Handelsgestzbuch sets out the agent's right to an indemnity. The method of calculation is set out in the Report itself.

In practice it appears that there has been no change in Germany as to the method of calculation of the indemnity following the implementation of the Directive in Germany as the indemnity provision of the Directive did not require change to German law. The change noted by industry was in relation to contracts with other EU countries, which prior to the Directive did not provide for an indemnity.

Greece

The implementation of article 17 of the Directive by article 9 of Presidential Decree 219 of 18 May 1991 did not conform with the Directive, in particular, in that it did not implement the second indent of article 17(2)(a) which requires that the indemnity be equitable. Greece has following correspondence with the Commission introduced a new law in 1995 which implements articles 17(2)(a).

Article 9(1)(c) states that the right to seek an indemnity does not prevent an agent from seeking damages under the Civil Code. Damages are payable and awarded according to whether the contract was fixed term or of indefinite duration.

An agent may also seek damaged for lack of proper notice.

Spain

Article 28 of Law No 12/1992 of 27 June 1995 provides for the payment of an indemnity. Article 29 of the law provides for the award of damages if the principal unilaterally breaks an agency contract which is for an indefinite period. The Directive has filled a legal gap in Spanish law in that prior to the law implementing the Directive there was no specific law covering commercial agents or commercial agency contracts. However, article 29 is not restricted merely to breach of contract and by virtue of this Spain has seemingly implemented both options contained in article 17 of the Directive unless the court interprets the scope of article 29 narrowly.

Owing to the recent coming into force of the law there is a lack of jurisprudence in this area. The case-law prior to the new law may be of relevance for the future since some of the principles may act as guidance for future judgment by the Spanish courts.

Under the old law, it was also possible to claim both damages and a goodwill indemnity and agents used to cumulate both claims. The difference between both remedies was sometimes blurred in practice. The Supreme Court has repeatedly recognised the possibility of obtaining an indemnity for goodwill. The judge is given a wide discretion to fix the level of the indemnity and in general it is calculated depending on the agent's earnings. As regards damages, the courts considered a number of different matters in arriving at the award, including the level of the last commission, the nature of the activity, loss of prestige and whether the contract was exclusive or not.

Finally, damages are payable for failure to respect the correct notice period which is the amount of commission the agent would have received if the notice period had been respected.

However, despite these judgments it is still difficult to reach general conclusions, particularly as in Spain the level of indemnity is fixed after the hearing and the decision is not published.

France

Unlike for many other Member States, the Directive has not brought about radical change to the pre-existing law in France. Under article 12 of Law No 91/593 of 25 June 1991, French law continues to give a right to compensation on termination of the agency contract. The change brought about relates to the circumstances in which compensation is payable and not in its calculation. The right to compensation now exists for the non-renewal of the contract and termination by the agent for reasons of old age, sickness or infirmity and on death.

Compensation is calculated as before according to the jurisprudence as neither the old law or the present law sets out the method of calculation. In the vast majority of cases it amounts to two years' gross commission which is calculated from the agent's average remuneration over the preceding three years or the global sum of the last two years' commission. This sum has become the customary award and is confirmed with court decisions applying the new law.

The indemnity is calculated on all remuneration, not just commission. It is based on the gross figure. No distinction is made between old and new customers and it includes special commission. There is no practice to reduce for professional costs. Finally, outstanding commissions must also be included in the calculation.

The indemnity represents that part of the market lost to the agent and his loss is fixed at that moment. Accordingly, future occurrences are not taken into account, such as the principal ceasing to trade, the agent continuing to work with the same clients or developments in the market place. Similarly, the agent is not required to mitigate his loss.

The French courts do not order the payment of two years' gross commission as compensation where it can be shown that the loss suffered by the agent is less, for example, because of the short duration of the contract. Similarly, the level may be increased, where, for example, an agent's loss is greater because of his age or length of the agency contract.

The Directive has brought about a greater interest in claiming damages for failure to respect the proper notice period. The amount taken is the highest of the period not respected calculated on commission received for the last two years or the commission received during the identical period the previous year.

Ireland

Ireland has not implemented this provision and therefore agents do not have either a right to compensation or an indemnity. Under the common law, an agent can seek damages for breach of contract. In a fixed term contract, this will allow the agent to claim the commission he would have received until the end of the contract, subject to the agent's duty to mitigate his loss. However, this is not sufficient for the purposes of implementing the Directive. In cases of contracts of indefinite period the claim is usually for remuneration during the notice period to be respected. In addition, in both cases, he may claim for the economic loss suffered as a result of the breach of contract.

To date there are no reported cases.

Italy

Italy amended article 1751 of the Civil Code by article 4 of legislative Decree No 303 of 10 September 1991 to introduce the indemnity system set out in the Directive. However, in the view of the Commission the implementation by Italy is incorrect in that Italy has treated the two indents in article 17(2)(a) of the Directive as alternative conditions whereas they are in fact cumulative. Accordingly the Commission has opened infraction proceedings.

It appears that the old system of collective agreements continues to apply. The Enasarco agreement of 30.10 1992 was agreed to by both principals and organisations representing agents. By doing so they have de facto re-introduced the criteria which were applicable under the previous text of article 1751.

In its judgment of 1 December 1994, the Viterbo Magistrate Court applied the collective agreement. The court held that article 1751 of the Civil Code could not be applied in practice as it does not fix any criteria for calculating the indemnity except the maximum. Accordingly, the court considered it appropriate to apply the collective agreement. The Court also stated that the circumstances in article 1751 were not intended for calculating the amount of indemnity, but for determining whether an indemnity was justified if at least one of the circumstances applied. Further, the court considered that wisely the social partners, in order to avoid practically insoluble problems, had replaced the old collective agreement thereby enabling article 1751 of the Civil Code to be applied in practice. It is not clear at this stage whether this judgment will be followed.

The system of the collective agreement is based on level of commissions and duration of the agency contract and the set percentages laid down in the agreement.

Under the collective agreement, the agent in most cases receives an amount which is much less than the maximum envisaged under the Directive.

Luxembourg

Luxembourg's law implementing the Directive of 3 June 1994 applies to all contracts existing before 1 January 1994 as well as to contracts entered into force after that date. Article 19 provides for an indemnity to be paid on termination. The new law introduced a right which did not exist under the pre-existing law. Those consulted also thought it was too soon to develop a theory about how the law would be interpreted.

Article 23(1) sets out the right to damages for unjustified failure to give due notice and article 23(2) provides for damages to be paid for a serious breach of contract. Article 24 states that this amounts to a sum equal to the remuneration that would have been received in the period between the breach and the normal end of the contract. To calculate this sum regard is to be had to the previous level of commissions and to other relevant matters. This sum can be reduced if the judge considers it too high in the circumstances of the case.

The Netherlands

Article 7:442 of the Civil Code provides for an indemnity to be paid on termination of the agency contract. Under article 7:439 damages are payable for unjustified failure to respect the correct notice period and articles 7:440 and 7:441 provide for damages to be paid for breach of contract. This covers the period from actual termination to the date on which the agency would have been terminated had proper notice been given. This amount is the amount of remuneration which would have been received and is based on the commission received prior to termination and other relevant circumstances. The judge can reduce the amount if he considers that it is too high having regard to the facts of the particular case. Under article 7:441.3, the party can seek in place of the sum under article 7:441.1 and 2, compensation for the actual damage suffered and he bears the burden of proving his loss.

There is no reported case to date concerning the new law nor are there any statistics.

Austria

The Austrian law of 11 February 1993 came into force on 1 March 1993. Under article 24, the agent has a right to an indemnity. To date there are no reported cases concerning the amount of indemnity or damages payable on termination of an agency contract under the 1993 law. The Directive has lead to a change in the previous law and in particular to a doubling of the maximum limit. Therefore, previous case-law is not useful guidance. Under the old law, there was a digressive reduction in the upper limit of compensation of aggregate amount of one year's commission calculated as a yearly average over the previous three years according to the length of the relationship.

In practice, it appears that commercial agents calculate the indemnity on the basis of the average income of the last five years taking into account the fluctuation of customers by computing a digression of income on the basis of five years. In most cases, this exceeds the upper limit set by law. On this basis, the parties negotiate in order to find a reasonable settlement. The method of calculation is based on German experiences.

It was considered too soon to make any judgment about the average level of indemnity paid. A claim for damages or performance of the contract can be made if a party terminates the contract prematurely without just cause under article 23. Article 23 also applies to a breach of article 21 which is concerned with notice periods. Any other claims for damages are dealt with in accordance with the provisions of the General Civil Code and the Commercial Code.

Portugal

Portugal adopted its law in 1986 which followed to a large extent the proposal for the Directive and included at article 33 the right to an indemnity. The law came into force on 2 August 1986. It has been amended by articles 33 and 34 of Decree No. 118/93 to bring Portuguese law in conformity with article 17 of the Directive.

In Portugal there have been a number of court judgments. The courts have calculated the level of indemnity taking into account the importance of new clients, the increased development of existing customers, the advantages to the principal after the termination of the contract and the loss of commission by the agent. The courts consider the indemnity as a measure of compensation for the agent for the benefits to the principal existing at the end of the contract with the clients developed by the agent.

Under article 32 of the law and under articles 562–572 of the Civil Code, there is also a right to be indemnified for the damages suffered for breach of contract. Article 29 specifically provides for damages for failure to respect the notice period or alternatively to damages for lack of due notice. The agent can seek, as an alternative to damages, a sum calculated on the basis of the average monthly remuneration over the previous year multiplied by the time remaining if the contract had continued to run. If the contract is of less than one year's duration then the whole contract period is to be used.

Finland

Under section 28 of Act No 417 of 8 May 1992, the right to indemnity on termination of an agency contract was introduced. The Directive has brought about a change in the pre-existing law. The law came into force on 1 November 1992 and there has been no court decision to date.

In practice, it appears that agents seek the maximum amount and the principal makes a counter-offer. The negotiations result in an amount which is not based on any specific calculation, rather it is the outcome of bargaining. Generally, the indemnity is in the region of three to six months' average commission. It was felt by the agents' federation that the amount of indemnity period was slightly higher under the new law than under the old law, but no statistics are available to support this.

Under section 9 of the law, the right to damages for harm caused by a violation of the agency contract is laid down or for when a party has neglected one of his obligations. Further, sections 26 and 27 of the Act provide for damages where notice periods are not respected.

Sweden

Article 28 of Law No 351 of 2 May 1991 introduced a right to receive an indemnity which did not exist under the previous law, which only sought to ensure that an agent received commission on orders concluded after the withdrawal of the agent's authority provided that the orders were brought about through the acts of the agent during the currency of the agreement.

As for other Member States, there has yet to be any court decision. In practice agents seek the maximum amount permitted under the law and the parties negotiate on this basis to reach an equitable sum. In doing so, the parties take into account, inter alia, the duration of the contract, the agent's promotional activities, the number of new customers, orders given after termination, the possibility of a new contract for the agent and the costs incurred and investments made by the agent.

There are no statistics but the Swedish authorities estimated that awards were typically between six months and one year commission calculated as an average over the last years of the contract. This would represent an increase in the amount of compensation.

Article 34 of the law provides for damages for breach of contract.

United Kingdom

The UK has adopted its own particular system in that under regulation 17 of Statutory Instrument No 3053 of 1993 the parties may choose whether an agent will have the right to an indemnity or compensation. It is only in default of a contractual provision that the law requires compensation to be paid. This method of implementation has of itself produced uncertainty, particularly since neither of the two options are familiar to the UK legal systems.

The law has only recently come into force in the UK and has caused a certain amount of confusion as parties and lawyers attempt to apply concepts with which they are unfamiliar and which are a certain degree alien to UK traditions. Various different approaches have developed.

In relation to compensation, lawyers try to apply traditional common law principles which does not work well since under the common law, termination of a contract in accordance with its terms or at the natural end of a fixed term contract does not give rise to a damages claim. Under the common law, the court tries to put the agent in the position he would have been in if the contract had been properly performed, but the injured party is expected to mitigate his loss and the court will have regard to future events. Typically for a fixed term contract, this would give the agent the right to claim commission for the duration of the contract. In the case of a contract for an indefinite period, the agent could seek damages for the notice period amounting to the remuneration he would have received in this period. The agent could also seek compensation for costs incurred in pursuance of the agency. Lawyers therefore have difficulties in reaching a view as to the level of compensation where the agent has died, become ill or retired. Typical compensation payments are between three to six months with some payments of 15 months depending on the level of service.

Some lawyers have therefore tried to apply by analogy the law relating to unfair dismissal or redundancy which is determined by age, length of service and the weekly wage.

As regards the indemnity provision, agents claim the maximum amount and then through negotiations a smaller sum is agreed. Typical payments appear to be between three and six months' commission based on what would have been earned rather than the average of the last five years.

Most contracts do not contain a provision providing for an indemnity, but this does not necessarily reflect a preference for the compensation option rather than the indemnity option.

To date, there have been no cases and parties are reluctant to litigate since lawyers are unconfident in advising what their clients' rights are and consequently what the courts will award. However, there are likely to be cases in the near future.

App2.3

[Note the Guidelines below are likely to be revised in 2020/21 – see https:// ec.europa.eu/competition/consultations/2018_vber/index_en.html.

The likely position after UK Brexit is that the guidelines will still remain useful and relevant as UK and EU competition law are currently similar.]

Commission Notice
Extract from
Guidelines on Vertical Restraints (OJ 2010/C 130/01)

2. AGENCY AGREEMENTS

2.1   Definition of agency agreements

(12) An agent is a legal or physical person vested with the power to negotiate and/or conclude contracts on behalf of another person (the principal), either in the agent's own name or in the name of the principal, for the:
— purchase of goods or services by the principal, or
— sale of goods or services supplied by the principal.

(13) The determining factor in defining an agency agreement for the application of Article 101(1) is the financial or commercial risk borne by the agent in relation to the activities for which it has been appointed as an agent by the principal.[1] In this respect it is not material for the assessment whether the agent acts for one or several principals. Neither is material for this assessment the qualification given to their agreement by the parties or national legislation.

(14) There are three types of financial or commercial risk that are material to the definition of an agency agreement for the application of Article 101(1). First, there are the contract-specific risks which are directly related to the contracts concluded and/or negotiated by the agent on behalf of the principal, such as financing of stocks. Secondly, there are

---

1 See judgment of the Court of First Instance in Case T-325/01 *Daimler Chrysler v Commission* [2005] ECR II-3319; judgments of the Court of Justice in Case C-217/05 *Confederación Espanola de Empresarios de Estaciones de Servicio v CEPSA* [2006] ECR I-11987; and Case C-279/06 *CEPSA Estaciones de Servicio SA v LV Tobar e Hijos SL* [2008] ECR I-6681.

the risks related to market-specific investments. These are investments specifically required for the type of activity for which the agent has been appointed by the principal, that is, which are required to enable the agent to conclude and/or negotiate this type of contract. Such investments are usually sunk, which means that upon leaving that particular field of activity the investment cannot be used for other activities or sold other than at a significant loss. Thirdly, there are the risks related to other activities undertaken on the same product market, to the extent that the principal requires the agent to undertake such activities, but not as an agent on behalf of the principal but for its own risk.

(15) For the purposes of applying Article 101(1), the agreement will be qualified as an agency agreement if the agent does not bear any, or bears only insignificant, risks in relation to the contracts concluded and/or negotiated on behalf of the principal, in relation to market-specific investments for that field of activity, and in relation to other activities required by the principal to be undertaken on the same product market. However, risks that are related to the activity of providing agency services in general, such as the risk of the agent's income being dependent upon its success as an agent or general investments in for instance premises or personnel, are not material to this assessment.

(16) For the purpose of applying Article 101(1), an agreement will thus generally be considered an agency agreement where property in the contract goods bought or sold

(a) does not contribute to the costs relating to the supply/purchase of the contract goods or services, including the costs of transporting the goods. This does not preclude the agent from carrying out the transport service, provided that the costs are covered by the principal;

(b) does not maintain at its own cost or risk stocks of the contract goods, including the costs of financing the stocks and the costs of loss of stocks and can return unsold goods to the principal without charge, unless the agent is liable for fault (for example, by failing to comply with reasonable security measures to avoid loss of stocks);

(c) does not undertake responsibility towards third parties for damage caused by the product sold (product liability), unless, as agent, it is liable for fault in this respect;

(d) does not take responsibility for customers' non-performance of the contract, with the exception of the loss of the agent's commission, unless the agent is liable for fault (for example, by failing to comply with reasonable security or anti-theft measures or failing to comply with reasonable measures to report theft to the principal or police or to communicate to the principal all necessary information available to him on the customer's financial reliability);

(e) is not, directly or indirectly, obliged to invest in sales promotion, such as contributions to the advertising budgets of the principal;

(f) does not make market-specific investments in equipment, premises or training of personnel, such as for example the petrol storage tank in the case of petrol retailing or specific software to sell insurance policies in case of insurance agents, unless these costs are fully reimbursed by the principal;

(g)   does not undertake other activities within the same product market required by the principal, unless these activities are fully reimbursed by the principal.

(17)   This list is not exhaustive. However, where the agent incurs one or more of the risks or costs mentioned in paragraphs (14), (15) and (16), the agreement between agent and principal will not be qualified as an agency agreement. The question of risk must be assessed on a case-by-case basis, and with regard to the economic reality of the situation rather than the legal form. For practical reasons, the risk analysis may start with the assessment of the contract-specific risks. If contract- specific risks are incurred by the agent, it will be enough to conclude that the agent is an independent distributor. On the contrary, if the agent does not incur contract-specific risks, then it will be necessary to continue further the analysis by assessing the risks related to market-specific investments. Finally, if the agent does not incur any contract-specific risks and risks related to market-specific investments, the risks related to other required activities within the same product market may have to be considered.

2.2   The application of Article 101(1) to agency agreements

(18)   In the case of agency agreements as defined in section 2.1, the selling or purchasing function of the agent forms part of the principal's activities. Since the principal bears the commercial and financial risks related to the selling and purchasing of the contract goods and services all obligations imposed on the agent in relation to the contracts concluded and/or negotiated on behalf of the principal fall outside Article 101(1). The following obligations on the agent's part will be considered to form an inherent part of an agency agreement, as each of them relates to the ability of the principal to fix the scope of activity of the agent in relation to the contract goods or services, which is essential if the principal is to take the risks and therefore to be in a position to determine the commercial strategy:

(a)   limitations on the territory in which the agent may sell these goods or services;

(b)   limitations on the customers to whom the agent may sell these goods or services;

(c)   the prices and conditions at which the agent must sell or purchase these goods or services.

(19)   In addition to governing the conditions of sale or purchase of the contract goods or services by the agent on behalf of the principal, agency agreements often contain provisions which concern the relationship between the agent and the principal. In particular, they may contain a provision preventing the principal from appointing other agents in respect of a given type of transaction, customer or territory (exclusive agency provisions) and/or a provision preventing the agent from acting as an agent or distributor of undertakings which compete

with the principal (single branding provisions). Since the agent is a separate undertaking from the principal, the provisions which concern the relationship between the agent and the principal may infringe Article 101(1). Exclusive agency provisions will in general not lead to anti-competitive effects. However, single branding provisions and post-term non-compete provisions, which concern inter-brand competition, may infringe Article 101(1) if they lead to or contribute to a (cumulative) foreclosure effect on the relevant market where the contract goods or services are sold or purchased (see in particular Section VI.2.1). Such provisions may benefit from the Block Exemption Regulation, in particular when the conditions provided in Article 5 of that Regulation are fulfilled. They can also be individually justified by efficiencies under Article 101(3) as for instance described in paragraphs (144) to (148).

(20) An agency agreement may also fall within the scope of Article 101(1), even if the principal bears all the relevant financial and commercial risks, where it facilitates collusion. That could, for instance, be the case when a number of principals use the same agents while collectively excluding others from using these agents, or when they use the agents to collude on marketing strategy or to exchange sensitive market information between the principals.

(21) Where the agent bears one or more of the relevant risks as described in paragraph (16), the agreement between agent and principal does not constitute an agency agreement for the purpose of applying Article 101(1). In that situation, the agent will be treated as an independent undertaking and the agreement between agent and principal will be subject to Article 101(1) as any other vertical agreement.

App2.4

Commission Staff Working Document, published on 17 July 2015
Evaluation of the Council Directive on the Coordination of the Laws of the Member States Relating to Self-Employed Commercial Agents (Directive 86/653/EEC)/ Refit Evaluation (Doc. Com (96) 354 final, 23.07.1998)

1.   Executive Summary

Background

The Commission Communication "REFIT – results and next steps"[1] identified the Commercial Agents Directive ('the Directive') as legislation that should be assessed given that it had never been evaluated since it entered into force in 1986 and there was an interest to know whether the Directive was still relevant to stakeholders and had EU added value. This evaluation therefore assesses performance of the Directive and examines whether it remains fit-for-purpose, delivers on its objectives at reasonable costs, is relevant, coherent and has EU added value.

The Directive affects a large and steadily growing market across a wide range of industrial sectors. It is estimated that in 2012 there were some 590 000 commercial agents in the EU, practically all SMEs, generating a combined turnover of EUR 260 billion (about 3 % of total commercial turnover) and providing employment to over 1 million people. On the other side of the commercial representation market, there are an estimated 1.7 million principals, 88 % of which are SMEs.

Historically, EU Member States had different rules regarding the rights and obligations of commercial agents and their principals. This created legal uncertainty and made it difficult in practice for market operators to use commercial representation across different Member States. Against this backdrop, the general objectives of the Directive, adopted in 1986, were to create a single market for commercial representation and eliminate barriers to the cross-border activities of commercial agents and their principals. More specifically, the Directive harmonises rules on: the rights and obligations of

---

1   COM(2013)685.

commercial agents and their principals; the remuneration of commercial agents; and the conclusion and termination of agency contracts, in particular any indemnity or compensation due to commercial agents when a contract ends.

Methodology

This evaluation assesses the functioning of the Directive, i.e. whether it has achieved its objectives and whether it is still fit-for-purpose today. The evaluation criteria are the Directive's: (1) effectiveness; (2) efficiency; (3) relevance; (4) EU added value; and (5) coherence with other policies.

Hard economic data to support the assessment has been difficult to find. Statistics and other quantitative data on the commercial agents market covering the period before and after the Directive's adoption do not exist.[2] Therefore, a counterfactual or comparative analysis is practically impossible to perform, at least in quantitative terms. This is particularly the case for the quantitative data needed for a comprehensive cost/benefit analysis of the Directive. To corroborate the findings of the evaluation, the evaluation process has built on a public consultation focused on stakeholders and a separate consultation of Member States. The consultation process aimed to collect evidence on the Directive's functioning and added value and to make it possible to assess the Directive's possible future. Other sources of information included data from Eurostat and information and data provided by representative associations and academics.

Findings

Effectiveness: The Directive meets its objective of facilitating cross-border activities. Long-term economic data supporting this conclusion is only available for two countries (Germany and Austria). However, stakeholder feedback received during the public consultation corroborates the finding with a large degree of consensus. Most Member States having responded to the consultation also state that the Directive functions well.

Efficiency: Due to the lack of quantitative data from the period preceding and following the adoption of the Directive, the efficiency analysis relies mostly on qualitative data and information. On this basis, the costs arising from the Directive are limited and affordable. While the Directive does not create administrative burden, it does possibly entail incremental operational costs for principals in those countries where commercial representation has not previously been regulated (e.g. UK, Ireland and Sweden). The Directive creates significant operational and commercial benefits by facilitating cross-border activities. An analysis of the costs and benefits at the level of individual businesses, based on responses to the stakeholder consultation, shows that the benefits of the Directive generally outweigh its costs.

---

2   Eurostat data for commercial representation is only available as from 2008.

<u>Relevance</u>: The Directive's objectives and its importance in establishing and maintaining a single market for commercial representation remain relevant today. The market for commercial representation is still growing and the attractiveness of the business model, especially for SMEs aiming to operate across borders, has not suffered from the emergence of other alternative sales channels, such as e-commerce. Feedback from stakeholders and Member States confirms the Directive's relevance.

<u>EU added value</u>: The Directive still adds value to the single market, because of the level of harmonisation it ensures. The benefits generated through the Directive remain valid, in particular for SMEs. Consumers also benefit from an EU-wide framework for commercial representation as it makes it possible for them to access products and goods that would otherwise not be available in their country.

These views were confirmed by stakeholders. Most operators were concerned about the possible risks related to the possible withdrawal of the Directive and believed that the benefits of the internal market for commercial representation were only secure if the Directive continued to ensure the current level of harmonisation throughout the EU. Specifically, both agents and most principals feared the risk that, without harmonised European legislation, future regulatory adjustments in some Member States may lead to increasing fragmentation, which would cause problems for SMEs (agents and principals) that provide and use commercial representation services across borders.

<u>Coherence with other policies</u>: The Directive's objective to increase the cross-border activities of commercial representation is in line with the wider objective of the single market. Due to the nature of commercial agents and their principals, a Directive that facilitates commercial representation also supports the Commission's SME policy. The evaluation has not found any possible conflicts with other policy fields.

The conclusion of the evaluation is that the Directive meets its objectives and functions well. The Directive's benefits outweigh its costs, it remains relevant and continues to have EU added value. Based on these findings, it is recommended that the Directive is maintained in its current form.

2. Introduction

In December 2012, the Commission launched a regulatory fitness and performance programme (REFIT).[3] The purpose of the REFIT programme is to identify opportunities to reduce regulatory costs and cut red tape, simplify regulation in order to meet policy goals, and achieve the benefits of EU regulation at the lowest possible cost. Fitness checks and evaluations of existing legislation are among the tools used by the REFIT programme to achieve these objectives.

The Commission's 'REFIT – results and next steps' communication[4] identified the Commercial Agents Directive as legislation that should be

3 COM(2012) 746.
4 COM(2013) 685 final.

assessed given that it had never been evaluated since it entered into force in 1986 and there was an interest to know whether the Directive was still relevant to stakeholders and had EU added value.

In June 2014, then DG Internal Market and Services (now DG Internal Market, Industry, Entrepreneurship and SMEs) launched an evaluation of the Commercial Agents Directive (hereinafter the 'Directive').[5] The purpose of the evaluation is to assess the functioning of the Directive and whether it remains fit-for-purpose in terms of effectiveness, efficiency, relevance, coherence and EU added value. This is the first time the Directive is evaluated since its entry into force. The Commission has previously submitted a report on the application of a specific article of the Directive[6] in 1996 (see 4.5).

3.   Background to the Initiative

3.1.   Objectives of the initiative

Commercial agents are self-employed intermediaries permanently authorised to negotiate the sale or purchase of goods in the name and on behalf of another person (the principal). Commercial agents may conclude transactions with another business (business-to-business or 'B2B') or directly with a final consumer (business-to-consumer or 'B2C'). Historically, EU Member States had different rules regarding the rights and obligations of commercial agents and their principals. This created legal uncertainty and made it difficult in practice for market operators to use commercial representation across different Member States.

Against this backdrop, the general objectives of the Directive are to:
- create a single market for commercial representation and
- eliminate barriers to the cross-border activities of commercial agents and their principals.

The Directive only applies to commercial representation in the sale and purchase of goods (as opposed to services). The focus area of the harmonisation envisaged by the Directive is the protection of commercial agents vis-à-vis their principals. Notwithstanding the focus on protection of agents, some provisions of the Directive can be considered as a protection of the principal, for example the clause on restraint of trade after the termination of the contract in Article 20.

As explained in the second recital of the Directive, coordination was necessary because the differences in national laws on commercial representation substantially affected the conditions of competition and how the activity could be carried out within the internal market. Such differences were detrimental to the protection available to commercial agents vis-à-vis their principals and to the security of commercial transactions, in particular when principal and

---

5   Council Directive 86/653/EEC of 18 December 1986 on the coordination of the laws of the Member States relating to self-employed commercial agents (OJ L 382 of 31.12.1986, p. 17).
6   COM(1996) 364.

commercial agents were established in different Member States. According to the third recital of the Directive, the existing rules concerning conflicting laws in the area of commercial representation were not sufficient to ensure the proper functioning of the internal market.

Against this backdrop, the key specific objectives of the Directive are to create harmonised rules on:

- the rights and obligations of commercial agents and their principals;
- the remuneration of commercial agents, and
- the conclusion and termination of agency contracts, in particular the indemnity or compensation due to commercial agents in case of a contract termination.

The rules established by the Directive on the compensation or indemnity due to commercial agents in the case of a contract termination built on existing legislation in Germany and France and its settled case law. When the Directive was adopted, only two Member States did not have rules on protecting agents in cases of contract termination: UK and Ireland.

Note that the Directive does not aim to fully harmonise the rules for self-employed agents, as it does not regulate all aspects of the relationship between principals and self-employed commercial agents. Instead, it offers options to Member States. Member States may go beyond the minimum protection requirements laid down by the Directive and offer greater protection to commercial agents.[7]

In summary, the Directive's intervention logic can be described as follows:

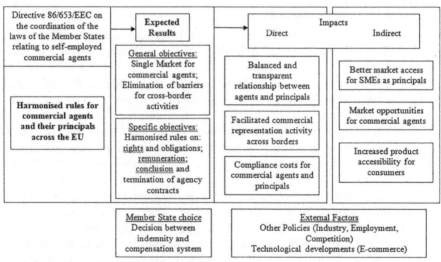

Figure 1 — The Directive's intervention logic

---

7   Judgment of the Court of 17 October 2013 in Case C-184/12, Unamar, p. 50.

3.2. Description of the initiative

3.2.1. Scope

Chapter I of the Directive (Articles 1 and 2) defines the commercial agents who fall under the Directive's scope. Under Article 1(2), the Directive applies to self-employed intermediaries who have continued authority to negotiate the sale or purchase of goods on behalf of another person (the 'principal') or to negotiate and conclude such transactions on behalf of and in the name of that principal. It follows from this definition that the Directive excludes from its scope the commercial agents who:

- are not self-employed;
- do not have continued authority;
- According to the case law of the Court of Justice, the number of transactions is normally an indicator of the continuing authority but it is not the sole determining factor.
- are not active in the sale or purchase of goods (for example those providing services, e.g. insurance brokers);
  Note that a number of Member States have extended the rules of the Directive to self-employed commercial agents selling services. Generally, where there might be a problem of protection of self-employed commercial agents in the sector of services, Member States may take the measures they consider necessary. The Directive does not constitute an obstacle to adopting such measures, as self-employed commercial agents in the area of services do not fall under the Directive's scope.
- do not conclude the sale or purchase of goods on behalf and in the name of the principal (e.g. independent car dealers).
  The Court of Justice ruled that commercial agents who act on behalf of a principal but in their own name do not fall under the scope of Directive 86/653/EEC.[8]

3.2.2. Rights and obligations of the parties

Chapter II (Articles 3 to 5) sets the rights and obligations of the parties (commercial agents and principals) from which they cannot derogate. According to the Directive, both parties must act dutifully and in good faith.

There are three particular obligations for commercial agents from which no derogation is possible: to make proper efforts to negotiate and, where appropriate, conclude the transactions he is instructed to take care of, to communicate to the principal all the necessary information available to the agent, and to comply with reasonable instructions given by the principal.

The Directive also imposes similar obligations on the principal who has to provide the commercial agent with the necessary documentation and other information, including in particular information within a reasonable period about a significantly lower future volume of transactions and information about the acceptance or refusal of transactions procured by the commercial

---

8   Order of the Court of 10 February 2004 in Case C-85/03, Mavrona.

agent. These two particular information obligations do not generally entail any costs for the principal and are necessary for the commercial agent in order to avoid useless efforts and costs and be able to correctly calculate his remuneration.

3.2.3. Remuneration of the commercial agent

Chapter III (Articles 6 to 12) deals with the remuneration of the commercial agent. The Directive does not bring prejudice to Member States' compulsory provisions concerning the level of remuneration of commercial agents. It follows that Member States may set the level of remuneration of commercial agents, if they estimate that there is a need to protect the principal or customers from excessive levels of commercial agents' remuneration.

The Directive deals in particular with the commission, the most usual form of remuneration of the commercial agent which varies with the number or the value of business transactions.

Under Article 7(1), the commercial agent is entitled to a commission during the period of validity of the contract not only when the transaction was concluded as a result of the agent's action, but also when the transaction was concluded with a third party previously acquired by the commercial agent as a customer for transactions of the same kind. Moreover, under Article 7(2) of the Directive, if the commercial agent was entrusted with or has an exclusive right to a specific geographical area or group of customers, the agent is entitled to a commission for transactions concluded with a customer belonging to that area or group.

Article 12 of the Directive gives commercial agents the possible means to be clearly informed about the commissions they are entitled to. It provides mandatory rules (without possibility of derogation by the parties to the detriment of the commercial agent) imposing on the principal the obligation to supply the commercial agent with a statement of the commission due. It also gives the commercial agent the right to demand all information, in particular an extract from the principal's books if this is provided for in national legislation.

3.2.4. Conclusion of the contract

Article 13(1) of the Directive gives every party the right to receive from the other one, on request, a signed written document setting out the terms of the agency contract. Waiver of this right is not permitted. Article 13(2) of the Directive gives Member States the possibility to provide that an agency contract is not valid unless there is written evidence.

It follows that the Directive imposes neither the written form[99] of the contract nor its registration. Therefore, it does not entail any costs or administrative burden for either party. It is up to the parties to request a signed written

---

9 According to a survey carried out in the UK by Dr Saintier, 67.5 % of commercial agents in the UK still do not have a written contract with their principal.

document and up to Member States to require a written document as a condition for its validity. It follows that the parties will only incur the cost of drafting a written document if they or the Member States make use of the possibilities offered under Article 13 of the Directive. In any case, the cost would be rather insignificant.

3.2.5. Termination of the contract

3.2.5.1. The prior notice obligation of the principal

Under Article 15 of the Directive, if an agency contract is concluded for an indefinite period,[10] either party may terminate it by giving prior notice. Prior notice is a classic obligation for terminating contracts concluded for an indefinite period. Both the principal and the commercial agent must respect this obligation, so both parties are treated equally, without particular protection for the commercial agent; violating the obligation entails responsibility for any damages.

However, the Directive does not affect national legislation that provides for the immediate termination of a contract because of one party's failure to carry out all or part of its obligations or if there are exceptional circumstances (Article 16 of the Directive).

3.2.5.2. Choice between indemnity and compensation system

Articles 17-19 of the Directive regulate the protection of the commercial agent after the termination of the contract. Article 17 is the Directive's central provision.

As the Court has already held, the system established under Article 17 of the Directive is mandatory.[11] Articles 17-19 of the Directive guarantee minimum protection for all commercial agents established in the EU. A principal cannot circumvent these provisions by using a choice-of-law clause without considering whether that choice could be detrimental to the commercial agent.[12] The Court of Justice held that Articles 17 and 18 of the Directive must be applied if the commercial agent carries out its activity in an EU Member State, even if the principal is established in a non-member country and a clause of the contract stipulates that the contract is to be governed by the law of that third country.[13]

Article 17(1) of the Directive sets up a system that enables Member States to choose between two approaches. Member States must take the measures necessary to guarantee that, if the contract is terminated, the commercial agent will receive either an indemnity determined according to the criteria

10 As such is considered also an agency contract for a fixed period which continues to
    be performed by both parties after that period expired (Article 14 of the Directive).
11 Case C-381/98 Ingmar [2000] ECR I-9305, paragraph 21.
12 Case C-381/98 Ingmar [2000] ECR I-9305, paragraph 25.
13 Judgment of the Court of 9 November 2000 in Case C-381/98, Ingmar.

set out in Article 17(2) or compensation according to the criteria set out in Article 17(3).[14]

Articles 17 and 18 of the Directive prescribe a precise framework within which the Member States may exercise their discretion as to the choice of methods for calculating the indemnity or compensation to be granted. Although the system established by Article 17 of the Directive is mandatory and prescribes a framework,[15] it does not give any detailed indications as regards the method for calculating the indemnity for terminating the contract.[16]

Under the indemnity system [Article 17(2)], the commercial agent is entitled to an indemnity if and to the extent to which s/he brought new customers to the principal or had significantly increased the volume of business with existing customers[17] after termination of the contract. The indemnity represents the continuing benefits (goodwill) to the principal after termination of the contract as a result of the agent's work. The agent receives a commission while the contract is valid, but this does not reflect the value of the goodwill generated for the principal; this is why payment of the goodwill indemnity is commercially justified. If no goodwill has been generated, the principal should not pay an indemnity. The Directive sets an indemnity level ceiling equal to one year of the agent's average annual remuneration over the preceding five years (or the average for the period in question if the contract lasted less than five years).

Under Article 17(2) (c), receiving an indemnity does not prevent the commercial agent from seeking damages. This provision governs situations where, in addition to the indemnity under Article 17(2) of the Directive, under national law the agent is entitled to seek damages, e.g. for the principal breaching the contract or failing to respect the notice period provided for in the Directive.[18]

Under the compensation system [Article 17(3)], the agent is entitled to compensation for the damage suffered as a result of the termination of the contract. The main differences compared with the indemnity system are that:
- the agent has to prove the actual loss suffered;
- there is no maximum level of compensation;
- there is no distinction between new and existing customers.

The Commission has submitted to the Council a report on the application of Article 17 of the Directive, as this was required under Article 17(6) of the Directive. The report provides detailed information on the actual calculation of the indemnity and is intended to facilitate a more uniform interpretation of Article 17.[19]

---

14 Judgment of the Court of 23 March 2006 in Case C-465/04, Honyvem, p. 20.
15 Judgment of the Court of 9 November 2000 in Case C-381/98, Ingmar, p. 21.
16 Judgment of the Court of 23 March 2006 in Case C-465/04, Honyvem, p. 34.
17 The German *Bundesgerichtshof* submitted a preliminary question to the Court of Justice of the EU relating to the definition of 'new customers' (Case C-315/14).
18 See the Commission's report on the implementation of Article 17 of the Directive, COM(96)364 final, p. 5.
19 Ibidem, p. 35.

4.   Evaluation Criteria and Evaluation Questions

The evaluation of the Directive has been carried out with particular attention to the following evaluation criteria and questions in order to guide the analysis of the Directive's functioning:

- Effectiveness: Has the Directive been effective in meeting, or moving towards, the defined objectives? Did the legislation help to facilitate the cross-border activities of commercial representations? What effects did the Directive have on SMEs (i) as commercial agents and (ii) as principals?
- Efficiency: Has the Directive delivered its results efficiently in terms of the resources used? Does it create administrative burden? What are the main costs and benefits of the Directive for (i) commercial agents and (ii) principals? At overall market level, did the benefits of the Directive outweigh its costs?
- Relevance: Are the objectives of the Directive still relevant today?
- EU added value: What is the ongoing added value of EU legislation in this field? Is the Directive still fit for purpose in meeting its objectives in the future? What would be the effects if the Directive were to be withdrawn and Member States were free to adjust their national regulatory frameworks?
- Coherence with other policies: To what extent is the Directive consistent with other policy objectives (i.e. other than the objective of a single market) at EU and national level?

5.   Method

The evaluation assesses the functioning of the Directive, i.e. whether the Directive has achieved it objectives, whether it is efficient, coherent and to which degree it is relevant today and still has an added value at the EU level.

Hard economic data to support the assessment has been difficult to find. Eurostat data for commercial representation is only available as of 2008. Other statistics and quantitative data on the commercial agents market covering the period before and after the Directive's adoption do not exist. This applies, in particular, to quantitative data for a comprehensive cost / benefit analysis of the Directive. There is limited academic literature. Therefore, the evaluation criteria and questions are assessed mostly qualitatively.

To gather information for the evaluation, the aforementioned evaluation questions were incorporated in a public consultation targeting interested stakeholders and a separate consultation of Member States. The objective of the consultation process was to collect concrete evidence on the functioning of the Directive and to enable an assessment of the Directive's possible future.

The consultation process was conducted between August and November 2014 and involved Member States, competent authorities, commercial agents and their principals, representative associations, academics, lawyers, consumers and citizens.

15 Member States contributed to the evaluation: Austria, Croatia, Cyprus, Czech Republic, Denmark, France, Germany, Hungary, Ireland, Luxembourg, Malta, Poland, Slovakia, Spain and Sweden. There are no Member State expert

groups or permanent committees dealing with legislation on commercial representation and the responsible ministries for such legislation vary between Member States. This implied that consultation enquiries had to be transmitted to the Permanent Representatives (ambassadors) of each Member State making direct follow-up enquiries difficult. This explains the limited response rate in the Member State consultation.

The public stakeholder consultation yielded 276 stakeholders responses, the vast majority of which came from commercial agents or their representatives (212 responses). There were also replies from 42 principals and 22 other stakeholders (industry federations representing both commercial agents and principals, as well as lawyers and academics).

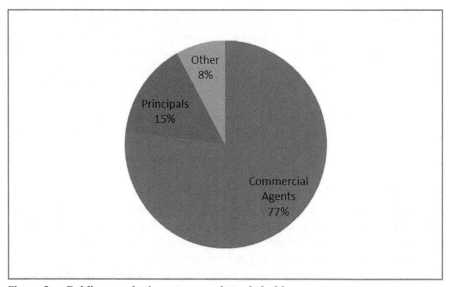

Figure 2 — Public consultation responses by stakeholder category

A large majority of stakeholder replies (more than 90 %) came from four Member States: France, Germany, Austria and the UK. The remaining responses came from stakeholders in nine Member States (Italy, Netherlands, Belgium, Finland, Denmark, Greece, Spain, Luxembourg and Sweden) and one non-EU country (Norway). Finally, there were seven responses from EU-wide associations or federations.[20]

Overall, the diversity of respondents to the stakeholder consultation was relatively low.

20 EDL (Association of European Distribution Lawyers), EuroCommerce (Association of European retailers and wholesalers), FECC (European Association of Chemical Distributors), UPEI (Union of European Petroleum Independents), DSE (Direct Selling Europe), ECFD (European Confederation of Fuel Distributors), CECRA (European Council for Motor Trades and Repairers).

Firstly, significantly more agents than principals contributed to the stakeholder consultation. This could result from the fact that commercial agents are organised in EU-wide and national associations which may have helped create awareness of the public consultation. Similar associations do not exist for principals of commercial agents. However, as shown by the results below, there was a significant level of consensus between agents and principals, which limits the risk of misinterpreting the consultation data due to a bias towards agents.

Secondly, as mentioned above, a high proportion of stakeholder responses originated from four Member States (France, Germany, Austria and the UK). Notably, the number of responses of individual agents from Italy was low in relation to the large proportion of Italian commercial agents in the European market. However, the national association representing Italian agents did reply to the consultation. Furthermore, 15 countries contributed to the separate Member State consultation — presumably on the basis of national stakeholder feedback including the views of principals. Again, the relatively strong level of consensus between Member States reduces the risk that a bias towards a small group of countries would distort the interpretation of the stakeholder responses.

Other sources of information included data from Eurostat (available only as of 2008) as well as information and data provided by representative associations and academics. As mentioned earlier, due to the fact that the Directive was adopted a long time ago, hard economic data for assessing the effects of the Directive is very limited. Therefore, the public stakeholder consultation and the Member State consultation were the main sources of information for assessing the Directive's effects.

6.   Implementation State of Play
The Directive was adopted in December 1986 and was fully transposed in all then-Member States in 1995. It is now fully transposed in all 28 Member States (see the national measures transposing the Directive in Annex 3). The Commission only received one complaint since the Directive's adoption. The complaint referred to a private conflict and was therefore reassigned to the competent national jurisdictions. European case law related to the Directive is provided in Annex 4 and is also referred to in the legal analysis in the following section.

Commercial agents in the EU are currently active in a wide range of industry sectors, such as:
- agricultural materials,
- textiles and footwear,
- fuels and chemicals,
- timber and building material,
- machinery and industrial equipment,
- furniture and household equipment,
- food and beverages, and
- medical industries.

Practically all commercial agents (between 90 % and 100 % depending on the Member State) are SMEs or micro-enterprises.

Producing businesses often use commercial representation to enter a new market in a different country, especially if they lack the resources to establish their own presence abroad. Therefore, the companies using cross-border commercial representation (principals) are also mostly SMEs (between 50 % and 90 % of all principals depending on the Member State).

It is estimated that in 2012 there were some 590 000 commercial agents in the EU-28, generating a combined turnover of EUR 260 billion (about 3 % of total commerce turnover) and providing employment to over 1 million people.[21]

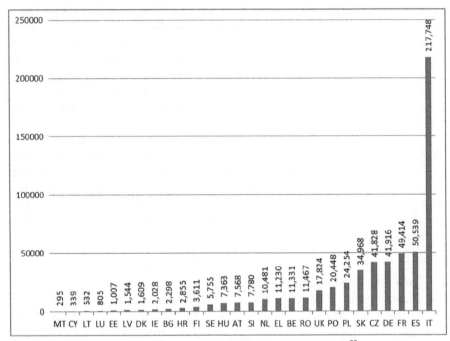

Figure 3 — **Number of commercial agents by Member State (2012)**[22]

Eurostat data shows that the number of contractual agents and people employed and the amount of turnover generated have increased between 2008 and 2012. On the other side of the commercial representation market, there are an estimated 1.7 million principals, 88 % of which are SMEs.[23]

Notably, the commercial representation market is growing, which implies that, despite the success of alternative sales channels such as e-commerce,

21 Source: EuroCommerce based on Eurostat data. According to further estimates based on data total number of commercial agents in the EU as it excludes the B2C segment. The total number of commercial agents is therefore around 740 000.
22 Source: Eurostat. Data for Malta dates from 2010.
23 Source: EuroCommerce based on Eurostat data.

commercial representation remains an attractive commercial proposition and is by no means a declining business model.

Annex 2 includes aggregated data and information provided by individual agents and principals during the public stakeholder consultation.

At national level, market characteristics (proportion of SMEs and micro-enterprises, proportion of cross-border relationships, etc.) vary between countries. The Commission received estimates related to these characteristics from six Member States (Germany, France, Spain, Sweden, Malta, and Cyprus). These numbers consistently confirm the importance of the commercial representation model for micro- and small enterprises.

In Germany, France, Spain and Cyprus, almost all commercial agents (between 99 % and 100 %) are SMEs or sole proprietors. In Sweden and Malta the percentage of SMEs and micro-enterprises is around 90 %, hence 10 % of commercial agents represent larger companies in these two countries.

As concerns principals, there is also a strong bias towards small companies. In the larger countries providing data (Germany, France, Spain), the vast majority of all principals (80 % or more) are SMEs. In the smaller countries, the percentage of SMEs among principals is lower but never below 50 % (80 % in Cyprus, 75 % in Malta and 50 % in Sweden).

The degree to which commercial agents operate across borders is correlated with the size of the domestic market. In smaller economies, i.e. Sweden, Malta and Cyprus, cross-border relationships dominate (more than 90 % of all relationships). For these countries, intra-EU commercial representation accounts for 70 % to 80 % of all relationships, with the exception of Malta where it accounts for only 20 %. Cross-border activities are less important but still significant for agents in larger countries and constitute 3 % in Spain, 25 % in Germany and 40 % in France.

7.   Answers to the Evaluation Questions

7.1.   *Effectiveness: Impact of the Directive on facilitating cross-border activities*

Although it is difficult to assess the impact of a Directive that was adopted almost 30 years ago in quantitative terms, there are strong qualitative indications that the Directive has had a significant impact on facilitating cross-border activities and creating a single market for commercial representation, and thus meeting its objectives.

A significant increase in the number of commercial representation relationships made across borders over the last 20-30 years is a good indicator for the Directive's actual market impact. Long-term data is available for Germany and Austria. The proportion of German agents representing principals from other EU Member States went from 26.5 % in 1984 to 68 % in 2014. A study from Austria shows that the proportion of Austrian commercial agents operating in at least one foreign country increased from 12 % in 2000 to 39 % in 2014, while the proportion of foreign principals using Austrian commercial agents increased from 30 % to 64 % in the same period.

Based on feedback from the relevant national associations, the developments described above could be attributed to a large extent to the Directive's impact.

In qualitative terms, these effects can be explained by a number of different reasons and observations:
- The Directive ensures legal certainty for agents and principals due to a common transparent framework across the EU.
- The Directive enables simplified and accelerated contract negotiations between agents and principals across borders.
- The Directive's harmonised definition of the rights and obligations of trading partners is particularly important for SMEs planning cross-border activities.
- The Directive's legal interpretation by the European Court of Justice makes it impossible for its provisions to be circumvented through choice-of-law outside the EU (see 4.5.2).

A number of Member States confirm these findings. Of the 15 Member States having responded to the consultation, eight specifically mentioned the Directive's effect on facilitating cross-border operations[24]. Six of these eight Member States saw a significant effect on facilitating cross-border operations and two saw a partial effect. The remaining seven Member States had not analysed the cross-border effect of the Directive and could not comment on the question.

The public stakeholder consultation underlined the Directive's importance for enabling cross-border activities, with a very large majority of responding stakeholders (85 %) attributing a significant impact to the Directive.

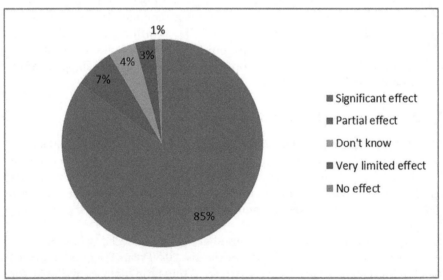

Figure 4 — Stakeholder responses on the Directive's effect on facilitating cross-border activities (N=276)

This view was even stronger among the commercial agents and their representatives who responded. More than 92 % of respondents in this group said that the Directive's effect was significant. The views of principals were

24 Germany, France, Spain, Poland, Czech Republic, Sweden, Cyprus and Malta.

more nuanced. Almost 60 % said that the Directive's effect was significant, while 21 % saw a partial effect and 10 % saw a very limited effect or no effect at all. The remaining 9 % stated that they were not in a position to assess the effect. The stakeholders who only saw a limited effect or no effect at all said that the framework provided by the Directive was too general and still allowed for inconsistent specific rules at national level. These respondents thought that a stronger degree of harmonisation would be desirable.

Conclusion

The Directive meets its objective of facilitating cross-border activities. Long-term economic data supporting this conclusion is available for two countries (Germany and Austria). Stakeholder feedback in the public consultation corroborates this finding with a large degree of consensus. Furthermore, eight of the 15 Member States having responded to the consultation state that the Directive had an effect in facilitating cross-border operations while the other seven Member States did not analyse this aspect. Specific suggestions by three Member States on the provisions of the Directive are discussed in section 6.4.

7.2.   *Efficiency: the Directive's costs and benefits for commercial agents and principals*

As already mentioned earlier in the report, quantitative data for a cost/benefit analysis does not exist due to the amount of time that has passed since the Directive was adopted. Therefore, the identified costs and benefits are described in qualitative terms.

Benefits

The following main benefits can be attributed to the Directive:

- The Directive sets out minimum standards for compensation and indemnity measures for commercial agents in situations where a principal terminates an agency contract. Although this is a benefit for agents, it is a cost for principals, at least in the Member States where similar compensation systems did not exist previously (e.g. UK). Nevertheless, the legal certainty and harmonisation achieved through the Directive in the areas of compensation and indemnity is a benefit for principals, especially SMEs, as well as facilitating cross-border commercial representation.
- The Directive eliminates or substantially reduces the need for in-depth research and analysis of the regulatory framework for commercial representation in other Member States. This makes it possible to avoid costs, to reduce administrative burden and to use contract templates across the EU. The Directive also helps avoid legal consulting and translation costs. These benefits apply to both agents and principals seeking to operate outside their country of origin.
- The Directive helps commercial agents from different countries to develop European cooperation networks, increasing the possible commercial reach for the benefit of principals.

Costs
Qualitative stakeholder feedback shows that the Directive does not cause administrative burden. Nevertheless, it could entail additional operational costs for principals as it ensures a minimum standard for the protection of commercial agents — at least in those Member States where a similar degree of protection was previously not granted to agents. This applies to the UK, Ireland and Sweden. The main element of this protection is that principals must pay indemnity or compensation after termination of the contract. Nevertheless, these potential costs incurred by principals are a compensation for the investments and efforts of commercial agents to increase the sales of the principals. Therefore, the Directive strikes a balance between the interests of the agents and principals.

Conclusion
The costs of the Directive are limited and affordable. Although the Directive does not create administrative burden it could possibly entail incremental operational costs for principals in those countries where commercial representation has not been regulated previously (UK, IE, SE). At the same time, the Directive creates significant benefits in operational and commercial terms by facilitating cross-border activities. A comparison between the costs and benefits at the level of individual operators follows in the next section.

7.3.   Effectiveness and efficiency: Overall effect on individual market participants
The Directive's effect on individual market participants can best be assessed based on the stakeholder consultations carried out during the evaluation process.
   An overwhelming majority of responding stakeholders (87 %) saw only positive effects for individual market players, especially better opportunities to participate in and benefit from the internal market.

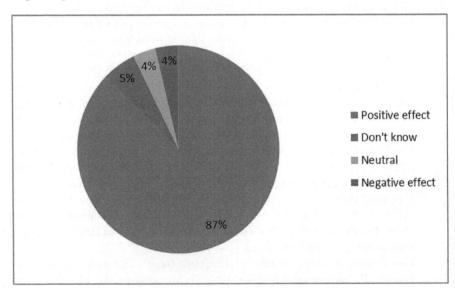

Figure 5 — The Directive's effect on market participants (N=276)

Those who saw a positive effect of the Directive said that by facilitating cross-border activities the Directive has helped commercial agents and principals, in particular SMEs, to grow their business outside their country of origin. In many cases, this had a direct and often significant impact on agents' revenue; it also clearly benefited the principals who would not have considered expanding their business abroad without the possibility for commercial representation.

A number of respondents to the consultation provided feedback on how much the number of their cross-border contracts increased due to the Directive.

Specific examples:
One commercial agent who responded to the public consultation said that their number of cross-border activities had tripled due to the Directive's adoption and its effects.
A commercial agent from Germany said that he was able to engage with five principals in Austria and Italy as a direct consequence of the Directive.

Figure 6 provides an overview of how agents and principals perceived the Directive's effects.

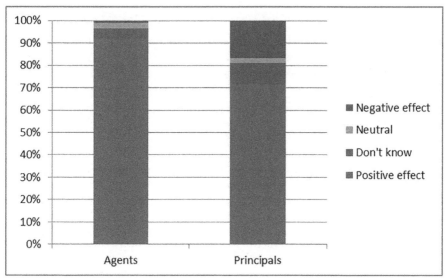

Figure 6 — The Directive's effects as perceived by agents (N=212) and principals (N=42)

All seven principals who saw a negative effect for market players were from the UK. Nevertheless, among all principals who responded, the number of those who saw a positive effect (30 respondents) clearly exceeded the number of those who saw a negative effect (seven respondents).

When asked how the Directive's benefits compared with its costs, stakeholders' responses had a strong tendency towards benefits outweighing costs, with 81 % of stakeholders saying that the benefits were much higher than the costs and 4 % saying that they were slightly higher.

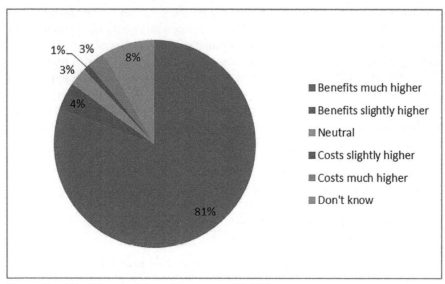

Figure 7 — The Directive's benefits vs costs (N=276)

A breakdown of the numbers based on the two main stakeholder categories shows that 87 % of commercial agents perceive the benefits as much higher than the costs, and 2 % as slightly higher.

For principals, these percentages are 55 % and 14 %, respectively. 14 % of responding principals said that the costs were much higher than the benefits, while 7 % said that the benefits and costs were comparable (10 % said they did not know whether the benefits or costs were higher).

The views of Member States were consistent with the ones received in the public stakeholder consultation. Around half of Member States stated that the Directive had a positive effect for commercial agents (8 out of 15 Member States) and for principals (7 Member States). One Member State responded that the general effect was neutral, and the remaining six Member States stated that they had not analysed the effect of the Directive on market participants.

7.4.   The Directive's relevance and EU added value

Relevance
The Directive's objectives and its importance in establishing and maintaining a single market for commercial representation remain relevant today. As described in section 2 of the report, the market for commercial representation is still growing and the attractiveness of the business model, especially for SMEs aiming to operate across borders, has not suffered from the emergence of other alternative sales channels, such as e-commerce. The feedback of stakeholders and Member States confirms the Directive's relevance.

Most market participants were very concerned about the risks related to the possible withdrawal of the Directive and believed that the benefits of the internal market for commercial representation were only secure if the Directive continued to ensure the current level of harmonisation throughout the EU. Specifically, both agents and most principals feared the risk that, without harmonised European legislation, future regulatory adjustments in some Member States may lead to increasing fragmentation, which would cause problems for SMEs (agents and principals) that provide and use commercial representation services across borders.

Added value

It can be assumed that, through the level of harmonisation it ensures, the Directive still adds value to the internal market today. The benefits generated through the Directive (described in the previous sections) remain valid, in particular for SMEs. Consumers also benefit from an EU-wide framework for commercial representation as it makes it possible for them to access products and goods that would otherwise not be available in their country.

Member States' views

Most Member States who contributed to the evaluation held a positive view of the Directive. Specifically, 11 Member States saw that the Directive had added value. The main advantages mentioned by these Member States were that the Directive ensured legal certainty and a predictable framework for cross-border contracts, thereby stimulating the internal market for commercial representation. The four remaining Member States who contributed to the evaluation said that they had not analysed the Directive's impact in detail and therefore did not have a view on whether it still added value or not. Only two of the 15 responding Member States had general doubts on whether the Directive was still required.

Stakeholder views

The positive views on the Directive's added value were confirmed in the stakeholder consultation. As many as 196 out of 276 respondents considered the Directive as 'perfectly fit for purpose', giving it a maximum rating of 10 on a 10-point scale. As should be expected due to the overall population of respondents, a significant majority of maximum ratings came from commercial agents. Nevertheless, 29 respondents from other categories, most of them principals, had the same view.

Only 14 respondents gave the Directive a rating of 5 or below. Most of these were principals based in the UK, so the low rating was presumably driven by the increase in operational costs described in the previous section (the Directive introduced measures to protect commercial agents where previously none existed).

The overall distribution of ratings from 1 (not at all fit-for-purpose) to 10 (perfectly fit-for-purpose) is shown in the figure below.

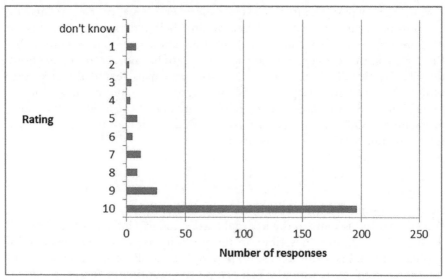

Figure 8 — Distribution of fit-for-purpose ratings across all respondents (N=276)

Although the distribution of ratings differs between commercial agents and principals, in both cases there is a clear tendency in favour of considering the Directive fit-for-purpose. The following two figures show the distributions for commercial agents and principals.

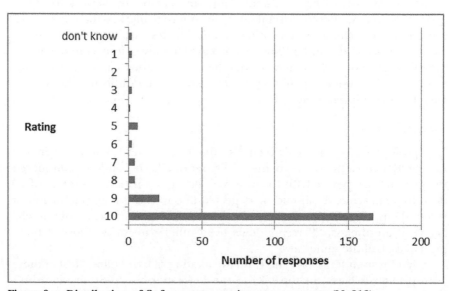

Figure 9 — Distribution of fit-for purpose ratings across agents (N=212)

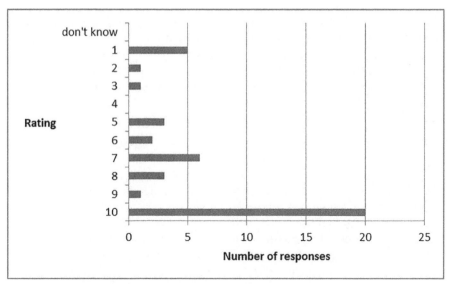

Figure 10 — Distribution of fit-for-purpose ratings across principals (N=42)

Based on the described benefits of the Directive and its importance in establishing and maintaining a single market for commercial representation, there is a risk of less harmonisation and, hence, possible fragmentation if the Directive were to be repealed.

The stakeholder consultation confirmed this. Most respondents were very concerned about the risks related to the Directive's possible withdrawal and believed that the benefits described previously were only secure if the Directive continued to ensure the current level of harmonisation throughout the EU. Specifically, both agents and most principals feared that, without harmonised European legislation, future regulatory adjustments in some Member States may lead to increasing fragmentation and cause problems for SMEs (agents and principals) in providing and using commercial representation services across borders.

Member States' suggestions for the Directive's provisions

Member States generally considered the Directive fit-for-purpose and did not identify any future national level requirements that would conflict with the Directive. Nevertheless, three Member States (Spain, Poland and Slovakia) suggested a number of specific modifications to the Directive. The proposed modifications and a brief analysis of their justification and feasibility follow below.

Slovakia

The Slovakian authorities suggested deleting the word 'self-employed' from the definition of 'commercial agent' under Article 1(2) of the Directive.

This suggestion is based on the idea that because the commercial agent negotiates and concludes agreements on behalf and in the name of the principal, the agent should not be considered as being self-employed.

Analysis: The suggested modification would cause a problem. A commercial agent who is not self-employed is already protected under national social laws applicable to salaried workers, so further protection under the Directive would not be justified.

Poland

The Polish authorities are in favour of more detailed provisions on calculating the indemnity due after a contract is terminated and of extending the Directive to actors other than commercial agents.

Analysis: Detailed provisions on calculating the indemnity or compensation due after a contract is terminated (Article 17 of the Directive) would mean less discretionary power and less flexibility for national authorities and jurisdictions. As regards extending the Directive's provisions to other categories of beneficiaries, the Directive does not exclude national legislation that has this purpose.

Spain

The Spanish authorities suggested changes to six provisions of the Directive:

1.   Amendment of Article 7(2) of the Directive in order to add a presumption of exclusivity in favour of the commercial agent.

     Analysis: Note that such a provision reinforces the protection of the commercial agent and imposes a significant burden on principals who do not mention in the contract that the agency is not exclusive. Such a provision may create problems in some Member States, for example the UK, where commercial agency contracts may not exist in written form, and could be a source of litigation with high legal costs.

2.   Amendment of Article 20(3) of the Directive to add that the clause on 'restraint of trade' for a maximum period of two years after the contract is terminated is valid only if the contract is in writing and to provide for compensation in addition to what is already provided for in the Directive.

     Analysis: Such an amendment would entail additional costs for the principal after termination of the contract and would further reinforce the protection of commercial agents. Therefore, it would put at risk the balance of interests achieved by the Directive in all Member States by adding costs for the principal and benefits in favour of commercial agents.

3. Amendment of Article 15 of the Directive to add a provision stating that the non-respect of the notice period entails the obligation of compensation based on past commissions.

    Analysis: The obligation of prior notice before terminating a contract (Article 15(1) of the Directive) is an obligation for both parties and not only for the principal. However, as Spain proposes to calculate the amount of compensation based on past commissions, the suggested amendment would exclusively favour the commercial agent.

    Moreover, an amendment of the Directive does not seem necessary as, according to the general rules on torts under national legislation, the lack of prior notice opens the possibility for both parties to claim damages. The Directive does not exclude this possibility for the commercial agent even if the agent was granted an indemnity for termination of the agency contract.

4. Amendment of Article 17 of the Directive to add a paragraph stating that agreements excluding an indemnity for the agent or containing criteria for its calculation which result in an indemnity lower than that under Article 17(2) are void before the contract is terminated.

    Analysis: Article 19 of the Directive states that 'the parties may not derogate from Articles 17 and 18 to the detriment of the commercial agent before the agency contract expires' and on this basis the Court of Justice ruled in Case C-465/04, Honyvem, that the indemnity for termination of the contract which results from the application of Article 17(2) of the Directive cannot be replaced by an indemnity determined in accordance with other criteria, unless the commercial agent is guaranteed in every case an indemnity equal to or greater than that which results from the application of Article 17.

    Therefore, the suggested amendment of the Directive does not seem necessary.

5. Clarification of Article 17(3) by adding that lost commissions are calculated based on the average commissions received the year before the unilateral termination of the contract by the principal.

    Analysis: Such a clarification would limit the margin of discretion granted by the Directive to Member States.

6. Amendment of Article 18 (b) of the Directive to clarify that the indemnity or compensation referred to under Article 17 of the Directive is not payable if the agent has reached the age of retirement provided for in the general national system of social security.

    Analysis: Such a provision could be considered as discrimination on grounds of age as it would entail that commercial agents at the legal age of retirement would never be entitled to an indemnity or compensation, and would be automatically excluded from these rights, although in reality self-employed commercial agents are able to continue to work beyond retirement age.

7.5. Coherence with other policies

The Directive's objective of increasing cross-border activities of commercial representation is in line with the wider objective of the single market. Due to the nature of commercial agents and their principals, a Directive facilitating commercial representation also supports the Commission's SME policy. The analysis and consultation carried out during this report's preparation have not shown any possible conflicts with other policy fields.

8. Conclusions

The findings of this report allow for a relatively clear assessment of the key evaluation criteria and questions despite the limited availability of quantitative data and certain limitations regarding the representativeness of responses to the stakeholder and Member State consultations.

The Directive seems to have been effective in achieving its objective to facilitate cross-border operations in commercial representation. The costs of the Directive are limited and affordable and the Directive does not create administrative burden. At the same time, the Directive creates benefits in operational and commercial terms through facilitating cross-border activities. Thus, the Directive is efficient in terms of costs and benefits.

The Directive's objectives and its importance in maintaining a single market for commercial representation remain relevant today. On the basis of the available data, the commercial representation market has steadily grown in terms of turnover and employed people. Therefore, the Directive has an ongoing added value, remains fit-for-purpose in fulfilling its objective, and is coherent with other policies. If the Directive were to be withdrawn, there would be a risk of fragmentation and ensuing impediments to the single market for commercial representation.

On this basis, it is recommended that the Directive is maintained in its current form.

Annex 1

Procedural Information

In June 2014, then DG Internal Market and Services (now DG Internal Market, Industry, Entrepreneurship and SMEs) launched an evaluation of the Commercial Agents Directive. The evaluation of the Directive is part of the Commission's Agenda Planning (2015/GROW/042) and Work Programme (COM(2014) 910 final – Annex 3).

An inter-service group steering group was set up at the launch of the evaluation. The Secretariat-General, the Legal Service, DG Employment, Social Affairs & Inclusion and then DG Enterprise and Industry (now DG Internal Market, Industry, Entrepreneurship and SMEs) participated in the group. The group met twice during the evaluation process (11 June 2014 and 24 April 2015).

The evaluation was performed internally. Hard economic data to support the assessment has been difficult to find. Eurostat data for commercial representation is only available as of 2008. Other statistics and quantitative data on the commercial agents market covering the period before and after the Directive's adoption do not exist. This applies, in particular, to quantitative data for a comprehensive cost / benefit analysis of the Directive. There is limited academic literature. Therefore, the evaluation criteria and questions were assessed mostly qualitatively.

Annex 2

Information on the Respondents to the Stakeholder Consultation

The feedback to the stakeholder consultation has been summarised in the main text of this document. The following provides more information on the respondents to the public consultation. It analyses the respondents' answers to questions regarding the size of commercial agents and principal undertakings, what sector they are involved in, and the cross-border relationships of the relevant market actors. The first part presents the results for commercial agents and organisations representing commercial agents; the second part presents the results for the principals and organisations representing principals.

Information provided by commercial agents during the consultation
All commercial agents responding to the public consultation were SMEs, and 65 % of these were sole proprietors. 32 % of the responding SMEs had between two and nine employees and only 3 % had more than 10 people on staff.

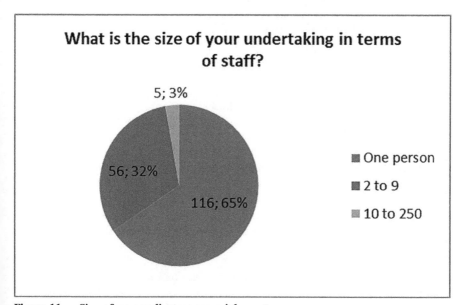

Figure 11 — Size of responding commercial agents

This picture is also confirmed by responses from organisations representing commercial agents. Austrian and German associations estimate that around 65 % of commercial agents are sole proprietors and the rest are SMEs. Similar estimates are made for France. In the UK, organisations estimate that 80 % are sole proprietors.

Commercial agents are primarily involved in business-to-business (B2B) transactions; only two commercial agents stated that they are primarily involved in business-to-consumer (B2C) transactions. Again, this picture of the market is confirmed by organisations representing commercial agents, with estimates of around 5–15 % of commercial agents being involved in the B2C sector.

83 % of commercial agents reported that they carry out cross-border activities. On average, cross-border business represents about 47 % of their total turnover. It is more common for commercial agents to operate cross-border within the EU than outside the EU. This has been confirmed by associations representing agents, with some variation between sectors.

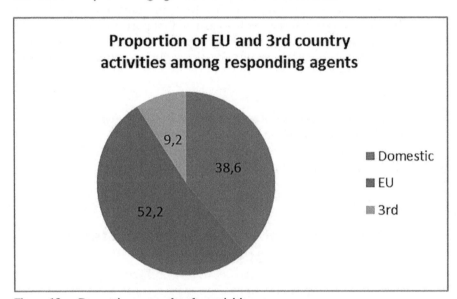

Figure 12 — **Domestic vs cross-border activities**

More or less all commercial agents and representatives of commercial agents agree that the market has developed positively during the last decades. Only four respondents consider the market to have been standing still or that turnover and the number of undertakings have decreased.

For example, the number of German commercial agents contracted by European manufacturers has doubled from 1984 to 2012, and in France the market increased by 5000 companies in 15 years, showing more than 14 % growth.

Information provided by principals during the consultation
The principals responding to the consultation are mainly SMEs, with only two companies that have more than 250 staff. Most organisations estimate

that about 90 % of the companies that use the services of commercial agents are SMEs. There is however some sectorial variation. In the German petrol station market, for example, two thirds of principals are estimated to be large multinational oil companies.

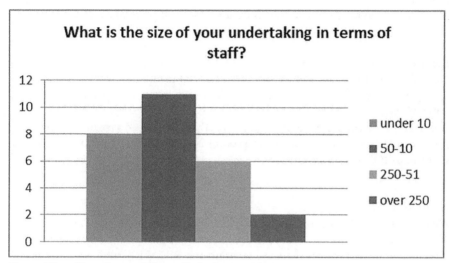

Figure 13 — Size of responding principal enterprises

Principals and organisations representing principals mention sectors such as retail, fashion, gifts, furniture, media companies and publishers, household appliances and merchandise, cosmetics, cleaning products, food supplements, craft supplies, wine, bags, candles and accessories, jewellery and energy services as areas where commercial agents are used.

Out of 28 principals who provided data, 15 use commercial agents across borders, of which four use commercial agents outside the EU. The main reason for principals to use commercial agents is that commercial agents have local market knowledge and proximity to the customer, which can also make commercial agents an effective way to internationalise and reach other markets. Principals also mention that commercial agents allow them to avoid hiring employees, and therefore related costs such as social security. Finally, using commercial agents is seen as a way of ensuring good customer contacts and they have a stronger incentive to be effective, as their profits depend on it.

Annex 3

National Measures Transposing the Directive

Austria
Handelsvertretergesetz (published in Bundesgesetzblatt für die Republik Osterreich (BGBl.), Nr. 88/1993).

Belgium
Loi du 13/04/1995

Bulgaria
Търговски закон (published in Bulgarian Official Journal of 21.7.2006)

Cyprus
Νόμος 51(Ι)/1992 που προνοεί για τη ρύθμιση των σχέσεων μεταξύ εμπορικού αντιπροσώπου καιαντιπροσωπευομένου (Cyprus Gazette of 1992-07-03).

Ο Περί Ρύθμισης των Σχέσεων Εμπορικού Αντιπροσώπου και Αντιπροσωπευόμενου (Τροποποιητικός) Νόμος 149 (Ι) του 2000 (Cyprus Gazette of 2000-11-17).

Czech Republic
Zákon č. 513/1991 Sb., obchodní zákoník (published in Sbirka Zakonu CR of 18.12.1991).

Zákon č. 370/2000 Sb., kterým se mění zákon č. 513/1991 Sb., obchodní zákoník, ve znění pozdjších předpisů, zákon č. 358/1992 Sb., o notářích a jejich činnosti (notářský řád), ve znění pozdějších předpisů, zákon č. 15/1998 Sb., o Komisi pro cenné papíry a o změně a doplnění dalších zákonů, ve znění zákona č. 30/2000 Sb., zákon č. 200/1990 Sb., o přestupcích, ve znění pozdějších předpisů, zákon č. 99/1963 Sb., občanský soudní řád, ve znění pozdějších předpisů, a zákon č. 328/1991 Sb., o konkursu a vyrovnání, ve znění pozdějších předpisů (published in Sbirka Zakonu CR of 25.10.2000)

Zákon č. 554/2004 Sb., kterým se mění zákon č. 40/1964 Sb., občanský zákoník, ve znění pozdějších předpisů, zákon č. 99/1963 Sb.,občanský soudní řád, ve znění pozdějších předpisů, zákon č. 358/1992 Sb., o notářích a jejich činnosti (notářský řád), ve znění pozdějších předpisů, zákon č. 513/1991 Sb., obchodní zákoník, ve znění pozdějších předpisů, a zákon č. 337/1992 Sb., o správě daní a poplatků, ve znění pozdějších předpisů (published in Sbirka Zakonu CR of 9.11.2004).

Zákon č. 89/2012 Sb., občanský zákoník ((published in Sbirka Zakonu CR of 22.3.2012).

Germany
Gesetz zur Durchführung der EG-Richtlinie zur Koordinierung des Rechts der Handelsvertreter vom 23/10/1989 (Bundesgesetzblatt Teil I vom 31/10/1989, Seite 1910).

Denmark
Lov nr. 272 af 02/05/1990 (Lovtidende A af 03/05/1990).

Estonia

Võlaõigusseadus n° 720389 (Elektrooniline Riigi Teataj num. RT I 2004, 37, 255).

Greece

Νόμοςαριθ. 9219 of 18.5.1991.

Spain

Ley número 12/92 de 27/05/1992, sobre Contrato de Agencia. [Boletín Oficial del Estado número 129 de 29/05/1992 Página 18314 (Marginal 12347)].

Finland

Laki kauppaedustajista ja myyntimiehistä (417/92) 08/05/1992

France

Loi n° 91-593 du 25.6.1991.

Croatia

Zakon o obveznim odnosima (Official Journal num. 35/05 of 17.3.2005).

Zakon o izmjenama i dopunama Zakona o obveznim odnosima (Official Journal num. 41/08 of 9.4.2008).

Hungary

2000. évi CXVII. törvény az önálló kereskedelmi ügynöki szerződésről (Magyar Közlöny of 2000-11-22 pages 7139-7144 num. 2000/113)

1959. évi IV. törvény a Magyar Köztársaság Polgári Törvénykönyvéről (Magyar Közlöny du 1959-08-11)

1952. évi III. törvény a polgári perrendtartásról (Magyar Közlöny of 1952-06-06 pages 00422-00495 num. 48).

Ireland

European Communities (Commercial Agents) Regulations, 1994. Statutory Instruments number 33 of 1994

European Communities (Commercial Agents) Regulations, 1997. Statutory Instruments number 31 of 1997

Italy

Decreto legislativo del 10/09/1991 n. 303, attuazione della direttiva n. 86/653/ CEE relativa al coordinamento dei diritti degli Stati membri concernenti gli

agenti commerciali indipendenti, a norma dell'art. 15 della legge 29 dicembre 1990, n. 428 (Legge comunitaria 1990),
Supplemento ordinario n. 57 alla Gazzetta Ufficiale — Serie generale — del 20/09/1991 n. 221 pag. 11.
Decreto legislativo of 15.2.1999 (published in GURI of 19.3.1999).

Lithuania

Lietuvos Respublikos civilinio kodekso patvirtinimo, įsigaliojimo ir įgyvendinimo įstatymas Nr. VIII — 1864
Lietuvos Respublikos civilinio kodekso 1.3, 2.55, 2.61, 2.72, 2.79, 2.112, 2.152, 2.160, 2.167, 4.176, 6.292, 6.298, 6.299, 6.747, 6.748.6.751, 6.753 straipsnių pakeitimo ir papildymo įstatymas Nr. IX-2172

Luxemburg

Loi du 03/07/1994 portant organisation des relations entre les agents commerciaux indépendants et leurs commettants et portant transposition de la directive du Conseil 86/653/CEE du 18/12/1986. Mémorial Grand-Ducal A Numéro 58 du 06/07/1994 Page 1088
Loi du 17/06/1992 relative 1) aux comptes annuels et comptes consolidés des établissements de crédit de droit luxembourgeois, 2) aux obligations en matière de publicité des documents comptables des succursales d'établissements de crédit et d'établissements financiers de droit étranger. Mémorial Grand-Ducal A Numéro 39 du 19/06/1992 Page 1184.

Latvia

Komerclikums (Latvijas Vēstnesis du 2000-05-04 pages num. 158/160).

Malta
Act of 5.1.2004

CHAPTER 13 COMMERCIAL CODE Part IV OF PRESCRIPTION AND INADMISSIBILITY OF ACTION IN CERTAIN COMMERCIAL MATTERS, OF THE JURISDICTION OF THE CIVIL COURT, FIRST HALL, AND OF COMMERCIAL FEES (The Malta government gazette of 1933-08-03)

The Netherlands

Wet van 05/07/1989 (PBEG Landbouwschap 382/17) (Herziening van dbepalingen inzake de agentuurovereenkomst), Staatsblad nummer 312 van 1989.

Poland

Ustawa z 23 kwietnia 1964 Kodeks Cywilny (Dziennik Ustaw du 1964-05-18 pages num. 1964/16/93).

Portugal

Decreto-Lei n. 178/86 de 03/07/1986. Regulamenta o contrato de agência ou representação comercial. Diário da Republica I Série n. 150 de 03/07/1986 Página 1575.

Decreto-Lei n. 118/93 de 13/04/1993. Altera o regime jurídico do contrato de agência. Diário da República I Série A n. 86 de 13/04/1993 Página 1818.

Romania

Lege privind agenţii comerciali permanenţi (Official Journal of 2002-08-06 num. 581).

Sweden

Lag om handelsagentur, Svensk författningssamling SFS) 1991:351

Slovenia

Obligacijski zakonik (Uradni list RS du 2001-10-25 pages 08345-08442 num. 83/2001).

Zakon o nepremičninskem posredovanju (Uradni list RS du 2003-05-09 pages 4793-4799 num. 42/2003)

Slovakia

Zákon č. 513/1991 Zb. Obchodný zakonnik (Zbierka zákonov SR du 1991-12-18).

Zákon č. 500/2001 Z. z., ktorým sa mení a dopĺňa Obchodný zákonník v znení neskorších predpisov (Zbierka zákonov SR du 2001-12-05 pages 5238-5283 num. 200). Act 500/2001 — Relevant provisions §§652-672a of the Commercial Code.

UK

The Commercial Agents (Council Directive) Regulations 1993. Statutory Instruments number 3053 of 1993

The Commercial Agents Ordinance, Legal Notice No 9 of 1994, First Supplement to the Gibraltar Gazette No 2 801 of 1994.

Annex 4

Case Law Related to the Directive

The Court of Justice of the EU replied to preliminary questions of national jurisdictions in the following twelve cases.

Case C-104/95, Kontogeorgas

1. *The first indent of Article 7(2) of Council Directive 86/653/EEC of 18 December 1986 on the coordination of the laws of the Member States relating to self-employed commercial agents must be interpreted as meaning that, where a commercial agent is responsible for a geographical area, he is entitled to commission on transactions concluded with customers belonging to that area, even if they were concluded without any action on his part.*

2. *Article 7(2) of Directive 86/653 must be interpreted to the effect that the meaning of the term `customer belonging to that area' must be determined, where the customer is a legal person, by the place where the latter actually carries on its commercial activities. Where a company carries on its commercial activity in various places, or where the agent operates in several areas, other factors may be taken into account to determine the centre of gravity of the transaction effected, in particular the place where negotiations with the agent took place or should, in the normal course of events, have taken place, the place where the goods were delivered and the place where the establishment which placed the order is located.*

Case C-215/97, Bellone

Council Directive 86/653/EEC of 18 December 1986 on the coordination of the laws of the Member States relating to self-employed commercial agents precludes a national rule which makes the validity of an agency contract conditional upon the commercial agent being entered in the appropriate register.

Case C-381/98, Ingmar

Articles 17 and 18 of Council Directive 86/653/EEC of 18 December 1986 on the coordination of the laws of the Member States relating to self-employed commercial agents, which guarantee certain rights to commercial agents after termination of agency contracts, must be applied where the commercial agent carried on his activity in a Member State although the principal is established in a non-member country and a clause of the contract stipulates that the contract is to be governed by the law of that country.

Case C-456/98, Centrosteel

Council Directive 86/653/EEC of 18 December 1986 on the coordination of the laws of the Member States relating to self-employed commercial agents precludes national legislation which makes the validity of an agency contract conditional upon the commercial agent being entered in the appropriate register. The national court is bound, when applying provisions of domestic law predating or postdating the said Directive, to interpret those provisions, so far as possible, in the light of the wording and purpose of the Directive, so that those provisions are applied in a manner consistent with the result pursued by the Directive.

Case C-485/01, Caprini

The answer to the question submitted must therefore be that, on a proper reading, the Directive does not preclude national legislation from making registration of a commercial agent in the register of undertakings subject to that agent's enrolment in a register provided for that purpose, on condition that non-registration in the register of undertakings does not affect the validity of an agency contract which that agent has concluded with his principal or that the consequences of such non-registration do not adversely affect in any other way the protection which that directive confers on commercial agents in their relations with their principals.

Case C-85/03, Mavrona

Council Directive 86/653/EEC of 18 December 1986 on the coordination of the laws of the Member States relating to self-employed commercial agents must be interpreted as meaning that persons, who act on behalf of a principal, but in their own name, do not come within the scope of that directive.

Case C-3/04, Poseidon

Article 1(2) of Council Directive 86/653/EEC of 18 December 1986 on the coordination of the laws of the Member States relating to self-employed commercial agents is to be interpreted as meaning that, where a self-employed intermediary had authority to conclude a single contract, subsequently extended over several years, the condition laid down by that provision that the authority be continuing requires that the principal should have conferred continuing authority on that intermediary to negotiate successive extensions to that contract.

Case C-465/04, Honyvem

1. *Article 19 of Council Directive 86/653/EEC of 18 December 1986 on the coordination of the laws of the Member States relating to self-employed commercial agents must be interpreted as meaning that the indemnity for termination of contract which results from the application of Article 17(2) of the Directive cannot be replaced, pursuant to a collective agreement, by an indemnity determined in accordance with criteria other than those prescribed by Article 17, unless it is established that the application of such an agreement guarantees the commercial agent, in every case, an indemnity equal to or greater than that which results from the application of Article 17.*

2. *Within the framework prescribed by Article 17(2) of Directive 86/653, the Member States enjoy a margin of discretion which they may exercise, in particular, in relation to the criterion of equity.*

Case C-19/07, Chevassus

The first indent of Article 7(2) of Directive 86/653/EEC of 18 December 1986 on the coordination of the laws of the Member States relating to self-employed commercial agents must be interpreted as meaning that a commercial agent entrusted with a specific geographical area does not have the right to a commission for transactions concluded by customers belonging to that area with a third party without any action, direct or indirect, on the part of the principal.

Case C-348/07 Turgay Semen

1. *Article 17(2)(a) of Council Directive 86/653/EEC of 18 December 1986 on the coordination of the laws of the Member States relating to self-employed*

commercial agents is to be interpreted to the effect that it is not possible automatically to limit the indemnity to which a commercial agent is entitled by the amount of commission lost as a result of the termination of the agency contract, even though the benefits which the principal continues to derive have to be given a higher monetary value.

2.   *Article 17(2)(a) of Directive 86/653 is to be interpreted to the effect that, where the principal belongs to a group of companies, benefits accruing to other companies of that group are not, in principle, deemed to be benefits accruing to the principal and, consequently, do not necessarily have to be taken into account for the purposes of calculating the amount of indemnity to which a commercial agent is entitled.*

Case C-203/09, Volvo

Article 18(a) of Council Directive 86/653/EEC of 18 December 1986 on the coordination of the laws of the Member States relating to self-employed commercial agents precludes a self-employed commercial agent from being deprived of his goodwill indemnity where the principal establishes a default by that agent which occurred after notice of termination of the contract was given but before the contract expired and which was such as to justify immediate termination of the contract in question.

C-184/12, Unamar — Judgment of 17 October 2013

Articles 3 and 7(2) of the Convention on the law applicable to contractual obligations opened for signature in Rome on 19 June 1980 must be interpreted as meaning that the law of a Member State of the European Union which meets the minimum protection requirements laid down by Council Directive 86/653/EEC of 18 December 1986 on the coordination of the laws of the Member States relating to self-employed commercial agents and which has been chosen by the parties to a commercial agency contract may be rejected by the court of another Member State before which the case has been brought in favour of the law of the forum, owing to the mandatory nature, in the legal order of that Member State, of the rules governing the situation of self-employed commercial agents, only if the court before which the case has been brought finds, on the basis of a detailed assessment, that, in the course of that transposition, the legislature of the State of the forum held it to be crucial, in the legal order concerned, to grant the commercial agent protection going beyond that provided for by that directive, taking account in that regard of the nature and of the objective of such mandatory provisions.

Two other cases (preliminary questions) were introduced in 2014 and they are still pending (Cases C-315/14 and C-338/14).

Appendix 3

Transcript of judgments

App3.1

Judgments – Lonsdale (t/a Lonsdale Agencies) (Appellant) v Howard & Hallam Limited (Respondents)

HOUSE OF LORDS
SESSION 2006-07
[2007] UKHL 32
on appeal from: [2006] EWCA Civ 63

OPINIONS
OF THE LORDS OF APPEAL
FOR JUDGMENT IN THE CAUSE
Lonsdale (t/a Lonsdale Agencies) (Appellant)
v
Howard & Hallam Limited (Respondents)
Appellate Committee
Lord Bingham of Cornhill
Lord Hoffmann
Lord Rodger of Earlsferry
Lord Carswell
Lord Neuberger of Abbotsbury
Counsel
Appellants:
Philip Moser
(Instructed by Morgan Cole, Oxford)
Respondents:
Oliver Segal
(Instructed by Harvey Ingram LLP, Leicester)
Interveners
Fergus Randolph
Ms Victoria Wakefield
(Instructed by APP Law on behalf of Winemakers' Federation of Australia)

Hearing dates:
16 and 17 May 2007
ON
WEDNESDAY 4 JULY 2007

HOUSE OF LORDS
OPINIONS OF THE LORDS OF APPEAL FOR JUDGMENT IN THE CAUSE
Lonsdale (t/a Lonsdale Agencies) (Appellant) v Howard & Hallam Limited (Respondents)
[2007] UKHL 32

LORD BINGHAM OF CORNHILL

My Lords,
1.   I have had the advantage of reading in draft the opinion of my noble and learned friend Lord Hoffmann. I am in full agreement with it, and for the reasons which he gives would dismiss the appeal and decline the appellant's request that a question be referred to the Court of Justice of the European Communities.

LORD HOFFMANN

My Lords,
2.   Mr Graham Lonsdale is a commercial agent in the shoe trade. On behalf of his principals he travels around his territory with catalogues and samples, calling on retailers and attending exhibitions. In 1990 Howard & Hallam Ltd ('H & H'), shoe manufacturers of Leicester, appointed him to sell their Elmdale brand in south-east England. A few years later he was appointed by a German manufacturer to sell their Wendel brand in a slightly larger territory.
3.   Wendel seems to have sold well and by 2000 accounted for two-thirds of Mr Lonsdale's business. Elmdale, on the other hand, was in terminal decline. Like many UK shoe manufacturers, H & H were unable to compete on style and price. Sales, and with them Mr Lonsdale's commission income, fell year by year. In 1997–1998 his gross commission was almost £17,000 but by 2002-2003 it had fallen to £9,621. In 2003 H & H ceased trading and sold the goodwill of the Elmdale brand to a competitor. There were no express terms about the termination of his agency – indeed, there was no written agreement at all. The agency was therefore terminable by reasonable notice. H & H gave Mr Lonsdale six months' notice. This is agreed to have been reasonable. He has been paid the commission on the sales which he generated. So he has no further contractual entitlement.
4.   Mr Lonsale has however a statutory entitlement to compensation under the Commercial Agents (Council Directive) Regulations 1993, which was made to give effect to Council Directive 86/653/EEC of 18 December 1986 on the coordination of the laws of the Member States relating to self-employed commercial agents. As the relevant regulations reproduce the language of the directive, it will be simpler to go straight to the directive.

It contains a number of provisions about commercial agents but we are concerned only with article 17, which deals with the termination of the agency contract:

Article 17

1.   Member States shall take the measures necessary to ensure that the commercial agent is, after termination of the agency contract, indemnified in accordance with paragraph 2 or compensated for damage in accordance with paragraph 3.

2.   (a)   The commercial agent shall be entitled to an indemnity if and to the extent that:

–   he has brought the principal new customers or has significantly increased the volume of business with existing customers and the principal continues to derive substantial benefits from the business with such customers, and

–   the payment of this indemnity is equitable having regard to all the circumstances and, in particular, the commission lost by the commercial agent on the business transacted with such customers. Member States may provide for such circumstances also to include the application or otherwise of a restraint of trade clause, within the meaning of Article 20;

(b)   The amount of the indemnity may not exceed a figure equivalent to an indemnity for one year calculated from the commercial agent's average annual remuneration over the preceding five years and if the contract goes back less than five years the indemnity shall be calculated on the average for the period in question;

(c)   The grant of such an indemnity shall not prevent the commercial agent from seeking damages.

3.   The commercial agent shall be entitled to compensation for the damage he suffers as a result of the termination of his relations with the principal.

Such damage shall be deemed to occur particularly when the termination takes place in circumstances:

–   depriving the commercial agent of the commission which proper performance of the agency contract would have procured him whilst providing the principal with substantial benefits linked to the commercial agent's activities,

–   and/or which have not enabled the commercial agent to amortize the costs and expenses that he had incurred for the performance of the agency contract on the principal's advice.

4.   Entitlement to the indemnity as provided for in paragraph 2 or to compensation for damage as provided for under paragraph 3, shall also arise where the agency contract is terminated as a result of the commercial agent's death.

    5.   The commercial agent shall lose his entitlement to the indemnity in the instances provided for in paragraph 2 or to compensation for damage in the instances provided for in paragraph 3, if within one year following termination of the contract he has not notified the principal that he intends pursuing his entitlement.

    6.   The Commission shall submit to the Council, within eight years following the date of notification of this Directive, a report on the implementation of this Article, and shall if necessary submit to it proposals for amendments.

5.   It will be noticed that although the purpose of the directive is said to be the coordination of the laws of the Member States relating to self-employed commercial agents, article 17 allows Member States to choose between two different rights, one or other of which must be accorded to a commercial agent on the termination of the agency. He must be given a right to either an indemnity in accordance with article 17(2) or compensation in accordance with article 17(3). The English words 'indemnity' and 'compensation' are not very illuminating in marking the distinction between these two rights. They are both ways of dealing with the unfairness which it was thought might arise if the termination of the agency leaves the agent worse off and the principal better off than if the agency had continued. It appears that the right under article 17(2), which the draftsman has chosen to label 'indemnity', is derived from German law and is now contained in section 89b of the *Handelsgesetzbuch*. The right to 'compensation' under article 17(3) is derived from French law and is now contained in article 12 of the *Loi no 91–593 du 25 juin 1991 relative aux rapports entre les agents commerciaux et leurs mandants*. The two systems can plainly lead to different results, so that, on this point at any rate, the extent of the coordination achieved by the directive is modest.

6.   The United Kingdom chose both systems, in the sense that it allowed the parties to opt for an indemnity under article 17(2) but provided that in default of agreement the agent should be entitled to compensation under article 17(3): see regulation 17(2). In the present case the parties made no choice and Mr Lonsdale is therefore entitled to compensation under article 17(3).

7.   The question in this appeal is how the compensation should be determined. But for this purpose it is necessary first to decide exactly what the agent should be compensated for. Only then can one proceed to consider how the compensation should be calculated.

8.   On this first question the directive is explicit. The agent is entitled to be compensated for 'the damage he suffers as a result of the termination of his relations with the principal.' In other words, the agent is treated as having lost something of value as a result of the termination and is entitled to compensation for this loss.

9.   As this part of the directive is based on French law, I think that one is entitled to look at French law for guidance, or confirmation, as to what it means. Article 12 of the French law says that the agent is entitled to 'une indemnité compensatrice en réparation du préjudice subi'. The French

jurisprudence from which the terms of the article is derived appears to regard the agent as having had a share in the goodwill of the principal's business which he has helped to create. The relationship between principal and agent is treated as having existed for their common benefit. They have co-operated in building up the principal's business: the principal by providing a good product and the agent by his skill and effort in selling. The agent has thereby acquired a share in the goodwill, an asset which the principal retains after the termination of the agency and for which the agent is therefore entitled to compensation: see *Saintier and Scholes,* Commercial Agents and the Law (2005) at pp 175–177.

10. This elegant theory explains why the French courts regard the agent as, in principle, entitled to compensation. It does not, however, identify exactly what he is entitled to compensation for. One possibility might have been to value the total goodwill of the principal's business and then to try to attribute some share to the agent. But this would in practice be a hopeless endeavour and the French courts have never tried to do it. Instead, they have settled upon compensating him for what he has lost by being deprived of his business. That is the *'préjudice subi.'* The French case law makes it clear that this ordinarily involves placing a value upon the right to be an agent. That means, primarily, the right to future commissions 'which proper performance of the agency contract would have procured him': see *Saintier and Scholes, op.cit,* pp. 187–188. In my opinion this is the right for which the directive requires the agent to be compensated.

11. Having thus determined that the agent is entitled to be compensated for being deprived of the benefit of the agency relationship, the next question is how that loss should be calculated. The value of the agency relationship lies in the prospect of earning commission, the agent's expectation that 'proper performance of the agency contract' will provide him with a future income stream. It is this which must be valued.

12. Like any other exercise in valuation, this requires one to say what could reasonably have been obtained, at the date of termination, for the rights which the agent had been enjoying. For this purpose it is obviously necessary to assume that the agency would have continued and the hypothetical purchaser would have been able properly to perform the agency contract. He must be assumed to have been able to take over the agency and (if I may be allowed the metaphor) stand in the shoes of the agent, even if, as a matter of contract, the agency was not assignable or there were in practice no dealings in such agencies: compare *Inland Revenue Commissioners v Crossman* [1937] AC 26. What has to be valued is the income stream which the agency would have generated.

13. On the other hand, as at present advised, I see no reason to make any other assumptions contrary to what was the position in the real world at the date of termination. As one is placing a present value upon future income, one must discount future earnings by an appropriate rate of interest. If the agency was by its terms or in fact unassignable, it must be assumed, as I have said, that the hypothetical purchaser would have been entitled to take it over. But there is no basis for assuming that he

would then have obtained an assignable asset: compare the *Crossman* case. Likewise, if the market for the products in which the agent dealt was rising or declining, this would have affected what a hypothetical purchaser would have been willing to give. He would have paid fewer years' purchase for a declining agency than for one in an expanding market. If the agent would have had to incur expense or do work in earning his commission, it cannot be assumed that the hypothetical purchaser would have earned it gross or without having to do anything.

14.   Mr Philip Moser, who appeared for Mr Lonsdale, objected that this method of calculation was likely to produce less than he would have been awarded by a French court. And it does appear that it is common practice for French courts to value agencies at twice the average annual gross commission over the previous three years. Mr Moser said that in stipulating that agents should receive compensation under article 17(3), the directive was adopting the French practice as Community law. This, he said, was confirmed by the report on the application of article 17 (COM(96) 364 final) which the Commission, pursuant to article 17(6), had issued in 1996. It noted that a body of case law had developed in France concerning the level of compensation. By 'judicial custom', this was fixed as two years' commission, which, they said 'conforms with commercial practice'. However, the courts retained a discretion to award less when 'the agent's loss was in fact less.' The report said that in France the directive had made no difference: 'pre-existing jurisprudence has continued to be applied.' In England, however, there had been difficulties of interpretation. There was, at that stage, no case law but 'the parties in practice are attempting to apply common law principles'. In particular, it was difficult to see how these principles would enable the courts to reach the figure of twice gross commission which was regularly awarded by French courts. The Commission said that there was 'a need for clarification' of article 17. But nothing has been done about it.

15.   Mr Moser invited your Lordships to treat the Commission as having indorsed the French method of calculating compensation under article 17(3) as the appropriate interpretation of that article as a Community instrument. It would follow that all Member States which adopt article 17(3) would be bound to treat twice gross commission as the normal compensation for termination of an agency, subject to variation in exceptional cases in which the principal could prove that the actual loss was less or the agent could prove that it was more. If your Lordships did not accept this as the plain and obvious meaning of the directive, he submitted that the question should be referred to the Court of Justice.

16.   My Lords, I do not accept this submission, to which I think there are at least three answers. First, the Commission report was not indorsing any method of calculation as a true reflection of Community law. That was not its function. The Commission was required by article 17(6) to report on the implementation of the Article, and, if necessary, to submit proposals for amendments. It reported on the basis of information supplied by Member States and noted that the UK position (so far as

it could be ascertained in the absence of any judicial pronouncement) was different from the French. But there is no suggestion that either approach would fail to implement the directive.

17. Secondly, the provisions of article 17(3) which say what the agent is entitled to be compensated for are perfectly plain. It is the damage which he suffers as a result of the termination. The French domestic law, as I have pointed out, says exactly the same. Where French and English courts differ is in the method by which that damage is calculated. But the Court of Justice has made it clear that the method of calculation is a matter for each Member State to decide. In *Case C-465/04 Honeyvem Informazioni Commerciali Srl v Mariella De Zotti* [2006] ECR I-02879 at paragraphs 34-36 the Court of Justice said:

> '34. . . . It must be observed that although the system established by article 17 of the Directive is mandatory and prescribes a framework . . . it does not give any detailed indications as regards the method of calculation of the indemnity for termination of contract.
>
> 35. The Court thus held that, within that framework, the Member States may exercise their discretion as to the choice of methods for calculating the indemnity [Case C-381/98 *Ingmar GB Ltd v Eaton Leonard Technologies Inc* [2000] ECR I-9305 at paragraph 21]
>
> 36. Therefore . . . within the framework prescribed by article 17(2) of the Directive, the Member States enjoy a margin of discretion which they may exercise. . .'

18. Thirdly, it seems that commercial agencies in France operate in market conditions which are different from those prevailing in England. It would appear that in France agencies do change hands and that it is common for the premium charged on such a transaction to be twice the gross commission. Whether the judicial practice of estimating the value of the agency at twice gross commission is based upon this fact of French economic life or whether vendors of agency businesses are able to charge such a premium because the purchaser knows that he will be able to recover that amount, either from the next purchaser or from the principal on termination of the agency, is unclear. *Saintier and Scholes, op.cit,* at p. 187 describe it as a 'chicken-and-egg process'. There does seem to be evidence that some principals demand payment of an estimated twice gross commission in return for the grant of a commercial agency (even if they have to lend the agent the money) because they know that they will have to return this amount to the agent on termination. At any rate, whatever the origins of the practice, it would appear that twice gross commission is often the real value of an agency in France because that is what you could sell it for in the market. As the Commission significantly remarked, the French system 'conforms with commercial practice'. There is no such market in England. It would therefore appear that the difference between French and English practice exists not because their respective courts are applying different rules of law but because they are operating in different markets.

19. Mr Moser said that the adoption of anything less favourable to commercial agents than the French method of calculation would not give effect to the purpose of the directive, which is to protect the interests of the commercial agent. No doubt this is one of its purposes: in *Page v Combined Shipping and Trading Co Ltd* [1997] 3 All ER 656, 660 Staughton LJ said, with more than a touch of irony, that the directive appeared to be based upon a belief that 'commercial agents are a downtrodden race, and need and should be afforded protection against their principals.' But these are generalities which do not help one to decide what protection is sufficient to give effect to the policy of the directive. One may however obtain a useful cross-check by considering what an agent could obtain under a system which provided him with an indemnity, since there is no doubt that this too would satisfy the policy of the directive.

20. It is a condition of the indemnity that the agent should have 'brought the principal new customers or . . . significantly increased the volume of business with existing customers' and that the principal 'continues to derive substantial benefits from the business with such customers': article 17(2)(a). It follows that in a case such as the present, in which the principal went out of business and therefore derived no benefit from the customers introduced by the agent, no indemnity will be payable: see *Saintier and Scholes, op.cit,* at p. 204. In addition, article 17(2)(b) limits the indemnity to one year's commission. In the face of these provisions which will satisfy the policy of the directive, it is impossible to argue that it requires a payment of twice gross commission whether the principal has derived any benefit from the termination or not.

21. In my opinion, therefore, the courts of the United Kingdom would not be acting inconsistently with the directive if they were to calculate the compensation payable under article 17(3) by reference to the value of the agency on the assumption that it continued: the amount which the agent could reasonably expect to receive for the right to stand in his shoes, continue to perform the duties of the agency and receive the commission which he would have received. It remains to consider some of the English and Scottish cases in which the question has been discussed.

22. The decision of the Court of Session in *King v Tunnock Ltd* 2000 SC 424 is the only appellate case containing a full discussion of the way compensation should be calculated. Mr King sold cakes and biscuits for Tunnock Ltd. He had taken over the agency from his father in 1962. It was his full time occupation. In 1994 the company closed its bakery and terminated the agency. The evidence was that over the previous two years he had earned gross commission amounting in total to £27,144. The sheriff held that he was not entitled to compensation because the principal, having closed the business, would not enjoy any benefits from the goodwill generated by the agent. But an Extra Division of the Court of Session reversed this interlocutor and awarded compensation in the sum of £27,144.

23. I respectfully think that the sheriff was right. In view of the closure of the business, the agency was worth nothing. No one would have given anything for the right to earn future commission on the sales of cakes and biscuits because there would be none to be sold. Nor had the principal retained any goodwill which the agent had helped to build up. The goodwill disappeared when the business closed. The reason why the business closed is not altogether clear but Mr King's low earnings for full time work over the previous two years suggests that it was not doing well. Even if one assumes that commission would have continued at the same rate, it is hard to see why anyone should have paid for the privilege of a full time job which earned him less than he would have been paid as a bus conductor.

24. I am bound to say that I do not find the reasoning of the Extra Division, delivered by Lord Caplan, at all convincing. He said that the agency had existed for many years and that it was likely that the agent had good relations with customers. That, no doubt, was true. But Lord Caplan then went on to say:

> 'In these circumstances we consider it likely that the pursuer would have expected and required a relatively high level of compensation to surrender his successful and long-established agency. The compensation would, of course, require to be tied to the commission he was earning. Thus this is a case where we can conclude, even on the limited information that is available, that the agent would have expected to receive a capital sum representing at least the total for the last two years of his earnings to be paid before he would voluntarily have given up his agency.'

25. '[He] would have expected to receive . . .'. I daresay he might. But would anyone have given it to him? Lord Caplan does not seem to have considered it relevant to ask. It appears that, following *King v Tunnock Ltd*, it is standard practice for the former agent to give evidence of what he would have expected to receive for his agency. In this case, Mr Lonsdale said in a witness statement that he had been advised by an accountant that an established method of valuation was to take the gross profits and multiply them by two and a half. For the last completed accounting year before closure his gross commission was £12,239.34 and he therefore valued the business at £30,598.35.

26. Mr Lonsdale at least claimed to have the support of an accountant for his valuation, although he did not call him as a witness. But the Court of Session appears to have arrived at the figure of twice gross commission without any evidence at all. Lord Caplan said that he was 'reassured' that this would be standard compensation in France, but, for the reasons I have explained, the French practice is of no evidential value whatever.

27. *King v Tunnock Ltd* was considered by Judge Bowers (sitting as a High Court judge) in *Barrett McKenzie v Escada (UK) Ltd* [2001] EuLR 567. The judge was not attracted by the formulaic approach of the Court of Session but said (at p. 575) that the point on which he agreed with Lord Caplan was that —

'one is valuing the agency and its connections that have been established by the agent at the time at or immediately before termination, and it is really a question of compensating for the notional value of that agency in the open market . . . .'

28. I agree that this is what compensation in article 17(3) means. My only caution is that one must be careful about the word 'notional'. All that is notional is the assumption that the agency was available to be bought and sold at the relevant date. What it would fetch depends upon circumstances as they existed in the real world at the time: what the earnings prospects of the agency were and what people would have been willing to pay for similar businesses at the time.

29. In *Tigana Ltd v Decoro* [2003] EuLR 189 the judge awarded the agent a sum equal to his commission less expenses over the 14 to 15 months during which the agency had subsisted. I would agree that prima facie the value of the agency should be fixed by reference to its net earnings because, as a matter of common sense, that is what will matter to the hypothetical purchaser. Furthermore, in the case of an agent who has more than one agency, the costs must be fairly attributed to each. He cannot simply say, as Mr Lonsdale did in this case, that the marginal cost of the Elmdale agency was little or nothing because he had to see the same customers and go to the same exhibitions for Wendel.

30. It may well be that 14 months commission adopted by the judge was a fair valuation. But he seems to have had no evidence that anyone would have paid this figure for a comparable business. Instead, he gave (at p. 221) a non-exhaustive list of 14 factors ((a) to (n)), some of them very wide ranging indeed, which he said would require consideration. The list gives no indication of the weight to be attributed to each factor.

31. More recently, in *Smith, Bailey Palmer v Howard & Hallam Ltd* [2006] EuLR 578 Judge Overend (sitting as a High Court judge) dealt with claims by other agents who had worked for the respondent in this case. He noted that the Elmdale brand had been sold to a competitor for £550,000 and that, over the three years before the sale, 42% of the sales and distribution expenses had consisted of agent's commission. On these figures, he considered that it would be right to attribute 42% of the value of the brand to the agents. This seems to me a flawed method of calculation. First, it treats the entire value of the brand, ie the goodwill of the Elmdale name, as attributable to sales and marketing. No allowance is made for the possibility that some of the goodwill may have been attributable to the fact that the company made good shoes. Secondly, no allowance is made for the fact that the commission, which is treated as the measure of the proprietary interest of the agents in the assets of the company, is what the agents were actually paid for their services. On this theory, the advertising agents should have acquired an interest proportionate to what they were paid. Thirdly, the valuation is based entirely on cost rather than what anyone would actually have paid for the agency.

32. That brings me to the judgments in the present case. The claim was heard by Judge Harris QC in the Oxford County Court and his judgment was, if I may respectfully say so, a model of clarity and common sense. I shall extract one or two of the most important passages:

    '18. If it is kept in mind that the damage for which the agent is to be compensated consists in the loss of the value or goodwill he can be said to have possessed in the agency, then it can be seen that valuation ought to be reasonably straightforward. Small businesses of all kinds are daily being bought and sold, and a major element in the composition of their price will be a valuation of goodwill.

    19. But neither side put evidence before the court about how commercial goodwill is conventionally valued. Nor was I told upon what basis claims of this type are conventionally settled. There was no evidence at all about how commercially to value such assets. It is of course for the claimant, as a seeker of compensation, to prove the value of what he has lost.'

33. The judge then found that net commission was running at about £8,000 a year and said:

    '20. ...T he value of that agency, the commercial value is what someone would pay for it; to acquire by assignment a business vehicle with a likely net annual income of £8,000 . . .

    22. Commonsense would indicate that few people wanting the opportunity to earn what the claimant was earning would be prepared to pay well over £20,000 for the privilege of doing so, still less would they do so in an industry in remorseless decline, and in which the likely buyers would be men of modest means . . .

    23. Given the absence of evidence about how commercially to value goodwill, or evidence about what price in practice might have been available, the court might be thought to be justified in simply finding that the claimant has failed to prove his case . . .

    30. This was an agency producing a modest and falling income in a steadily deteriorating environment. There is no evidence that anyone would have paid anything to buy it . . . I am strongly tempted to find that no damage has been established . . . But perhaps that conclusion, though I regard it as logical, is a little over rigorous given that the defendant has already made a payment. Doing the best I can, I find that the appropriate figure for compensation is one of £5,000.'

34. The Court of Appeal approved of this approach. After a thorough review of the authorities, Moore-Bick LJ quoted paragraph 18 of the judgment (see above) and said that the judge was right in his approach. I agree. Furthermore, I do not think that the judge could have been faulted if he had simply dismissed the claim.

35.   That is sufficient to dispose of the appeal, but there are three additional comments to be made. First, Mr Moser urged your Lordships not to adopt a principle which required valuation evidence. Valuations, he said, were expensive and most claims were too small to justify the cost. Moore-Bick LJ said (at paragraph 57) that 'in most cases' the court would be likely to benefit from the assistance of an expert witness but that in some cases it might be sufficient to place all the material before the court and invite the judge to act as valuer. It seems to me that once it is firmly understood that the compensation is for the loss of the value of the agency, relatively few cases will go to court. As Judge Harris said, small comparable businesses are bought and sold every day and it should not be difficult for the parties, with the benefit of advice about the going rate for such businesses, to agree on an appropriate valuation. It should not always be necessary for them to obtain a full scale valuation, involving the checking of income and expenditure figures and the application of the going rate to those figures. But I do not see how, if the matter does go to court, the judge can decide the case without some information about the standard methodology for the valuation of such businesses. In this case, the judge was simply invited to pluck a figure out of the air from across the Channel and rightly refused to do so. Nothing is more likely to cause uncertainty and promote litigation than a lottery system under which judges are invited to choose figures at random.

36.   It may also be possible, after a period of experience in such valuations, for the court to take judicial notice of what would be the going rate in what I might call the standard case, namely an agency which has continued for some time and in which the net commission figures are fairly stable. It should not be necessary to repeat boilerplate evidence in every case. But the judge must be reasonably confident that he is dealing with the standard case. Adjustments would be needed if, as in this case, the market was in decline or had disappeared altogether.

37.   Secondly, there is the question raised by the Winemakers' Federation of Australia Inc, who were given leave to intervene and made submissions. They are concerned about the case in which the agent is able to transfer the goodwill he has created with customers to another principal: for example, to persuade the supermarkets to whom he has been selling the produce of one winery to transfer to another. In such a case the former principal would not retain the goodwill which the agent had created and it would be unfair to have to pay compensation on the basis that the agent had gone out of business.

38.   In my opinion circumstances such as these will be reflected in the process of valuation. The hypothetical purchase of the agency does not involve an assumption that the agent gives a covenant against competition. If the situation in real life is that the hypothetical purchaser would be in competition with the former agent and could not have any assurance that the customers would continue to trade with him, that would affect the amount he was prepared to pay. If it appeared that all the customers

were likely to defect to the former agent (or, for that matter, to someone else), he would be unlikely to be prepared to pay much for the agency.

39. What matters, of course, is what would have appeared likely at the date of termination and not what actually happened afterwards. But I do not see think that the court is required to shut its eyes to what actually happened. It may provide evidence of what the parties were likely to have expected to happen.

40. Thirdly and finally, there is the question of whether a reference should be made to the European Court of Justice. Mr Moser says that the differences in opinion between the Scottish and the English courts and between various English judges show that the law is uncertain. That is true, but what is uncertain is not the meaning of the directive. It is clear that the agent is entitled to compensation for 'the damage he suffers as a result of the termination of his relations with the principal' and that the method by which that damage should be calculated is a discretionary matter for the domestic laws of the Member States. It is the way in which our domestic law should implement that discretion which has been uncertain and the resolution of that uncertainty is the task of this House and not the European Court of Justice.

41. I would therefore dismiss the appeal.

LORD RODGER OF EARLSFERRY
My Lords,

42. I have had the privilege of considering the speech of my noble and learned friend, Lord Hoffmann, in draft. I agree with it and, for the reasons he gives, I too would dismiss the appeal.

LORD CARSWELL
My Lords,

43. I have had the advantage of reading in draft the opinion prepared by my noble and learned friend Lord Hoffmann. For the reasons which he has given, and with which I fully agree, I too would dismiss the appeal and decline to make a reference.

LORD NEUBERGER OF ABBOTSBURY
My Lords,

44. I have had the privilege of reading in draft my noble and learned friend Lord Hoffmann's speech, with which I fully agree, and to which there is nothing I can usefully add. Accordingly, I too would dismiss this appeal.

App3.2

Tigana Limited v Decoro Limited [2003] EWHC 23 (QB)

High Court of Justice, Queen's Bench Division 3 February 2003

MR JUSTICE DAVIS:

Introduction

1. By a written Sales Agreement dated the 1st January 1999 and made between Decoro Limited ('Decoro': a company incorporated in Hong Kong) and Tigana Limited ('Tigana': a company incorporated in the Isle of Man) Decoro appointed 'Tigana' its sales representative for the purpose of procuring sales of Decora's leather furniture products in the United Kingdom and Eire, on the terms there set out. The initial term of the agreement was stated to be one year beginning on the 1st January 1999. There was provision for renewal for further yearly terms if the parties mutually so agreed. In the event there was no such further agreement and the Sales Agreement accordingly expired by effluxion of time on the 31st December 1999.

2. By its Claim Form, issued on the 20th September 2000, Tiganaclaims commission and compensation said to be due to it under the terms of the Sales Agreement and by reason of the application of the Commercial Agents (Council Directive) Regulations 1993 ('the Agency Regulations') which came into force on the 1st January 1994. The issues arising in this litigation include issues as to the true meaning and effect of certain of the Agency Regulations.

The background

3. The background facts, as I find them to be, are as follows.

(a)   Mr Coleman

4. Mr Stuart Coleman has since 1978 acted as a manufacturer's and seller's agent in the furniture business, with particular emphasis on the leather upholstery market. He became very well known in the trade in the United Kingdom and also had significant international connections. In the course of his business he had frequent dealings with major UK furniture groups such as DFS, Land of Leather, Queensway, Leatherland and many others. Mr Coleman's practice was to act on a commission basis for manufacturers (who were usually foreign based). His usual role was to seek to introduce the importer, and its goods, to prospective UK customers (who ordinarily would be retailers of considerable size or, sometimes, wholesalers) with a view to securing the placing of orders. Thereafter Mr Coleman would act as a point of contact between the importer and retailer, seeking to secure repeat or further orders, organising the necessary administration, ensuring that deliveries were made on time and helping to deal with any service and specification

problems that might arise. Mr Coleman (operating, as I understand, primarily from his home address) traded under the name Stuart Coleman and Associates. In most years, he was a sole trader but there were occasions, as he told me, when his wife was in partnership with him. He also employed between two and three administrative and secretarial staff to assist him in his work.

5. The nature of Mr Coleman's business involved frequent trips abroad: not only to international trade fairs but also to the factory premises of manufacturers with a view to inspecting their methods of manufacture and to assessing their products. Frequently Mr Coleman would be accompanied by buying representatives of existing or prospective UK customers. Nevertheless, customers (who in the first instance would have little more to go on than the manufacturer's brochure and product specifications) would place considerable reliance on Mr Coleman's own views as to the marketability of particular furniture products.

6. In 1998 Mr Coleman held five agencies, all of which had lasted for a number of years. One was for an Italian furniture manufacturer called Ital Design. Another (relatively recently taken on) was for an Italian leather furniture manufacturer called Calia/Maxim. A third agency was for a Dutch manufacturer called Hetanker; a fourth was for an Italian manufacturer, specialising in marble topped furniture, called Stone International; and a fifth was for another Italian manufacturer called Presotto. The turnover of each in the United Kingdom was quite significant; the largest being Ital Design, which was, in 1999, in the region of £4 million. In handling these agencies, Mr Coleman dealt with several of his contacts in the UK retail market. Not all required products from each of these manufacturers: although some took orders from more than one of them. On such orders Mr Coleman was paid a commission: the rate varied, depending on the nature of the product and whether it was a promotional or non-promotional sale. Although the commission might be as much as 10%, usually it was in the region of 5% (being in respect of promotional sales).

7. For the leather furniture industry the most important international trade fairs are those held at High Point, North Carolina, USA. Such fairs are held twice in each year, in April and October. Some manufacturers retain permanent show rooms at High Point.
    Tigana Limited v Decoro Limited 205

(b) *The introduction at High Point and subsequent events in 1998*

8. Mr Coleman (as was his practice) attended the High Point fair in October 1998. Before he went he had been told by an American agent, whom he had known for some time, that a new Chinese based company, with Italian backing, called Decoro had been taking the US leather furniture market by storm. Decoro was, and is, a company based in Hong Kong and China, with its manufacturing operations sited at Shenzhen in China. Mr Coleman, with his experience, was aware that the US leather furniture market was very different to the UK market: the preference in the USA,

for example, was inclined to large studded suites which was not the UK fashion. On the other hand, leather quality was not of prime importance to the UK market: and Mr Coleman also perceived that, for larger pieces, Chinese manufacturers with their lower labour costs could produce pieces at very favourable prices compared to, for example, Italian manufacturers. Moreover, Mr Coleman understood that, in Decoro, there would be the benefit of Italian know how and designs. Mr Coleman accordingly resolved to make contact with Decoro's representatives at the October 1998 fair, which took place between around the 18th and 24th October.

9.   This he did. He spoke to Mr Giovanni Pratti, Decoro's International Sales Director. Mr Pratti suggested that he return to speak to Mr Lucca Ricci, the president (and a shareholder) of Decoro. Later that day, Mr Coleman and Mr Ricci discussed the possibility of Mr Coleman's acting as Decoro's agent in the UK. The discussions ranged over model ranges, prices and production capacity. Mr Ricci was very keen on the proposal. The following day Mr Coleman introduced a number of UK corporate buyers to Mr Pratti and Mr Ricci, including representatives of Sterling Furniture, Dansk Design, Conroys and Cousens. Orders for some five containers of samples were taken. One buyer was heard to say, 'What's the catch?' reflecting his surprise at the perceived value of the product. In addition, Mr Coleman telephoned Mr Paul Briant, Managing Director of Land of Leather, from High Point. Land of Leather is one of the UK's largest leather furniture retailers. On the strength of Mr Coleman's recommendation, Mr Briant ordered some $40,000 worth of pieces, leaving it to Mr Coleman to select the models and colour ranges.

10.   There is no doubt, and I find, that each of Mr Coleman and Mr Ricci and Mr Pratti was at this stage very keen on the prospect of Mr Coleman's acting as Decoro's UK agent. Mr Coleman considered that products of the quality and value which Decoro were manufacturing would be capable of finding a ready market in the UK and, as he saw it, he had the right connections to enable Decoro to break into that market. For its part, Decoro wanted to expand into the UK market: but, as I find, it had at that time no presence at all there and perceived itself as requiring just such a person as Mr Coleman to enable its products to be introduced to UK retailers and wholesalers.

11.   On his return to the UK from High Point, and before any formal agency contract had been agreed, Mr Coleman took steps to contact other potential customers in the UK whom (from his knowledge of them) he assessed as being likely to be interested in Decoro's products. These included Furniture Village, Barker & Stonehouse and Kingdom of Leather. All in due course placed orders. In addition Mr Coleman discussed Decoro's leather furniture with Julian Cox (a long-standing business contact) who was a director of Furnitureland. Furnitureland was to go on to become, for a while, Decoro's largest UK customer.

12.   The intention was that orders placed in October and November 1998 should catch the Christmas and New Year sales markets. At various stages

Mr Coleman communicated with the various customers, as well as with Decoro itself. Mr Coleman gave certain advice to Decoro, amongst other things concerning labelling requirements, referring to the Furniture and Furnishings (Fire)(Safety) Regulations 1988 (1988 SI No 1324).

(c)   The agency contract

13.   In the meantime, although orders were being solicited and placed with Decoro for the UK market, the terms of the proposed agency had not yet been finalised. At the initial meeting at High Point, Mr Ricci had proposed 2% for promotional models and 7% for highly priced models, those rates corresponding to the rates Decoro paid in the US market. Mr Coleman's counter proposal was 5% on promotional models and 10% on larger items. Mr Coleman made the point that Decoro maintained a US office whereas in the UK the administration would be undertaken by Mr Coleman who would bear the overheads. Nothing was finalised at this time.

14.   On 6th January 1999, Mr Coleman flew out to China via Hong Kong to visit Decoro. There were two reasons for the visit. The first was to introduce Mr Briant (of Land of Leather) and Mr O'Kane (another prospective customer) to Decoro and to enable them to view Decoro's operation: those two individuals accompanying Mr Coleman for that purpose. The second was to enable Mr Coleman to finalise the terms of the agency: which he discussed with Mr Ricci in Hong Kong.

15.   On his return from Hong Kong Mr Coleman wrote to Mr Ricci a letter dated 12th January 1999. The letter enclosed copies of orders placed by Land of Leather and also referred to orders to be placed by Mr O'Kane. The letter went on to say, amongst other things:

> 'As for our discussions regarding my contract
> 1)   I will have total exclusivity to promote your range in the UK. This covers England, Wales, Scotland, and Ireland south and north.
> 2)   5% commission will be paid on all models where the price of the 3.2.1 combination does not exceed dollars 1130. This also applies to part orders of items in these price points.
> 3)   the contract should run for one year with 3 months notice minimum on either side. European agents laws with an English Court jurisdiction . . .'

The letter went on to cover other points, including a proposal to convert a barn at Mr Coleman's premises in Stowmarket, Suffolk, with a view to displaying Decoro leather suites in conjunction with Stone International marble top tables. This letter, it may be observed, connotes that (as one would expect) Mr Coleman was aware of the Agency Regulations and also that he desired them to apply to the agency contract, and expressly alluded to them accordingly. However, although Mr Coleman expressly alluded to them, it would appear that Decoro did not consider such regulations (or, if it did, see fit to seek to modify their application to the proposed agency). It would seem that neither side took legal advice at this time.

16. On the 4th February 1999, Mr Ricci sent a draft Sales Agreement to Mr Coleman. This proposed rather lesser commission rates. It also provided that Mr Coleman should not during the period of the agency contract act as a representative for any competing products. Mr Coleman responded (having, in the interim, again referred to the European Law on Sales Agents): in particular he queried the proffered commission rates and also the 'no competition' provision, in view, in particular, of his agencies with Ital Design and Calia/Maxim. Mr Ricci in due course indicated agreement to the various revisions to the draft put forward by Mr Coleman. In the event there were further discussions between the parties in Hong Kong during March 1999 (on a further visit by Mr Coleman, with his wife). Also during those discussions Mr Coleman recommended that Decoro should apply to become a member of FIRA (The Furniture Industry Research Association), providing some literature in that regard including a Technical Data Sheet which referred to the 1988 Fire Safety Regulations.

17. As a result of those discussions the Sales Agreement was finalised. It was given the date of 1st January 1999 (being backdated for the purpose). The Agreement provides as follows:

'THIS AGREEMENT, made and entered into this the 1st day of January, 1999, by and between DECORO LTD, a Hong Kong Company (hereinafter referred to as the 'Company'), and **TIGANA** LTD (hereinafter referred to as 'Sales Representative').

In consideration of the mutual covenants, the parties hereby enter into the following Agreement:

1. **Duties. Term** Sales Representative agrees to sell for the Company in the Capacity of Sales Representative for an initial term of one year beginning on the 1st day of January 1999. The parties may by mutual agreement in writing renew this Agreement for additional one (1) year terms with such changes and amendments, if any, as may be mutually agreed upon and set forth in the renewal agreement.

2. **Position** The Sales Representative as an independent contractor will use his Best efforts to sell the Company's products on a commission basis. This Sales Agreement is personal to the Sales Representative named herein and cannot be assigned without the prior written approval of the Company. The rights and obligations of the Company hereunder shall accrue to its successor and assigns. The Sales Representative shall bear all of his own selling expenses, without reimbursement by the Company.

3. **Commission a.** The Sales Representative shall be paid a commission of five (5%) percent on all promotional merchandise, and a commission of ten (10%) percent for all non-promotional merchandise. All commissions

shall be paid on the published factory price, and exclusive of freight and transportation charges, duty or customs fees, sales or similar taxes, and adjusted for returns, rejections, damage allowance, and uncollectible accounts. All orders must have credit clearance from the Company prior to shipment or delivery.

b. Promotional merchandise is defined as a sofa group (sofa, loveseat and chair) that arrives paid in the UK for ONE THOUSAND ONE HUNDRED THIRTY US DOLLARS ($1,130.00) or less.

c. Commissions shall be due and payable to the Sales Representative within thirty (30) days of full payment being received by the Company.

d. The Company shall have full control of and full discretion as to the collection, adjustment or compromise of all accounts sold by Sales Representative, and shall not be liable to Sales Representative for any loss of commission or other claim whatsoever arising thereby.

4. **Assigned Country** UNITED KINGDOM and EIRE.

5. **Trade and Business Secrets** Sales Representatives will not, at any time, either during this employment or thereafter, reproduce, disclose or use any confidential information, trade or business secrets, customer lists, or confidential records of the Company unless specifically authorized in writing by the Company.

6. **Termination** This Agreement may be terminated by either party, with or without cause, upon giving ninety (90) days written notice certified mail to the other party.

7. **Entire Agreement** This Agreement constitutes the entire agreement between the Company and Sales Representative and supersedes all prior and contemporaneous statements, understandings or agreements.

8. **Return of Company Property** Upon termination of this Agreement, the Sales Representative shall return to the Company all samples, customer lists, price lists and other property furnished to the Sales Representative by the Company.

9. **Applicable Law** This Agreement shall be governed by and construed by the laws of the Country of the United Kingdom.'

18. **Tigana** was named as the Sales Representative, rather than Mr Coleman, because, as Mr Coleman told me, he had been advised by his accountants that there might be advantages in using an Isle of Man company in this context. **Tigana** had previously been acquired as an 'off the shelf' company for this purpose. In practical, if not legal, terms **Tigana** was Mr Coleman.

(d) Trading during 1999

19. As has been mentioned, orders procured by Mr Coleman had been placed with Decoro from October 1998. These orders had to a considerable

extent (although not solely) been by way of sample orders. Further orders came in January 1999, in the period before the Sales Agreement was finalised, including those resulting from the visit to China of Land of Leather (Mr Briant) and European Furniture (Mr O'Kane) in January 1999. On 20th January 1999 Furniture Village placed an order with Decoro. On the 19th February 1999 Furnitureland (Mr Julian Cox) placed a substantial prospective order with Decoro, via Mr Coleman, for its Easter promotion. In May 1999 Mr Coleman made a further visit to China, this time accompanied by representatives of Furnitureland and Conroys. Furnitureland were calculating that by that time their orders would come to as many as 170 container loads. It is clear that throughout this period Decoro was shipping to the UK very substantial quantities of leather furniture to the UK – Furnitureland alone placed orders of around $3.65 million for the period April, May, June 1999. It is further clear that the purchases were all by customers introduced through the agency of Mr Coleman.

20.   During this period there had been some difficulties. On occasion the shipping paperwork was defective. Also there were various problems with scuffmarks on some of the furniture, lack of feet (or screw holes for the feet) for some of the chairs, inadequate labelling and so on. Mr Coleman, and his staff, did his best to handle such complaints, communicating with Decoro when necessary. There is nothing to suggest that these particular problems, although tiresome, were such as to affect to any significant extent the overall saleability of Decoro's furniture in the UK or its relations with its customer base.

21.   However, a far more significant problem was emerging.

22.   The fire safety regulations applicable to furniture sold in the UK would appear to be amongst the most stringent, if not the most stringent, in the world. Decoro appreciated in broad terms (if not specific terms) that the requirements might be different to other countries in which its products were sold. The Far Eastern manufacturers of foam required for Decoro's leather furniture, Wah Tung and latterly Tung Ah, in due course obtained certificates from Intertek Testing Services ('ITS') in Hong Kong at the end of 1998 which stated that the foam provided satisfied the UK 1988 Fire Safety Regulations. On the 4th February 1999 Mr Coleman wrote to say that certificates would be needed from the foam manufacturers that the foam satisfied British Safety requirements. The request was repeated by fax of 11th March 1999. By this time rumours were beginning to circulate – perhaps to some extent fostered by trade competitors of Decoro and of its customers in the UK who had been making their own inspections – that Decoro's foam was not fire retardant to the requisite standard.

23.   On the 17th March 1999 Mr Coleman wrote to all of Decoro's UK customers enclosing copies of the ITS certificates and informing them that Decoro was applying to become a member of FIRA, and was sending FIRA a sample for testing. In the meantime, as has been mentioned, substantial orders continued to be placed with Decoro.

24.   On the 25th May 1999 a sample from Decoro eventually arrived at FIRA for testing. On the 7th June 1999 FIRA notified Mr Coleman that the sample had failed the test with regard to the foam, the full report following on 9th June 1999. At that time Furnitureland indicated that it would not accept Decoro furniture without FIRA test certificates, and that it required an acceptance of full liability on the part of Decoro if the furniture was not compliant. In the meantime further tests were sought at FIRA. A replacement foam sample also failed. By this time local trading standards officers were taking an interest and visiting stores in order to inspect Decoro furniture products. On the 28th June 1999 a sample taken by Cardiff trading standards officers for non-foam filling testing failed as to the fibres incorporated in the cushioning. Mr Coleman notified Mr Ricci of this on 28th June 1999, asking for confirmation from Decoro's fibre suppliers that the fibre was compliant with UK safety regulations.

25.   On the 29th June 1999 Furnitureland formally suspended all further deliveries from Decoro, and all further sales out of stock of Decoro products. In the meantime the rumours were gaining widespread currency within the furniture trade. Furnitureland commissioned a test of the fibre, which was recorded as failing on its being tested on 5th July 1999.

26.   A further testing session in respect of the fibre was held on the 12th July 1999 at the furniture technology laboratory of the independent testing organisation SATRA at Kettering. Present, among others, were several representatives of Furnitureland; Mr Ricci; Mr Pratti; and Mr Coleman. When the test was undertaken, the fibre failed. In consequence there were further discussions with Furnitureland. An arrangement was concluded on the 13th July 1999; it involved (amongst other things) the agreed recall of 63 containers, in storage or in transit, to China for reworking, at the expense of Decoro. Those goods, when reworked, and further outstanding orders amounting to 179 containers, were to be provided to Furnitureland at a discounted price of 7% to compensate Furnitureland for its own anticipated losses. Subsequently, on around 11th August 1999, Decoro agreed to bear $485,000 in respect of the ex-factory costs of recall.

27.   Other customers were notified that the furniture had failed the fibre tests and an article appeared in the 'Cabinet Maker' (the trade magazine) to that effect. In addition, however, on a further test by SATRA at the request of Cardiff trading standards officers, the (grey) foam was also failed in a test undertaken on the 29th July 1999 (there being at this time two foams proffered by Decoro for testing – grey and yellow). Samples of Decoro products taken by West Yorkshire trading standards officers in early August 1999 failed both as to foam and as to fibre.

28.   On the 8th August 1999, Mr Coleman and two representatives of Furnitureland visited Decoro's factory in Shenzhen, China. With them, at the behest of Furnitureland, went Mr Feltham-White, then employed by SATRA as a technical consultant. Mr Feltham-White submitted a detailed report as to the requirements for Decoro's furniture to enable

it to comply with UK regulations. He also stated that the foam, if of the yellow variety, was compliant.

29.   Throughout this time other retailers (such as Conroys) were putting pressure on Decoro and Mr Coleman to come up with solutions and also were seeking recompense. The position was sufficiently serious for Mr Ricci to be expressing concerns as to whether Decoro could survive. On the 19th August 1999 Mr Coleman advised that all Decoro products sent to the UK to date must be recalled. On the 26th August 1999 a meeting was held in London with Decoro's major UK retailers (other than Furniture Village). An arrangement was reached which was reflected in a letter sent out the following day by Mr Coleman. That provides as follows:

> Further to our meeting yesterday in London please find my confirmation of the agreements reached by Decoro and the retailers present.
>
> 1)   As from 1st September all materials used in the production of Decoro's sofas will be fully compliant to the UK spec and batch tested prior to productions.
>
> 2)   Decoro will grant an ongoing invoice discount of 6% to cover the costs of replacement orders for previous deliveries. All future deliveries will be a mix of special orders and replacement orders to ease the pain.
>
> 3)   Any unused stock presently held by you can be sent back to China for reworking and redelivery. The transport costs of this will be met by the retailer and reimbursed by Decoro under their discount on ongoing orders.
>
> 4)   Paul Briant will investigate the possibility of exporting the return stock to Belgium at £80 per seat.
>
> 5)   I have booked the same hotel for next Wednesday 1st September from 9am to 3pm for a meeting with Cabinet Maker, the various T.S.O.'s and a solicitor provided by Furnitureland to discuss the law regarding compliance and numerous press releases.
>
> 6)   All clients should provide Decoro with detailed lists of replacement stock broken down as:
>
> a)   Replacement delivered stock
>
> b)   Replacement warehouse stock to be returned
>
> c)   Showroom models stock
>
> I trust this covers all of the items we discussed but if you require any further information please let me know.'

30.   Notwithstanding all these difficulties, it is the fact (as I find) that overall most of Decoro's customers – Furniture Village being the principal exception – were supportive of Decoro. That may well have been in part because of the terms and discounts being offered by Decoro to help rectify the situation; but I have no doubt that it was primarily due to the customers' perception that these were essentially good products, competitively priced. In the beginning of September 1999 Mr Coleman

arranged a meeting with Cabinet Maker, the trade magazine, attended by representatives of Decoro's major customers. The upshot was an article in that magazine of 10th September 1999. It was headed: 'Stockists unite to back Decoro and defy critics'. The article started:

'Main Decoro stockists have issued a bullish message to trade critics. "It's a good quality product and we will continue to sell it".'

The article went on to name the four retailers – Land of Leather, Sterling, Conroys and Furnitureland – as participating in a product recall and recorded them as stating that they would continue to stock the product and were happy with the measures taken. The managing director of Furnitureland was quoted as saying with regard to Decoro: 'Our relationship is more of a partnership now'. I have no reason to think that the article does not accurately record the views of these retailers. By this time, as I find, by 1st September 1999 Decoro was in a position to manufacture UK compliant furniture.

31. Throughout 1999 Mr Coleman had been receiving infrequent payments of commission which he calculated were due to him. On the 20th August 1999 Mr Ricci wrote to him, complaining of all the disruption and cost to Decoro and intimating that outstanding commission might not be paid and, indeed, such as had been paid should be repaid. Mr Coleman took the view that Mr Ricci was seeking to blame everyone but Decoro itself for the Fire Safety Regulations debacle. At all events he continued to act as its agent and continued to deal with its customers: for example, on one occasion he even held certain sums proffered by a customer as a kind of stakeholder. He sought to persuade Furniture Village to enter into an arrangement similar to that offered to the other retailers. He continued to deal with queries. He arranged for visits to the China operation by representatives of Kingdom of Leather and Conroys, Furnitureland and World of Leather. He continued to seek new introductions and attended the High Point fair in October 1999, where orders for Decoro products for the UK market were taken, and where he entered into preliminary discussions with other potential new customers, Allders and Reids. He also visited Decoro's factory in China during November 1999, primarily to check that production and shipment was on course for pre-Christmas orders. On his return, he entered into negotiations with a furniture outlet called Crazy George, which had many UK stores, seeking to interest it in Decoro products.

32. Nevertheless Mr Coleman's contact with Decoro was diminishing. By October 1999 some of Mr Coleman's staff had been complaining at the lack of information they were receiving from Decoro. On 14th September 1999 Land of Leather had (unbeknown to Mr Coleman) written to Decoro indicating that it was agreed they deal directly with each other (although this did not always happen: for example, provisional Heads of Agreement reached at High Point in October 1999 between Mr Pratti and Land of Leather were copied by the latter to Mr Coleman). During November Furnitureland were communicating directly with Mr Pratti and Mr Feltham-White on various matters. For example on 7th December

1999 Furnitureland's managing director, Mr Peddar, wrote to Mr Ricci saying among other things. '. . . we are very keen to promote heavily your models early in the New Year . . . . The success we have enjoyed together can be repeated during the year 2000 and we look forward to working with you . . . . I confirm our absolute desire to increase our turnover with Decoro. . . .'. Further by the end of November 1999 Decoro was in discussion with Mr Feltham-White with a view to Mr Feltham-White becoming Decoro's UK representative in place of Mr Coleman.

33.   On the 20th December 1999, Mr Ricci, in response to Mr Coleman's query as to his payments of commission, wrote to stress the losses caused by the fire regulation problems but 'notwithstanding the loss your commission have (sic) been and will be completely paid'. The letter also stated that it was not Decoro's intention to renew the contract when it expired on 31st December 1999. This was a great disappointment to Mr Coleman. A further letter of 27th December 1999 confirmed that intention and stated that Decoro considered the contract terminated at the expiry date of 31st December 1999. On the 21st December 1999 Decoro had notified all its UK customers that Mr Coleman would cease to be its representative from 1st January 2000. On the 4th January 2000 the customers were formally notified that Mr Feltham-White would be Decoro's representative. Mr Feltham-White in fact started in post on 1st February 2000, having served out his notice with SATRA, on a salaried basis (his current salary being around £60,000 p.a). The ostensible reactions of Decoro's UK customers, expressed to Decoro, were mixed. Some expressed surprise and concern at Mr Coleman's departure; others, however, indicated some unhappiness at Mr Coleman's after-sales service (although they had never voiced such dissatisfaction to Mr Coleman himself) and a lack of concern at his departure.

(e)   *The events of 2000*

34.   During the early part of 2000 Decoro continued to take substantial orders from UK customers. A considerable quantity of orders, for example, was placed by Land of Leather in January 2000. (Land of Leather told Mr Feltham-White on 5th January 2000 that they had sold nearly 30 containers over the Christmas/New Year holiday alone). These orders had been contemplated and, indeed, discussed with Mr Coleman at High Point in October 1999. The orders were, however, only formally confirmed and placed after discussions at a trade fair in Paris on around the 12th January 2000 and the orders entered into Decoro's system on around 17th January 2000. (Notwithstanding the absence of the original order forms I accept Mr Pratti's evidence, given in re-examination, to this effect). Orders from other customers continued to flow in, although Furniture Village, at least, seemed disinclined to deal further with Decoro in the early part of 2000 (mainly owing to a stated desire, as Mr Coleman told me and I accept, for 'the dust to settle'). Comparative figures are set out in Appendices 1, 2 and 3 to Mr Coleman's witness statement dated 31st October 2002. These were subsequently revised and, as so revised,

are appended to this judgement: they are based on the details provided by Decoro on disclosure in these proceedings.

35. Mr Pratti in his 3rd witness statement also provides some figures. In paragraph 62 he records the approximate UK sales revenue of Decoro for 1999 as being in the region of $10m–$12m; for 2000, as $22m; for 2001 $17m; and for 2002 $24m. He goes on to record that in the year 2000 of the then 3 major customers, Furnitureland provided Decoro with nearly $11m of business; Land of Leather $6.8m of business; and Sterling $2.2m of business. Mr Pratti's particular point was that those volumes were principally to be explained by the customers availing themselves of the discount arrangement reached with them to compensate for the problems with the non-compliant furniture delivered in 1999. I have no reason to doubt that this was a significant factor (a point illustrated by the heavily reduced orders from those customers in 2001 – in Sterling's case, to nil – as set out in paragraph 64 of Mr Pratti's statement). Nevertheless the fact remains that Decoro in 2000 (and thereafter) undertook considerable volumes of business with customers initially introduced by Mr Coleman. Paragraph 18 of Mr Pratti's fourth witness statement indicates that Decoro makes a significant gross profit margin (before deduction of transport and other costs) on its products – doubtless reflecting its low cost base in China – and at no stage has Mr Pratti sought to deny that the sales in 2000 (even allowing for the discount arrangement) were anything other than profitable to Decoro.

36. Mr Feltham-White commenced work full-time for Decoro on the 1st February 2000. His principal role at that time was to ensure compliance with the regulations and to provide good customer aftersales service. Subsequently, since 2000, Mr Feltham-White has succeeded in bringing in new customers for Decoro (in particular Reids, Allders and various other companies). However Mr Feltham-White in cross-examination openly accepted, and I find, that the orders which flowed into Decoro during 2000 primarily (and, at least up to October, exclusively) derived from the customers whom Mr Coleman had initially introduced: and that effectively during 2000 Mr Feltham-White administered those customers whom Mr Coleman had so introduced. The aim, at that stage, as he told me, was to consolidate the business which had been introduced by Mr Coleman: in Mr Feltham-White's words, he was 'handed the reins' for the customers introduced by Mr Coleman. Since Mr Feltham-White was on a salary, he did not receive any commission himself for these orders.

37. Mr Coleman was pressing in the meantime for sums he was claiming were due to him. The only sums that had previously been paid to **Tigana** for commission totalled (as was ultimately agreed) $215,432. One point concerned expenses. Although the Sales Agreement had provided that **Tigana** should bear its own selling expenses, a separate agreement had been reached between Mr Ricci and Mr Coleman (as was common ground) that Decoro should pay the costs of Mr Coleman's flights to and hotel expenses for Hong Kong and China, as well as those of his

commercial invitees. Mr Coleman was pressing for reimbursement of such expenses. Eventually, after service of a Statutory Demand for the sum of £34,987 these were for the most part paid. On the 4th March 2000 Decoro sent a statement showing $404,703 due to **Tigana** for commission. However, notwithstanding Mr Ricci's assurance given in his letter of 20th December 1999, this was not paid.

38.   A letter before action was sent on the 26th April 2000. This was met with a response from Decoro's solicitors to the effect that **Tigana**, in breach of duty, had failed properly to advise as to 1988 Fire Safety Regulations; that no compensation or indemnity was due because the termination of the agency was by reason of Mr Coleman's 'fault'; and that Decoro's own rights were reserved in respect of loss and damage which it had suffered as a result of **Tigana's** alleged breach of contract.

39.   The Claim Form, with Particulars of Claim, was issued on 18th September 2000.

The course of the proceedings

40.   By its claim form, **Tigana** claims sums said to be due to it under Clause 3 of the Sales Agreement. The amount said to be due (based on the details provided by Decoro itself) is pleaded as $404,703. In addition sums are claimed by reference to Regulations 7 and 8 of the Agency Regulations. Further a claim for compensation (amounting to the equivalent of two years gross commission based on the earnings of the Claimant) pursuant to Regulation 17 is made. There is also raised in the claim form an unquantified claim for damages.

41.   By its Defence and Counterclaim served in April 2001 (and amended in April 2002) it was admitted that the sum of $404,703 was owed to **Tigana** for unpaid commission. It was denied that any sums were due under Regulations 7 and 8. It was denied that any sums were due by way of compensation under Regulation 17 since (a) the Sales Agreement expired by effluxion of time and Regulation 17, on its true interpretation (so it is alleged), has no application in such circumstances and in any event (b) the Sales Agreement was terminated by reason of the default of **Tigana** (reliance being placed on Regulation 18 in this regard). Further a substantial counterclaim was pleaded (plainly also intended to operate by way of set-off to the claim, as well as constituting a cross claim). What was alleged (to summarise) was that the failure of Decoro to supply furniture which was compliant with the 1988 Fire Safety Regulations, and the resulting loss, was caused by alleged breach of duty on the part of **Tigana** (by Mr Coleman) in failing to advise properly as to the existence and effect of such 1988 Fire Safety Regulations. Damages put at some $2,735,000 (and interest) were claimed.

42.   The Claimant took the view that the original defence and counterclaim contained no real defence and applied for summary judgment. Detailed evidence was put in: that put in by Decoro did not, in a number of respects, correspond to what had been alleged in previous correspondence or the Defence and Counterclaim as originally pleaded.

43. The application came before Master Rose. By Order dated 1st November 2001, he dismissed **Tigana**'s application for summary judgment. In his careful and detailed judgment (judgment having been reserved) the Master made clear that his dismissal of the application was on the basis that the evidence of Decoro showed an arguable set off and counterclaim. Costs were ordered to be in the case. Subsequently the Defence and Counterclaim was amended in a way that, so it is said, does not seem altogether to mirror the way in which the matter was put before the Master. In due course, detailed witness statements and experts reports were put in which (so it is said by **Tigana**) advances a different case yet again.

44. The trial was listed to start before me on Monday the 2nd December 2002. On the afternoon of Friday 29th November 2002 a note was sent by counsel for Decoro indicating that Decoro did not propose to pursue its counterclaim (and also abandoning certain other points under the Agency Regulations, including the argument under Regulation 18). One consequence of this was greatly to shorten what otherwise would have been potentially a very lengthy trial. Another consequence was that there was, after all, no defence raised as to the entitlement of **Tigana** at least to receive the unpaid commission.

45. As has been mentioned, it was admitted in the Defence that the sum of $404,703 was due in respect of such unpaid commission. However at the outset of the trial before me Mr Antony White QC (who, with Mr Algazy, appeared for **Tigana**) very fairly indicated that the latest figures available indicated that may be an incorrect quantification and that he did not seek to hold Decoro to its admission. Ultimately the parties agreed that the correct figure was $350,000. Total commission earned for 1999 was agreed at $558,725 (with a further $6,707 earned for 1998).

46. On the pleaded case, **Tigana** had also sought to argue (by reference to Clause 6 of the Sales Agreement) that Decoro had failed validly to terminate the Agreement on 31st December 1999 in that it had not given 90 days written notice. However at trial Mr White – mindful of the express provisions of Clause 1 – disclaimed that point: in my view, rightly. Further it ultimately became common ground between Mr White and Mr Charles Hollander QC (who, with Mr Dhillon, appeared for Decoro) that, on the evidence and in the circumstances of this particular case, no further sums were payable under Regulation 7 or Regulation 8 (b). Further, Mr White advanced no separate claim for damages. Thus the only issues remaining were:

    46.1 To what sum (if any) is **Tigana** entitled under Regulation 8 (a) of the Regulations?

    46.2 To what sum (if any) is **Tigana** entitled under Regulation 17 of the Agency Regulations?

    These raise issues of fact and law. I thus turn to them: but before doing so I should say a little about the witnesses who gave evidence before me at trial.

47.   Mr Coleman was cross-examined for almost a day. He struck me as an astute man and as a careful witness. I gained the impression on occasion that he was somewhat exasperated by what he considers to be tactical manoeuvering on the part of Decoro to avoid paying him what he considers to be his due: but, if so, he kept that under control. I considered his evidence reliable and not prone to exaggeration. So far as the Defence witnesses are concerned, Mr Pratti was also cross-examined for about a day. He, too, is an astute man. Although English is not his first language, his comprehension is excellent. However his answers on occasion tended to be rather long and diffuse, and did not always address the question actually asked. In the course of cross-examination, a number of discrepancies between his various witness statements were exposed, and also certain inconsistencies between them and his oral evidence were revealed. Overall, I was minded to prefer the evidence of Mr Coleman to Mr Pratti where they were in conflict; although in truth the differences were not, for the most part, very great. Mr Feltham-White gave candid evidence: albeit that, in some respects, it significantly modified his various witness statements. Mr Imrie, a director of Furniture Village, gave brief, but valuable and palpably reliable, evidence. I also allowed to be admitted in evidence (without objection from Mr White, subject always to questions of weight) two written witness statements of Mr Peddar, director of Furnitureland, who was said to be unavailable owing to business commitments.

The Agency Regulations

48.   The Agency Regulations (SI 1993 No 3173) came into effect on 1st January 1994. Their origin is EC Directive 86/653 ('the Directive'), relating to the 'co-ordination of the laws of the Member States relating to self-employed commercial agents.' The relevant recitals of the Directive read as follows:

> 'Whereas the restrictions on the freedom of establishment and the freedom to provide services in respect of activities of intermediaries in commerce, industry and small craft industries were abolished by Directive 64/224/EEC;
>
> Whereas the differences in national laws concerning commercial representation substantially affect the conditions of competition and the carrying-on of that activity within the Community and are detrimental both to the protection available to commercial agents *vis-à-vis* their principals and to the security of commercial transactions; whereas moreover those differences are such as to inhibit substantially the conclusion and operation of commercial representation contracts where principal and commercial agent are established in different Member States;
>
> Whereas trade in goods between Member States should be carried on under conditions which are similar to those of a single market, and this necessitates approximation of the legal systems of the Member States to the extent required for the proper functioning of the

common market; whereas in this regard the rules concerning conflict of laws do not, in the matter of commercial representation, remove the inconsistencies referred to above, nor would they even if they were made uniform, and accordingly the proposed harmonisation is necessary notwithstanding the existence of those rules;

Whereas in this regard the legal relationship between commercial agent and principal must be given priority; Whereas it is appropriate to be guided by the principles of Article 117 of the Treaty and to maintain improvements already made, when harmonising the laws of the Member States relating to commercial agents;

Whereas additional transitional periods should be allowed for certain Member States which have to make a particular effort to adapt their regulations, especially those concerning indemnity for termination of contract between the principal and the commercial agent, to the requirements of this Directive.'

49. There are then set out in the Directive the relevant Articles, being twenty-three in number. Article 22 provided that Member States should bring into force provisions necessary to comply with the Directive before 1st January 1990. However, by Article 22(3), such time limit was extended to 1st January 1994 for Ireland and the United Kingdom: connoting that the UK was one Member State which would have to 'make a particular effort' to adapt its regulations to the requirements of the Directive. It is also to be noted that Article 17 (which provides for indemnification or compensation of a commercial agent 'after termination of the agency contract') expressly provides, by Article 17(6), for the submission by the Commission to the Council, within 8 years of the notification of the Directive, of a report on the implementation of the Article, providing (if necessary) proposals for amendments.

50. The Agency Regulations are in lay out and in language very similar, although not identical, to that of the Directive. But there are differences – thus the lay out and wording of, for example, Regulation 17 is different to that of Article 17.

51. In the respects relevant to these proceedings the Agency Regulations (as subsequently amended in relatively minor respects) provide as follows:

'1 **Citation, commencement and applicable law**

(1) These Regulations may be cited as the Commercial Agents (Council Directive) Regulations 1993 and shall come into force on 1st January 1994.

(2) These Regulations govern the relations between commercial agents and their principals and, subject to paragraph (3), apply in relation to the activities of commercial agents in Great Britain

(3) A court or tribunal shall:

(a) apply the law of the other Member State concerned in place of regulations 3 to 22 where the parties have agreed that the agency contract is to be governed by the law of that Member State;

361

> (b) (whether or not it would otherwise be required to do so) apply these regulations where the law of another Member State corresponding to these regulations enables the parties to agree that the agency contract is to be governed by the law of a different Member State and the parties have agreed that it is to be governed by the law of England and Wales or Scotland.

2   Interpretation, application and extent

> (1) In these Regulations—
>
>> 'commercial agent' means a self employed intermediary who has continuing authority to negotiate the sale or purchase of goods on behalf of another person (the 'principal'), or to negotiate and conclude the sale of purchase of goods on behalf of and in the name of that principal; . . . .'

. . .

'Form and amount of remuneration in absence of agreement

6. (1) In the absence of any agreement as to remuneration between the parties, a commercial agent shall be entitled to the remuneration that commercial agents appointed for the goods forming the subject of his agency contract are customarily allowed in the place where he carries on his activities and, if there is no such customary practice, a commercial agent shall be entitled to reasonable remuneration taking into account all aspects of the transaction.

(2) This regulation is without prejudice to the application of any enactment or rule of law concerning the level of remuneration.

(3) Where a commercial agent is not remunerated (wholly or in part) by commission, regulations 7 to 12 below shall not apply.

Entitlement to commission on transactions concluded during agency contract.

7. (1) A commercial agent shall be entitled to commission on commercial transactions concluded during the period covered by the agency contract —

(a) where the transaction has been concluded as a result of his action; or

(b) where the transaction is concluded with a third party whom he has previously acquired as a customer for transactions of the same kind.

(2) A commercial agent shall also be entitled to commission on transactions concluded during the period covered by the agency contract where he has an exclusive right to a specific geographical area or to a specific group of customers and where the transaction has been entered into with a customer belonging to that area or group.

Entitlement to commission on transactions concluded after agency contract has terminated.

8.   Subject to regulation 9 below, a commercial agent shall be entitled to commission on commercial transactions concluded after the agency contract has terminated if—

(a)   the transaction is mainly attributable to his efforts during the period covered by the agency contract and if the transaction was entered into within a reasonable period after that contract terminated; or

(b)   in accordance with the conditions mentioned in regulation 7 above, the order of the third party reached the principal or the commercial agent before the agency contract terminated.

. . .

When commission due and date for payment

10   (1)   ICommission shall become due as soon as, and to the extent that, one of the following circumstances occurs:

(a)   the principal has executed the transaction; or

(b)   the principal should, according to his agreement with the third party, have executed the transaction; or

(c)   the third party has executed the transaction.

(2)   Commission shall become due at the latest when the third party has executed his part of the transaction or should have done so if the principal had executed his part of the transaction, as he should have.

(3)   The commission shall be paid not later than on the last day of the month following the quarter in which it became due, and, for the purposes of these Regulations, unless otherwise agreed between the parties, the first quarter period shall run from the date the agency contract takes effect, and subsequent periods shall run from that date in the third month thereafter or the beginning of the fourth month, whichever is the sooner.

(4)   Any agreement to derogate from paragraphs (2) and (3) above to the detriment of the commercial agent shall be void.

11   Extinction of right of commission

(1)   The right to commission can be extinguished only if and to the extent that—

(a)   it is established that the contract between the third party and the principal will not be executed; and

(b)   that fact is due to a reason for which the principal is not to blame.

(2)   Any commission which the commercial agent has already received shall be refunded if the right to it is extinguished.

(3)   Any agreement to derogate from paragraph (1) above to the detriment of the commercial agent shall be void

. . .

Conversion of agency contract after expiry of fixed period.

14. An agency contract for a fixed period which continues to be performed by both parties after that period has expired shall be deemed to be converted into an agency contract for an indefinite period.

. . .

Entitlement of commercial agent to indemnity or compensation on termination of agency contract

17. (1) This regulation has effect for the purpose of ensuring that the commercial agent is, after termination of the agency contract, indemnified in accordance with paragraphs (3) to (5) below or compensated for damage in accordance with paragraphs (6) and (7) below.

(2) Except where the agency contract otherwise provides, the commercial agent shall be entitled to be compensated rather than indemnified.

(3) Subject to paragraph (9) and to regulation 18 below, the commercial agent shall be entitled to an indemnity if and to the extent that—

    (a) he has brought the principal new customers or has significantly increased the volume of business with existing customers and the principal continues to derive substantial benefits from the business with such customers; and

    (b) the payment of this indemnity is equitable having regard to all the circumstances and, in particular, the commission lost by the commercial agent on the business transacted with such customers.

(4) The amount of indemnity shall not exceed the figure equivalent to an indemnity for one year calculated from the commercial agent's average annual remuneration over the preceding five years and if the contract goes back less than five years the indemnity shall be calculated on the average for the period in question.

(5) The grant of an indemnity as mentioned above shall not prevent the commercial agent from seeking damages.

(6) Subject to paragraph (9) and to regulation 18 below, the commercial agent shall be entitled to compensation for the damage he suffers as a result of the termination of his relations with his principal.

(7) For the purpose of these Regulations such damage shall be deemed to occur particularly when the termination takes place in either or both of the following circumstances, namely circumstances which—

    (a) deprive the commercial agent of the commission which proper performance of the agency contract would have procured for him whilst providing his principal with substantial benefits linked to the activities of the commercial agent; or

(b)   have not enabled the commercial agent to amortise the costs and expenses that he had incurred in the performance of the agency contract on the advice of his principal.

(8)   Entitlement to the indemnity or compensation for damage as provided for under paragraphs (2) to (7) above shall also arise where the agency contract is terminated as a result of the death of the commercial agent.

(9)   The commercial agent shall lose his entitlement to the indemnity or compensation for damage in the instances provided for in paragraphs (2) and (8) above if within one year following termination of his agency contract he has not notified his principal that he intends pursuing his entitlement.

Grounds for excluding payment of indemnity or compensation under regulation 17.

18.   The [indemnity or] compensation referred to in regulation 17 above shall not be payable to the commercial agent where—

(a)   the principal has terminated the agency contract because of default attributable to the commercial agent which would justify immediate termination of the agency contract pursuant to regulation 16 above; or

(b)   the commercial agent has himself terminated the agency contract, unless such termination is justified—

(i)   by circumstances attributable to the principal, or

(ii)   on grounds of age, infirmity or illness of the commercial agent in consequence of which he cannot reasonably be required to continue his activities; or

(c)   the commercial agent, with the agreement of his principal, assigns his rights and duties under the agency contract to another person.

Prohibition on derogation from regulations 17 and 18

19.   The parties may not derogate from regulations 17 and 18 to the detriment of the commercial agent before the agency contract expires.

Restraint of trade clauses

20.   (1)   IA restraint of trade clause shall be valid only if and to the extent that—

(a)   it is concluded in writing; and

(b)   it relates to the geographical area or the group of customers and the geographical area entrusted to the commercial agent and to the kind of goods covered by his agency under the contract.

(2)   A restraint of trade clauses shall be valid for not more than two years after termination of the agency contract.

(3)   Nothing in this regulation shall affect any enactment or rule of law which imposes other restrictions on the validity or enforceability of restraint of trade clauses or which enables a court to reduce the obligations on the parties resulting from such clauses.'

. . .

52.   Mr White and Mr Hollander were agreed that **Tigana** fell within the definition of 'commercial agent' and that the Agency Regulations (as amended) applied to the Sales Agreement.

The claim under Regulation 8(a)

53.   As has been mentioned, the claim for unpaid commission is now agreed in the sum of $350,000 and, further, no issues under Regulation 7 or Regulation 8(b) now arise. The essential task, therefore, under Regulation 8(a) is to identify those transactions (if any) concluded after 31st December 1999 where (a) the transaction was 'mainly attributable' to **Tigana**'s efforts during the period of the Sales Agreement *and* (b) the transaction was entered into within a 'reasonable period' after 31st December 1999. The overall task, therefore, is one of judgment and assessment (but not of discretion) by reference to the facts of the case.

54.   The wording of Regulation 10 and 11, as compared to that of Regulations 7 and 8, indicates that it is deliberately contemplated that (for the purposes of Part III of the Agency Regulations) a distinction is to be drawn between the 'execution' of a transaction and the 'conclusion' of a transaction. In the circumstances of the present case, I take that a view that a transaction is to be taken as concluded when the relevant order is placed. It is also clear that the phrase 'mainly attributable' connotes a causative link between the efforts of the commercial agent and the conclusion of the transaction (albeit after the agency contract has terminated). One might perhaps see an analogy with the familiar English legal phrase 'effective cause': but it is perhaps better not to gloss the words actually used in Regulation 8(a).

55.   It is tersely said in Bowstead and Reynolds on Agency 17th ed. para 11–030 that: 'The requirements of [Regulation 8(a)] are somewhat imprecise and may give rise to difficulty'. That may, or may not, be so in any given case: but there is no conceptual difficulty involved and the Regulation self-evidently designedly confers a degree of flexibility available to each case under consideration: for example, what may be a 'reasonable period' in one case will not be in another case. Everything, therefore, will depend on the circumstances of each case.

56.   On behalf of **Tigana**, Mr White submitted that the evidence shows that the introductions effected by Mr Coleman continued through 2000 and thereafter. Mr White did not focus on each individual transaction concluded in 2000 and 2001 (which would have been a mammoth task); rather, he approached the matter as one of generality. He acknowledged, for example, that Furnitureland chose to engage as consultant Mr Feltham-White (as the evidence of Mr Feltham-White and

Mr Peddar shows) from around mid-1999, via Satra, Mr Peddar then appreciating that it was essential to ensure technical compliance with the 1988 Regulations and perceiving Mr Feltham-White (not Mr Coleman) as the person to achieve that. Indeed Mr Feltham-White, on behalf of Furnitureland, visited the factory in China on several occasions in the second half of 1999 to ensure the procedures to achieve compliance were in place. But Mr White submitted that, even so, the business from Furnitureland (which had been introduced by Mr Coleman) was 'mainly attributable' to Mr Coleman's efforts. So also, he submitted, were the orders placed by all the other customers – who did not even use Mr Feltham-White in this respect – 'mainly attributable' to Mr Coleman's efforts. Mr White's overall submission was that Regulation 8 (a) should apply to all orders placed with Decoro by customers initially introduced by Mr Coleman until at least the end of June 2001 – that is, a period of 18 months after the agency came to an end.

57. For his part, Mr Hollander submitted that no orders placed after 31st December 1999 were 'mainly attributable' to the efforts of Mr Coleman at all and he submitted, accordingly, that no payment under Regulation 8(a) should be ordered at all. He submitted that, after the debacle concerning the 1988 Fire Safety Regulations, Mr Coleman's influence and involvement greatly decreased; and thereafter the customer connection was fostered (and, indeed, retrieved) by Decoro itself directly, through Mr Pratti and Mr Ricci and (latterly) Mr Feltham-White, and by the offer of the discount arrangements to customers. He cited the position of Furnitureland as one example: and Land of Leather as another example (which company concluded in principle Heads of Agreement on 19th October 1999 relating to future dealings by negotiating directly with Mr Pratti). He also pointed out, by way of example, that although Land of Leather had indicated an intention to place orders at the High Point fair in October 1999 (when Mr Coleman was present) it did not in fact place such orders until after discussions and communications with Mr Pratti at a trade fair in Paris between 10th and 12th January 2000 (by which time Mr Coleman had ceased, of course, to be Decoro's agent). He drew attention to the position of customers such as Furniture Village (initially introduced by Mr Coleman) which refrained from placing further orders until well into 2000, after the 'dust had settled' and Mr Feltham-White had satisfied them that all was now in order. Overall, Mr Hollander's submission was that by the end of December 1999 Mr Coleman had been sidelined; that he 'created' none of the orders placed in 2000 or thereafter; and that none such were mainly attributable to his efforts. Mr Hollander's alternative submission was that no more than a proportion of the orders placed in a relatively short period (he suggested 3 months from the end of December 1999) could be said to be mainly attributable to Mr Coleman's efforts.

58. Considering the evidence, I am in no doubt that Mr Hollander's submissions are to be rejected. It seems to me that Mr Coleman's role was intended to be primarily introductory – that was the main purpose

for which he had been retained as agent. To a considerable extent the agency was, if I may put it this way, 'front loaded': that is, dependent on his activities at the outset (although also, of course, it was intended that he bring in yet more customers thereafter). Of course an important part of his role was thereafter also to maintain regular liaison with customers (and, not least, secure repeat orders) and assist in after sales service: but that too was an aspect of cementing the relationship created by the initial introduction. Mr Imrie in his second witness statement made clear that the buying director of a customer is one who makes the decisions as to what models and ranges, and at what prices, he will buy. I accept that. But in cross-examination Mr Imrie (a conspicuously fair and objective witness) also gave evidence to the effect that he set store by having had a business relationship with Mr Coleman for some 25 years; and he relied on him for his knowledge and experience and that he expected to be able to rely on Mr Coleman's indication given to him that Decoro products were saleable products in the UK. Mr Coleman's reliable recommendation was, as he put it, 'the extra ingredient' in the decision making process. I think that applied equally to other customers introduced by Mr Coleman. It was just because Mr Coleman had real standing and real clout in this particular business that these major customers were induced to be interested in Decoro's products. Mr Imrie also – and in my view importantly – stated that in general business terms the key role of an agent such as Mr Coleman was at the first stage: that is, in arranging sales to the retailer rather than in procuring sales by the retailer to the public.

59.   As it seems to me, but for Mr Coleman's efforts at the end of 1998 and during 1999 in introducing customers Decoro would have had no customer base. It is noticeable that in January 2000 Decoro was able to obtain substantial orders (from customers introduced by Mr Coleman) when it had no agent at all; and even when Mr Feltham-White started work for Decoro in February 2000 his initial activities were solely to service customers introduced by Mr Coleman. He was not in a position to achieve any new introductions until October 2000 (when there was the High Point fair at that time) and even during 2001 a very significant amount of Decoro's business still derived from customers who had been introduced by Mr Coleman. It is of some note that at that time Mr Feltham-White's experience had been entirely as a technical consultant: he simply did not have the general knowledge and experience of the retail customer side of the furniture industry, or the wide trade connections, which Mr Coleman had. It was Mr Coleman who, by his introductions, enabled Decoro to break into the UK market: and his efforts were, in my judgment, not significantly less causative of the conclusion of transactions in 2000 with customers introduced by him than they had been in 1999.

60.   Mr Hollander, however, submitted that the placing of the orders in 2000 was mainly attributable to the efforts of Decoro and Mr Feltham-White themselves. I reject that on the facts. It is of course true that the non-compliance with the 1988 Fire Safety Regulations had in 1999 been a

very serious problem. Mr Hollander submitted that Mr Coleman had sought to minimise that in his evidence. I reject that. Mr Coleman accepted in cross-examination that it had indeed been a very serious, indeed potentially disastrous, problem. But his simple point was that the problem had, by September 1999, been overcome. That evidence – which is borne out by the subsequent conduct of most of the customers and by, for example, the article in Cabinet Maker – I accept. No doubt that overcoming of the problem was in part due to the preparedness of Decoro to offer discounts to retailers to help compensate for their own losses and business disruption (as well as by its acting on its technical appraisals, through Mr Feltham-White while at Satra, and incorporating compliant foam and fibre in its manufacturing processes by 1st September 1999); but in my view that does not detract from the essential and continuing importance of Mr Coleman's role in having effected and maintained the introductions in the first place.

61. I thus also reject the suggestion of Mr Hollander that it was Decoro and Mr Feltham-White who restored the customers' confidence and that it was to their efforts (not Mr Coleman's) that the orders placed in 2000 were mainly attributable. Mr Feltham-White's witness statements on one reading might suggest that the fire-retardancy problems and customers' perception of such problems, and lack of confidence, persisted into 2000. However it became clear in the course of his cross-examination that Mr Feltham-White was saying no such thing. The principal technical problems in 2000 (which were addressed) were certain difficulties with the flattening of Dacron contents in some of the cushions. As Mr Feltham-White expressly accepted, the fire-retardancy problems had been eradicated by the time he was appointed to act as agent. The overall effect of Mr Feltham-White's evidence conveyed to me the same impression as the documents and other evidence (and as confirmed by the actuality of what happened): that at the end of 1999 most of Decoro's existing customer base – Furniture Village being the one significant 'doubter' – remained extremely keen to place orders for Decoro products, and had confidence in such products. For example, Sterling Furniture stated as much in a letter to Decoro of 21st January 2000; Cresta Furniture was another so to indicate at a meeting with Mr Feltham-White on 7th January 2000. By way of further example, Land of Leather alone sold over 30 containers of such furniture in the post-Christmas/New Year holiday period and placed substantial further orders in 2000: as did many other customers. As Mr Feltham-White conceded, he effectively took over the administration of customers Mr Coleman had previously introduced: he had the list of such customers from Decoro and his aim was to consolidate business with those customers so introduced by Mr Coleman. Moreover, many of the orders were repeat orders of models in existence in 1999.

62. I was unimpressed by the submission that Mr Coleman had by the end of 1999 minimal involvement with the customers and that this indicated that the orders placed in 2000 were not mainly attributable

to his efforts. Not only does this submission again unjustifiably down-play the importance of his initial introductions; it also downplays the extent of his continued dealings with customers in the second part of 1999. Mr Coleman, I am satisfied, did still have a continuing significant involvement – albeit reduced by reason of Decoro's unilateral (and uncommunicated) decision to seek itself to deal with customers direct. I also find as a fact that Mr Coleman was doing his best to help Decoro, during 1999, sort out the problems that had arisen relating to the 1988 Fire Safety Regulations: albeit that his ability to do so was reduced by reason of his own comparative lack of expertise in the relevant technical aspects and by reason of Decoro's appropriating to itself much of the dealing with concerned customers. I add that I further find as a fact that Decoro felt able to deal directly with customers, and ultimately felt able not to renew **Tigana**'s agency at the end of December 1999, just because it felt it had now secured a sufficient UK customer base represented by the customers introduced by Mr Coleman.

63. Ordinarily the lapse of time in any given case will, sooner or later, be likely to result in transactions ceasing to be 'mainly attributable' to the efforts of the original agent. I find, in the present case, that UK orders placed with Decoro during 2000 (save in respect of those – relatively few – placed after October 2000 from new customers introduced by Mr Feltham-White) were mainly attributable to the efforts of Mr Coleman during the agency. I include Furnitureland in this, for the reasons above given. I attach no weight to the statement of Mr Peddar (who was not tendered for cross-examination) that Furnitureland's decision to place new orders had 'nothing to do with Mr Coleman': since, among other things that statement was made in the context of a witness statement blaming Mr Coleman for inaction in dealing with the 1988 Fire Safety Regulation problems (which was not a matter pursued with Mr Coleman in evidence) and where Mr Peddar makes no reference to the potential significance of the initial introduction at all.

64. It is to be noted, however, that the provisions of Regulation 8(a) are conjunctive and cumulative: the transaction concluded is to be mainly attributable to the agent's efforts during the period of the agency contract *and* if the transaction is entered into within a reasonable period after the agency contract terminated. Thus the second part of Regulation 8(a) delimits the first part.

65. What is a reasonable period in this case? I have come to the conclusion it is nine months. I so conclude for essentially the following reasons:

65.1 By October 2000 Mr Feltham-White had become established as Decoro's agent in place of Mr Coleman.

65.2 Up to October 2000, Mr Feltham-White's activities had been confined to consolidating and administrating the customers introduced by Mr Coleman: by then, he had become familiar with existing customers and thereafter he also started to introduce some new custom himself.

65.3 By October 2000, there had been (or were about to be) High Point, and other trade fairs, where new Decoro models were displayed. Repeat orders for 1999 models were thus tending to disappear.

65.4 The significance of Mr Coleman's erstwhile involvement with Decoro would by October 2000 be likely substantially to have diminished in the eyes of even his most loyal supporters.

65.5 For the purposes of Regulation 8(a), nine months seems to me to be a fair reflection, in the circumstances, both of the nature of **Tigana**'s agency and of the actual period of such agency.

66. Accordingly, while I think that a proportion of the orders placed up to the end of 2000 (and, perhaps, even in the first part of 2001) could be said still to be mainly attributable to Mr Coleman's efforts, in my judgment nine months is to be determined as the reasonable period for the purposes of Regulation 8(a).

Quantum of commission payable under Regulation 8(a)

67. In the bundles before the court were included helpful revised schedules (based on the documentary disclosure of Decoro, and, as has been mentioned, containing some – albeit relatively minor – departures from the Appendices to Mr Coleman's witness statement) setting out the details of orders and totals of orders placed by customers over the relevant periods (including each quarter in 2000 and 2001). For the period from 1st January 2000 to 30th September 2000 the cumulative total orders placed (all being customers introduced by Mr Coleman, and the most significant being Land of Leather and Furnitureland) amounted to $12,867,613.61 (before transport costs). The commission payable was put at $606,836.64: see Appendix 2. If that were an agreed figure that (subject to one possible trifling arithmetical adjustment to $606,839.39) would be the sum accordingly payable.

68. That Appendix was prepared before trial by Mr White's solicitors, based on the then disclosed documents and then witness statements. In opening his case, however, Mr White said, without elaborating, that the evidence might indicate that the figures in Appendix 2 may not be accurate and that an account might be needed. Mr Hollander expressed disappointment at that stage that the figures, as set out in the Appendix, were not agreed. The trial continued. In due course, Mr Pratti verified his witness statements. Paragraphs 63 and 64 of his 3rd witness statement dated 7th November 2002 seem to indicate rather greater volumes of orders for 2000 than the schedules in Appendix 2 set out and thus that Appendix 2 may be something of an understatement of the true figure. Accordingly Mr White in his closing submissions duly sought an account in respect of the commission properly payable.

69. In written submissions presented after the conclusion of the trial, Mr Hollander submitted that was a misunderstanding: that it was a regrettable that **Tigana** had not sought clarification earlier; and a further (6th) witness statement of Mr Pratti was proffered. This was designed to show that paragraphs 63 and 64 of his 3rd witness statement had set out inaccurate approximate figures and that the true position was indeed as

revealed on disclosure and thus as reflected in Appendix 2. In a written response, Mr White protested at this further evidence (sought to be adduced after conclusion of the hearing without the leave of the court or the consent of the Claimant).

70.   I am not prepared at this stage, given the circumstances, to have regard to Mr Pratti's 6th witness statement. Mr White, in my view, was and is entitled to take the stance that he has (given the evidence proffered at the trial) and it would be unjust for Mr Pratti's 6th witness statement now to be accepted with no opportunity of challenge. Accordingly, if the parties cannot agree on the quantum of commission payable under Regulation 8(a), having regard to my determination in principle on that point, there will have to be an assessment of the sums due. In the circumstances, I reserve such assessment to myself. Decoro will be free at that stage to seek leave to adduce Mr Pratti's 6th witness statement (and other evidence) and to seek to make good Mr Hollander's assertion that **Tigana** now takes a 'thoroughly bad point'.

Does Regulation 17 apply to an agency contract expiring by effluxion of time?

71.   I turn then to the issues arising under Regulation 17. The essential issues are these

  71.1 Should the question of **Tigana**'s claimed entitlement in principle to compensation under Regulation 17 be referred to the European Court of Justice for a preliminary ruling?

  71.2 If not, as a matter of interpretation of the Agency Regulations is **Tigana** entitled to compensation at all under Regulation 17, given that the Sales Agreement expired by effluxion of time?

  71.3 If **Tigana** is entitled to compensation under Regulation 17, in what amount should that compensation be assessed?

72.   The first two issues arise in this way. Regulation 17 has effect, by Regulation 17 (1), 'after termination of the agency contract'. Shortly put, therefore, the issue is whether such regulation can apply at all where – as here – the agency contract has expired by effluxion of time.

73.   Mr Hollander's first submission was not, as it happens, that such Regulation (on its true interpretation) had no application at all to the Sales Agreement as having expired by effluxion of time. His first submission was that it was not clear whether Regulation 17 (itself based on Article 17 of the Directive) applied to agency contracts which expired by effluxion of time. The matter was not acte claire, he submitted, and accordingly there should be a reference to the European Court of Justice for a preliminary ruling, without more. In seeking a reference he placed reliance on certain general observations made by Sir Thomas Bingham MR in the Court of Appeal decision in *R v International Stock Exchange of the United Kingdom and Republic of Ireland Ltd, ex.p Else* [1993] QB 534. For his part, Mr White submitted that the discretion of a first instance Judge to refer, pursuant to CPR Pt. 68 and Article 234 of the EC Treaty,

was not so circumscribed and that a degree of doubt did not necessitate a reference; but that in any event the matter was sufficiently clear so as not to warrant a reference.

74.   It is a necessary consequence of Mr Hollander's case, in this context, that his own submission to the effect that Regulation 17 does not apply to agency contracts which have expired by effluxion of time is not plainly right. In my view, not only is that submission not plainly right: it is plainly wrong.

75.   The word 'termination' can readily – and in English legal terminology frequently does – carry with it the notion of a unilateral act of bringing to an end. I agree with Mr Hollander on that. But all depends on the context in which the word is used. 'Termination', for example, can also be taken to connote simply 'the coming to an end.'

75.1   Thus under Regulation 8 of those very Agency Regulations commission is payable (in the circumstances there set out) 'after the agency contract has terminated'. It is evident that Regulation 8 extends to agency contracts which have expired by effluxion of time: were it otherwise, the clear purpose behind that Regulation would stand to be seriously undermined. Indeed, Mr Hollander expressly conceded that Regulation 8 applies to contracts which have expired by effluxion of time in the course of his submissions by reference to what sums (if any) should be paid to **Tigana** under that regulation.

75.2   Again, in Regulation 20(2) it is expressly provided that a restraint of trade clause (which, by Regulation 2(1), is defined to mean an agreement restricting the business activities of a commercial agent 'following the termination of the agency contract') should be valid for not more than two years after 'termination of the agency contract'; again, it would be senseless to conclude that such provision did not apply to agency contracts which have expired by effluxion of time; again, Mr Hollander expressly conceded as much. That being so, it is plain that, within the Agency Regulations themselves, 'termination' can extend to expiry by effluxion of time; and it is difficult indeed to see why 'termination' should have any different meaning for the purposes of Regulation 17.

75.3   That interpretation also is consistent with Regulation 19. The restriction on derogation from Regulations 17 and 18 'before the agency contract expires' connotes that it is contemplated that Regulation 17 extends to agency contracts expiring by effluxion of time. Such interpretation also is at least consistent with the use of the word 'termination' in the other sub-paragraphs of Regulation 17 itself: and, in particular, is consistent with the entitlement to compensation or indemnity on the termination of the agency contract by death. It is also consistent with the provisions as to retirement through age or ill-health under Regulation 18(b). Indeed it would seem surprising that Regulation 17 could apply to agency contracts 'terminated' by death or retirement but not when they expire by effluxion of time. That view also, in my view, is consistent with the use of the word 'damage' in Regulation 17(6), which plainly in this context has a broad meaning.

76. It is true that Regulation 14 (contained in Part IV of the Agency Regulations, which is headed 'Conclusion and Termination of the Agency Contract') relates to an agency contract for a fixed period after that period has 'expired'. The word 'terminated' is not used. But that is readily to be explained by that regulation being deliberately designed to cover contracts being performed after the agreed fixed period has ended: the Regulation self-evidently does not deal with the termination of contracts generically.

77. In my judgment, therefore, all the intrinsic indications are that the phrase 'termination of the agency contract' in Regulation 17 extends to agency contracts which have expired by effluxion of time. But if there be adopted what is called a purposive approach to construction – and after all the court is positively required to seek to construe the Agency Regulations to accord with the Directive – then that conclusion is confirmed. Mr Hollander could advance no reason of policy or purpose for excluding agency contracts expiring by effluxion of time from the ambit of Regulation 17. To the extent that he submitted that it was simply a consequence of the bargain made (a) that does not fit well with Regulation 19 (b) that could be said of agency contracts which are (under the terms of the contract) terminable on notice: and yet Regulation 17, as is conceded, at all events applies to those. On the other hand, as the recitals to the Directive show, a principal purpose of the Directive was to afford protection to a commercial agent. Moreover one can discern from the Directive (and Article 17 and Regulation 17 themselves) a desire to prevent a principal from, as it were, unjustly enriching itself by appropriating to itself, without recompense, the goodwill and customer connection to which the efforts of the commercial agent have contributed; and to compensate the agent for the loss to him of his agency. There is no identifiable reason for there being an intention that that purpose should not be applicable to agency contracts which expire by effluxion of time: indeed that would seem to involve a major inroad into the protection otherwise designed to be offered.

78. There is a yet further consideration. As has been mentioned, Article 17 of the Directive itself contemplated the submission in due course of a report by the Commission to the implementation of the Article. Such report ('the 1996 Report') was in due course submitted on 23rd July 1996. Since it was sanctioned by the Article itself, I think it legitimate to have regard to it on these issues. At page 2 of the 1996 Report, it is expressly stated that the indemnity system (which, it is said, was modelled on Article 89b of the German Commercial Code) clearly provides for payment, inter alia, on the end of a fixed term contract. Accordingly, since Regulation 17 of the Agency Regulations extends both to indemnity and to compensation, it is very difficult to discern, as Mr White pointed out, any purpose in distinguishing, in principle, on so fundamental a

point the position applicable to awards under Regulation 17 in the case of compensation. I might add that it is of some interest also to note from the 1996 Report that, subsequent to the Directive, France changed its own laws expressly to apply the right of compensation to non-renewal of contracts expiring by effluxion of time. It is further of some note that the comments with regard to the United Kingdom contained in Appendix B of the 1996 Report include the following:

> 'In relation to compensation, lawyers try to apply traditional common law principles which does not work well since under the common law termination of a contract in accordance with its terms or at the natural end of a fixed term contract does not give rise to a damages claim.'

This suggests that the 1996 Report considers that refusal to make payment at the 'natural end of a fixed term contract' does not 'work well' with the Directive.

79. I therefore conclude that Regulation 17, on its true interpretation, extends to agency contracts which have expired by effluxion of time.

80. I was referred to a number of authorities: and all reach the like conclusion. In Bowstead and Reynolds on Agency (17th ed) at para 11–041) there is a detailed discussion of this very issue. After noting that, without further background, a common lawyer might conclude that there was nothing due on the regular expiry of a fixed term contract, the text goes on:

> 'The general background of the directive, however, and the way in which it is understood, and similar forms of legislation have been understood, in other European countries suggests almost conclusively that not only indemnity, but also compensation where there is no indemnity, should be available in this case.'

And in Chitty on Contracts (28th ed) Vol 2 para 32–147 (in the chapter on Agency, the editor of which was Professor Reynolds) this is said:

> 'To a common lawyer it might appear that it should not apply where the contract is for a fixed term which has run, on the basis that in such a case the contract is not terminated but simply expires. This is clearly contrary to the intention of the Directive and the laws of other EU countries make clear that [that] interpretation is not correct . . . .'

81. In *Page v Combined Shipping and Trading Co. Ltd* [1997] 3 All ER 656 (an interlocutory decision involving consideration of Regulation 17) Lord Justice Staughton, after referring to the recitals to the Directive, said this:

> 'Now, that indicates to my mind at least two purposes. The first is harmonisation of the law of Member States of the Community so that people compete – in the popular cliché of today – on a level playing field. It should not make any significant difference whether one employs a commercial agent in country "A" or country "B", they will compete on equal terms. The second objective is one which appears to be a motive of social policy, that commercial agents are a downtrodden race, and need and should be afforded protection against their principals.

> Those reasons seem to me to point fairly strongly to an intention to depart from the domestic legal provisions of the various countries in the Community or at any rate some of them, and achieve a regime which is new to some and will be the same for all.'

Those general observations at least accord with an approach which does not treat the word 'termination', as used in Regulation 17, in what might be styled the prima facie common-law sense; although, in any case, as I have sought to show, there are overwhelming reasons why, as a matter of ordinary construction, it is in any event not to be given such an interpretation. In *Whitehead v Jenks & Cattell Engineering Ltd* [1999] Eur LR 827 Judge Alton (sitting as a Judge of the High Court) in a carefully reasoned decision held that Regulation 17 of the Agency Regulations was apposite to include agency contracts which expired by effluxion of time. She placed – as would I – considerable emphasis on the fact that 'termination', depending on the context, variously may be focusing on the time of cessation of the contract or may be focusing on the mechanism by which the contract is brought to an end; and on the use of that word in the former sense in Regulations 8 and 20. Likewise, in the Scottish case of *Frape v Emreco International Ltd* [2002] Eur LR 10, Lord McEwan (sitting in the Court of Session, Outer House), who placed particular emphasis on the policy behind the Directive and on the requirement to seek to construe the Agency Regulations purposively so as to fulfil the policy behind the Directive, reached a similar conclusion. As he put it, the word 'termination' was, in this context, 'habile' to cover agency contracts which expire through effluxion of time. He expressly agreed with the decision of Judge Alton. I agree with the conclusion of each of Judge Alton and Lord McEwan.

82. I would only add (although it is not strictly, I think, relevant) that in this case, in practical terms, as a matter of mechanism the Sales Agreement was brought to an end by the decision of Decoro. True it is that in law the contract expired by effluxion of time, no agreement for renewal having been reached as provided by Clause 1. But the mutual hope and expection at the outset of the agency was, I am satisfied, that the agency would last for considerably more than a year (that indeed in part explains the existence of Clause 6): and Mr Coleman wished it to continue. In the circumstances, it did not: Decoro unilaterally communicating its intention not to renew the contract by its letters of December 1999. I find it wholly unsurprising that Regulation 17 (and Article 17) should provide for compensation on effluxion of the Sales Agreement in such circumstances.

83. In my judgment, as a matter of interpretation of the Agency Regulations by reference to their intrinsic terms; as a matter of interpretation of the Agency Regulations by reference to their (and the Directive's) perceived purpose and policy; and on consideration of the authorities to which my attention is drawn, the answer to the question raised is clear. Since all the arrows point in the same direction, that is the direction I propose to follow. Accordingly, I decline to direct a reference to the European

Court of Justice for a preliminary ruling; and I hold that Regulation 17 is capable of applying, and does apply, on the expiry of the Sales Agreement by effluxion of time on 31st December 1999.

To what amount of compensation is Tigana entitled under Regulation 17?

84. Regulation 17 is, in some respects, drafted in a way significantly different to Article 17. Article 17 provides as follows:

'1. Member States shall take the measures necessary to ensure that the commercial agent is, after termination of the agency contract, indemnified in accordance with paragraph 2 or compensated for damage in accordance with paragraph 3.

2 (a) The commercial agent shall be entitled to an indemnity if and to the extent that:

- he has brought the principal new customers or has significantly increased the volume of business with existing customers and the principal continues to derive substantial benefits from the business with such customers, and

- the payment of this indemnity is equitable having regard to all the circumstances and, in particular, the commission lost by the commercial agent on the business transacted with such customers. Member States may provide for such circumstances also to include the application or otherwise of a restraint of trade clause, within the meaning of Article 20;

(b) The amount of the indemnity may not exceed a figure equivalent to an indemnity for one year calculated from the commercial agent's average annual remuneration over the preceding five years and if the contract goes back less than five years the indemnity shall be calculated on the average for the period in question.

(c) The grant of such an indemnity shall not prevent the commercial agent from seeking damages.

3. The commercial agent shall be entitled to compensation for the damage he suffers as a result of the termination of his relations with the principal.

Such damage shall be deemed to occur particularly when the termination takes place in the circumstances:

- depriving the commercial agent of the commission which proper performance of the agency contract would have procured him whilst providing the principal with substantial benefits linked to the commercial agent's activities,

- and/or which have not enabled the commercial agent to amortize the costs and expenses that he had incurred for the performance of the agency contract on the principal's advice.

377

4. Entitlement to the indemnity as provided for in paragraph 2 or to compensation for damage as provided for under paragraph 3 or to compensation for damage as provided for under paragraph 3, shall also arise where the agency contract is terminated as a result of the commercial agent's death.

5. The commercial agent shall lose his entitlement to the indemnity in the instances provided for in paragraph 2 or to compensation for damage in the instances provided for in paragraph 3, if within one year following termination of the contract he has not notified the principal that he intends pursuing his entitlement.

6. The Commission shall submit to the Council, within eight years following the date of notification of this Directive, a report on the implementation of this Article, and shall if necessary submit to it proposals for amendments.'

85. Article 17 itself (as the 1996 Report observes) represents a compromise between the German system of indemnity and the French system of compensation. It seems there was a reluctance (notwithstanding the stated desire to remove differences between Member States as to the treatment of commercial agents and to achieve 'approximation' and 'harmonisation') to achieve uniformity by plumping for just one type of reparation. Most Member States have since opted for the indemnity system. France has continued with its compensation system. The United Kingdom, however, has compounded the compromise, as it were, by providing for both. Thus if the overall policy is that parties compete on a level playing field (in Lord Justice Staughton's phrase) parties, in the context of Regulation 17 and depending on whether the indemnity system or compensation system applies, could be said to be competing on different football pitches.

86. One difference in the wording of Regulation 17 as compared to Article 17 is that under the Agency Regulations an indemnity only applies where the agency contract so provides. It also is to be noted that Regulation 17 (here reflecting Article 17) provides that there is to be a 'cap' of one year's remuneration (as averaged) where the indemnity approach applies: and that, in cases of indemnity, damages may also be awarded. No such cap is provided by Regulation 17 with regard to compensation. Nor is there any provision with regard to payment of damages in addition to compensation. This indicates, in my view, that, in cases of compensation where there is also loss caused by a breach of contract or duty, 'damages' that would otherwise be payable are to be subsumed into, and taken into account as part of the assessment of, the compensation for the 'damage' which is to be awarded.

87. Mr White and Mr Hollander were agreed in this case on a number of points:

87.1 Since the Sales Agreement contains no provision for indemnity, compensation is the only relevant remedy in this case. This is obviously right.

87.2 Common law principles of mitigation and avoidable loss have no part to play in the assessment. Mr Hollander's concession in this respect is, in my view, also obviously right: having regard, for example, to the availability of compensation on the death or retirement of the agent (Regulations 17(8); 18(b)). As Mr Hollander put it, the focus is on the position at the time of termination: one looks back, not forward.

87.3 The amount of commission awarded under Regulation 8(a) is in this particular case (although not necessarily in all cases, as each of them expressly stated by way of qualification) a matter to be taken into account in deciding what compensation, if any, should be awarded under Regulation 17. Although Mr White did not accept this in his opening submissions, he did in his closing submissions; and in any case, in the circumstances of this particular case and given the nature of this particular agency, (and including the point that repeat orders would feature significantly) I am in no doubt that it is a factor that should be taken into account. Otherwise there might be an unfair element of potential double counting in favour of **Tigana**.

87.4 No question of breach of contract or duty now arises.

88.   Mr White and Mr Hollander were also agreed that, in assessing compensation, the court necessarily had to adopt something of a broad brush approach: as put in *King v Tunnock Ltd* 2000 SLT 744; [2000] Eur LR 531 (a decision of an Extra Division of the Inner House, Court of Session) 'a broad approach is both inevitable and a practical requirement of the law'. I agree with this: but I also agree with the submission of Mr Hollander that a court cannot simply alight on a figure by reference to its 'feel' of a particular case. There must be some methodology to the assessment, even though the approach is necessarily broad.

89.   The question then is: what are the factors to be taken into account in making the assessment and in deciding what compensation (if any) to award? I would venture to suggest that the following factors are likely to feature or to require consideration in such cases. I would not for one moment seek to offer this as an exhaustive list: further, some may not in fact feature at all in some cases; yet further, the weight (if any) to be given to each of such factors will vary from case to case. But at least the following can, I think, be identified:

89.1 The period of the agency, as provided for in the contract.

89.2 The period for which the agency in fact lasted up to termination.

89.3 The terms and conditions attaching to the agency as provided in the agency contract.

89.4 The nature and history of the agency and of the particular market involved.

89.5 The matters specifically mentioned in Regulation 17(7) (a) and (b).

89.6 The nature of the client base and of the kind of contracts anticipated to be placed (for example, 'one-off' or repeat).

89.7 Whether the principal has appointed the agent as its exclusive or non-exclusive agent.

89.8 The extent to which the agent has bound himself during the agency to act exclusively for the principal and the extent to which the agent is free to act for others (and whether in the same field of goods or services or not).

89.9 The extent to which the principal retains after termination of the agency benefit (for example, by way of enhanced trade connection or goodwill) from the activities of the agent during the agency.

89.10 The extent to which an agent is free, after termination, to have dealings with customers with whom he dealt during the agency (A restraint of trade clause will be a relevant consideration in this context).

89.11 Whether there are any payments under Regulation 8 (or other Regulations) which ought to be taken into account.

89.12 The manner in which the agency contract is ended: for example by notice given by the principal; or by notice given by the agent; or by effluxion of time; or as the case may be.

89.13 The extent to which the principal and agent respectively have financially contributed to the goodwill accruing during the period of agency.

89.14 The extent to which there may have been loss caused by any relevant breach of contract or duty.

90. It is clear that the 'damage' suffered by a commercial agent as a result of the termination of the agency (Regulation 17 (6)) is – generally speaking (and breach of contract cases aside) – to be regarded as a putative loss and not simply (by common law standards) actual loss. This is shown by the exclusion of principles of mitigation and applicability of the compensation provisions to termination on death or retirement. Clearly one important element, as the recitals to the Directive show, is to avoid a principal being unjustly enriched by retaining for itself without payment the entirety of the benefit of goodwill to which the activities of the agent during the agency have contributed. But another element (which finds both reflection and emphasis in Regulation 17(7) (a)) is to compensate the agent for the loss of a beneficial agency contract. One can perhaps there see some analogy with redundancy payments in an employment context: although the analogy cannot be pushed too far, since the policy considerations behind redundancy payments for employees are rather different.

91. A very striking illustration of the potential reach of Regulation 17 is to be found in the case of *King v Tunnock* itself. In that case, the pursuer's father had acted for many years as agent for the defenders, Tunnocks, a manufacturer of cakes and biscuits, selling their products at wholesale prices to retailers. In 1962 the pursuer took over the business for his father, his business consisting exclusively of selling Tunnock's products. On 14th July 1994, Tunnocks closed down their bakery operations and the agency was terminated on that date in consequence. The pursuer was held entitled in the Sheriff Court to payment of £4,762 in lieu of any notice given (cp Regulation 15 of the Agency Regulations) but, notwithstanding that his agency had lasted over 30 years, not entitled to

any compensation under Regulation 17: since it was not shown that he had suffered any loss entitling him to compensation. The decision was upheld by the sheriff principal; but reversed by the Inner House of the Court of Session. The Court awarded the pursuer an additional £27,144 (and interest), representing the total gross agency earnings in the last two years of the agency contract. Thus although Tunnocks retained no benefit from the termination of the agency (since they had closed down their bakery operation) and although the pursuer suffered, on the common law approach, no actual loss (in that he was compensated for the failure to give 3 months notice and there would thereafter have been no Tunnocks bakery products for him to sell) he nevertheless was awarded substantial compensation.

92. That decision was much debated before me, and in consequence I will have to deal with Counsel's submissions on it. I would at the outset like to point out, however, that it is (as a matter of decision) clearly distinguishable on the facts from the present case: not least because, as I find, in the present case Decoro has received very substantial benefits by reason of the activities and efforts of Mr Coleman as agent which it has, after termination of the agency contract, retained and used for itself (without payment): viz the customer base introduced by Mr Coleman; and because here the agency lasted for a very much shorter period than in *King v Tunnock.*

93. In the course of giving the reserved judgment of the court (the court having been supplied with, and referred at length to, materials as to French Law) Lord Caplan said this:

> '33. In our view there can be little doubt as to the objectives of the 1986 Directive. The preamble to the Directive states its objectives very plainly. It is quite clear that the Directive is aimed at removing restrictions on the activities of commercial agents caused by the differing laws of the Member States. The aspiration is to harmonise the laws so that conditions for commercial agents throughout the European Community are equivalent to those of a single market. A major aim is to remove inconsistencies in the laws of Member States as they relate to commercial agents. Moreover, the differences in the national laws are said to be detrimental to the protection available to commercial agents *vis-à-vis* their principals, particularly where principal and agent are established in different Member States. It must be noted that the requirement of protection is focused on the position of the agent and not on that of the principal who, presumably, will normally be in a stronger position and thus able to look after himself. The aspect of a Directive in protecting the agent is reinforced by a reference in preamble to Article 117 of the European Community Treaty. This narrates that Member States agree upon the need to promote improved working conditions and an improved standard of living for workers.

34. No matter what objectives underlie the legislation there can
never be a guarantee that it will deliver the required results.
However, in the present case if the national courts treating
their country's application of the Directive under their own
national regulations continue to produce divergent results
then the whole objective of the Directive has failed.

. . .

38. Looking therefore to the terms of Regulation 17(6) and
Regulation 17(7) we must say that in the eyes of UK lawyers
the draughtsmanship is at best somewhat clumsy. However,
by construing these provisions within the context of the
Regulations there is an obvious pattern. In doing so we take
into account that Regulation 17(1) appears to envisage that
paragraphs (6) and (7) should be read together for the
purpose of giving compensation for damage. The governing
principle is that expressed in Regulation 17(6). The agent is
entitled to compensation for damage he suffers as a result of
the termination of his relationship with the principal. The
word 'suffers' is in the present tense, which suggests that
the point of time defining damage is the termination of the
agency. Moreover, what is compensated is 'the termination
of his relations with his principal'. The emphasis is not on
his future loss but on the impact of the severance of his
agency relationship with his principal. An agency generally
has commercial value. This is acknowledged by the fact that
under Regulation 18(c) the commercial agent may, with
the agreement of his principal, assign his agency contract
to another. If he does that he does not get compensation
since he has an opportunity to cash in on the value of his
agency (assuming it has value at all). He thus has suffered
no damage through loss of agency. There are two aspects of
the termination situation which must be considered. The
first is the fact and circumstances of the termination (certain
causes of termination excluding compensation). The word
'damage' is used to connote the factor that mainly introduces
the eligibility for compensation. However, it is important
to keep in mind that the reference is to damage or iniura
and not to 'damages'. Looking, therefore, at damage, he is
entitled to compensation. The question of course remains as
to the level of compensation and the specific reference to
circumstances deemed to be damage is even more immediate
than it is in the Regulations.

. . .

40. Transferring attention to Regulation 17(6), the entitlement
to compensation is not stated to be dependent on any
particular type or extent of loss. The only requirement is
damage through the termination of the agent's relation

with his principal. Reference to the termination of the relationship with the principal is important. There is no equivalent provision regarding indemnity. Indemnity can arise if the agency is terminated and the principal continues to gain through the agent's efforts. Thus one has to pay regard particularly to commercial factors such as commission lost to quantify the indemnity. However, compensation is payable upon rupture of the relationship with the principal. At that point of time the value of the lost agency must be ascertained and there is simply no reference to the actual course of events to be expected after termination. Indemnity hinges upon the principal continuing in business and exploiting the agent's connection. Unless Regulation 17(7) represents a restriction or qualification of Regulation 17(6), it is not necessary for the agent to project his actual prospective loss. All he needs to prove is that after termination he had lost the value of an agency asset which, prior to the termination, existed. The importance of the asset to the agent is emphasised by consideration of the definition of a commercial agent with his 'continuing authority' (Regulation 2(1)) and the obligation of the principal to notify a downturn below that which the agent 'could normally have expected' (Regulation 4(3)). If what is lost has little or no value than of course the level of compensation may be fixed at a low level, but that is a different matter.

41. Under Regulation 17(7) damage is deemed to occur 'particularly' when termination takes place in various defined circumstances. Now the sheriff and sheriff principal construe Regulation 17(7) as meaning, in effect, that damage will be deemed to occur 'only when the specified circumstances apply' or at least 'in particular' when these circumstances apply. It must be observed that if the intention had been to provide that compensation should be paid when Regulation 17(7) (a) or (b) apply then it would have been much easier to say that rather than to employ the circuitous draftsmanship occuring in Regulation 17(6) and (7). In any event the deemed damage is said to occur not 'only' in certain circumstances, but 'particularly' in certain circumstances. The meaning of the word 'particularly' received careful consideration in the debate before us. We agree with the view that 'particularly' is used in its normal meaning of 'especially noted' or 'more than others'. It has to be observed that in the French text the word 'notamment', which is defined as meaning 'notably' or 'among others'. Why two special situations should be expressly directed is not clear. It may be that the directive was seeking to say that in these particular circumstances there can be no doubt that damage will have been suffered. The

agent is safe from having to demonstrate that he has suffered damage when these particular situations arise.

42. However, once one were to accept that Regulation 17(7) does not set out the exclusive circumstances giving rise to compensation the only guidance that is left as to what other circumstances might give rise to compensation are the governing provisions of Regulation 17(6). If it can be shown that damage has been done to the agency relationship, then compensation will arise and the remaining question is the level of that compensation. We do not claim that the import of Regulation 17(7), when it is viewed in isolation, is without difficulty, but the matter becomes much clearer if the whole of the regulations are considered. First, there is no particular equitable requirement to link compensation to what the principal gains from the termination. Exploitation of the agent by the principal would generally be prevented by Regulation 8, which gives the agent a right to commission on sales to his own customers even after this agency has ended. Regulation 17 obviously acknowledges that compensation can be payable to an agent even over and above what he will gain from commission from sales gained by the principal, with the agent's customers, after the agency ends.

43. Regulation 18 is curious because the heading to the regulation refers to 'grounds for excluding payment of indemnity or compensation under Regulation 17'. The terms of the regulation thereafter relate to 'the compensation referred to in Regulation 17'. The regulation itself distinctly differentiates between 'compensation' and 'indemnity'. Be that as it may, the agent who has given up his agency because of age, infirmity or illness remains eligible for compensation. Under Regulation 17(8) the agent who dies is likewise entitled to compensation. These arrangements suggest that the entitlement is not limited to a situation where the agent's future earnings are critical to his entitlement. The vital difference between indemnity provisions and the compensation provisions is that indemnity requires that the principal should continue his business. If theȳ20principal does not continue in business after the termination the requirements of Regulation 17(3) cannot be satisfied. In the case of compensation there is no prerequisite to entitlement that the principal continues in business. Thus compensation may arise where (as in this case) the principal shut down the relevant part of his business, or, say, ceases to trade because the company goes into receivership. We can thus conclude that in so far as entitlement to compensation is concerned, the Directive is not troubled with what happens after the date of termination. It is the value of the rupture of

the agency relationship that is the source and justification of compensation.

. . .

48.   It is obvious in our view, that on the basis of their own terms Regulation 17(6) and (7) provides for a different basis of making compensation than our traditional common law approach. However, as stated, the regulation does fit in well with the French approach to such compensation. The legislation provides for valuation at the date of termination rather than requiring an explanation of the future prospects for the agency. During the currency of the agency the agent has owned a valuable asset and what he chooses or omits to do after he has lost that asset has no bearing on the value of what he has lost. If he had assigned the agency he would normally have received some compensation for that assignation, observing that he could do so only with the principal's agreement and been free thereafter to do as he chose. Thus the French conclusion that mitigation of loss by agent is not a factor when compensation is approached as we have described, is, in our view, persuasive. The implication would be (and in our view we consider this to be inevitable) that in the present case the post-termination activities of the pursuer and any sums of sickness benefit he received have no application to the measure of his loss. The Directive and Regulations, as presented, seem to harmonise with the French approach and, given their terms, and the general objective of achieving harmonisation, we see no justification for construing the Regulations as being radically different from the French approach.

49.   The matter of fixing an appropriate level of compensation remains. It seems that even in France the two-year rule is only a benchmark and can be varied at the discretion of the judge. However, this does not mean that we are precluded from considering what will happen in France, for the rulings of a judicial system applying the same legislation (intended, indeed, to operate in the same way between the relevant systems) must be entitled to some respect. There are also practical considerations. The French law obviously considers that there is some merit in finding a clear and practical basis for determining a fair level of loss. We equally consider that given the particular type of loss we are dealing with, a broad approach is both inevitable and a practical requirement of the law. This approach is emphasised when we consider that they are seeking an overview of the commercial situation where one of the dominant aims is to protect the agent.'

The Court went on to award a figure representing the total of the last two years of the pursuer's gross earnings. The court indicated that that figure represented a sum he would have been likely to have required to have surrendered his agency and further stated (at the end of paragraph 51): 'We are reassured that under French law compensation of two years commission would be regarded as a standard compensation for the loss of the agency, so that it is difficult to believe that in the present case such compensation could be other than reasonable.'

94. Mr White supported that decision, both as to its reasoning and its conclusions. In his opening written submissions, indeed, he submitted that I was bound by that decision: although, in this context, Mr White disclaimed, on my query, any reliance on the choice of law clause in the Sales Agreement identifying the applicable law as that of 'the United Kingdom' (sic). Mr White referred me to the decision of Mr Justice Morland in *Ingmar GB Ltd v Eaton Leonard Inc* [2001] Eur LR 756 – a case involving questions of compensation under Regulation 17. In the course of his judgment Mr Justice Morland, having referred at length to *King v Tunnock* said this (at paragraph 39): 'In my judgment, in so far as the Court of Session interpreted the purpose of the Regulations and enunciated principles of law, I am and should be bound by the decision of the Inner House as a first instance Judge.' Mr Justice Morland went on to stress the desirability of courts in England and Wales (Northern Ireland has its own regulations) in applying the same principles as the courts of Scotland by reference to the Agency Regulations: which in terms apply to the activities of commercial agents in Great Britain.

95. Whilst there is a general practice that in revenue and taxation cases English courts will regard themselves as bound by relevant decisions of superior Scottish courts, I am not aware of any practice or precedent (and none was cited to me) that in other cases an English court is so bound: although there are, of course, cases stressing the desirability of English and Scottish courts reaching the same conclusion on common legislation. Of course, the English court will treat a decision of the Scottish Court with the greatest respect and will be disinclined to depart from it (the more so, in the present context, given the general applicability of the Agency Regulations to Great Britain). But that is a different matter to being *bound* by the decision. In the event, Mr White in his closing submissions withdrew his suggestion that I was strictly bound by the decision in *King v Tunnock*: and I have to say that, in my own view, I am not strictly bound to follow it. But in any case the actual decision was, as I have said, one on its own facts.

96. I would state my respectful agreement, however, with the Inner House of the Court of Session in its ruling that an award of compensation is not solely confined to situations where one or other of the sets of circumstances set out in Regulation 17 (7) (a) and (b) is established and the Regulation does not delimit the kind of loss for which compensation may be awarded. I think that is so, in agreement with the Court of Session, because, firstly, Regulation 17(7) 'deems' damage – which is to be contrasted with 'damages' – to have occurred 'particularly when' those circumstances occur: the word 'particularly' clearly connotes

that there may be situations where compensation can be awarded (and 'damage' has occurred) even though those circumstances specified in Regulation 17(7)(a) or (b) are not shown to exist; and, secondly, because (as explained by the Court of Session) such interpretation better accords with the policy of the Directive.

97. Where I must, with great respect, express reservations as to certain aspects of the judgment in *King v Tunnock* is with regard to the degree of primacy apparently given by the Inner House to French law and practice in deciding on the general level of awards of compensation. In the 1996 Report there is a useful summary of the applicable French law. It seems that the French courts customarily award compensation of two years gross remuneration on termination of an agency contract (although that is a bench-mark only and the court retains a discretion). The Inner House of the Court of Session, citing the 1996 Report and passages from a French text-book and other materials as to French law, and stressing the importance of harmonisation as between Member States on these provisions, seems to endorse the general application of a 'two-year rule' (albeit the court stressed that it is a bench mark only and can be 'varied' at the discretion of the Judge: see paragraph 49 of the judgment). That decision was, in due course, described by Judge Bowers (sitting as a Judge of the High Court) in *Barret Mckenzie v Escada (UK) Ltd* (unreported: 1st February 2001) as setting a 'tariff'. As to that, Judge Bowers stated that he disagreed with *King v Tunnock*.

98. My approach is as follows.

98.1 First, it seems to me as a matter of principle that if it were intended by the Directive that, on matters of compensation, French law were to apply, then it would and should have said so. Thus in *Nicolaus Corman & Fils SA v Hauptzellamt Groman* [1982] ECR 13, the court said (at paragraph 8):

'... the Community legal order does not in fact aim in principle to define its concepts on the basis of one or more national legal systems without express provision to that effect.'

In *R v Customs & Excise Commissioner ex p. EMU Tabac* [1998] ALL ER (EC) 402, the court said (at paragraph 30):

'First it is clear from the case law of the court that the Community Legal order does not, in principle, aim to define concepts on the basis of one or more national legal systems unless there is express provision to that effect ...'

Accordingly in the case of *Bell Electric Ltd v Aweco Systems Appliance GmbH* [2002] EWHC (QB) 872 (8th May 2002) to which Mr Hollander referred me, Mr Justice Elias, speaking in the context of the approach to assessing compensation under Regulation 17, observed that courts in England and Wales are not obliged as a result of European Union law itself to apply the principles of French law in determining compensation. I agree.

98.2 This general principle is not alluded to in the judgment in *King v Tunnock*. This may be because the Court of Session was taking the view that the court was not seeking to apply French law, as such, as a matter of decision but only having regard to it with a view to achieving a harmonised approach: cp the comments of Lord Hamilton in *Roy v M.R Pearlman Ltd* 1999 SC 459 at p 469 G-H and the comments of Mr John Mitting QC (sitting as a deputy Judge of the High Court) in *Moore v Piretta PTA Ltd* [1999] 1 ALL ER 174 at p 176. I can, at all events, certainly see that a court which is concerned with questions of compensation under Regulation 17 would wish to have regard to statements as to French law and practice – which in my view can sufficiently be garnered from the 1996 Report itself – as explaining the background to and purpose of the Directive. I would also regard it as unexceptionable for a court to choose to have regard to it as one factor, by way of a comparator, in the overall consideration of an award of compensation under Regulation 17. Indeed it may well be, judging by the contents of paragraphs 50 and 51 of the judgment in *King v Tunnock* (and particularly the last sentence of paragraph 51) that the Court of Session considered that that was what it was doing: although it must be said there are passages elsewhere in the judgment which seem to be putting it rather more strongly. Be that as it may, I do not think what is said to be French law and practice can be used to dictate the approach to, or operation of, the assessment of compensation under Regulation 17; and to the extent that Mr White's submissions went that far I reject them.

98.3 The Directive has left it to each of the Member States to implement the Directive. Courts in England and Wales will be assessing compensation awards under Regulation 17, applying the Agency Regulations under an agency contract governed (ordinarily) by English law. Where an English court is concerned to construe, or give effect to, a contract governed by French law then of course it will (on production of appropriate expert evidence) seek to ascertain what the French law is and then apply it (see, indeed, the express provisions of Regulation 1(3), as amended). Apart from that, however, it seems to me wrong for the English court, when considering the issue of compensation under Regulation 17, to attempt to put itself in the shoes of a French court in the case of a contract governed by English law to which the Agency Regulations (applicable in Great Britain) apply. Otherwise (in the words of Judge Hallgarten QC in the County Court decision of *Duffen v Frabo* [2000] ILL Rep 180) 'it will find itself drawn into attempting to mimic what a French court would actually have done, a task which it is ill-equipped to perform'. Besides, given that under French law the Judge has a discretion to depart from the 'two year rule', it would seem to be an impossible hypothetical task to identify on the facts of a particular case how or to what extent a French court would exercise such a discretion. It is, surely, for the court actually seised of the case to make its own decision and exercise its own judgment under Regulation 17.

98.4 The approach indicated in *King v Tunnock* could lead to the conclusion that in particular cases evidence as to French law may be needed. Indeed the Court of Session so indicated: see paragraphs 44 and 47 of the judgment. But many of these cases for compensation will be for relatively modest sums and will involve claims brought in the County Court or Sheriff Court. It seems very doubtful that it was contemplated by the drafters of the Directive or Regulations that local solicitors should be required to familiarise themselves with and adduce expert evidence of the French law (or, in cases of indemnity, German law) and obtain access to French (or German) legal advice – even if they had the resources and facilities to do so – with regard to a particular case; or that parties should have to pay for that.

98.5 The Court of Session thought that if application of the Directive under a country's own national regulations produced divergent results then the 'whole objective of the Directive had failed.' Obviously 'approximation' is the aim and 'harmonisation' is the object and it is clear that the Directive was concerned to protect commercial agents generally. Such agents' *right* to indemnity or compensation, equally applicable to all Member States, is spelled out in the Directive. But the *remedy* (that is to say, whether the indemnity or compensation approach is to be adopted and how quantification is to be worked out) is to a significant degree left to each Member State. Thus not only does the Directive build into itself a divergence by allowing for a choice between an indemnity system or compensation system (or, as the UK has chosen to interpret it, both) in the first place: the Directive also ascribes to Article 17 a further degree of divergence by letting Member States (and the courts of Member States) work out – subject to the requirements spelled out in Article 17 – the method of assessment for themselves. The report contemplated by Article 17(6) (and as submitted in 1996) was, in part, I infer, to assess whether the anticipated divergence might prove to be too great to be acceptable. Moreover, Regulation 17 of the Agency Regulations having then chosen to build into its own provisions the potential divergence between indemnity and compensation, by allowing for both, it seems – to me at least – odd positively to enhance the potential divergence by applying a two year tariff for compensation cases whereas indemnity cases are capped (and it is a cap, not a tariff) at one year. One would have thought that a court might at least be rather slow (save in a very meritorious case) to make an award of compensation very significantly in excess of the maximum available under the indemnity provisions of Regulation 17.

98.6 Finally, it is a point of comment that aspects of the French Civil Code applicable to commercial agents have since been significantly modified, as the 1996 Report notes – the clear inference being that the Civil Code was modified to bring it in line with the Directive.

That is not consistent with an understanding that French law (as it stood in 1986) with regard to compensation was to be taken as determining the whole approach as to compensation under Article 17 of the Directive.

99. Mr White urged that the two year 'tariff' led to certainty and that it was desirable for parties to know where they stood. If it were otherwise, he submitted, they, and their legal advisers, would be unable to predict, in any given case, the outcome. (He did not altogether demur when I put it to him that, if he were anatomically to be judged, he seemed to prefer to be judged by a rule of thumb rather than a rule which he feared would accord to the length of a judge's foot). But uncertainty, I am afraid, is not uncommon in legal contexts; and in any event there must be occasions when the desideratum of certainty should, in the interests of justice, yield to the desideratum of flexibility. Besides, an appeal to certainty is rather weakened when it is seen that in any event the court has a broad discretion to depart from the asserted two-year rule when justice so requires in a particular case. Moreover, my wariness as to a two-year rule, so called, being applicable to the Agency Regulations is considerable. I find it difficult, speaking for myself, to think there is, or at all events should be, precisely the same benchmark for a commercial agency which has been lawfully terminated in circumstances where the principal has retained no benefit resulting from the agency itself and where the agent would have derived no benefit from the agency after termination in any event, on the one hand, as compared to a commercial agency which has been terminated by the principal in circumstances where the principal retains substantial benefit (by way of enhanced goodwill and trade connection) arising from the efforts of the agent and where the agent would have continued to derive considerable sums of commission had the agency continued, on the other hand. Nor is it clear as to whether the 'two year' rule is designed (presumably by use of projected or extrapolated figures) to apply to agency contracts lasting less than two years and (if so) on what basis. These are but examples reflecting the wide variety of circumstances that may apply in each case; and point against a tariff system being designed to apply under Regulation 17.

100. In my judgment, therefore, and in rejection of Mr White's submissions on this point, I am not bound to seek to apply what is said to be French law and practice, and I am not bound to apply a 'two year tariff' (albeit subject, as Mr White accepts, to a discretion to depart from it) in this case. There is no 'tariff' applicable under English law, in my judgment, for the purposes of determining compensation under Regulation 17. Nor, in my view, is an English court, where the agency contract is governed by English law, bound to enquire into French (or any other Member State) law. Rather, in my view, the court has to make its assessment of the compensation (if any) to be paid under Regulation 17 having regard to the 'balance sheet' (as Mr Hollander put it) of relevant considerations, by reference to the circumstances of each case.

101. In the present case, it is plain, on the facts, that the circumstances identified in Regulation 17(7) (a) obtain here. 'Damage' is thus deemed to have occurred. Further, in the present case, it is plain, on the facts, as I have already said, that Decoro has retained for itself – thus far, without any payment – the 'substantial benefits' of the customer connection introduced by Mr Coleman (I unhesitatingly reject, on the facts, for the reasons already given, Mr Hollander's submission that, as at 31st December 1999, there was a 'negative goodwill'). For these reasons alone I take the view that **Tigana** is entitled to significant compensation under Regulation 17. Mr White also stressed the continuing availability of these customers to Decoro and that Decoro, notwithstanding that it had in effect dispensed with Mr Coleman's services (relieving itself of the obligation to pay him commission in the process), had been able seamlessly to continue to manufacture and deliver its furniture for the UK market through the year 2000. Mr White further submitted that the agency had been of some length; that its very nature, in particular the introductory element, meant that it was to a significant extent 'front-loaded'; that it came to an end, in practical terms, by the choice of Decoro, not **Tigana**; and that upon termination Mr Coleman and **Tigana** were in practical terms to an extent restricted in their ability to offer corresponding leather furniture made by other manufacturers to those customers, given that they had now established a connection with Decoro. Mr White submitted that in all the circumstances of this case compensation of not less than the equivalent of two years gross remuneration should be awarded.

102. For his part, Mr Hollander pointed out that, on the other side of the balance sheet, the agency had been relatively short: the situation thus was very different to that in *King v Tunnock* and *Ingmar GB Ltd*. In formal terms it had lasted just for one year: and in practical terms no more than 15 months (Mr Hollander fairly and realistically disclaiming any argument to the effect that in the months of October and November and December 1998 it might be said that it was Mr Coleman, not **Tigana**, who was acting). He also stressed – and I think these are points of considerable weight – that the agency had not been exclusive: Mr Coleman thus had been free to carry out (and had carried out) his valuable agency contracts with other furniture manufacturers; and Mr Coleman (and **Tigana**) had been subject to no restraint of trade provision and had been free, after termination, to solicit business from the customers he had introduced to Decoro. He also validly pointed out that, in the circumstances of this case, commission payable under Regulation 8(a) – and, in the result, I have determined that such is payable in a substantial sum – was a relevant factor, to ensure that there was no element of double benefit in favour of **Tigana**. He further added that **Tigana** had gained significant commission already under the Sales Agreement and, for good measure, that an award assessed as at 31st December 1999 involved a degree of accelerated payment.

103. Mr Hollander re-emphasised the point that he had made in his argument on Regulation 8(a), to the effect that much of the success was due to

the fact that the products of Decoro were excellent products, keenly priced: further, that the customer base had, after the problems with the 1988 Fire Safety Regulation, been retrieved, and then consolidated, by Decoro's own efforts: not least by its preparedness to offer substantial discount arrangements to customers affected by the problems under the 1988 Fire Safety Regulations. I again attach little weight to these points in the circumstances. That the product was, essentially, an excellent product, keenly priced, was a given: it was, indeed, a fundamental reason for Mr Coleman entering into the agency contract in the first place. That Decoro itself greatly assisted in retrieving the position, after the problems with the 1988 Fire Safety Regulations, has to be set in context: these problems arise through no default of Mr Coleman (as evidenced by the abandonment of the counterclaim and of reliance on Regulation 18(a)). More generally, I consider that an enquiry as to the respective non-financial contributions by principal and agent to achieving the business of particular customers is likely, in the usual case (and at all events in this case) to be unhelpful. As pointed out by Mr John Mitting QC in *Moore v Piretta PTA Ltd* at p 182:

> 'The parties have after all agreed a percentage to reward the agent for his efforts which reflects their judgment of the value of his efforts.'

There may be cases where such an enquiry is appropriate: for example, where the agreed remuneration is significantly out of step with the industry norm; or perhaps – albeit generally the performance of an agent retained on a commission basis will in any event find reflection in the commission he earns – where the performance of the agent has been lamentable (albeit falling short of 'default' for the purposes of Regulation 18 (a)). This is not such a case. It is, I think, sufficient for me simply to reaffirm my finding that **Tigana** (through Mr Coleman) throughout carried out the agency effectively (being instrumental in introducing major customers) and diligently.

104. Mr Hollander also submitted that it was a relevant consideration that it was Decoro which had to bear all the losses occasioned by the non-compliant furniture, whereas (so he said) **Tigana** had not borne any part of those losses. I am not moved by that. Decoro must (at least vicariously) bear the responsibility for what happened: **Tigana** itself (the counterclaim being abandoned and it not being put to Mr Coleman that he had been at fault) does not bear the responsibility. Further, **Tigana** was, on Mr Hollander's own approach, adversely affected: to the extent that sales were lost, **Tigana** itself lost commission. Moreover, **Tigana** had to bear an extra administrative burden in dealing with the complaints and Mr Coleman himself had to devote much time to helping sort out the problems.

105. A further issue arose, in that Mr White submitted that compensation awarded under Regulation 17 should be assessed by reference to gross remuneration. Mr White again relied heavily on *King v Tunnock* in this regard and on French practice – whereby, as the 1996 Report states,

compensation is usually awarded by reference to gross remuneration. For his part, Mr Hollander submitted that it should be by reference to net remuneration (that is, after making allowance for expenses incurred in the operation of the agency). Mr White did not seek to say that the court was always required to make an award on a gross basis: it had, he said, a discretion to make an award on a net basis; but he submitted that a court ordinarily should. For his part Mr Hollander, as I understood him, submitted that it would never be appropriate for an English court to award compensation under Regulation 17 on a gross remuneration basis. In this context, Mr Hollander referred me to comments of Judge Hallgarten QC in *Duffen v Frabo* to the effect that it would be 'offensive' to award the claimant compensation on a gross basis (although I think Judge Hallgarten QC may have been speaking by reference to the facts of the particular case before him); and to the use of the like word 'offensive' by Judge Bowers (speaking more generally on the operation of Regulation 17) in *Barret Mckenzie v Escada (UK) Ltd.* Both judges clearly and understandably were concerned that otherwise there might be something of a windfall for the agent.

106. For myself, I do not think it would be wrong in principle, or necessarily 'offensive' in all cases, for an English court to award compensation by reference to gross remuneration. I say this for three reasons in particular:

106.1 First, under Regulation 17, an indemnity can be calculated by reference to gross remuneration (see Regulation 17(4) and the comments on the indemnity system in the 1996 Report). Why should the compensation system necessarily and invariably be different?

106.2 Second, it seems clear that the Directive contemplates that goodwill established by an agent for the benefit of the principal can be treated, as it were, as a quasi-proprietary right in which the agent is taken to have a share and of which he is divested on termination. It would not necessarily be commercially unusual, for example, for the price for the sale of the goodwill of an agency (if assignable) to be calculated by reference to gross earnings. Indeed it is of note that in *King v Tunnock* the court adopted that very approach in deciding on the level of compensation to be awarded to the pursuer, on the facts of that particular case: see paragraph 51 of the judgment.

106.3 Third, once it is accepted (as it has to be) that common law principles of loss and damage do not govern the operation of Regulation 17, it is no real extension to the assessment of the compensation for 'damage' under Regulation 17(6) to permit an award of compensation by reference to gross remuneration.

107. Nevertheless, I am also firmly of the view that an English Court is fully entitled to award compensation by reference to net remuneration, rather than gross remuneration; and it is not required to take gross remuneration as a starting-point or to treat it as the norm. To the extent that (if relevant) this may involve some degree of divergence from what

may be standard French practice (albeit the position in any event is discretionary in France) then that divergence seems to me to be within the margin of divergence which is contemplated by the Directive. After all, as Mr Hollander cogently pointed out, the fact that common law principles as to loss and damage do not govern awards of compensation under Regulation 17 does not mean that the English court is required altogether to shut its eyes to what the actual loss is: and in any case considerations of loss are consistent with the wording of Regulation 17 itself.

108. Considering the various factors which I have mentioned in paragraph 89 above, and the 'balance sheet' of points advanced on behalf of **Tigana** and Decoro respectively, I have come to the conclusion that the compensation to be awarded to **Tigana** should be assessed by reference to the net remuneration of **Tigana** in the period of its agency. That is not just a period of 12 months: it should also, in my judgment, extend the first two and a half months or so in which Mr Coleman acted (before the agency contract formally commenced) since these were very important in initiating some of the valuable introductions of customers to Decoro. The total (gross) is thus $558,725 + $6,707 = $565,432. I consider that expenses should be deducted, in all the circumstances of this case, not least because it was agreed that **Tigana** would bear its own expenses (excluding flights to and hotel costs in China and Hong Kong) and because I consider to do so fairly reflects the nature and history of this particular agency. I had no precise figures as to these expenses (**Tigana** not, it seems, having prepared any accounts). Moreover a considerable part of Mr Coleman's overall overheads and expenses are attributable to his other agencies. Mr Coleman told me, however, that of the $215,432 that was paid to **Tigana**, all went to Stuart Coleman & Associates to defray expenses. Some in fact went to pay expenses properly payable by Decoro for flights to and hotel costs to China (including the £34,987 ultimately recovered in that regard from Decoro in 2000); some, I anticipate, having regard to Mr Coleman's evidence, were in respect of extra secretarial costs incurred by **Tigana** to deal with customers complaints about fire regulation problems. I do not think an inquiry need be directed as to the expenses. I assess the appropriate deduction as 20% of the gross remuneration. Thus the award of compensation which I make is in the sum of $452,346.

109. In making that assessment, I have also asked myself, by way of a check, whether such an award is fair and proportionate: if it seemed to be prima facie to be too high (or too low) I would have reconsidered the weight I had been minded to give to the various factors. (I observe that a similar approach seems to have been adopted by Mr Justice Morland in the *Ingmar GB Ltd* case in deciding, in the event, not to adopt a two year purchase approach: see paragraph 52 of his judgment). In my view, an award of $452,346 (reflecting the net remuneration in the effective period of the agency) is, in the circumstances of this case, the appropriate award under Regulation 17.

110. I add that, even if I had regarded myself as bound to take a 'two year gross remuneration' starting point, I would in my discretion unhesitatingly have departed from that in all the circumstances – in particular, given that the agency here lasted for significantly less than two years, that it was non-exclusive, that there has been the award under Regulation 8(a) and that Mr Coleman had free access to the customers after termination. I would thus in any case not have reached any different conclusion on the ultimate assessment of compensation under Regulation 17.

Conclusion

111. In conclusion, therefore, I will order that:
    - 111.1 Decoro is to pay **Tigana** the agreed sum of $350,000 by way of commission due under the Sales Agreement.
    - 111.2 Decoro is to pay **Tigana** commission under Regulation 8(a) in an amount to be assessed (but being not less than $606,836.64).
    - 111.3 Decoro is to pay **Tigana** compensation under Regulation 17 in the amount of $452,346.
112. I will hear counsel as to any further directions or orders that may be needed and on questions of interest and of costs.

Appendix 4

Sample agency agreements

App4.1

1. Sample agency agreement drafted from perspective of principal

NON-EXCLUSIVE UK/EU/EEA AGENCY AGREEMENT

THIS AGREEMENT IS made the . . . . day of . . . . BETWEEN:

(1) (principal's name), whose principal place of business is at address) and Company Number ; [ ] ('Principal'); and
(2) (agent's name), whose principal place of business is at (address) [(either – trading as or a limited company, Company No . . .)] ('Agent')

1   Appointment

1.1   Principal appoints Agent as independent sales agent to represent and sell its products as constituted and notified to Agent from time to time ('the Products') for the duration of this Agreement on a non-exclusive basis in the following territory:

. . . .
. . . .
'the Territory')

1.2   Principal reserves the right from time to time on written notice to Agent:
(a)   to alter the Territory;
(b)   to exclude particular retail accounts within the Territory from this Agreement including (without limitation) where small accounts are taken over by large accounts and where a particular customer refuses to deal with Agent;
(c)   to alter, increase or decrease the range of, the Products.

1.3   Agent undertakes not to appoint any assistant, sales representative or sub-representative or otherwise subcontract or delegate its obligations under this agreement, nor to assign its rights under this Agreement. Where Agent is a limited company Agent shall obtain

Principal's prior written consent before using any employee to undertake the obligations of this agreement.

2   Best efforts: competitive lines and other business

2.1   Agent shall devote its best efforts to marketing the Products and servicing accounts which carry the Products in the Territory. The Agent shall act in good faith in its performance of its obligations under this Agreement and take all due care and diligence in soliciting sales of the Products.

2.2   Agent shall not engage in any business which creates a conflict of interest with Agent's obligations under this Agreement for the duration of this Agreement, whether directly or indirectly.

2.3   Agent undertakes not to carry any other lines of (*specify*) products, whether competitive with the Products or not, except with the prior written consent of Principal for the duration of this Agreement. Principal hereby gives permission for the Agent to carry the following:

. . . .
. . . .
. . . .
. . . .

2.4   Agent shall attend such exhibitions at which Principal is present for the full duration of the exhibition as notified by Principal to the Agent at the agent's own expense. In particular, but without limitation, Agent shall pay its own travel and accommodation expenses in relation to such attendance. Agent shall bring its current samples of the Products with it to such exhibitions.

2.5   Agent shall pay for samples of the Products as required by Principal.

3   Confidential information, trade marks and data protection

3.1   Agent shall not divulge, disclose or communicate to any person nor use for its own benefit any information concerning any matters affecting or relating to the business of Principal, including without limitation, customer names and order details, Principal products, technical and financial information and the terms of this Agreement and documents referred to in this Agreement ('the Confidential Information').

3.2   Agent undertakes to return all Confidential Information on demand to Principal and forthwith on termination of this Agreement and in each case cease to use the same and not retain any copies of it.

3.3   Agent shall assist Principal in the registration of trade marks in the name of Principal in the Territory and undertakes to inform Principal of any potential infringements of Principal's trade marks or other intellectual property rights in the Territory.

3.4   Agent shall not register any trade mark, patent, registered design, internet domain name or other registered intellectual property right or company name in the name of 'Principal', any existing registered or unregistered trade mark or Principal, the design of any of the Products or any invention contained therein or in any other way arising from or related to this Agreement. Any goodwill which Agent accrues from the operation of this Agreement shall vest in Principal. Agent shall not be involved in any activity for the duration of this Agreement which may bring the trade marks or other rights of Principal into disrepute.

3.5 Where the Agent handles any personal data (as defined in the General Data Protection Regulation and Data Protection Act 2018) for the Principal, it shall handle such data in accordance with the Principal's privacy policy supplied to the Agent and all relevant data protection and email marketing legislation in force from time to time and shall follow the Principal's instructions in relation to all such personal data at all times.

4 Sales manual: opening accounts: principal approval and orders: advertising

4.1 Agent undertakes to follow the procedures and requirements set out in, and otherwise comply with, the Sales Manual of Principal in current version from time to time ('the Sales Manual'). (The current version is attached as Appendix 1. Principal reserves the right from time to time to update the Manual.)

4.2 All account applications solicited by Agent shall be subject to acceptance by Principal in its discretion, including without limitation where an applicant is a bad payer or has a poor credit rating or is a slow payer.

4.3 No orders from a prospective retailer shall be accepted by Principal prior to the approval of the account application and otherwise than where the procedures in the Sales Manual have not been followed.

4.4 All orders solicited by Agent shall be subject to acceptance by Principal. Such orders shall not be deemed finally accepted until shipment of those orders and Principal reserves the right to reject those orders at any time prior to shipment.

4.5 All orders submitted to Principal by Agent must be signed, submitted with VAT numbers where relevant and with the accompanying credit application forms. Agent must ensure that all orders are submitted with the correct name of the customer, including whether or not the customer is a limited company, partnership or sole trader and if a sole trader the name of the individual sole trader as well as his or her trading name, with full address and post code and other details required for invoicing as notified by Principal to Agent from time to time.

4.6 Agent shall transmit all orders received from clients to Principal in the format decided by Principal on a weekly basis. All costs of sending such order information, including but not limited to the purchase of equipment required to complete the delivery, shall be for the cost of Agent. Copies of the information shall be retained by Agent for the purposes of verifying commission payable.

4.7   In the event that an order taken by Agent and imported by Principal is completely or partially cancelled by a customer Agent undertakes to assist in selling off that order to another customer prior to the end of the relevant Selling Season.

4.8   Agent undertakes to provide in advance of each Selling Season, in a format to be advised by Principal, a list of customers to be visited by Agent with an expected Selling Season forecast figure attributed to each customer.

4.9   Agent shall maintain at all times during the Selling Season a complete presence of all the Products on Principal's season price lists in the offices or sales showroom of Agent and in the event that this is a shared showroom in which agreed non competing brands are present, Agent shall devote a part of its showroom or office, the amount of space allocated to the Products shall be similar in area to that occupied by other brands.

4.10   Agent shall report in advance in writing to Principal details of all advertising, publicity, press public relations, shows, conferences and other marketing and promotional activities and costs thereof that will be undertaken by Agent at its own expense and to assist in the sale of the Products. Principal shall determine whether such advertising may proceed.

5   Principal's obligations

5.1   Principal shall provide Agent with all necessary materials and documentation such as (*specify*) and other information necessary for Agent to perform its obligations under this Agreement prior to the beginning of each Selling Season, details of which shall be communicated to Agent from time to time.

5.2   Principal shall deliver to Agent all sample collections of the Products ordered by Agent, subject to availability. Agent agrees to pay for such samples not later than [ninety] (*90*) days after the end of each Selling Season.

5.3   Principal shall notify Agent within thirty [30] days following the end of the Selling Season of non-acceptance of orders which have been sent to Principal, which the parties agree is a reasonable time.

5.4   Principal shall provide sales training, support and assistance for which Principal shall quote charges in advance to Agent.

6   Commission

6.1   Principal shall pay Agent a commission on Products on delivery of the Products on orders solicited by the Agent and accepted by Principal under the terms of this Agreement.

6.2   Commission shall be paid in accordance with and at the rates set out in the Commission Plan in the Sales Manual and as set out in Appendix 2.

6.3   Commission is at the rate of 8% of net sales in accordance with this clause which shall rise to 9% where the target set out in Appendix 3 is met. Agents are paid 5% on accounts designated by Principal as (*specify*).

6.4   Any changes to such commission rates or details of commission and dates of payment shall only be made effective on written notice of Principal to Agent.

7   Changes in prices and/or terms of sale

7.1   Agent shall solicit sales from customers on the prices and terms of sale notified to it from time to time from Principal and only in accordance with the procedures and detail set out in the Sales Manual. Principal reserves the right at any time to change dealer list prices and terms of sale. Principal shall immediately notify Agent of any such changes.

7.2   Agent is given no power or authority to vary such terms and prices as set out in the Sales Manual or otherwise notified to it and is given no continuing authority to negotiate any matter on behalf of Principal.

8   Targets and minimum sales

8.1   Principal and Agent shall meet periodically to establish target figures which Agent shall aim to achieve over the next (. . .) month period. The current figures at the date of this Agreement are set out in Appendix 3. In addition at these meetings the performance of Agent during the prior (. . .) months shall be reviewed. Where in any period the parties fail to reach agreement within a period of one month the target figures for the following such period shall be fixed at a minimum of [ ]% more than the target figures for the previous such period.

8.2   In addition to the obligations under clause 8.1, the Agent shall achieve at least 80% of the previous Selling Season's achieved sales figures which is recognised as a fundamental term of this agreement. Failure to achieve this binding minimum figure shall entitle Principal, at its discretion, to terminate the Agreement on written notice forthwith once the sales Figures for such Selling Season are ascertained and such breach shall be material.

9   Non payment or late payment by accounts

9.1   Where a customer of Principal does not pay an invoice on which Agent has received or is entitled to receive commission, Agent shall be charged back a sum equal to its commission rate on the unpaid balance owing by the customer, save where such failure to pay is wholly attributable to default by Principal.

9.2   If any such customer's account is unpaid 120 days after the date of invoice Agent shall be charged back a sum equal to his commission rate on the arrears balance of the account; payment of

> such commission to Agent shall not be re-instated, save where such failure to pay is wholly attributable to default by Principal.

9.3   Where a customer in default of payment subsequently makes a payment after Agent has repaid or been charged back its commission under clauses 9.1 and 9.2 above, the Agent shall be repaid such commission less a 2% handling charge.

9.4   Where this Agreement replaces one with another Agent, the new Agent shall be required to share its commission on an equitable basis with the old representative for a reasonable period to be agreed in writing between the outgoing representative, the Agent and Principal.

9.5   Principal shall not be liable to or otherwise responsible to Agent for any loss, liability, whether consequential, financial, indirect or direct, for any delay or failure in filling orders nor filling orders with defective goods and all such liability is hereby excluded, save for liability for death and personal injury which may not as a matter of English law be excluded, save for any obligation to pay Agent commission under clause 9.1 above.

10   Independent contractor

Agent is acting solely as an independent contractor and nothing in this Agreement shall constitute the creation or establishment of partnership, joint venture or employee/employer relationship between the parties.

11   Compliance with laws and regulations

Agent agrees to comply with any respective national laws and regulations concerning illegal, unfair trade practices and anticompetitive or restrictive practices. In addition Agent shall comply with all business procedures and policies which Principal announces or publishes, including, without limitation the Sales Manual.

12   Indemnification

Agent shall indemnify and hold Principal harmless from all claims, costs, expenses, including legal fees, arising from Agent's misrepresentations of the quality, use or purpose of the Products, Agent's disparagement of Principal's competitors or their merchandise, any promises or representations made by Agent contrary to Principal's policies or instructions or Agent's acts of unfair competition or unlawful conduct or any breach of any provision of this Agreement by Agent.

13   Term and termination

13.1   Agent is appointed as Agent by Principal for a fixed term of 12 months from the date of this Agreement ('the Term'). This Agreement may be renewed for subsequent [twelve] (*12*) month periods by agreement between the parties at any time before the expiry of the Term or any subsequent twelve month term. Where this Agreement is not so renewed it shall expire without notice.

13.2 Either party may terminate this Agreement on written notice to the other at any time as follows:

(a)   one month's notice in the first year of this Agreement;

(b)   two months' notice during the second year of this Agreement where the Agreement is renewed under clause 13.1 above; and

(c)   three months' notice after completion of the second year of this Agreement where the Agreement is renewed under clause 13.1 above.

13.3 Notwithstanding the above this Agreement may be terminated immediately on written notice by one party to the other where the other party is in breach of any provision of this Agreement, including without limitation, failure to meet the minimum sales figure described in clause 8.2 above or by operation of law or where the other party goes into liquidation or becomes bankrupt or equivalent such events in the jurisdiction to which the other party is subject or there is a change in control of Agent, where a company or the death of the majority shareholder or owner of Agent.

13.4 Where the Commercial Agents (Council Directive) Regulations 1993 apply to this Agreement and the Agent is so entitled, the Agent may claim to be indemnified under such Regulations on termination of this Agreement where such termination brings with it an entitlement to such an indemnity.

14   Return of materials upon termination

14.1 On termination of this Agreement by either party, Agent shall return promptly to Principal all sales materials, price lists, customer account lists, copies of invoices, mailing lists and other materials, including computer software if any, supplied to the Agent by Principal or any customer or contact arranged through the operation of this Agreement. Agent shall forthwith cease to use such documents and shall not retain any copies of them.

15   Payment of commission on termination

15.1 Where this Agreement is terminated, Principal shall pay commission to Agent on orders written and solicited by Agent and accepted by Principal as at the date of termination. Such commission shall be paid to Agent after the orders have been shipped, invoiced and paid for in cleared funds by the customer. The Agent shall also be paid commission on orders received for a period of two months after termination where the Agent generated such order, which period the parties agree is reasonable.

[16   Restrictive covenant

On termination of this Agreement Agent may not engage in any business which conflicts with the interest of Principal in the Territory for a period of [twelve] (12) months from the date of termination.]

17 Waiver

The failure or forbearance of either party to exercise any of its rights or remedies under this Agreement shall not operate as a waiver as to any other or subsequent non performance or breach of contract.

18 Entire agreement

This Agreement and its appendices and documents referred to herein is the entire agreement between the parties and supersedes any prior agreement, understanding or correspondence between the parties. All such prior agreements are terminated on the date of this Agreement.

19 No third party rights

Nothing in this Agreement shall confer any right on a third party except where expressly so stated, whether under the Contracts (Rights of Third Parties) Act 1999 or otherwise.

20 Governing law and jurisdiction

This Agreement is subject to the laws of England and the parties agree to submit to the exclusive jurisdiction of the English courts in connection with any dispute under this Agreement or otherwise in relation to their contractual relationship.

Signed by . . . .
[for and on behalf of Principal UK LIMITED]

Signed by . . . .
[for and on behalf of . . . .

APPENDIX 1
(CLAUSE 4)

CURRENT SALES MANUAL OF PRINCIPAL

APPENDIX 2
(CLAUSE 6.2)

COMMISSION RATE FOR AGENT

APPENDIX 3
(CLAUSE 8.1)

MINIMUM SALES REQUIREMENTS

2.   Example of agency agreement drafted from principal's point of view

THIS AGREEMENT is made the day . . . . of . . . .

BETWEEN:

(1)   (*principal's name*) Company No.(. . .), whose registered office is at (*address*) ('the Principal'); and

(2)   (*agent's name*), whose principal place of business is at (*address*) ('the Agent')

1   Definitions

1.1   'House Accounts' means those customers sales to whom result in nil or reduced commission to the Agent which are listed in the Schedule (if any).

1.2   'Net Sales Value' means the price charged to customers for Products sold under this Agreement less any value added, or other sales, tax.

1.3   'Normal Price' is defined in sub-clause 7.6.

1.4   'The Products' means the products set out in the Schedule (if any) or if none are so listed the Principal's product range from time to time.

1.5   'The Term' means the period specified in clause 9.1 unless earlier terminated.

1.6   'The Territory' means the territory set out in the Schedule.

2   Appointment

2.1   The Principal appoints the Agent as its agent for the sale of the Products in the Territory, and the Agent accepts such appointment, for the Term and subject to the terms and conditions of this Agreement. The Principal reserves the right to vary the Products from time to time including to reduce the number and range of Products which the Agent may market under this Agreement.

2.2   The Principal shall not appoint another agent for the Products during the Term for the Territory where this appointment is specified to be exclusive in the Schedule.

2.3   Whether the appointment of the Agent is exclusive or non-exclusive the Principal shall be free to sell the Products to customers in the Territory, provided that commission is paid to the Agent in accordance with clause 7 below.

2.4   The Agent shall not during the Term market products, whether as agent or distributor, in the Territory, which compete with the Products or otherwise be directly or indirectly involved in the manufacture, sale, promotion, marketing or importation of competing products in the Territory.

2.5   The Agent may only represent as agent or distributor up to three additional companies in the (*specify*) industry for non-competing products and undertakes that before signature of this Agreement the Agent has notified the Principal of all other agencies held by the Agent and activities undertaken by the Agent whether with competing companies or products or not and whether relating to (*product area*) or not, both in the UK and abroad on the Schedule.

2.6   The Agent shall ensure that the Net Sales Value of the Products sold by the Agent on behalf of the Principal in the Territory during any year of this Agreement is at or higher than the required minimum set out in the Schedule. For each subsequent 12-month period such minimum shall be increased by a figure to be agreed by the parties and in default of such agreement shall be no less than 110% of the previous year's required minimum sales level.

3   Principal's duties

The Principal shall act dutifully and in good faith and shall:

(a)   provide the Agent with the necessary documentation relating to the Products and any other information necessary for the performance of the agency;

(b)   inform the Agent within three months of the Principal's refusal or acceptance of any potential order or lead passed by the Agent to the Principal and of when the Principal is not proceeding with any order for any reason; the parties agree that three months is a reasonable period for these purposes;

(c)   notify the Agent within three months where the Principal finds that the number of orders will be significantly lower than that which the Agent would normally have expected; the parties agree that three months is a reasonable period for these purposes.

4   The agent's duties

4.1   The Agent shall use its best endeavours to promote and market the Products to existing and prospective customers in the Territory.

PROMOTIONAL ACTIVITIES

4.2   The Agent shall:

(a)   make such personal visits to existing and potential customers as are necessary to promote and sell the Products;

(b)   advertise and distribute publicity material concerning the Products in the Territory, subject to obtaining prior approval in writing from the Principal on the form and extent of such advertising and publicity materials;

(c)   attend relevant trade exhibitions or other sales outlets in the Territory, comprising at least two such exhibitions in each calendar year;

    (d)   promptly refer enquiries concerning the Products from customers and prospective customers outside the Territory to the Principal;

    (e)   maintain a list of customers and potential customers for the Products in the Territory and on request from the Principal from time to time supply a copy of the list, which list is proprietary information and trade secrets of the Principal;

    (f)   from time to time keep the Principal fully informed of the Agent's promotional and marketing activities in respect of the Products and within 30 days after the end of each calendar quarter provide the Principal with a detailed report of those activities; and

    (g)   from time to time keep the Principal informed of market conditions for the Products in the Territory and the activities and products of the Principal's competitors in the Territory.

GENERAL

4.3   The Agent shall act at all times in good faith towards the Principal and not let its own personal interest conflict with the duties owed to the Principal under this Agreement nor under the general law.

4.4   The Agent shall comply with all reasonable instructions given by the Principal concerning the sale and promotion of the Products.

4.5   The Agent shall comply with all applicable laws and regulations concerning the conduct of agents and the sale of the Products and will obtain all necessary licences, permits and consents, where relevant.

4.6   The Agent shall not engage in any conduct which in the opinion of the Principal is prejudicial to the Principal's business or to the sale or promotion of the Products.

4.7   The Agent shall not institute legal proceedings in the name of the Principal nor as agent for the Principal without the consent in writing of the Principal.

5   Conduct of business

The Agent shall:

(a)   promptly inform the Principal of any complaints or after-sales enquiries concerning the Products received by the Agent;

(b)   not pledge the Principal's credit nor hold itself out as having any authority for the sale of the Products, other than as agent;

(c)   in all dealing concerning the Products describe itself as the sales agent of the Principal;

(d)   assist the Principal with debt collection where required by the Principal.

6   Sales of the products

6.1   The Agent shall market the Products to customers only on the Principal's standard terms and conditions of sale and at the prices stipulated by the Principal from time to time. Any variation to such prices or terms must be approved in advance by the Principal and the Agent is given no continuing authority to negotiate sales under this Agreement.

6.2   The Agent shall, in the course of dealing with customers and prospective customers, bring to their notice such terms and conditions.

6.3   The Agent shall give such advance notice to the Principal of potential orders as may reasonably be required to enable the Principal to maintain adequate stocks of the Products.

6.4   The Agent shall inform the Principal of each order for the Products obtained by the Agent.

6.5   The Principal shall be entitled to accept or reject any order for the Products in the Territory at its discretion.

7   Commission

7.1   The Agent shall be entitled to the percentage commission set out in the Schedule on the Net Sales Value of the Products sold in the Territory as provided below.

7.2   Within 14 days of the end of each month the Principal shall send the Agent a statement showing the total Net Sales Value of each type of the Products sold in the Territory by the Principal during such preceding month, whereupon the Agent shall issue an invoice to the Principal for commission on such orders.

7.3   The Principal shall send the Agent a cheque in settlement of the commission no later than 30 days from the date of the Agent's invoice.

7.4   The Agent shall be entitled to commission on all orders received from the Territory where the appointment is specified to be exclusive in the Schedule, subject to any reduction for House Accounts. Where the appointment is non-exclusive the Agent shall be paid commission on transactions (i) which are concluded, demonstrably, in the opinion of the Principal, as a result of the Agent's marketing actions and (ii) where the transaction is concluded with a customer acquired by the Agent for the Principal for the Territory (if any) during the Term of the Agreement or any agreement which this Agreement replaces, for transactions of the same kind.

7.5   Where a customer negotiates a discount from the normal price charged for the Products ('Normal Price' for this purpose being a band comprising the published list price of the Principal less 5%) then the Agent shall be entitled to a lower commission specified in the Schedule.

7.6   Where for the purposes of promotions (including winter and summer sales) the Principal charges customers less than its list price the Agent shall be paid a reduced commission to be specified by the Principal, but which shall not be less than a commission rate of 2%.

7.7   After termination of this Agreement the Agent shall be entitled to commission on orders accepted after that date where the order was mainly due to the efforts of the Agent during the period of this Agreement and was entered into within a period of three months of termination. The parties agree that three months is reasonable for such a period. An order is mainly due to the Agent's efforts where the Agent can show to the satisfaction of the Principal that it expended significant effort in bringing the customer in as a customer of the Principal.

7.8   Where an order reaches the Principal or Agent before this Agreement is terminated commission is payable to the Agent even where the goods are sent after termination, where the order resulted from the Agent's efforts or it relates to a customer who had previously been acquired by the Agent for transactions of the same kind. The Agent shall supply within seven days of receipt of such an order details of it to the Principal, including sufficient evidence of the date of receipt of the order to prove, to the satisfaction of the Principal, that the order was received before this Agreement was terminated.

7.9   Where this Agreement is for the appointment of a new agent in place of another, the Agent shall not be entitled to commission on orders mostly attributable to the efforts of the agent which the new Agent is replacing unless the Agent can show that it is equitable in all the circumstances that it share the commission with the previous agent. Where the Principal gives the new Agent a customer list or contacts at the date of appointment such list is attached in the Schedule.

7.10 Where a customer or potential customer does not place an order for three months from its last order to the Principal in the Territory or the introduction by the Agent to the Principal of the customer, then the Agent's right to commission on orders from that customer shall be extinguished, where the agency herein is not exclusive.

7.11 The Principal may in its absolute discretion reject any potential customer or repeat order from an existing customer, for any reason, including without limitation where such customer has a bad credit rating or the Principal is restrained by an existing agreement from serving such customer if the customer is a competitor.

7.12 Where a customer does not make payment to the Principal for Products on which commission has already been paid or obtains a refund, then the Principal may deduct the commission already paid from subsequent commission payments to the Agent or, on termination, require repayment thereof by the Agent, save where the Principal is to blame for such payment being made such as where defective Products were supplied.

7.13 All sums under this Agreement are exclusive of value added, or other sales, tax which the Agent may be obliged to charge the Principal.

8   Confidentiality and data protection

8.1 The Agent shall not during the Term, or thereafter, disclose, or permit to be disclosed, any business information of the Principal, including (without prejudice to the generality of the foregoing) details of this Agreement, terms and conditions, prices, customer lists, details of the Products and financial information of the Principal and shall not use information other than for the purposes of this Agreement. On termination of this Agreement all such information, whether in written form or on computer disk or in any other form, shall be returned to the Principal forthwith and the Agent shall not keep a copy.

8.2 Where the Agent handles any personal data (as defined in the General Data Protection Regulation and Data Protection Act 2018) for the Principal, it shall handle such data in accordance with the Principal's privacy policy supplied to the Agent and all relevant data protection and email marketing legislation in force from time to time and shall follow the Principal's instructions in relation to all such personal data at all times.

8.3 This clause shall continue after termination of this Agreement without limit as to time.

9   Term and termination

9.1 This Agreement is for a period specified in the Schedule from the date in the Schedule and shall expire at the end of such period ('the Term').

9.2 Three months prior to the expiry of the Term the Principal and Agent shall discuss whether or not they wish to enter into another agency agreement for another period. Neither shall be under any obligation to enter into a new such agreement.

9.3 This Agreement may be terminated during the Term by either party on giving written notice to the other of at least one month in the first year, two in the second and three thereafter.

9.4 The Principal may terminate this Agreement forthwith by notice in writing to the Agent, without prejudice to the Principal's other rights and remedies in such circumstances, where:

(a) the Agent is in breach of any provision of this Agreement, provided that if the breach of capable of remedy the Agent has been given 30 days' notice to remedy such breach and it has not been remedied in that period;

(b) the Agent (where the Agent is a limited company) goes into liquidation (either compulsory or voluntary) save for the purposes of reconstruction or amalgamation or if a receiver is appointed in respect of the whole or any part of its assets or makes an assignment for the benefit of, or composition with, its creditors generally or threatens to do any of these actions;

(c) the Agent, where an individual or partnership, has a bankruptcy order made against it or a petition for such an order presented or if an application is made for an interim order under s 256 of the Insolvency Act 1986 or the Agent appears to be unable to pay, or to have a reasonable prospect of being able to pay, any debt as defined in s 268 of the 1986 Act or if a person is appointed by the court to prepare a report in respect of the Agent under s 273 of the Act or if an interim receiver is appointed of the property of the Agent under s 286 of the Act;

(d) where the Net Sales Value of the Products sold, by the Agent on behalf of the Principal in the Territory during any year of this Agreement is less than the required minimum set out in this Agreement;

(e) the Agent (or its key staff where a Company) is unable, or cannot reasonably be required, to continue its activities under this Agreement as a result of age, infirmity, death or illness; the Agent shall inform the Principal in writing as soon as any illness interferes with its activities in any way and undertakes to submit to a medical examination by the Principal's nominated doctor where so required;

(f) the Agent ceases or threatens to cease to carry on business;

(g) where the Agent, being a company, suffers a change of control or change of directors or other key personnel.

9.5 [Where the Agent is an individual sole trader this Agreement shall expire without prior notice when the Agent reaches the retirement age of 65 years and where the Agent is a partnership where the last of the partners reaches the age of 65.]

9.6 The right to terminate this Agreement is without prejudice to any other right or remedy in respect of the breach.

9.7 Where the Commercial Agents (Council Directive) Regulations 1993 apply to this Agreement and the Agent is so entitled, the Agent may claim to be indemnified under such Regulations on termination of this Agreement where such termination brings with it an entitlement to such an indemnity.

9.8 On termination the Agent shall cease to hold itself out as having any authority or fight to represent the Principal and shall not directly or indirectly for two years after termination solicit customers of the Principal in relation to the Products in the Territory.

10 General

10.1 Nothing in this Agreement shall create a partnership or relationship of employer and employee or joint venture between the parties.

10.2 This is the entire agreement between the parties and any earlier agency or similar agreement, letter or document, is hereby terminated and superseded. This Agreement may only be modified by agreement in writing of both parties.

10.3 In entering into this Agreement both parties agree they have not relied on any representation or warranty and all such warranties implied by statute or common law are hereby excluded, to the fullest extent permissible under the law. In particular any forecast by the Principal of possible commission earnings by the Agent in the Territory is not legally binding.

10.4 If any provision of this Agreement is held by a court to be void or otherwise unenforceable the Agreement shall continue to be valid as to its other parts.

10.5 Failure by either party to enforce a right under this Agreement or delay in doing so will not amount to a waiver of such right.

10.6 The Agent shall not assign or otherwise dispose of its rights and obligations under this Agreement without the prior written consent of the Principal, including, without limitation where the Agent, being a partnership, proposes to take on a new partner or dissolve the partnership or where the Agent being a limited company, wishes to transfer or dispose of its business.

10.7 The Agent, where an individual or partnership, shall carry out its obligations personally under this Agreement and may not delegate or contract out its obligations or appoint sub-agents without written permission of the Principal. Where the Agent is a limited company the Agent shall notify the Principal of the employees or directors who will carry out the activities under this Agreement and shall not alter such details without the prior written consent of the Principal. Any act or omission of an approved sub-agent or employee shall be deemed to be the act or omission of the Agent.

10.8 This Agreement is governed by English law and the parties agree to submit to the exclusive jurisdiction of the English courts in connection with any dispute hereunder.

10.9 Nothing in this Agreement shall confer any right on a third party except where expressly so stated, whether under the Contracts (Rights of Third Parties) Act 1999 or otherwise.

10.10 Any notices sent between the parties shall be sent by first class post to the addresses given in this Agreement or variations to those addresses notified to each other for such purpose from time to time. Notices shall be deemed served 48 hours after posting.

IN WITNESS the parties have entered into this Agreement on the day and dates given on page 1.

Signed by . . . .

[for and on behalf of. . . . .

Principal's full name

Signed by:

. . . .

[(*where a limited company is agent*)
for and on behalf of]

. . . .

Agent's full corporate name

SCHEDULE

The Products are:
(*insert details*)

The Territory is:
(*attach map where possible*)

The Agency is exclusive/non-exclusive (*delete as appropriate*)

House Accounts:
(*name house accounts and give commission rates on them including where 0%*)

Starting date of the Agency and period:
(*start date and period –12 months, 2 years etc*)

Declaration of Agent's existing other agencies and distribution activities for all types of products and services.

List of customers given to the Agent by the Principal on the date of this Agreement:
(*specify*)

Commission rate where customer negotiates a discount:
(*specify*)

Annual minimum sales requirement:
(*insert details*)

3. Short sample agency agreement written from agent's perspective

(This agreement attempted to avoid provocative clauses or those unlikely to be accepted by a principal. Some agents may have more commercial muscle and be able to negotiate better terms.)

EXCLUSIVE AGENCY AGREEMENT

THIS AGREEMENT is made the day . . . . . . of . . . . . .

Between:
    (1)   (*principal's name*) ('Principal'); and
    (2)   (*agent's name*), whose principal place of business is at (*address*) ('Agent')

1   Appointment

Principal appoints Agent as its exclusive agent for the Products in the Territory listed on the Schedule and undertakes that for the duration of this Agreement Principal will neither sell nor market the Products in the Territory other than through Agent and shall not appoint any other agent for the Territory.

2   Best efforts: Competitive lines and other business

2.1   Agent shall devote its best efforts to marketing the Products and servicing accounts which carry the Products in the Territory.

2.2   Agent shall neither market nor sell in the Territory any products which compete with the Products.

2.3   Agent shall be given samples of the Products and marketing literature by Principal.

2.4   Agent shall pass all orders for the Products to Principal who shall deal with such orders promptly and ensure goods supplied are of satisfactory quality.

3   Commission

3.1   Principal shall pay Agent a commission of the percentage set out on the Schedule on all sales of the Products in the Territory, whether such sale is generated by the Agent or not. Such commission shall be on the invoiced value, less VAT, charged by Principal to customers.

3.2   Commission shall be paid each month by the first week of the month on sales invoiced by Principal in the preceding month. Where a customer subsequently defaults in payment of any invoice where Principal is not to blame for such default then Principal may deduct commission already paid for such sale from the next commission due to Agent.

3.3   With each such monthly commission payment Principal shall send Agent a full commission statement showing all sales of the Products made to the Territory in the preceding month sufficient to enable Agent to check the commission due.

4   Term and termination

4.1   This Agreement is for an initial minimum period of two years and shall continue after unless and until terminated by at least one year's written notice by one party to the other to expire on the third or any subsequent anniversary of the date of this Agreement.

4.2   On termination of this Agreement commission shall be paid to Agent on all orders received up to the date of termination and for a period of three months thereafter.

5   General

5.1   This Agreement is subject to English law and the parties agree to submit to the jurisdiction of the English courts in respect of any dispute.

5.2   This Agreement replaces any earlier agreement or arrangement between the parties, verbal or written, and is the entire agreement between them. It may only be modified by written agreement of both parties.

5.3   Nothing in this Agreement shall prevent Agent from subcontracting its obligations under this Agreement nor from using a sub agent. Either party may assign all its rights under this Agreement to a third party but only with the prior written consent of the other party.

SCHEDULE

The Products are:
(*insert details*)

The Exclusive Territory is:
(*specify*)

The Commission Rate is:
(*specify*)

SIGNATURES
Signed by. . . . .
[for and on behalf of
Principal. . . . .]
Signed by. . . . .

App4.4

4.   Sample letter making agency claim

Dear Sirs,

We act for Mr (*name*) who was your commercial agent appointed under agency agreement dated (*date*). On (*date*) you gave Mr (*name*) one month's notice of termination of his agency. We are writing formally to make our client's claim under the Commercial Agents (Council Directive) Regulations 1993 as amended ('the regulations').

1.   The regulations entitled our client to three months' notice of termination to expire at the end of the month of (*specify*). Our client is therefore entitled to £ (. . .) being the commission he would have earned in that period.

2.   The regulations also entitle our client to all commission due on orders received up to the date of termination. He estimates he is due at least (*amount*). The Regulations give us a right to see extracts from your books to verify commission due so please provide satisfactory explanation with your calculations in reply.

3.   The regulations give our client the right to commission on orders received after termination for a reasonable period, which we suggest here should be a period of [three months]. Based on the last year's commission earnings we would estimate this sum to be £ (. . .).

4.   Finally our client is entitled to a lump sum on termination under regulation 17. This would normally be of the order of about two years' gross commission. On this basis our client is entitled to at least £ (. . .). He reserves the right, however, if this matter proceeds to trial, to claim a sum in excess of this where his loss is greater.

5.   Our client has attempted himself to obtain compensation from you to no avail. He will therefore require that his legal costs be paid if the matter goes forward.

As we are keen to have this matter settled as soon as possible we look forward to receiving your proposals for settlement within seven day otherwise our client will consider issuing proceedings. Please confirm if you have a firm of solicitors who would accept service of any such proceedings on your behalf.

Yours faithfully,
(*signature*)

[(*1. If proceedings will be issued, say in 7 days, then the letter should say so and the letter could be headed Letter Before Action). (2. In some cases a without prejudice offer letter written pursuant to the Civil Procedure Rules 1998 Part 36 could be sent at the same time).*]

App4.5

5. Letter rejecting agent's claim

Dear (*name*)

We refer to your letter of (*date*). We cannot entertain any compensation claim from you.

1. The regulations to which you refer do not apply to you. (*give reason – see Chapter 1 etc*)

2. Even if they did your efforts have not led to substantial benefits accruing to us/or your contract was terminated for breach of contract as we earlier indicated so no compensation is due.

3. We would warn that if you do bring proceedings these would be vigorously defended and our lawyers inform us we have a very good chance of successfully defending your claim. [In addition you owe us £ (. . .) and we will be counterclaiming for that sum, in any event please remit such monies forthwith otherwise we shall have to consider taking legal action.]

Yours faithfully,
(*signature*)

App4.6

6. Sample particulars of claim – county court

IN THE COUNTY COURT at [...............]Case No. (. . . . .)

BETWEEN:
(*Claimant's name*)
and
(*Defendant's name*)

PARTICULARS OF CLAIM

1. The Claimant was at all material times a self employed commercial agent of the Defendants appointed in or around (*date*), (*no written agreement in this case*)

2. Under the verbal agreements between the parties confirmed by commission statements the Claimant was paid commission normally of . . . . . % of the net sales value of the Defendant's products sold in the exclusive territory of (*specify area*).

3. On (*date*) the Defendant terminated the Claimant's agency agreement with effect from (*date*).

4. The Commercial Agents (Council Directive) Regulations 1993 as amended apply to the agency arrangements.

5. The said regulations in regulation 15(2)(c) entitle the Claimant to three months' notice in writing to expire at the end of a calendar month. The notice given on (*date*) was therefore insufficient. The Claimant therefore claims commission under regulation 7 of the said Regulations on the basis of what he would normally have earned in a period lasting from (*date*) which would have comprised the proper notice period.

6. The Claimant further claims commission on all orders received after termination for a reasonable period in his territory under regulation 8(1), which reasonable period should be three months.

7. Further, or in the alternative, the Claimant claims compensation under regulation 17(2) of the regulations. The Claimant brought substantial benefits to the Defendant from which the Defendant shall continue to benefit after termination.

PARTICULARS

Please see attached Schedule.

8. The Claimant claims damages for breach of contract.

PARTICULARS

The availability of stock by the Defendant to customers in the Claimant's territory was so poor as to reduce the numbers of orders received and thus commission was reduced below what it should have been had the Defendant acted properly.

9.   The Claimant claims interest pursuant to s 69 of the County Court Act
     1984 on any damages awarded.

     AND the Claimant claims:
     (1)   Commission for a notice period to expire on (*date*)
     (2)   Commission for three months after termination
     (3)   Damages for breach of contract and/or pursuant to regulation 17
           of up to £50,000 (*limiting to a particular sum is required to determine
           county court fee and correct court*)
     (4)   Interest
     (5)   Costs

STATEMENT OF TRUTH

The Claimant believes that the facts stated in these Particulars of Claim are true. I
am duly authorised as a director to sign this statement on behalf of the Claimant.

Datedthis. . . . .

. . . .
(*signature*)

IN THE COUNTY COURT at . . . . Case No. (. . . . .)

BETWEEN:
(*Claimant's name*)
and
(*Defendant's name*)

SCHEDULE OF FINANCIAL LOSS

[Or attach Valuer's report if one has been obtained]
(A)   Income consists of commission on sales turnover normally calculated at
      . . . . . % of net sales value on orders received in the agent's territory.
(B)   Average commission was £ . . . . . plus VAT per annum averaged over the
      period (*specify*).
(C)   The notional value of the agency at the date of termination to a willing
      buyer following the principles in the Lonsdale decision [2007] UKHL 32
      is [xxx] on the following basis [add details] and the Claimant therefore
      claims a sum of up to £50,000.

IN THE COUNTY COURT at (. . . . .) Case No. (. . . . .)

BETWEEN:
(*Claimant's name*)
and
(*Defendant's name*)

PARTICULARS OF CLAIM

. . . .
(*signature*)

App4.7

7.   Example of defence and counterclaim

IN THE COUNTY COURT at (.........) Case No. (. . . . .)

BETWEEN:
(*Claimant's name*)
and
(*Defendant's name*)

DEFENCE AND COUNTERCLAIM

1.   Paragraphs (*insert number*) of the particulars of claim are admitted, save that (*direction*)
2.   Paragraph (*insert number*) of the particulars of claim is denied. The Commercial Agents (Council Directive) Regulations 1993 ('the Regulations') apply to 'commercial agents' as therein defined. Regulation 2(1) provides that such an agent must have:
> 'continuing authority to negotiate the sale or purchase of goods on behalf of another person (the 'principal'), or to negotiate and conclude the sale or purchase of goods on behalf of and in the name of the principal.'

The Claimant was given no such authority whether in the written agreement between the Claimant and the Defendant dated (*date*) ('the Agreement') or otherwise.

PARTICULARS

Clause (*insert number*) of the said Agreement provides that the Agent must not:

> 'accept orders or make contracts on behalf of the Principal other than subject to the confirmation and acceptance by the Principal.'

Clause (*insert number*) of the said Agreement provides that the Agent must not:

> 'offer any of the Products for sale other than at the prices specified from time to time by the Principal.'

Clause (*insert number*) of the said Agreement provides that the Agent must not:

> 'receive orders for the Products except for such payment or such cash or credit terms as the Principal shall from time to time notify in writing to the Agent and the Principal reserves the right to refuse to grant credit to any customers.'

The Defendant has given no powers to the Claimant to negotiate. The Claimant's duty is to find customers for the products. The Claimant is given no power to vary terms or prices and no authority to negotiate at all.

Regulation 18(a) will be relied upon to the effect that if, which is denied, the Regulations apply, no entitlement to compensation arises as the Agreement was terminated through default attributable to the Claimant, justifying immediate termination. In particular the Claimant in breach of regulation 3 of the Regulations failed to act dutifully and in good faith in the interests of the Defendant in performing his duties and/or in breach of clause (*insert number*) of the Agreement to use '*his best endeavours to promote and extend the sale of the Products throughout the Territory*'.

PARTICULARS

1.   (*set out breaches such as reductions in sales as against targets etc.*)
2.   The Claimant is not entitled to compensation under Regulation 17 as: [*set out reasons*]
3.   Paragraph (*insert number*) of the Particulars of Claim is denied. The Defendant gave notice to the Claimant of termination of the Agreement by letter dated (*date*) and the Agreement terminated on (date), through the application of clause (*insert number*) of the Agreement which provided for the said such three month notice period.
4.   Paragraph (*insert number*) of the Particulars of Claim is denied, save that the Defendant admits that the Claimant built up the said area. There were (*specify*) not (*specify*), customers at the date of termination, reducing to (*specify*) in (. . .) and (. . .) in (. . .). The Defendant has not reaped substantial benefits from the Claimant's efforts after the Agreement was terminated. Turnover in the Claimant's final year was £ . . . . .
and currently in (date) £ . . . . . and the value of the agency to a third party notional buyer would be very low if not zero.
5.   Paragraph (*insert number*) of the Particulars of Claim is admitted, save that the said entitlement claimed is denied.
6.   Paragraph (*insert number*) of the Particulars of Claim is admitted.
7.   Further or alternatively the Defendant will rely upon its counterclaim herein by way of set-off in extinction or diminution of the Claimant's claim.
8.   In the circumstances the Claimant is not entitled to the relief claimed or any relief.

COUNTERCLAIM

9.   Under Clause (*insert number*) of the Agreement the Claimant must pay the Defendant for necessary samples of the Products for which the Claimant has not paid.

PARTICULARS

£ . . . . as set out on statement of account attached
10.   The Claimant has refused to pay for such samples.
11.   The Defendant claims interest pursuant to s 69 of the County Courts Act 1984 at such rate and on such sums as the Court considers appropriate.

AND the Defendant counterclaims:

(1)   £ . . . . .
(2)   Under paragraph 11 hereof interest for such periods and at such rates as to the court shall seem just.

STATEMENT OF TRUTH

The Defendant believes that the facts stated in this Defence are true. I am duly authorised as a director to sign this statement on behalf of the Defendant.

DATED. . . . .

. . . .

(*signature*)

Solicitors for the Defendant

To: The District Judge

To: The Claimant

IN THE COUNTY COURT at (............) Case No. (. . . . .)

BETWEEN:
(*Claimant's name*)
and
(*Defendant's name*)

DEFENCE AND COUNTERCLAIM

App4.8

8. Consent order

IN THE COUNTY COURT at (............) Case No. (. . . . .)
BETWEEN:
(*Claimant's name*)
and
(*Defendant's name*)

The parties having agreed terms of settlement and consent to an order in the following terms:

BY CONSENT it is ordered that:

1. The Claimant be at liberty to accept the sum of £ . . . . . in full satisfaction of his claim to damages herein.
2. The Defendant having paid such sum on (date) to the Claimant's solicitors [or shall pay such sum within seven days of the date of this order]
3. There be no order for costs.
4. The Defendant undertakes to indemnify the Claimant against any value added tax subsequently levied by HMRC on the said sum on presentation by the Claimant to the Defendant of a VAT invoice
5. The defendant be discharged from any further liability in respect of the Claimant's cause of action herein.

WE CONSENT TO AN ORDER IN THE ABOVE TERMS

. . . .

(signature)   (signature)

Claimant's solicitors   Defendant's solicitors

Ref: Ref:

DATED THIS DAY OF . . . . .

Notes
1. In this example no confidentiality obligations were imposed post settlement.
2. There was no counterclaim to settle.
3. In some cases the defendant will need an invoice before he can pay.
4. For settlement 'letters' before proceedings are launched the same types of issues need to be addressed but without the requirement of stating the parties and claim number etc. The full and final settlement clause should be carefully worded to ensure it covers all claims – for breach of contract, commission owed, compensation/indemnity for all agreements and for agents, that it also settles any counterclaim.

5.   Where proceedings have been launched one party must agree to lodge the consent order at court so the court knows the proceedings are over and pay the court's fee for this.

6.   Always check the relevant court rules for consent order. For example, for the Chancery Division of the High Court, see the example in https://www.judiciary.uk/wp-content/uploads/2016/02/chancery-guide-feb-2016.pdf.

Index